House of Hits

BRAD AND MICHELE MOORE ROOTS MUSIC SERIES

UNIVERSITY OF TEXAS PRESS ☩ AUSTIN

The Story of
Houston's Gold Star/SugarHill
Recording Studios

house of hits

by ANDY BRADLEY *and* ROGER WOOD

Requests for permission to reproduce material
from this work should be sent to:
Permissions: University of Texas Press
P.O. Box 7819, Austin, TX 78713-7819
www.utexas.edu/utpress/about/bpermission.html

∞ The paper used in this book meets the minimum requirements
of ANSI/NISO Z39.48-1992 (R1997) (Permanence of Paper).

Designed by Lindsay Starr

Library of Congress Cataloging-in-Publication Data

Bradley, Andy, 1951–
House of hits : the story of Houston's Gold Star/SugarHill Recording
Studios / by Andy Bradley and Roger Wood. — 1st ed.
p.   cm. — (Brad and Michele Moore roots music series)
Includes bibliographical references and index.
ISBN 978-0-292-71919-4 (cl. : alk. paper)
1. SugarHill Recording Studios. 2. Gold Star Studios. 3. Sound recording
industry—Texas—Houston—History. I. Wood, Charles Roger, 1956–   II. Title.
ML3792.S84B73 2010
781.6409764'1411—dc22
2009044441

Contents

Foreword

I **FIRST CAME TO SUGARHILL STUDIOS** in the year 1991. I had been out of the business of recording for a decade and was eager to get back into the studio. My friend and former bandmate in Radio Birdman, Chris Masuak, had asked me to help out on an album he was doing with his group the Hitmen. I flew in to Houston's Hobby Airport, and we stopped at a Two Pesos for cheap tacos on the way.

The building is on Brock Street in a quiet and old neighborhood. Although in the city, it has a rural feel. It rains a lot, so stuff grows fast here. Primal life energy flows freely. Trees, vines, flowering shrubs of all kinds mingle with old stuff lying around and threaten to engulf the pavement. If people went away, there would be no sign of civilization within a decade. Small mid-century vintage wood-frame houses needing paint line the street, some with beer coolers on the front porch. Kids and dogs run around outside, their shouts mingling with a hint of charcoal smoke and the aroma of tortillas. I got the feeling there was some voodoo in that humid air.

Inside the building, the small reception area has some glass cases displaying Gold Record awards, album covers, and other memorabilia. Down the narrow hallway, Studio B is on your left; the original gold star emblem is emblazoned in the floor. Go on down past there, through the coffee lounge, and into the control area with the big Neotek desk that adjoins the big room known as Studio A. You suddenly get hit with the impression you are in a parallel world. It looks like an old Mexican cantina, but with a grand piano out front—a surreal juxtaposition, but somehow perfect. There are painted palm trees and white adobe walls fronting the various booths. Staff members told me that Freddy Fender wanted those palms in there, and they just left 'em. I felt immediately at home. If I could afford the rent, I'd live there.

Behind the control room there is a narrow staircase that leads up to Huey Meaux's old tape archives. I went up there and had a quick look around the dusty shelves, and was astonished to lay hands on original four-track masters of the 13th Floor Elevators and the Sir Douglas Quintet, among others numerous and amazing. Those tapes were as hot and heavy in my hands as a box of plutonium. I felt like Indiana Jones finding the Ark.

SugarHill and the Houston music scene have living treasures too. All it took was a phone call from Andy to get Grady Gaines (who played with Little Richard, among others, back in the 1950s) to come down and blow tenor sax on one of my sessions. After the killer tracks that he recorded, and the fan photos we had to take of Grady in his blue cardigan with Chris and me, I handed him a wad of cash. He said, "You boys can call me anytime!" A great moment at SugarHill, but maybe the greatest was Huey Meaux wandering into the control room during a playback. He listened for a minute, then shook his head. He looked up and said, "Y'all need to record in *mono*."

Magic is a recurring theme in this history. Maybe it is the central theme. Much has been said and written about other magical studios—Abbey Road, Olympic, the Hit Factory, to name a few. There is certainly more to these places than bricks, mortar, wires, and electrons. Take the trip through these pages, and enjoy the ride. But after you read about SugarHill magic, be sure to get hold of some of the wonderful recordings made here. When you listen, you'll hear it and you will feel it, somewhere in the beat. You'll know, because it will make you want to dance.

DENIZ TEK
Billings, Montana

Acknowledgments

THE COAUTHORS HEARTILY THANK Andrew Brown, whose knowledge of and passion for the history of independent recording in Texas inspired and informed this book.

Andy Bradley adds: Thanks to the numerous musicians and engineers, past and present, who participated in our research. The staff at SugarHill Studios and my business partners have gone the extra mile. My wife Donna gave me the idea and kept me focused. And I must acknowledge my two mentors, Bill Holford and Calvin Owens. Bill galvanized my love of analog recording and taught me how to edit with a razor blade. Calvin taught me patience and, with his many sessions featuring big brass and strings, how to record such instrumentation effectively. Johnny Bush, a Texas legend and my friend, has given me invaluable insight into country music. Roger Wood's involvement has been critical in developing and documenting the narrative and preparing the manuscript.

We have lost quite a few colleagues since the inception of this project. May this book keep their memories alive.

Roger Wood is grateful to Marla, his wife. He also thanks his many friends who love the music and stories of Texas and the Gulf Coast, especially James Fraher, Edwin Gallaher, Mack McCormick, John Nova Lomax, Tomas Escalante, Pete Mitchell, Reg Burns, Chris Gray, William Michael Smith, Pete Gordon, Ruben Duran, Chris Strachwitz, Rick Mitchell, Gary Hartman, Tom McClendon, the folks at KPFT-FM radio, and his two brothers, Glen and Terry. For professional support and more, he thanks Alan Ainsworth of Houston Community College—Central, Andy Bradley and the SugarHill staff, as well as Theresa May and Allison Faust of the University of Texas Press.

Roger Wood's involvement in the writing of this book was supported by an Individual Artist Grant Award provided by the City of Houston through the Houston Arts Alliance.

QUOTATIONS FROM OUR MANY oral historical sources, unless otherwise indicated, come from the interviews documented in Appendix A, which follows the main text.

Quotations from, or references to, published sources are each cited by the relevant writer's name and other necessary identifying data, corresponding to full documentation in the Bibliography.

Most of the photographs in this book come from the in-house archives of SugarHill Studios, and unless otherwise indicated, the photographers are unknown. We thank Tony Endieveri, Doug Hanners, Frank Juricek, Gaylan Latimer, Gina R. Miller, and Chris Strachwitz for the use of additional images.

In the main text, when referencing a recording, we generally include the issuing label's catalogue number, signified by a parenthetical reference containing the # sign.

Introduction

THE CASE FOR GREATNESS

THIS BOOK APPROACHES postwar Texas music history through the epic story of a single entity—a Houston-based sound engineering and recording facility that started in 1941 and is still operating today. Over the years its founder and subsequent engineers have produced a multitude of influential hit records and classic tracks for numerous labels in a diverse range of popular genres. Combining firsthand accounts from insiders and musicians with research-based historiography and discography, we make the case that the structure that houses the enterprise now known as SugarHill Studios, a place first famous for several decades mainly under the name Gold Star Studios, is the most significant studio site in the rich legacy of popular music recording in the state of Texas.

That argument is based on several criteria, including this studio's unique longevity of continuous operation, its production of so many hits and popular standards in so many different styles of music, and its key role in the careers of scores of major musicians, songwriters, and producers.

Regarding that last point, among the hundreds of Gold Star/SugarHill–affiliated artists, a brief sampling of the roster includes blues giants (ranging from Lightnin' Hopkins to Albert Collins to Bobby Bland), country legends (from George Jones to Willie Nelson to Roger Miller), early rockers (from the Big Bopper to Roy Head to Sir Douglas Quintet), seminal figures in Cajun and zydeco (from Harry Choates to Clifton Chenier), architects of R&B (from O. V. Wright to Junior Parker), pioneers of psychedelia (from 13th Floor Elevators to Bubble Puppy), the phenomenal Freddy Fender, Tejano performers (from Little Joe y La Familia to Emilio Navaira), Texas jazz ambassadors (from Arnett Cobb to Conrad Johnson), revered song-crafters (from Guy Clark to Lucinda Williams), satirists (such as Kinky Friedman), gospel greats (such as the Mighty Clouds of Joy), neo-swing bands (such as Asleep at the Wheel), contemporary pop icons (such as Beyoncé Knowles and Destiny's Child), rappers (such as Lil' Wayne) . . . and many more.

Of course, there are many other important studios that have also made their mark on the history of music recording in Texas. Elsewhere in Houston, for example, ACA Studios did much important work documenting regional music for commercial release. Founded in 1948 by Bill Holford, its legacy extends all the way to 1985—impressive, for sure.

Likewise, as Gary Hickinbotham relates in *The Journal of Texas Music History*, Dallas has been home to several noteworthy facilities over the years. Included among those are the one Jack Sellers and Jim Beck built in the 1950s, as well as Sumet Studio (built in 1962 by Marvin "Smokey" Montgomery), Autumn Sound Studio (built in 1974 and later renamed Audio Dallas), Dallas Sound Labs (founded in 1980), and others. In Lubbock there was Bobby Peebles' Venture Recording Studio; in El Paso there was the one Bobby Fuller built in 1962; in San Antonio, there were studios created by engineers such as Bob Tanner, Jeff Smith, Abe Epstein, and Eddie Morris, and so on. Meanwhile, to quote Hickinbotham, "there were no real commercial studio facilities for recording in Austin until the 1970s." During that era and thereafter, famous enterprises such as Austin Recording Studio, Pedernales Recording Studio, Arlyn Studios, Riverside Sound Studio, Electric Graceyland Studios, and the Hit Shack came into being.

Granted, studios such as these have made many salient contributions, in varying degrees, to the grand-scale history of music recording in the state. Their individual roles and accomplishments could likely provide worthy material for articles or books by other writers. However, none of the aforementioned studios got started as early as the one Bill Quinn created in 1941. Not only was it one of the first, but also in terms of longevity and diversity it is surely the most impressive. For, as this book shows, during almost seventy years of continuous operation, this studio company has had a wide-ranging impact on so many different facets of popular music that no other independent recording facility in the state—and only a few in the nation—can rival its achievement.

We also concede that some of the most influential recordings ever to come out of Texas were not made in any studio. In the earliest days of recording technology, well before the advent of any established studio sites in the region, the Lone Star State profoundly affected recording history, particularly in terms of the evolution of certain folk-ethnic musical styles and their impact on popular tastes.

For instance, as far back as 1908 the groundbreaking folklorist John A. Lomax was transporting his newfangled portable equipment across Texas to make the earliest field recordings of many previously undocumented cowboy songs that are now considered American classics. Then, in the 1920s and '30s during the first major wave of commercial recordings of popular music, New York–based companies (such as RCA Victor and Columbia) regularly sent engineering teams to Texas to conduct sessions in hotel rooms and other makeshift locations, producing some of the most momentous music recordings of the era in the process.

A case in point: In 1936 at the Gunter Hotel in San Antonio, such arrangements yielded the first recordings by the iconic Mississippi-born blues guitarist and singer Robert Johnson. A year later, he made his only other recordings at a temporary facility rigged up in the Brunswick Records warehouse in Dallas. Thus, no sonic documentation of Johnson exists outside of sessions in Texas. These are profoundly crucial tracks whose influence still resonates today.

Yet, like the earlier field recordings by Lomax, the Johnson sessions did not take place in any professionally designed, quasi-permanent studio space devoted exclusively to sound recording. There was none in Texas at the time. In fact, before World War II, such facilities simply did not exist in most American cities other than New York and Chicago, where they were owned and utilized by the few early major record labels. These were companies that guarded zealously their in-house innovations and trade secrets. But by the 1940s that situation was starting to change.

Across the nation various self-taught or military-trained technophiles and inventors, as well as other people involved in commercial music performance, were beginning to tinker curiously with existing equipment and to ponder the possibilities of devising a way that they, solely on their own, could capture and play back sound. Other hit-seeking entrepreneurs, usually with dreams much larger than their budgets, were discovering new performing talent and analyzing the logistics of where and how to make records. The independent recording industry was about to be born.

Meanwhile, working entirely on his own in southeast Houston, Quinn did things that ultimately made him part of that process. A native of Massachusetts, he had previously been employed to handle sound equipment for a carnival company before circumstances prompted him to settle unexpectedly in Houston. Keen on electronics, Quinn had long been intrigued by the way sound vibrations could be captured in grooves on a disc and then duplicated and played back on a machine. Utilizing primitive or improvised equipment and substandard raw materials, and guided evidently by an inquisitive endurance of trials and errors, he eventually taught himself how to make records. Despite wartime shortages of basic materials that had generally paralyzed the industry, he·independently started commercially recording and pressing discs.

By 1941 he had changed the name of his one-man business operation from Quinn Radio Service to Quinn Recording Company. Initially he focused his commercial work on spoken text or jingles, documenting it direct to disc on acetate masters. His first clients typically were making advertisements for radio broadcast or creating novelty gifts in the form of individualized personal greetings or songs.

By 1944, however, the maverick Quinn decided to augment his business plan to encompass straight-up music production. He created his own labels, first Gulf and then Gold Star, specializing originally in what he called "hill-billy" songs. Soon, though, he was recruiting and recording African American blues singers, of which there were plenty in mid-twentieth-century Houston. By the time that the postwar boom years were underway, Quinn had become a legitimate but eccentric one-man record company doing his small-scale business far removed from the industry centers.

Starting in 1950, following a bit of success on the regional market and some consequent legal entanglements with the Internal Revenue Service, Quinn made some changes. Closing his shop on Telephone Road, he moved the whole enterprise into his family residence, conveniently located just a few blocks away. That modest homestead was also situated on a larger tract of land, which would later offer valuable space for expansion. Meanwhile, Quinn, his wife, and their son continued to live upstairs while he set up and ran his recording studio and company on the first floor.

Today that business is still in operation, under a different name, on the same site. Moreover, the large, remodeled-many-times-over building located there still uses some of the aged structure of Quinn's old house. And just beyond the property boundaries, various working-class families still reside nearby.

One might ask: How could such a significant recording studio be located in such an odd edifice on such an obscure street? Blame it on the "anything goes" mentality that, past and present, has defined Houston, the nation's largest city to reject zoning laws regulating land use. Blame it also on the fact that this particular mixed-use southeast-side neighborhood has somehow been bypassed by the regentrification that has altered so much other inside-the-Loop real estate. Blame it too perhaps on the incongruousness inherent in the strange business of independently recording music. Whatever the case, the most historic continuously operated studio in Texas remains almost hidden from public consciousness, even in Houston. But there it is, nestled on a dead-end street among a gritty hodgepodge of residential bungalows, machine shops, small businesses, and warehouses serviced by the nearby railroad line.

This book is largely the story of that place, the house where the studio founder once lived and made records. A lot has happened to it, and a lot has happened in it over the years. That modest structure has been expanded, re-modeled, and subsumed into a more intricate network of hallways, offices, storage rooms, and studio spaces. One could easily overlook the currently extant architectural clues, but to the keen observer its original foundation, main walls, and roofline remain detectable even today within the larger footprint. Known with changing times under a variety of business names—including Quinn Recording, Gold Star, International Artists, and SugarHill—it is the unlikely home of one of the most noteworthy independent recording enterprises in the history of postwar popular music.

AS WITH ALL ACCOUNTS, THIS ONE HAS A NARRATOR, a role overtly assumed by me, Andy Bradley, abetted by the writing skills, research, and historical insights of my collaborator Roger Wood. Speaking in the first person at various points in the book, I sometimes directly relate experiences and observations that are part of my ongoing professional relationship with the historic recording facility now known as SugarHill Studios.

But there are many voices that ultimately inform this story. Beyond Roger's own distinctive coauthorial voice (which invisibly influences the texture, tone, and shape of the entire narrative), there are scores of musicians, producers, engineers, and others who share their own oral historical accounts. These portions are culled mostly from a series of documented interviews I conducted (over several years) and are interwoven into the text in the form of quotations, most of which adopt a personal perspective too. Otherwise, except when thus signified, only I shall wield the first-person singular pronouns.

So who am I?

I am a Japanese-born Canadian of Russian and Anglo parentage who grew up in Asia and Australia and moved to Houston in 1980. A large part of my life was, is, and will always be music—as a fan and as a longtime professional audio recording engineer. Growing up overseas did not stop me from amassing a large record collection filled with American rock, blues, and country music. Some of my favorite recordings came from artists such as the Big Bopper, Sir Douglas Quintet, Bubble Puppy, 13th Floor Elevators, and Lightnin' Hopkins. I also grew up intrigued by records produced by Pappy Daily, Huey P. Meaux, and Don Robey. Today it still blows my mind to realize that I work in the space where they made so many classic recordings.

In the 1970s in Australia I worked as an audio engineer and roadie for various bands and sound companies. Under a pseudonym ("Supermort") as well as my own name, I also worked as a part-time journalist writing a rock column and music-related articles for several Australian magazines.

Then in 1980 I moved to Houston and started working at the ACA Studios. After four years of being mentored by the veteran audio man Bill Holford, I approached Meaux, then the owner of SugarHill, with a proposal to bring my client base and take over his studio operations. Meaux agreed, and I became the latest in a long lineage of engineers to work in this historic place. So I was thrilled years ago to have the gig, and I still am. It comprises the bulk of my professional work (though I also have served for many years as the senior audio engineer at Rice University's Shepherd School of Music).

But I actually came to the profession circuitously, all thanks to Radio Birdman.

You see, as a journalist some of my work (published in magazines such as *Rolling Stone, Ram,* and *Juke*) focused on the extraordinary Australian alternative rock band known by that bizarre moniker. I was a big fan and eventually worked for Radio Birdman as a roadie. I soon developed deep friendships with all the principals, interacting with them professionally and personally on the road, on stage, in recording sessions, and at home. These guys are integral to my life's path.

Today Radio Birdman is widely considered to be one of the all-time greatest Australian bands. For example, John Dougan, writing in the *All Music Guide to Rock,* credits these "highly regarded punk forefathers" with "changing the course of Australian rock forever." Led by Deniz Tek, Radio Birdman's sound and style disregarded many established rock band conventions. They also established an independent record company that enabled them to sidestep the major label morass.

Working as a sound technician and roadie for Radio Birdman first brought me into recording sessions and set in place the chain of events that led to my career as a professional recording engineer, my part-ownership of a famous studio, and my coauthorship of this book.

Many factors have coalesced to facilitate the research and inspire my efforts, ultimately including my invaluable collaboration with Roger Wood to bring this book to fruition. Our work together has taught us many things— not only about the history of a rare, almost unique studio complex but also about Houston, the upper Gulf Coast region, the state of Texas, and American popular music at large.

As early R&B star Joe Hinton sings in the title line of a 1964 hit record that was written by Willie Nelson and recorded at Gold Star Studios: "Ain't it funny how time slips away?" This book seeks to reclaim slippery time, or at least a meaningful portion of it, the part that relates to a place that has produced a huge quantity of great music in many different eras and styles. May you enjoy your journey back in time, back to what was originally a simple residential structure in an unzoned neighborhood, back to the place where Bill Quinn founded the enterprise that would become, however unlikely, a house of hits.

House of Hits

The Raid

SHE SAID, "PUT THAT DOWN, and put your hands up!" I thought, *hmm, some anonymous chick singer with a sense of humor.*

It was ten o'clock in the morning, Friday, January 26, 1996. I was walking across the hall, from the Studio A control room toward Studio B, with a rack full of expensive microphone preamps in my arms. My mental focus at that moment had been solely on an upcoming recording session. Otherwise, I was just awaiting the arrival of the producer whose mixing session I had scheduled. But then this attractive black woman in jeans, black sweater, sneakers, and a light-blue satin jacket was suddenly walking toward me shouting her outrageous requests.

I was about halfway into the studio before I felt a large gun barrel stuck in the middle of my back. She sternly repeated her command. Exasperated, I said, "OK, but I'm carrying five thousand bucks' worth of gear here, and I am going to put it down on this table."

Upon depositing that equipment, I turned and faced her with my hands meekly up in the air. It was only then that I saw the automatic pistol and the words "Houston Police" inscribed on her jacket.

The officer immediately asked who else was in the building, and I said that my client, Joel Stein, was in the other studio. Then I thought frantically and quickly added that a guy was upstairs in the tape vault. She motioned her gun and said, "Let's go find them and talk." We crossed the hall back into Studio A. She summoned Joel to join me and then marched us both to the front of the building, where we were turned over to a uniformed officer.

Unbeknownst to all of us, legendary record producer and former studio owner Huey P. Meaux was already handcuffed and sitting in the back of an HPD patrol car in the middle of the studio's parking lot.

As I also later learned, at the onset of the raid my colleague Dan Workman had instinctively hidden himself in the drum booth of Studio B, from which vantage point he observed the exchange between that gun-toting plainclothes cop and me. Unaware of her professional status, he inferred that the studio was being robbed at gunpoint (as was reported to have occurred elsewhere a couple of months earlier). As Workman reflexively headed toward a telephone to call the police, another female officer, pistol pulled, quickly apprehended him.

He was escorted back into the section of the building that housed Meaux's company called Music Enterprises, Inc. It was private office and warehouse space that Meaux rented from the current property owners, Modern Music Ventures, Inc. (MMV).

Elsewhere, Brian Thomas, a musician who was temporarily living in the tape vault, was getting a wakeup call from HPD officers wearing riot gear and pointing pump shotguns at his face. His makeshift quarters and personal belongings were thoroughly searched, and then, wearing nothing but his jockey shorts, he too was brusquely marched down to Meaux's office.

Other plainclothes officers had apprehended Maria Garcia, secretary to the studios and MMV, and directed her to the front of the building.

Meanwhile, in the back corner of Meaux's space, police used battering rams to crash through unlocked doors—a pointlessly dramatic scene that evoked an assault on a fortified crack house. But it was not really a drug raid that shook Meaux's door frames, and what the police found inside was actually rather mundane: two people working on music publishing files and one cleaning lady.

The HPD squad leaders kept Maria, Joel, and me in the front reception room under official supervision. The others were similarly held in other areas. Meanwhile, the search-warrant-sanctioned raiders forcefully proceeded to access and assess the structure and contents of the entire building.

It seems that anywhere a door was locked or even merely closed, they broke through it rather than asking for it to be unlocked or opened. It was a frightening scene to witness, perhaps more so for some of us than for others. For instance, Rosie, a nearby resident and mild-mannered matriarch who provided janitorial services for the building, was verbally harassed (in her native Spanish, by some of the Hispanic officers in the crew) to the point of fearful humiliation. From my perspective, it was a particularly galling abuse of power. But given the circumstances there was little that Rosie, I, or anyone else looking into the barrels of those HPD firearms could do. Nothing, at least, but wait for the search frenzy to conclude—and hope that the mild terror provoked by this unexpected turn of events would soon subside.

The whole experience was exasperating. We had no idea what was going on; or rather, we could see and hear what was going on but had no knowledge of why. And despite the evident gusto with which HPD was executing the raid, there were anomalies that made it all a bit surreal.

About two hours into the disruption, producer David Thompson appeared in the doorway and reported that Meaux was cuffed and detained outside. We had speculated covertly that perhaps someone from one of the bands that stored equipment in the warehouse had been busted for running drugs, or who knows what? Now we began to wonder about Meaux.

About three in the afternoon—some five hours after my plans for a normal workday had disintegrated at gunpoint—the head of the task force announced that they had procured the evidence and collected the necessary information, and then they released us. Until that point, the numerous phones in the building had been ringing sporadically, going unanswered while we waited in limbo. Now it was time, however, for the various enterprises housed at SugarHill Studios to resume contact with the outside world.

Most of the police soon departed, except for a couple of officers who supervised the remaining confiscation and loading of the contents of Meaux's offices and storage spaces for transfer to a bonded warehouse.

By four o'clock Workman was finally able to start his recording session. Meanwhile, I focused on mixing an album. Around eleven o'clock that night David Lummis of MMV handed me the keys to the back of the building and asked me to lock up when the authorities were done.

Early the next day numerous TV station trucks were parked outside SugarHill Studios. All day long the façade of the structure served as the on-the-crime-scene background while various reporters addressed their respective camera lenses and relayed the scandalous news: Meaux, the famous Gulf Coast music producer and promoter, had been busted on drug and sex charges regarding activities with underage females that allegedly took place right here, behind locked doors in some mysterious private chamber that he maintained.

Meanwhile, journalists bombarded the phone lines of various other independent companies based inside the building with requests for statements and interviews. Suddenly everyone, it seemed, had a keen interest (mostly salacious) in this obscurely tucked-away place of business called SugarHill.

The HPD spokesperson, who had been duly told that the property now belonged to MMV, apparently nonetheless misinformed the media, which first reported that the studios were owned by Meaux. The general misperception was thus that the whole multifaceted SugarHill enterprise was somehow complicit in Meaux's treachery and therefore permanently tainted. In truth, however, Meaux had sold the studios to MMV over nine years prior to this arrest. In other words, without knowledge or consent on the part of the

SugarHill Studios, front entrance, 2009 (photo by and courtesy of Tony Endieveri)

actual landlord, the criminal behavior with which Meaux was charged had occurred in privately accessed space (with its own backdoor entrance) that he legally rented and occupied merely as a tenant. His misdeeds should never have been linked with the ownership of the studio, but erroneously they were. Eventually the media were forced by MMV's attorney to correct and retract their false statements. However, some damage had been done.

After the Meaux scandal broke, SugarHill Studios lost a lot of business, and it took nearly six months to recover from the residual paranoia induced by the widespread misreporting and presumed guilt by association. Most prominent among those clients who quickly canceled recording sessions were the gospel artists and church-related producers. But there were many others who followed suit.

The legal aftermath of the Meaux arrest played out over the next five months, as reported in a series of articles in the *Houston Chronicle*. First, Meaux posted bail in the amount of $130,000. Then when he later failed to report to authorities as ordered, he became a fugitive from justice, eventually ending up in Mexico—where in March of 1996 he was arrested in a Juárez hotel and turned over to the FBI. After being extradited to Houston, Meaux initially entered a plea of not guilty. However, two months later he avoided a trial by pleading guilty to all charges: two counts of sexual assault of a child, one count of possession of cocaine, one count of child pornography, and one count of bond jumping. He was sentenced to fifteen years' imprisonment at a Texas Department of Corrections unit in Huntsville.

Following the sentencing, most of the nonevidentiary contents of Meaux's rented office were returned to the building. As time passed, most of us at SugarHill went about our business as usual, albeit with a heightened appreciation of a normal workday. Nevertheless, through the end of the 1990s it seemed that I was regularly encountering people who inquired whether SugarHill had closed or, presuming it had, asked where I was now working.

The night following the raid, I had walked silently through the debris within Meaux's trashed-out office, exhausted yet trying to fulfill my assignment to close and somehow lock the mutilated doors. As I surveyed the damage and thought about the unsettling events that had transpired, I wondered if this was perhaps the darkest day in the history of this venerable recording studio complex. Like others familiar with the lore of the building, I had heard stories of misdeeds and convictions of one of its previous affiliates. But the sensationalism generated by the Meaux arrest certainly topped that one, especially in terms of media exposure and public disdain. To say it made me uneasy is an understatement.

However, even then something inside me realized that this was likely eventually to be, in retrospect, just one small chapter in the story of this historic building. I thought of the hundreds of musicians, singers, producers, and engineers who had previously done such significant work here. Then I wished, and I believed, that all of this Meaux-induced bad karma would dissipate like a violent storm and that, yes, the sun would shine on SugarHill again.

Domestic Crude

IN MANY RESPECTS, the recording studio company currently known as SugarHill aptly reflects the unusual city in which it came into being and evolved. Given the eccentricities of its origin, its expanded physical structure, and its development into a nexus for the recording of so many variant types of music, it seems reasonable to surmise that such a unique studio complex could exist, and for so many years, only in Houston.

The largest municipality in Texas, and the fourth-largest in the nation, Houston is still at its core a supersized boomtown characterized in part by the crap-shoot speculation, grimy realities, and occasionally lucrative windfalls of its signature major industry: oil. Though named in honor of the first president of the Republic of Texas, the city was founded in 1836 as a moneymaking venture by a pair of real estate developers from New York. Relatively free of pretension regarding its social history, this international port city has been consistently receptive to a diverse influx of newcomers offering skills, capital, or ideas to exploit in the open marketplace. Despite its various shortcomings, Houston has proven itself to be a pretty good place to find a job, build a business, or, in these ways or otherwise, start over in life. Local government has long championed free enterprise and the entrepreneurial spirit, seemingly taking a kind of perverse pride in its no-zoning policy—unique for an American city of its size.

In these ways Houston reflects the origins and evolution of the recording company that Bill Quinn launched there in 1941. For both this multifaceted studio enterprise and the metropolis that is its home emerged from humble origins far removed from the established centers of financial or cultural power. Yet both—through ingenuity, hard work, a no-zoning mentality, and a capacity for unmitigated expansion—evolved into forces that have impacted the world at large.

The Gold Star/SugarHill legacy is thus inextricably a Houston story—and, as such, a Texas story. Key elements of the city's character and composition are essential factors in the studio's very existence, its independence, and its uncanny success.

As David G. McComb notes in *The Portable Handbook of Texas,* Houston had first established itself in the 1800s as a rail center and market hub for cotton and lumber, but it was the discovery of oil in 1901 at the nearby Spindletop field that "dramatically changed the Houston economy in the twentieth century." With that discovery, and the opening of the Houston Ship Channel in 1914, the city soon established itself as the petrochemical capital of the nation, attracting thousands of immigrants each year in the process. After 1945 Houston's postwar economy accelerated rapidly, and its population followed suit, soaring from approximately 500,000 to over 1.5 million inhabitants by the early 1960s. This tremendous influx of people also stimulated a blossoming club scene for regional strands of popular music. In turn, the vibrant live-music market encouraged the talent that became the basis for the growth of independent record companies and the studios that served their needs.

In these facilities singers, musicians, record producers, songwriters, and audio engineers from all over the area would gather in controlled environments in hopes of creating a hit record. If that elusive goal was fulfilled, it then became a source of revenue for the principals and perhaps a way of making a career. In terms of big dreams, disappointments, calculated risks, and potential rewards, independently prospecting for a hit record was a lot like wildcat drilling for oil. The Houston mentality, of a piece with that of oil-rich Texas at large, not only understood but seemed to relish such challenges. Whether one were hoping for hit records or oil deposits, nothing was ever guaranteed. But the allure of proving one's instincts to be trustworthy, almost as much as the desire for a lucrative payoff, proved irresistible to a certain breed of speculator.

One of the most prominent of such individuals in the local music business was Don Robey (1903–1975), a native son of the city and a self-described gambler. Between 1949 and 1973 he owned and developed at least five record labels—and sometimes used Gold Star Studios to produce his sessions. As Nelson George says in *The Death of Rhythm and Blues,* "Don Robey built an empire worth millions in a city far removed from the main line of entertainment." His remarkable success was the equivalent of hitting a series of huge gushers in the oil fields, and it surely stimulated lots of would-be imitators in the city, some of whom succeeded too.

But other factors also fueled the sudden rise of the independents both in and beyond Houston. Following a period of commercial dormancy during World War II, the mainstream American recording industry resumed operations but substantially altered its ways, in part because the rise of broadcast television was quickly changing the nature of the game. As the established companies began to make enormous profits from nationwide hit singles produced in their own recording studios (and sometimes promoted to millions of potential customers via national television exposure), major-label executives soon decided that the expenses and risks of recording localized talent for regional markets were no longer justified. In short, the big record labels stopped going out into the field to make their recordings. Their withdrawal thus opened the door for the growth of the independent recording industry in places such as Texas, despite a dearth of studio facilities there at the time.

Another scenario was the sudden postwar presence of recently discharged veterans who possessed previously rare knowledge and skills concerning electronics. Bill Holford of ACA Studios, the chief competitor to Bill Quinn's Gold Star Studios, was one such military-trained innovator. He and various other entrepreneurs and independent engineers like him built most of the early studios and manufacturing plants in Houston, Dallas, and San Antonio. Quinn's original pressing plant and, some years later, Gaspar Puccio's Houston Records were among the first. These were all self-reliant projects, for it was not until the early 1970s (when technological groundbreakers such as Rupert Neve began producing high-quality recording equipment in quantities to supply the needs of the burgeoning field) that studio owners generally stopped designing and building their own equipment.

Since the 1930s Houston had been a particularly fertile area for country singers and dance bands, the original focus of Quinn's involvement in the music recording business. Bill C. Malone, in *Country Music, U.S.A.*, cites Gold Star Studios as his first example of the many small recording companies that had come into being by the 1950s. Yet, despite the fact that it originally announced itself to the world via the slogan "King of the Hillbillies," Quinn's fledging enterprise, as far back as 1947, was already crossing the racial barriers of the time to record African American music. Why? More so perhaps than any other city in the state, Houston was the center of a thriving black community. Hence, by the late 1940s, it was making its mark on the popular genres of blues, R&B, and gospel, with artists such as Lightnin' Hopkins and moguls such as Robey leading the way. Despite the rigid segregation in place at the time, Quinn was, almost from the start, a major documentarian of the sounds of mid-century black Houston.

By the 1950s Quinn's studios were also home to the Starday and D Records labels owned by Harold W. "Pappy" Daily (1902–1987), a native of Southeast Texas who became a prominent music publisher, producer, and promoter.

Among other achievements, Daily helped to launch the recording careers of George Jones, the Big Bopper, Johnny Preston, Frankie Miller, Roger Miller, and several other members of the Country Music Hall of Fame.

Almost from the start Quinn was recording both country music by whites and blues by black performers. These two categories of roots music represent the dominant sounds of the otherwise mostly segregated white and black working classes of the era. Quinn recorded Mexican American music too. Together these styles formed the foundation not only for the early success of the Gold Star venture but also for the larger music culture of Houston—and that of Texas in general.

However, although country and blues sensibilities best characterize the music first produced by Quinn, multiple varieties of rock, jazz, zydeco, pop, Tejano, R&B, rap, classical, contemporary Christian, and other genres ultimately become part of the story too. Now well into the twenty-first century, this historic studio company still exists in a structure built onto what was once his family home. Where else could such a phenomenon occur? Only in a city that has always allowed property owners to build pretty much whatever they want on their land, even if it is situated in a residential neighborhood. And only in a city that has been a hotbed of talent for so many different styles of music. And, even more to the point, only at a studio company that has long embraced a no-zoning philosophy in its approach to music recording.

Like Houston itself, the Gold Star/SugarHill complex is a sprawling, seemingly unplanned and unrestricted, multicultural place. Compared to certain high-class counterparts elsewhere, both the city and the recording facility may seem unimpressive at first glance. Yet beyond their funky exteriors, both share some rare achievements and distinctions. One is tempted to say that they share a common spirit or soul, a certain intangibility.

Perhaps noted rock journalist Chet Flippo sums it up best when he defines the essence of Texas music as "crude grace." That oxymoronic phrase may refer to the musical heritage of the Lone Star State at large, but it also evokes the particular essence of Houston, of Quinn's self-taught genius, and of many of the producers and artists who have made music on the site that he established.

Maybe it is just a certain Texan instinct, informed as it is by the mythos of defiant independence that is part of the state's lore. Perhaps it comes down to a kind of stubborn self-trust, fueled by a tinge of healthy disdain for East Coast or West Coast cultural hegemony. For here in the largest city on the Gulf Coast, many folks—including oil-field wildcatters and record producers alike—have dared to define their own paths, whatever the consequences.

That mentality, of course, implies a type of strong-willed, critics-be-damned motivation that some outsiders might consider to be cocky, naïve, or even crazy. And yes, it is brash, sometimes reckless, and often more than a bit crude in its various manifestations. But at its core lies a self-sufficiency that can sometimes lead to rare and, despite the contradictions, even wonderful phenomena—such as a major metropolis without zoning laws, for instance.

Given his peripatetic background, Quinn could have just as well settled somewhere else. Perhaps elsewhere he could have even successfully started a career in the recording studio business. Yet the fact that he came to and stayed in Houston, becoming a naturalized Texan of sorts in the process, is essential to understanding how and why this particular man was ultimately able to transform his very residence into a storied studio complex in which the no-zoning mentality extended to musical styles and performers—a place where anything might have seemed possible for anyone who dared to dream big and trust his gut.

The Independent Quinn

WILLIAM RUSSELL ("BILL") QUINN was born in Amesbury, Massachusetts, on January 8, 1904, the son of an Irish immigrant mother and a father about whom we have no information. Not quite seventy-two years later, on January 4, 1976, he passed away in Houston, a death apparently noted in print at the time only in a brief *Houston Post* obituary. Though he may have departed this life and his adopted home city without much fanfare, during the many years that he resided there, Quinn created, expanded, and eventually sold the ongoing multifaceted enterprise that Ray Cano Jr. defines in *Texas Music History Online* as "the oldest continuously operating recording facility in Texas."

Known during most of Quinn's proprietorship as Gold Star and today as SugarHill, this studio complex has been, as described by William Michael Smith in *Paste* magazine, "a virtual open mic for the sounds swirling through the honky-tonks and juke joints that dot the Gulf Coast." Thus, as both a businessman and a music documentarian, Quinn is a significant figure in state history and American culture. Yet in some respects, it seems he only casually aspired to achieve much success in either arena, making his accomplishments all the more remarkable.

Despite being an amateur musician himself (who reportedly played the button accordion, organ, and bass), Quinn may have originally been more interested in the technology of recording and disc pressing than in the regionally distinctive styles of music that his self-taught skills would eventually capture and preserve. For example, as Andrew Brown writes in his *Harry Choates* essay, Quinn operated "more in the manner of a glorified hobbyist . . . [who had] realized his ambition when he discovered the secret to pressing records" and who "essentially had no guiding vision when it came to the record business." However, Quinn had settled in the right place at an opportune time to make some important recordings.

The exact starting date of Quinn's Houston residency is unknown. The aforementioned obituary, almost certainly composed or informed by a family member who would know, identifies Quinn as a "Houston resident for 36 years"—suggesting that he had made the move by late 1939 or 1940. Producer Chris Strachwitz, in his liner note essay to *Texas Blues: The Gold Star Sessions*, suggests that Quinn's decision to settle in the city was motivated in part by chance. It happened while Quinn was on winter break from his seasonal job as a sound technician for a New Jersey–based traveling carnival company (Royal American Shows). On their way back to the East Coast, Quinn and his first wife Lona had come through Houston to visit her sister, but their car broke down, leaving them stranded without funds to pay for repairs. "Bill, however, . . . was soon earning money repairing radios," Strachwitz writes.

Operating at first out of his sister-in-law's house, Quinn encountered a customer who asked him to fix a nonfunctioning home disc recorder. Quinn was so intrigued by the contraption that he purchased his own disc-recording device and began to experiment with it. By 1941, he had opened his first shop at 3104 Telephone Road and soon started recording individual voice messages direct to disc—mostly birthday greetings and such, novelty items sent to relatives and friends. This unexpected new direction in his vaguely defined business plan led him to change the name of his one-man operation from Quinn Radio Service to Quinn Recording Company, and—just like that—what was formerly a "shop" was transformed into a "studio." The proprietor soon was profitably producing radio jingles and other types of audio commercials, most likely his main source of income throughout the World War II years.

Fortunately for Quinn, Houston was a rapidly growing city where the demand for locally produced sound recordings, particularly those used in radio advertising, likely exceeded the supply of businesses that could accommodate the need. In a Houston telephone directory from April 1944, for example, Quinn Recording Company is one of only two clearly defined recording services listed in the Yellow Pages. The other is a now long-gone establishment called Sound Sales & Engineering Company, which advertised in-store and on-location recording. Two other businesses, Lil' Pal Exclusive Radio & Record Store and a place called The Groove, were probably only retail outlets for the sale of prerecorded discs and players.

The war years and their aftermath were obviously a time of many changes throughout America, but especially so in the media that dispersed recorded music. Thus, though he probably never imagined such a possibility when he settled in Houston, Quinn would soon discover another grand opportunity, one that would cause him to develop new technological skills far beyond those required merely for engineering the single-disc recording of sound for radio ads. Still working out of his Telephone Road storefront through the end of the 1940s, Quinn would metamorphose into a maverick music producer and studio proprietor and, for a while, even a record label owner.

During this period, the Quinn family lived in a house located at 1313 Dumble Street in southeast Houston, not far from the Telephone Road studio. (Incidental numerological trivia: 1313 is also the first number that Quinn used in cataloguing the productions of his Gold Star Record Company.) By 1950 Quinn's family would move nearby in the same neighborhood to a two-story house at 5628 Brock Street, as would his studio facility, which he would rename also as Gold Star.

Today there is a small retail strip center at 3104 Telephone Road where Quinn's original studio once stood. According to Clyde Brewer (a fiddler, pianist, and guitarist who recorded first at Quinn Recording and then later at its Gold Star and SugarHill incarnations), the now demolished original building, before becoming a studio, had housed a corner grocery store and gas station. Brewer's earliest memories of the studio date back to 1947, when, as a teenager, he played fiddle on a session with his uncle in the group Shelly Lee Alley's Alley Cats.

Brewer recalls walking in off the street directly into "a fairly good-sized" studio room with a small control room off to the right side, visible through a tiny window. In the main studio room stood a baby grand piano and a single microphone on a tall stand. Behind the studio room was another section, which contained the pressing plant and a bathroom. The walls of the studio were plain white-painted surfaces with no appreciable soundproofing elements. In the control room there were a large disc-cutting lathe made by Presto and a Rek-O-Kut turntable driven by a motor with a huge fan belt.

Another longtime country musician who played on many sessions, steel guitar master Frank Juricek, provides his own description:

> Bill Quinn's studio on Telephone Road was an old gas station with the pumps taken out—and might have had a grocery store also in the main building. It still had the canopy in the front, which made it easy to unload equipment even if it was raining. . . . You walked right into the studio when you walked in the front door. There really wasn't any real entryway. In the back right corner of the room was his booth where the acetate cutter and turntable and such were. The piano would sit right in front of his booth. . . . He had added on to the back of the building, and that's where he had his pressing plant and all the equipment he needed to do the plating and all that other stuff.

Juricek's references to "plating" and the "other stuff" allude to basic production techniques employed by Quinn in the late 1940s. For starters, the disc recorder with which he had begun in 1941 had soon given way to more sophisticated equipment. However, he had no tape recorders, which had been invented in Germany and largely kept secret through the war years. Such technology was not yet readily available or affordable to pioneering independent sound technicians such as Quinn. (Ampex premiered its later widely adopted 300 series in late 1949 and 1950.) In Quinn's early phase, recording was still done direct to disc on masters made of wax (or in later years, acetate) at the speed of 78 revolutions per minute (rpm). The 45 rpm disc did not proliferate until the 1950s. Moreover, shellac was a key ingredient for making disc material, and it was generally in short supply for nonmilitary purposes during the war.

To make a record in the studio, one or more microphones would be plugged directly into a tube mixer and/or tube preamp. While the musicians performed into the microphone(s), the resulting sound signal was passed straight to the cutting lathe, and the needle of the lathe etched this sonic information directly onto the disc. Later that wax disc would be doused repeatedly in a liquefied nickel bath and thus plated. The disc then became a "mother" that could spawn as many stamping plates as necessary.

The creation of the stamping plates, or stampers, was a time-consuming and delicate process. It started by placing shellac (or in subsequent years, vinyl), as well as the preprinted front and back paper labels, in proper alignment between the plates. Then the presses compressed those materials together, creating duplicates of the original, one at a time. These records were typically referred to as "singles," with an A-side and a B-side, totaling two songs per disc. During this era producing an album-length recording was very difficult. Why? The artists would essentially have to perform all of the material for a whole long-play (LP) side straight through, in a single sitting, with only a brief pause between each song in a set of five or more. In other words, since the recording process was strictly direct to disc, there was no option for editing, adding, subtracting, or rearranging separate tracks. It is important to remember also that standard audio recording at this time was mono, not stereophonic.

Nevertheless, these wax masters were capable of rendering good recordings. The main obstacle to excellent sound fidelity, until the early 1950s, was related to the use of shellac as the primary ingredient in the copies. The subsequent introduction of vinyl (or vinylite) vastly improved the quality of pressings, allowing records to more closely represent the nuances and tones of the original musical performance.

Frank Juricek, 1948 (courtesy of Frank Juricek)

Juricek performed on numerous Quinn-produced tracks starting in the late 1940s, including sessions with fellow musicians such as Hank Locklin, Leon Payne, Ernie Hunter, Lester Voytek, Red Novak, Pete Machanga, and singer Frances Turner. Later, after the studio moved to Brock Street, he played also on Quinn-engineered tracks produced by Pappy Daily. Reflecting on those experiences, Juricek emphasizes the unique role that Quinn played in the regional music scene at the time:

> He was the first man doing the real recordings in Houston. . . . I used to hang out at the studio all the time, and I wanted to know how you took those acetate discs and turned them into masters. So he took me back there and showed me the whole process. . . . He showed me the plating process, and then he showed me what I called the "waffle" that he put between the labels in the press—and out came the record. It looked like a waffle iron because of the excess that came out around the edge of the press that had to be trimmed off.

According to Brewer, Quinn's early recording sessions typically involved only one microphone—with the musicians arranged around it and the singer and primary instrumental soloist positioned closest. Because it was a direct-to-disc recording process, during each session Quinn had to hover watchfully with a clean paintbrush in hand, gently pushing toward the center of the disc the shavings dug out by the needle. By the end of the song, Quinn would have "a big glob of wax" to discard.

As for the ambient environment, Brewer also notes that there was no heat or air-conditioning in Quinn's Telephone Road building—a factor that could affect the whole recording process. He shares the following anecdote:

> We were on a two-day session when a wicked cold snap came through Houston during the night, following the first day of recording. The next morning Bill had to use a blowtorch to heat up the motor in the lathe so that it would maintain a constant speed during the second day.

Accounts such as these illustrate only some of the challenges and problems that an early recording engineer such as Quinn had to address to create his products. Because the few major record companies were zealously protective of industry secrets and technology, he had to figure out the process and acquire workable studio equipment on his own. Moreover, because the federal government still controlled most of the nation's shellac supply (and the major record companies dominated the limited market for the rest), he also had to scramble to procure the raw material for making records.

But Quinn ingeniously pulled it off. He somehow arranged to purchase an older, phased-out pressing-plant machine from an unidentified source. Then he inquisitively began to tinker with it—experimenting, modifying, and updating it until it could meet his needs. He also scoured the city's resale shops and garage sales, buying all the old 78 rpm records that he could find. He then pulverized them in a coffee bean grinder, melted down the resulting shards and dust, and thereby reclaimed the reconstituted shellac-based material. However, the paper labels attached to the recycled records somewhat contaminated the resulting substance, and that lack of purity negatively affected the sound quality it was capable of reproducing. Nonetheless, the process worked. Because the recycled matter was pliable and doughy, it was generally nicknamed "biscuit." Mack McCormick, who knew Quinn firsthand, says that Quinn regularly scheduled "biscuit days" devoted to acquiring old records for reprocessing to yield ingredients for making new ones.

As a result, Quinn achieved a rare status for the 1940s, one unprecedented in Texas and throughout most of the South: self-sufficiency not only in making recordings but also in mastering them, electroplating them, and then pressing multiple copies for distribution and sale. As Brown writes in the aforementioned liner notes, Quinn "had found an independent way to go from the studio to the warehouse, and so was free to put regional talent in record stores. He sneered at the monopoly, thereby helping to end it."

Gold Star Records

ILL QUINN MUST HAVE HAD an open mind about the music he recorded. Being an outsider to the region, he perhaps lacked the generally ingrained social prejudices of most middle-aged white men in the South at the time. His initial focus was simply on making the kinds of records that might get stocked on jukeboxes and in music stores in Houston and along the Southeast Texas coast. As a result, by 1947 he was readily producing sessions featuring black musicians as well as white, or featuring lyrics sung in either French or English. The styles he recorded predominantly reflect the working-class tastes and demographics of the time and place: country, Cajun, gospel, and blues.

As a pioneer in the nascent business of independently recording, reproducing, and distributing roots music for popular consumption, Quinn faced many challenges. Having mastered the studio and pressing plant process, he next needed to align with a record label—a separate company that would handle business relationships with performers and product marketing. Ever the self-reliant individual, Quinn opted to create his own record label—twice, in fact. However, both would be relatively short-lived enterprises. More proficient as an engineer than as a music mogul, for most of his career Quinn chose to concentrate solely on studio and plant operations. Yet during the approximately six years that he owned record labels, Quinn produced many historic discs.

Ownership of a record label should not be confused with ownership of a recording studio or pressing plant. A record company signs individual artists or groups to contracts, pays for recording sessions in studios and the creation of products in plants (but does not necessarily own those facilities), arranges for distribution and marketing of products, accounts for and pays royalties (ideally, at least), and so on. On the other hand, a studio is the physical facility (equipped with sound-recording technology and serviced by in-house engineers) in which a recording session takes place and in which the results are subsequently mastered for reproduction. A pressing plant is a factory, separate from the studio, in which multiple duplicate copies of that product are rendered.

Grasping those distinctions is particularly important because Quinn would ultimately use the same brand name, Gold Star, for both a record label and, after relocating to Brock Street, his major studio facility. In other words, Gold Star Records is a separate enterprise from Gold Star Studios, though Quinn was proprietor of both. But before he ever began using the Gold Star name, back when he was doing business as Quinn Recording Services, he would make his initial foray into label ownership.

In league with someone—though exactly who is not clear—Quinn first launched the Gulf Record Company label in July of 1944. In his *Harry Choates* liner notes, Andrew Brown cites Frank Sanborn and Orville "Bennie" Hess as the original partners, based on a DBA statement acknowledging the same. Nevertheless, Brown also points to evidence suggesting that W. Kendall Baker may have been involved rather than Hess. Moreover, Quinn later is reported to have insisted, to musicologist Paul Oliver, that Vernon Woodworth was his only business partner at the time. Whatever the case, the Gulf gamble failed, coming as it did before Quinn had discovered the right artists, built his own pressing plant, or established any distribution strategy. Within a year of its creation, it was abandoned and replaced by Quinn's Gold Star imprint.

According to Chris Strachwitz, Quinn told him that the first commercial release on the doomed Gulf label was a 78 rpm disc featuring an artist identified as Tex Moon performing an A-side song entitled "When We Planted Old Glory in Japan." To date we have not been able to verify, however, that this record was ever actually issued to the retail market. It seems more likely that a Gulf disc attributed to Woody Vernon, "I'm Lonesome But I'm Free" backed with "A Rainy Sunday Night," was the first actually to be marketed. This recording was released with the catalogue number Gulf 100 (a numeration often used for the start of a series in recording). Moreover, Woody Vernon is known to have been the stage name of Vernon Woodworth, the man whom Quinn later identified as his sole partner in the Gulf venture. Complicating matters, however, is Strachwitz's implication that Tex Moon may have also been a stage name for Woodworth.

Whoever the singer might have been, the novice label owner Quinn first struggled to get from the recording studio to the retail marketplace because he had no pressing equipment. In fact, the main significance of Quinn's Gulf Records debacle may be that it prompted him to build his own pressing plant. As Quinn soon discovered, the big record companies that controlled the only extant pressing facilities did not generally do custom pressings for small independent firms. He searched widely for a pressing service, thinking for a while that he had found one in Janette Records of Richmond, Virginia. However, when it became clear that Quinn needed pressings not for some vanity project but for discs intended for commercial distribution on jukeboxes, that company (which had recently been absorbed by a major label, Decca Records) also refused. Quinn could have given up then, assuming that such obstacles, reinforced as they were by the policies and powers of the dominant corporations, were insurmountable. The only alternative, once again, was self-reliance. So Quinn located, bought, and transported the previously described used pressing machine and began to refurbish it and learn, entirely on his own, how to make duplicate discs of his recordings.

Only four singles released on the Gulf label have been accounted for to date, those identified by the catalogue numbers 100, 103, 105, and 3000. The missing numbers in the 100 series may have been assigned to other releases, but so far no evidence of that has been discovered. Of that group, the most significant is arguably "Nails in My Coffin" (#103), written and performed by Jerry Irby. Although the record did little for Irby's performing career, the song was good enough to soon be covered by both Floyd Tillman and Ernest Tubb, two giants of country music. Tillman's version, recorded for the Columbia label (#36998), debuted in August of 1946 and peaked at number two on the country charts. Tubb's treatment, released by Decca (#46019), came out in December of 1946, charting as high as number five. Bolstered by such professional acknowledgment of his skills, Irby established a reputation as a songwriter. Incidentally, he returned to the studios in 1959 and rerecorded "Nails in My Coffin" for Hi-Lo Records (#1244/1245) as the flip side to "The Sea."

Gulf single number 3000 is also noteworthy. It presents an African American group called Jesse Lockett and His Orchestra performing the songs "Blacker the Berry" and "Boogie Woogie Mama." Dating from early 1946, this recording features an incipient R&B sound, and it may well be the first of such recordings ever made in Houston. Thus, it set the stage for the many important blues and R&B recordings that Quinn would soon produce on the Gold Star label.

BY 1946 QUINN HAD DROPPED THE GULF RECORDS brand and founded a new company, Gold Star Records, which became one of the earliest and most successful independent record labels in the South. More importantly, it was the first in Texas devoted to country, blues, and Cajun music—and the first to produce a national hit.

Under the Gold Star name, Quinn scored a major success with his premiere release. It came unexpectedly from an old song, the title of which Quinn had incorrectly documented as "Jole Blon" (#1314). That was his double misspelling of the French phrase "Jolie Blonde" ("Pretty Blonde"), the title of a traditional South Louisiana waltz lyric. The performer was Harry Choates (1922–1951), whose surname was also misspelled on the first pressings of the disc label within the artist identification "Harry Shoates & & His Fiddle" (yes, the ampersand was incoherently doubled too). A native of Vermilion Parish, Louisiana, Choates had grown up across the Sabine River in Port Arthur, Texas, a Cajun stronghold approximately ninety miles east of Houston. Accompanying himself on fiddle and backed by a string band, Choates sang on his Gold Star debut disc with such plaintive enthusiasm that many listeners, whether they could translate the French lyrics or not, wanted their own copies of "Jole Blon."

The result was a commercial success that twice in 1947 (January and March) hit the number four spot on the *Billboard* charts for "Most Played Juke Box Folk Records." In so doing it also signaled the arrival of Gold Star Records on the national music scene. That recording was the first and only Cajun song ever to make *Billboard*'s Top Five in any category—hence, its longstanding reputation as "the Cajun national anthem."

Initially, however, Gold Star's "Jole Blon" was only a regional hit, which introduced a new problem for Quinn to solve. Triggered by heavy airplay on a Houston radio station, the sudden local demand for copies quickly overstressed Quinn's capacity to make them in the little one-man pressing plant he had recently set up. Assessing the desperate situation, he realized the need to press more discs faster and to deliver them for sale while the record was still popular. So, despite his inclination for working solo, Quinn wisely arranged a licensing agreement with Modern Records, an independent West Coast company that thereafter handled much of the pressing, national distribution, and promotion of this erstwhile Gold Star single.

The strategy worked, for thousands of people far beyond the upper Gulf Coast were soon buying "Jole Blon" or punching its number on jukeboxes. It would later also be leased and reissued outright on other labels, including not only Modern (#20-511), but also Starday (#187), D Records (#1024), and Deluxe. Surely a novelty to many, this recording nonetheless established the beloved Cajun song as a country music standard. As Texas Country Music Hall of Fame member Johnny Bush (b. 1935) says,

When I was a young boy living in Kashmere Gardens [in northeast Houston], my parents played Harry Choates' "Jole Blon" on our Victrola, and that was a

Harry Choates, Austin, ca. 1950

giant smash hit in our area! It must still be a big hit today because if people come to your show and see fiddles on the bandstand, you can't leave without playing it at least once that night.

In search of similar hits, Quinn subsequently recorded Choates numerous times, singing in French and in English, before the latter's untimely 1951 death. Some of the resulting tracks were issued on Quinn's Gold Star label; others were recorded by Quinn but issued on labels such as Starday, Hummingbird, or D Records. Among those titles are several blatant attempts to capitalize on "Jole Blon," including a version of the same song delivered in English, plus "Mari Jole Blon" ("Jole Blon's Husband"), "Jole Blon's Gone," and "Jole Brun" ("Pretty Brunette"). However, none of these follow-up releases sold much, nor did any of the more than forty other Choates tracks that Quinn ultimately recorded.

Like his relatively short lifespan, Choates's stint on the *Billboard* charts was brief; there would be no second act for him. There would be, however, other hits for Quinn and his record label. Though Choates was the man who first put the "gold" in Gold Star, Quinn would have to discover other artists to achieve commercial success again.

ONE OF THE MOST INFLUENTIAL SINGERS and guitarists in postwar blues history, Texas native Sam "Lightnin'" Hopkins (1912–1982), had already made his first recordings when Quinn met him and they began their uneasy professional affiliation. In 1946 Hopkins had been recruited by Houston-based talent scout Lola Anne Cullum (1903–1970) to travel to California, where, accompanied by pianist Wilson "Thunder" Smith, he cut a total of six tracks, his earliest, for the Los Angeles–based concern Aladdin Records. During his affiliation with that label through early 1948, Hopkins recorded over forty songs, the majority of which were produced in sessions staged in rented studio space back in Houston. Quinn Recording Company was conveniently located in close proximity to the Third Ward, the southeast Houston neighborhood where Hopkins (who reputedly disliked traveling) resided for most of his life, and in 1947 Hopkins first came there to record, yielding four tracks issued on Aladdin. Observing the interest of a West Coast company in this down-home local blues singer, Quinn seized the opportunity.

Hopkins soon was making records directly for Quinn and Gold Star. Their sporadic relationship continued through the demise of Quinn's label in 1950. During that span Hopkins recorded over one hundred songs at Quinn's Telephone Road studio, reportedly usually at a flat rate (for example, seventy-five or one hundred dollars cash) per session.

Hopkins's first Gold Star release (#3131) was a remake of a song previously recorded in California for Aladdin: "Short Haired Woman," backed with "Big Mama Jump." Almost immediately in demand on jukeboxes in the African American districts of metropolitan Houston, it became a bona fide regional hit. Its success also prompted Quinn (who still used the now-misleading slogan "King of the Hillbillies" on the labels affixed to his records) to create a completely new category of Gold Star recordings, the 600 series. It was devoted to blues music performed by black artists and intended for distribution primarily to black audiences—what was called the "race records" market at the time. "Short Haired Woman" was thus the commercially successful follow-up to "Jole Blon" that Quinn had been seeking, and Hopkins was his dark-skinned new star.

Lightnin' Hopkins, inside Gold Star Studios, 1961

Other Hopkins records produced by Quinn likewise garnered national attention on the *Billboard* R&B charts. For instance, in November 1948, "T-Model Blues" (Gold Star #662) peaked at number eight. Moreover, in February 1949, Hopkins's performance of the poignant sharecropper's protest song "Tim Moore's Farm" (which Quinn had licensed to Modern Records) peaked at number thirteen. The many songs Hopkins cut for Quinn established his reputation as an innovator with wide appeal among black audiences. Those tracks, licensed and reissued on CD in 1990 by Arhoolie Records as *The Gold Star Sessions, Vol. 1 and Vol. 2*, are today ranked by many aficionados to be essential recordings by one of the greatest blues artists of all time.

Consider, for example, a *Paste* magazine article by Steve LaBate entitled "Just for the Record: 10 Classic Sessions and the Studios That Shaped Them." Purporting to recognize "the greatest albums and singles . . . crafted in the polyphonic pantheons of the music industry," it memorializes the sessions and studios that produced acclaimed masterpieces such as *Pet Sounds* by the Beach Boys (1966), *Abbey Road* by the Beatles (1969), "What's Going On" by Marvin Gaye (1971), and *The Unforgettable Fire* by U2 (1984). Notably, only two recordings made before 1966 are commemorated, both from 1948: the Nashville session for "Lovesick Blues" by Hank Williams and the Houston session for "T-Model Blues" by Lightnin' Hopkins. Though few Houstonians might have believed it at the time, Quinn's modest Telephone Road studio was producing music that impacted popular culture at large—then and now.

Having occasionally harnessed Hopkins's fertile, improvising genius was crucial for Gold Star Records. It was the payoff for the risks Quinn had taken in spontaneously producing a session whenever Hopkins dropped in, usually without advance notice, and offered to record immediately for cash on the spot. As Chris Strachwitz explains in an interview:

Lightnin' liked to make records, and no wonder, when he could sit down a few minutes, make up a number, and collect $100 in cash. And local record producer Bill Quinn had him doing just that. Whenever Lightnin' needed some money, he would go over to . . . Gold Star Studios to "make some numbers." And he had a fantastic talent to come up with an endless supply of these numbers. Many were based on traditional tunes he had heard in the past, but all of the songs received his personal treatment and they came out as very personal poetry.

Strachwitz had originally visited Houston in 1959 as a neophyte producer specifically hoping to meet and record Hopkins—a mission that would lead to the founding of Arhoolie Records, for which Hopkins eventually made numerous recordings. Consequently, the California-based Strachwitz developed a long friendship with both this iconic Texas bluesman and Quinn, whose facilities he sometimes rented and used over the years. Of the relationship between Hopkins and Quinn, Strachwitz says, "Just occasionally Lightnin' would talk about Quinn, you know. He referred to Bill as 'the right sucker' [or] he was 'mister money bags.' Of course, he appeared to call him these things in an affectionate way."

Affection notwithstanding, the Hopkins-Quinn affiliation was often somewhat strained, particularly because the singer nonchalantly ignored previously signed Gold Star contracts whenever another opportunity arose to make a record with—and collect more cash from—someone else. As Alan Lee Haworth points out in *The Handbook of Texas Music*, ultimately "Hopkins recorded for nearly twenty different labels." Nevertheless, as Alan Govenar asserts in *Meeting the Blues*, the many tracks Quinn documented for Gold Star Records constitute Hopkins's "finest work." As such, those Hopkins recordings at Quinn's studio are both aesthetically and historically significant—and not exclusively in relation to the blues genre.

For instance, Hopkins's Gold Star sessions yielded one track that signaled the incubation of a new genre of music along the upper Gulf Coast. The song titled "Zolo Go," produced around 1949 or '50 as the B-side to "Automobile" (#666), is one of the first recordings ever to use an approximation of the word "zydeco" to refer to a musical form. On it Hopkins eschews guitar and instead accompanies himself on organ, evoking the sound of an accordion and a Creole backbeat.

As Roger Wood states in *Texas Zydeco,*

The "Zolo Go" title was surely assigned by Quinn after the session, most likely based on his misunderstanding (he was a Caucasian native of Massachusetts, after all) of the exotic word that he had heard Hopkins articulate in the studio. As Chris Strachwitz says in his liner notes to the CD *Lightnin' Hopkins: The Gold Star Sessions, Vol. 1*, ". . . Lightning is singing about his impressions of going out to a zydeco dance. When Bill Quinn heard this, he probably had no idea what zydeco was or how to spell it."

Along with Clarence Garlow's 1949 hit "Bon Ton Roula" on the Houston-based Macy's label (#5002-A), the novel Hopkins song helped to introduce zydeco—the word and the sound—to larger audiences.

Though Quinn's Gold Star Records label would fold before other producers started deliberately recording the accordion-based black Creole music now recognized as zydeco (the standard spelling of which originated also in Houston), the aforementioned single by Hopkins is a seminal track. Among other things, it signifies the early presence of this newly syncretized musical form in the Gulf Coast's largest city. Incidentally, after Quinn quit the label business and moved his recording facility to his Brock Street residence, his renamed Gold Star Studios would host Clifton Chenier (1925–1987), a long-time Houston resident and the eventual "King of Zydeco," on many sessions for the Arhoolie Records label. But more than a decade before Chenier would cut the tracks that ultimately defined this vibrant new genre, Hopkins and Quinn were already, despite the awkward spelling, spreading the word.

MEANWHILE, QUINN'S WILLINGNESS TO PAY CASH to record Hopkins attracted many other African American blues singers to his studio. The most notable and prolific among these were Lil' Son Jackson and L. C. Williams, but Quinn also issued singles credited to Thunder Smith, Leroy Ervin, Lee Hunter, Buddy Chiles, Andy Thomas, Perry Cain, and others. Some of the backing musicians who appeared on these tracks include Elmore Nixon, Leroy Carter, Luther "Ricky" Stoneham, Buster Pickens, and Skippy Brown. The roster of performers on the Gold Star 600 series reads like a virtual "Who's Who" of mid-twentieth-century East Texas blues. These recordings are now invaluable historical documents tracing the fusion of the country blues sound with modern urban influences.

Granted, some of these records made little or no profit for Quinn. But there were some commercial successes too. For instance, in November 1948, Lil' Son Jackson's "Freedom Train Blues," the flip-side to "Roberta Blues" (#638), climbed to number seven on the national R&B charts. Born as Melvin Jackson (1915–1976), the singer-guitarist known as "Lil' Son" ultimately recorded at least ten of his compositions on the Gold Star label in 1948 and 1949, including "Ground Hog Blues" and "Bad Whiskey, Bad Women" (#642), "Gone with the Wind" and "No Money, No Love" (#653), "Cairo Blues" and "Evil Blues" (#663), and "Gambling Blues" backed with "Homeless Blues" (#668). These records, some of which were released as late as 1950 or '51, did well enough to elevate Jackson's status as a regional blues star to that of Hopkins. However, by 1949 Jackson had left Houston (a city he had come to from Dallas, specifically to audition and record for Quinn), and he recorded thereafter only for Modern Records and the Imperial label.

Though not as big a player on the national scene as Jackson, L. C. Williams (1924–1960) was regionally popular during his affiliation with Gold Star Records, producing at least eight tracks for Quinn. He had started out as a sideman drumming for Hopkins and others. But he soon became a vocalist, one who could imitate his mentor so well that Quinn identified him as "Lightnin' Jr." on his first record. After initially affiliating with Quinn's label, Williams later recorded locally for various others (including Eddie's, Freedom, Jax, and Mercury).

Conrad Johnson (1915–2008) was a saxophonist who went on to become one of the most distinguished music educators in Texas history. Affectionately known to several generations of musicians as "Prof," Johnson directed the multiple-award-winning Kashmere High School Stage Band, among other achievements during his thirty-seven years in public education. After retirement from teaching, he continued, well into his nineties, to lead his own orchestra and to record. But back in 1947, Johnson too launched his recording career at Quinn's studio.

His song "Howling on Dowling" (the title of which alludes to a Houston street) appears on a 78 rpm Gold Star single backed with "Fisherman's Blues" (#622). Performed in a fully orchestrated, upbeat style with witty lyrics, it evokes the popular mid-century sound of national phenomenon Louis Jordan. This record also establishes that Quinn's 600 series not only featured the down-home blues of guitar-wielding singers such as Lightnin' Hopkins but also the more refined big band sounds of jazz and early R&B.

The blues artist best known as Peppermint Harris (1925–1999) also got his start on Gold Star Records. Actually born Harrison D. Nelson Jr., he moved to Houston in 1947 and reportedly soon met Hopkins, who introduced him to Quinn. Shortly thereafter, he cut "Peppermint Boogie" backed with "Houston Blues" for Gold Star (#626). Since clever monikers were popular in blues music, Quinn credited the 1947 record to Peppermint Nelson as a promotional tactic. The nickname stuck for a while, but when a subsequent producer mistakenly recalled the name as Peppermint Harris, that replaced the others. Harris would go on to make hit records on various labels, settle in California, and establish himself as a songwriter. But like so many others, he launched his career with Quinn.

Another such expatriated Texas artist was Houston-born saxophonist and bandleader Curtis Amy (1927–2002), who become an acclaimed session musician and jazz artist in his own right after moving to the West Coast. However, his rookie outing in the studio occurred in 1947 when he recorded "Realization Blues" and "Sleeping Blues" on the Gold Star label (#618). These tracks, credited to Curtis Amy and His Orchestra, offer big band blues rendered in a jazzy style. Amy later established himself, first in New York and then in Los Angeles, as a first-rate sideman on popular recordings by the likes of Ray Charles, Carole King, Marvin Gaye, Smokey Robinson, Lou Rawls, the Doors, and many others.

So many distinguished and diverse musicians saw the inside of a recording studio for the first time at Quinn's original facility. Others of note include Deacon Anderson, a steel guitarist best known as coauthor of the oft-recorded novelty song "Ragg Mopp," which was first a hit for the Ames Brothers in 1950. That same year Anderson had come to Quinn Recording with Cotton

Thompson and the Village Boys (as part of a lineup that included Clyde Brewer and Pee Wee Calhoun) to cut "How Long" and "Hopeless Love" for the Gold Star label (#1381). Hank Locklin (1918–2009) is another example of an esteemed country music veteran who got his start recording for Quinn, releasing "Rio Grande Waltz" and "You've Been Talking in Your Sleep" (#1341) in 1947. Similarly, vocalist Frances Turner first appeared on Gold Star in 1947 performing "The Moment I Found You" and "The Curse of an Aching Heart" (#1342).

Frank Juricek says, "A lot of people came to record with Bill. It was a fascinating time to be around while all that was happening." Among the tracks on which he performed as a sideman were "I Left a Rose" and "Blue Eyes" by Tex Looney and His Western Stars (#1315/1316), "Drinkin' My Life Away" and "Blue Schottische" by Leon Jenkins and the Easterners (#1317), and the hit "Kilroy's Been Here" backed with "Delivery Man Blues" by Aubrey Gass with the Easterners (#1318). In 1947, though still a teenager, Juricek even got Quinn to record one of his compositions. "I wrote a song back then called 'Green Bayou Waltz,'" he explains. "Old Bill Quinn said, 'That's a great song! Let's put it out.' So we went into the studio and recorded it. . . . It was a simple old thing, but Bill put it out [#1334], and we got some airplay."

Country singer and acclaimed songwriter Eddie Noack (1930–1978), who would later record for numerous labels (including 4-Star, TNT, Starday, D, Mercury, Dixie, Faith, and Allstar), introduced himself to the record-listening public with sides he made for Quinn. In a 1976 interview by Bill Millar for *New Kommotion* magazine, Noack relates how he got started:

> I just called Quinn one day and he said, "Well, come on out." My cousin
> Ollie and I rode a bus out there. His studio at the time seemed an adequate
> set-up. He had only one microphone and we cut directly to an acetate disc . . .
> so you didn't stop if you made a mistake, you just kept going. Our first rec-
> ord, "Gentlemen Prefer Blondes," was Gold Star #1352.
>   . . . My second record, Gold Star #1357, "Pyramid Club," was about the
> pyramid club craze that was storming the country. Quinn would blankly
> ship my record to the cities where the distributors told him the craze was
> happening. We sold quite a few records and got reviewed in *Billboard* maga-
> zine. . . . My biggest seller on Gold Star was probably the next one, "Hungry
> But Happy"/"Raindrops in a River" [#1371], which Bob Wills recorded about
> eighteen years later.

Noack adds, "On the strength of the Gold Star recordings, I was able to perform at better gigs." He notes too that by 1951 Quinn "was about out of the record company business," a time that signaled the end of Gold Star

Records and Quinn's remarkable four-year run as a label owner. But, like many other musicians, Noack maintained his relationship with Quinn even after he signed with other labels "because he was renting out his studio to anyone who wanted to record."

QUITE A NUMBER OF EVENTS CAUSED QUINN to get out of the record label business and concentrate on simply running his studio. For example, Hopkins had broken his contract and was recording for anyone who paid cash, while many imitation artists were diluting his blues market niche. Choates had tragically died. The label's third-best-selling artist, Lil' Son Jackson, following a disagreement with Quinn, had departed in a huff to record elsewhere. Coinciding with these developments was a personal situation, the death of Quinn's first wife, which may well have dispirited him too. But the last straw was likely his legal entanglement with the Internal Revenue Service.

During this era, the government imposed a luxury tax on phonograph records. Quinn had dutifully paid the government for his own pressings, but he erred in assuming that the plants with which he had subcontracted for additional pressings had also paid the tax. It turned out they generally had not, and it was Quinn's responsibility, so the IRS eventually came after him demanding settlement of a substantial tax bill. In disgust with the whole experience, Quinn shut down the label and went back to making custom recordings and pressings for other record companies.

QUINN'S INDEPENDENT RECORD COMPANY would likely have been more successful if he had simply understood copyright law and the concept of registering songs, as well as leasing songs under copyright to other companies. However, naïve upstart that he was, he never copyrighted any of the songs that he recorded on his label. This oversight was augmented by the parallel ignorance of most of the songwriters who recorded for him in the late 1940s. Consequently, other performers would sometimes rerecord Gold Star–released material for other labels, even have hits with them, register the copyright for themselves, and Quinn and the original creators of such songs would not be acknowledged or compensated, nor would they have any viable legal recourse.

Another flaw was that Quinn only sporadically established a viable system of distribution beyond Houston, a problem that limited public exposure and availability of his products. Quinn filled orders for Gold Star records strictly on a COD basis, and he stubbornly refused to maintain any open accounts. Again and again, he had turned down out-of-town requests for shipments of his records if the outlets would not agree to pay the full wholesale price up front. That also meant the retailers had no possibility of returning products that failed to sell. Rather than accept such a risk, many of them balked at stocking Gold Star discs.

Quinn's preference for cash-only relationships is reflected also in Juricek's memories of the man, as are other insights about his basic character. He says,

> Bill Quinn was a great guy, and he always had cash on him . . . didn't trust banks and buried money in tin cans in his yard. . . . You couldn't help but like Bill. He was easygoing. And he dressed just as simple as could be—no shirt or tie on Quinn. We all had a good time working with Bill Quinn.

Yet even if musicians generally enjoyed their collaborations with Quinn, their interests were not always well served by his approach to the record business.

In addition to the problems outlined above, there was also Quinn's unsophisticated approach to publicity. His sole strategy for calling attention to new Gold Star releases seems to have been occasionally to include a few free samples of new records with orders sent out to distributors. Thus, if there were no demand for these new records, then the few original copies were all that were ever pressed.

Yet despite his retreat from the label business, Quinn would remain a key figure in the Texas recording industry for years to come. And when his IRS troubles finally forced him to close the Telephone Road shop and move his equipment into his house on Brock Street, he would soon resurrect the Gold Star brand name to christen the new studio facility he would devise there.

Label's Demise, New Studio's Rise
RECORDING IN THE HOUSE

BY LATE 1950 OR EARLY 1951 all recording for his own Gold Star Records label had ceased, and Bill Quinn had returned to the considerably less demanding life of making custom recordings and pressings for others. With the dissolution of his label, Quinn sold or leased much of his catalogue of Gold Star master recordings to other companies. Most notably, in September 1951 Modern Records bought the rights to thirty-two unreleased masters by Lightnin' Hopkins and Lil' Son Jackson for the sum of $2,500. This was quite a large transaction for its time, significant enough to merit an article in *Billboard* magazine. In 1955 the local entrepreneur known as Pappy Daily (co-owner of Starday Records and the sole owner of D Records) bought the rights to all the Harry Choates masters. In later years, Quinn would also lease numerous tracks by Hopkins and others to Arhoolie Records. Thus, though Gold Star Records was no longer releasing product on its own, many of its recordings were still being issued, or reissued, and heard.

In late 1951 Modern Records released the first of the Hopkins tracks purchased from Quinn, "Bad Luck and Trouble," followed through 1954 by "Lonesome Dog Blues," "Jake's Head Boogie," "Last Affair," "Another Fool in Town," "Black Cat," "Santa Fe," and others. However, Modern could not duplicate Gold Star's previous chart success with Hopkins.

Though no longer working for Quinn's label as he had done from 1947 through 1950, the prolific blues composer continued to record frequently at Quinn's studio from 1951 through 1964. These sessions occurred at the new facility that Quinn created in (and later expanded into a newly constructed building adjacent to) his residence on Brock Street, and various other labels issued these Hopkins recordings.

Sleepy LaBeef, a rockabilly musician who first visited Quinn's studio in the mid-1950s, recalls his impressions of a typical Hopkins session at this time:

> One of the outstanding things was when Sam "Lightnin'" Hopkins would come over. . . . Sam came over once after having a falling out with his wife. He'd say, "Bill, turn on the mic. I'm ready to sing some blues." Just him and his guitar, ready to record. I think Bill would sometimes pay him ten bucks a day just to sit in there and record. He might get three or might get ten different songs, just him and his guitar. You'd hear him just stomping his foot, playing guitar and singing.

Sometime in 1950 Quinn had ceased to record at his old Telephone Road location and begun converting the bottom floor of his house at 5628 Brock into a recording studio. He likely continued to fill orders for pressings at his original shop for a while longer. Clyde Brewer, who had recorded in Quinn's first studio, says he did sessions at Quinn's house in the summer of 1950. With the relocation, Quinn also changed his business name from Quinn Recording to Gold Star Recording Studios, thereby retaining the brand identity he had established with his former Gold Star label. From later federal tax records (for 1958) we have ascertained that Gold Star Studios was a Subchapter S Texas corporation formally owned by Mr. and Mrs. Bill Quinn, with C. M. Faber (of 6731 Harrisburg Street in Houston) listed as Vice President and Richard Greenhill identified as the Secretary-Treasurer.

Quinn was almost certainly oblivious to the fact that, around the same time that he renamed his company, a place called Gold Star Recording Studios was opening in Los Angeles. That famous recording center, which operated from 1950 to 1984 and produced multitudes of hits, was in no way affiliated with Quinn's business.

Meanwhile, following the relocation and name change, Quinn continued operating one of the major recording studios in the region. Yellow Pages listings in the 1952 Houston telephone directory show twelve companies categorized under "Recording Service." Only two of the four identified in the previously cited 1944 Yellow Pages were still in operation: Lil' Pal and the renamed Quinn enterprise. And of the twelve businesses listed in 1952, only two advertised a full range of professional recording services and air-conditioning. Those two companies were Gold Star Studios and ACA Recording Studios, then located at 1022 Washington Avenue. Bill Holford, Quinn's chief competitor over the years to come, owned the latter.

In May 1950 Holford had opened his own facility, ambitiously dubbed ACA for Audio Company of America. For the eighteen months prior to this, Holford had been operating an audio business out of his house. ACA soon became an important Houston recording base for various labels (such as Freedom, Peacock, Macy's, and Trumpet) and hundreds of musicians. As writer Gary Hickinbotham says, it was "one of the premier Texas studios of the post–World War II period."

Nonetheless, Quinn's new recording facility, installed on the ground floor of his family residence, was a worthy rival—and even more so after it would be expanded and refurbished several times in years to come. From the start, it provided ample space outfitted with proven professional equipment manned by a first-rate audio engineer. Following Quinn's initial transformation of his house, the bottom floor contained the main studio room, a control room, a vocal booth, the interior staircase, and the kitchen. The overall dimensions were twenty-eight feet long by twenty-eight feet wide, with a ten-foot-high ceiling.

From the front door perspective, the control room was in the back right-hand corner of the house. At first, however, it offered no window into the main studio. So the musicians had to wait for a red "record" light to know when to begin playing.

The baby grand piano was located in the opposite back corner, by the stairway. Quinn had removed its top and used a cable attached to the ceiling to suspend a microphone above it.

In the left front corner of the first-floor room was the vocal booth. Musician Glenn Barber describes the basic recording setup:

> Bill built that booth around 1952 or so. It had wheels on it so he could move it around, but it stayed on the left as you walked in the front door most of the time. He had one of those classic Shure mics in the vocal booth, one of those chrome-plated-looking things. Then out in the studio he was using one of those big diamond-shaped RCA ribbon mics.

Judging from photographs and oral histories, the flooring was likely a vinyl product. Johnny Bush, who first recorded there in 1956 as a drummer behind country singer Mickey Gilley, describes it as "kind of an asphalt tile floor."

The studio walls were covered in a sound-baffling material improvised from egg cartons. Ted Marek's 1957 *Houston Chronicle* article quotes Quinn's explanation:

> I found that regular sound-proofing killed the echo but made a "dead" room. I tried material after material on the walls to no avail, but then I discovered the egg carton. I found that the compressed papier-mâché cartons with the peaks and valleys were the answer. I tacked thousands of the cartons up on

the walls and came up with the perfect room sound. There is no echo but the room is "live" and musicians can hear their own voices and instruments in all parts of the studio.

This space, fully remodeled, is now the state-of-the-art Studio A at the present-day SugarHill Studios complex. But in the Gold Star era, the Quinn family (and their Afghan hounds, which reportedly often lounged in the studio) maintained private residential quarters on the now-removed second floor.

Record producer, promoter, and entrepreneur Slick Norris adds his memory of the place: "The front door of the house led straight into the studio. He had no waiting room or reception room at all. It was pretty primitive, but the man had some ability to get a sound."

Shelby Singleton (1931–2009), former owner of the famous Sun Records Studio in Memphis, recalls his impressions of the Gold Star space and Quinn, both before and after a major expansion: "I remember the first time I met him. I was working for Pappy Daily, and I thought it was very strange to be recording in someone's living room. But then he built the big studio in the back, and that was much better."

NOT ONLY WOULD THE SIZE AND FEATURES of the Gold Star building be significantly upgraded during the 1950s, but so would the fundamental technology that Quinn utilized there. By this time, tape recorders had become the main medium for documenting and reproducing sound. Originally they did so only in mono, but by the late 1950s the stereophonic revolution was underway. Taping introduced a new step in the recording process, one that came between the actual musical performance and the wax or acetate mastering. This development surely reduced the in-studio stress on the performers and engineers. Unlike before, an imperfect "take" no longer meant a wasted piece of valuable wax. Instead, if a flaw occurred, they simply kept the tape rolling and did another take, or they rewound the tape and recorded over the previous take as it was being erased.

Likewise, long-playing record albums became practical to conceive and produce, triggering new ways that recordings could be packaged and experienced. With a session preserved on tape, the producer could select preferred tracks and resequence them to establish material for each side of an LP disc. Then the set of songs comprising one whole side could be transferred as a group to a wax or acetate master.

The recording medium was a ferric oxide–based tape that came on metal or plastic reels. In layman's terms, audio recording tape was a thin strip of plastic or Mylar with a chemical solution affixed to the backing via a special type of glue. This mix of ferric oxide and glue contained enough silicone lubricant to allow tape to slide easily past metal guideposts and recording heads with minimal degradation of material or depositing of debris. However, thorough cleaning of the tape path has always been necessary between recording sessions, sometimes between reels. The mono and stereo tape decks both used one-quarter-inch magnetic recording tape on ten-and-a-half-inch reels that each held approximately 2,500 feet of tape. The National Association of Broadcasters established a recording speed standard of fifteen inches of tape per second, which allowed for a little over thirty minutes of recording time per reel.

The first multitrack tape recorders, in the form of three-track machines that recorded on half-inch tape, were in use by the end of the 1950s. Stereo (or two-track) machines had achieved limited availability by 1952, and certain innovative engineers, most notably Tom Dowd of Atlantic Records, were recording in mono and stereo simultaneously. However, the major record companies did not start pressing stereo records for sale to the general public until near the end of the decade.

By 1957 Ampex had manufactured a pair of experimental eight-track machines, designed by the famous electric guitar pioneer Les Paul, and these utilized one-inch tape. Dowd ordered a third machine custom-built, and by 1958 he was recording on it. However, the recording industry at large did not adopt eight-track technology until approximately ten years later.

Prior to purchasing his own Ampex machines in the late 1950s, Quinn was using a monophonic Berlantz Concertone Recorder, with ten-and-a-half-inch reels running quarter-inch tape. This machine was an older, heavily worn contraption, but it yielded a fantastic sound by prestereo standards. Quinn later switched over to a Magnacord mono tape deck before upgrading to stereo.

Back in those days, neither tone controls nor equalizers existed. Thus, when a client requested that the sound be "brightened" (by increasing treble) or "darkened" (by decreasing treble or increasing bass), Quinn would remove a capacitor and resistor or two from the rear of the machine and replace them with alternates that sometimes achieved the desired effect.

Musicians Clyde Brewer and Herb Remington say they made a habit of requesting more bass or "bottom end" at the start of a session. Apparently Quinn's recordings tended to be trebly, no matter how much he fiddled with capacitors or resistors. Yet the musicians report that he was usually willing to strive to achieve the desired sonic results.

Country singer James O'Gwynn says, "Bill Quinn was a good guy and he took a lot of pains with us to get a good sound. He did the best you could with the type of equipment you had in those days." Remembering the origi-

Musicians (left to right: Lou Frisby, Herb Remington, Ernie Hunter, and Doc Lewis) in front of Gold Star Studios, 1955

nal setup at the Brock Street facility, he adds, "He had egg crates all over the walls, and his recording equipment was kind of primitive, but he got a good sound."

O'Gwynn's eventual Starday Records label-mate Frankie Miller concurs: "Bill Quinn was so good to work with because he would work hard to try to get you a good sound. In his day he was real good."

Starday Records president Don Pierce, after signing a deal to merge with Mercury Records in 1957, assessed Quinn's skills as quoted by John Tynan in *Country and Western Jamboree* magazine: "Bill is an old timer in the business and knows how to work with country artists and musicians. He knows how to get a real twangy country sound that sells."

The eventual Grand Ole Opry star O'Gwynn (b. 1928—and billed as "The Smiling Irishman of Country Music," even though he was born in Mississippi) recorded frequently for various labels at Quinn's facility in the 1950s. "I did about twenty-six or twenty-eight sides over there at Gold Star Studios," he says. Today O'Gwynn is best remembered for the 1958 hit "Talk to Me Lonesome Heart," which he recorded at Gold Star Studios for D Records (#1006). But his earliest affiliation with Quinn yielded "Love in an Old Fashioned Way" and "Bottle Talk" (#2020), as well as "I Wish You Wuz My Darling But You Ain't" and "Love Made Slave" (#2023), both on Nucraft Records. Quinn next recorded O'Gwynn singing "Your Love Is Strong (But Your Heart Is Weak)" and "Ready for Freddy" for the Azalea label (#106).

Country music defined much of Quinn's studio career. Though the stylistic pursuits of his clientele remained somewhat varied, the entrepreneur who had envisioned his short-lived label as "King of the Hillbillies" was surely in his element now working with artists such as O'Gwynn.

THROUGHOUT THE 1950S, QUINN RECORDED numerous other tracks for independent record labels, with the results being issued on the newer 45 rpm discs. One such label was Nucraft Records, owned and operated by Boyd Leisy, a would-be mogul who ran his record companies out of his Houston tamale restaurant. From 1953 through 1959 Leisy released at least nineteen singles, all recorded at Gold Star Studios, featuring artists such as James O'Gwynn, the Hooper Twins, the Harmonica Kid, Link Davis, and Floyd Tillman.

Another of Quinn's regular clients was Freedom Records (not to be confused with a later jazz label of the same name), a local company owned by the Kahal family. Representative examples of the many country music sessions that Quinn engineered for that label include "Jelly Roll Blues" by Cotton Thompson, backed by Olin Davidson and His Village Boys (#5010), produced in 1950. Drew Miller and Wink Lewis's Dude Ranchers cut a song called "What's a Matter Baby" (#5016) featuring a solo by steel guitarist Ralph "Dusty" Stewart. Johnny Nelms and the Sunset Cowboys, who had recorded earlier for the Gold Star label, came to Quinn's new studio to record the song "If I Can't Have You" for Freedom (#5018).

For the same label, Charlie Harris with R. D. Hendon and His Western Jamboree Cowboys cut "No Shoes Boogie" (#5033), issued in March 1951. Of all the Freedom releases, this track perhaps best exemplifies the hard-rocking, shuffle-beat swing style that defined so much of the Texas music scene prior to rock 'n' roll. In addition to the superb electric guitar of Charlie Harris, the band featured Theron Poteet on piano, Johnny Cooper on rhythm guitar, Tiny Smith on bass, Don Brewer on drums, and (as was often the case on Freedom recordings) veteran Herb Remington (a former member of the seminal Texas Playboys swing band) on steel guitar.

Beyond the Freedom label, there were many other independent companies that hired Quinn to record their country artists during this time. Deacon Anderson, working for Bayou Records, cut the single "Just Looking through These Tears" backed with "Daddy's Waltz." In 1954 Quinn recorded Eddie Noack singing "How Does It Feel to Be the Winner" and "Too Hot to Handle" (#110) for Bob Tanner's San Antonio–based TNT Records.

Of special note, master songwriter and singer Floyd Tillman (1914–2003) came to Gold Star Studios for the first time in late 1954 or early '55 to record

Eddie Noack, publicity photo, 1950s

a single for Houston-based Western Records. The A-side, written and sung by the eventual Country Music Hall of Fame inductee, was called "Save a Little for Me." The label text credits the performance to Floyd Tillman with Link Davis and the Bayou Billies. The B-side, "Big Houston," was written and sung by Davis "with Floyd Tillman and all the boys."

Davis, a tenor sax player and singer, often recorded at Gold Star Studios—playing on hits such as "Chantilly Lace" by the Big Bopper and "Running Bear" by Johnny Preston. Meanwhile, Tillman and Davis would reunite at Gold Star Studios about a year and a half later on sessions produced for Charlie Fitch's Sarg Records label.

Although Tillman (who had cut his first record as a featured singer with Leon "Pappy" Selph's Blue Ridge Playboys back in 1938) never scored a hit with the records he made at Gold Star Studios, his presence there was significant, especially in its impact on other musicians. As indicated by the title of his final album, *The Influence* (released posthumously in 2004 on Heart of Texas Records), Tillman's sixty-plus-year career in country music directly inspired countless singers and songwriters. Among the long list of classic songs that Tillman penned are "It Makes No Difference Now" (a hit for Bing Crosby in 1939) and his own early hits, the 1942 chart-topping classic "They Took the Stars out of Heaven" and the 1944 song "Each Night at Nine."

Tillman is remembered today as a seminal country music composer, particularly because he wrote one of the first "cheating" songs, which would become a staple of the genre in subsequent decades. His widely covered 1949 number one hit "Slippin' Around," as recorded by Margaret Whiting and Jimmy Wakely (Capitol #40224), helped to usher in a movement toward confessional social realism in country songwriting.

Though the most fertile period of Tillman's career was in the 1940s, he returned to record again at Gold Star Studios in 1964 and 1967, and again in 1973 (by which time Quinn's facility had been sold and renamed SugarHill).

While numerous independent labels utilized Quinn's expertise during the 1950s, there was one in particular for which the Brock Street facility would prove to be an especially worthy base for taking its sound to the world.

6

Pappy Daily and Starday Records

A MAJOR BEHIND-THE-SCENES FIGURE in twentieth-century popular music, in Houston and beyond, was Harold W. "Pappy" Daily. This Marine Corps veteran, ex-semipro baseball player and manager, and former accountant for the Southern Pacific Railroad was an early jukebox distributor, record store proprietor, record wholesaler, and music publisher, but also a hit-making producer and label owner with close ties to Gold Star Studios during a major phase of his illustrious career.

By the early 1970s, when he ceased record production in Nashville and concentrated solely on his Glad Music publishing firm in Houston, Daily had owned part or all of at least four record labels. Artists whom he had signed, recorded, published, and promoted had scored numerous Top Ten hits on the country and pop charts and become national stars. Stephen Thomas Erlewine, in *All Music Guide*, describes him as "one of the most important record executives and producers of the postwar era."

Daily got into the music business around age thirty. Concerned about possibly losing his railroad company position during the Great Depression, he opted to become the first Bally's jukebox distributor in Houston. As Daily told writer Barbara Wesolek, "I would have stayed with the railroads if there had been any security, but they were cutting people off. I didn't know anything about the coin business or phonograph records or music."

This new field proved so lucrative that by 1932 he had created his own jukebox distributing operation, South Coast Amusements. Throughout the rest of the 1930s his company dominated the regional market for jukeboxes, coin-operated pool tables, and slot machines. In *The Complete D Singles Collection*, writer Colin Escott notes, "At one time, South Coast Amusements had offices in Dallas, Amarillo, Shreveport, San Antonio, Beaumont, and Corpus Christi, but Daily later closed them all down and centralized his operation . . . in Houston."

Daily's ventures prospered during World War II, but even more so after. By 1946 he had opened his first record store, Daily's Record Ranch. In 1951 Daily also established a record wholesale business that covered the entire Southwest region—a well-timed and profitable undertaking, as the public appetite for hearing and collecting the latest hit discs was growing fast.

A shrewd businessman, Daily soon realized that there was potentially even more money to be had in also producing the records that he stocked on jukeboxes or distributed for sale. Though he claimed to have had no preexisting affinity for it, Daily had, as writer Linda Hellinger puts it, "developed an ear for country music by listening to the records in his jukeboxes." He was likely well aware too of Bill Quinn's recent run as a local independent record company owner (since Quinn had probably placed Gold Star Records releases such as "Jole Blon" in Daily's store). Daily may have been prescient enough to infer that he could locate and promote regional talent more effectively than the reticent sound engineer. Moreover, as Escott's essay points out, Daily had some previous experience, though "only a marginal involvement," in a short-lived mid-1940s label called Melody, which had issued a couple of records by Jerry Jericho and Ben Christian. He had also made initial recordings and placed "some marketable singers" with the 4-Star Records label in California. Drawing from that background, in 1952 or early '53 Daily formed a partnership with a Beaumont nightclub owner and talent booker named Jack Starnes, and together they launched a new record label.

They called it Starday, based on a combination of the first syllable from each of their surnames. That fledging company would be the Southeast Texas home of some of the essential country music of the 1950s, as well as a regional launching pad for the newly defined rockabilly genre. Daily and his partner had started out self-reliantly recording in makeshift fashion on a Magnacord tape deck in the Starnes family house in Beaumont. Before long they had graduated to a more professional setting, doing sessions for a while at Bill Holford's ACA Studios in Houston.

However, within two years of Starday's birth, they had established their primary recording base at Quinn's Gold Star Studios. This affiliation was significant not only for the classic songs it produced (such as the first hit by George Jones), but also because the Daily-Quinn relationship would later lead to renovation and expansion of the Gold Star property.

Ted Marek's 1957 feature article on Gold Star Studios yields some insights regarding Daily's role there. While an accompanying photo depicts Quinn doing studio work, others show Starday singer Jeanette Hicks cutting songs for upcoming release (according to the text: "Tomorrow I'll Be Gone" and "Extra, Extra, Read All about It"). There is also a shot of another Starday artist, rockabilly singer Rudy Grayzell. Along with various session musicians (such as Clyde Brewer and Frank Juricek), the only non-musician other than Quinn who appears in these images is Daily. Most tellingly, the article identifies him as a "co-owner" of the studio with Quinn and quotes him philosophizing on the record business as follows:

> It helps to be luckier than smart in the tune-picking industry. I've given up trying to predict which tune will click. I let the artists pick the ones they like. If they're enthusiastic about a number I'll go along with them because they'll put something extra into the recording. I wish I could pick 'em.

Despite his modest self-assessment as a forecaster of hits, by the time this article ran, Daily had already produced several big sellers, especially with Jones. Moreover, within a year, he would record—again at Gold Star Studios—one of his all-time greatest hits, "Chantilly Lace" by the Big Bopper, for D Records.

Musician Slick Norris says, "Pappy had the knowledge of how to sell records. He was both a wholesaler and a retailer from his own shop. Pappy really didn't know the making part of it as well as he knew how to sell and market them." Indeed, given Quinn's technical skills and facility, he could record and master whatever product Daily might choose to pay for.

By the late 1950s Daily evidently was willing, and certainly financially able, to invest in some improvements at Gold Star Studios. In fact, a fairly common rumor among musicians who worked there was that Daily was not a co-owner but actually funding the whole operation for a while. For instance, James O'Gwynn says, "Somebody told me that Pappy really owned the recording studio back then, and Bill Quinn was running it for him." While there is no clear evidence, beyond such oral historical impressions, to establish that Daily ever assumed full control of Gold Star Studios, the Marek article and statements such as O'Gwynn's point to the powerful presence that Daily established at Quinn's facility. There he mastered the hit-making process, first for the Starday label that he owned in part and later for the D label that he owned outright.

Though the Starday brand name would later survive for decades in Nashville, its Texan cofounders would both ultimately disassociate from it. In 1953, the year after creating Starday, Daily and Starnes allowed the West Coast–based businessman Don Pierce (1915–2005), whom Daily knew from 4-Star Records, to buy into the company. The college-educated Pierce soon assumed the corporate presidency, and Daily formally took the role of the A&R

man—the person in charge of "artists and repertoire." In other words, Daily made the corporate decisions concerning which artists, supporting players, styles, and songs would be recorded for the label. Thus, he was not merely a titular producer who only provided funding and accounted for profits; he was a music producer, directly involved in the creative process of crafting records aimed at becoming hits. Generally speaking, Daily excelled at this assignment, though he would fulfill it for a variety of different companies over the following years.

As for Daily's work with Starday, it lasted through the end of 1957 or early 1958. Pierce had also independently purchased Hollywood Records of Los Angeles, and shortly after joining Starday, he consolidated the two label offices there. With Pierce running the company in California and Daily working the studio in Houston, the Beaumont-based Starnes became a less active partner, and in 1955 he sold out his interest to the other two. In 1957 Pierce moved the Starday-Hollywood offices to Nashville. Meanwhile, Daily, riding on the heels of the early hit singles, had produced the first Starday LP, *Grand Ole Opry's New Star* by George Jones (#101), in 1956. Daily's proven capacity for commercial success led to a 1957 Starday distribution agreement with the larger Nashville-based branch of Mercury Records.

John Tynan, writing about that merger in the March 1957 issue of *Country and Western Jamboree* magazine, refers to Houston as "Hillbilly Heaven" due to the number of "down home" country singers it was introducing to the world via Starday Records—artists such as George Jones, Hank Locklin, Leon Payne, Benny Barnes, James O'Gwynn, Tibby Edwards, Jeanette Hicks, Eddie Noack, and many others. This article also quotes Pierce explaining the company's approach to recording at Gold Star Studios:

> At the session we try for a relaxed atmosphere so the artist and the musicians can create with feeling. In this connection we are pleased with the results we have obtained through Bill Quinn and his studio in Houston. . . . We try not to duplicate sounds from other records. We prefer musicians who play well and who have a style and sound that is fresh and new—but it must be country.

Suddenly this little upstart label from Southeast Texas was positioning itself as a major player in the Nashville-centric country music business. More to the point, its savvy A&R man—the guy everyone called "Pappy"—was gaining fame. And they were doing it as a result of recordings created at Gold Star Studios. Within another year Pierce bought out Daily's share of the Starday company, and Daily began producing for Mercury in Nashville and for his own new label, D Records, down in Houston.

"Pappy was a great man, and he done a lot for me. He carried me a long way, and I stayed with him for nearly four years," said the singer O'Gwynn in 2004. "Pappy's publishing company still is my publishing company, Glad Music."

O'Gwynn's rise to country star status was fueled in large part by the Daily magic, which propelled him straight from Starday to the higher-profile Mercury Records. As O'Gwynn relates,

> We cut "Losing Game" and "If I Never Get to Heaven" [#266]. I cut that in 1956, and it was the only one that I did for Starday itself. I was voted "Most Promising [Country] Artist" in *Billboard* magazine on [the basis of] that record, and it also got me on the *Louisiana Hayride* [radio program]. Then Pappy made a deal with Mercury Records, and he put me and George Jones out on Mercury/Starday. . . .

Though O'Gwynn soon found himself recording for a prestigious Nashville label, he was still making those records at Gold Star Studios. He continues,

> I cut a whole bunch of sides, nearly twenty, for Pappy over there at Quinn's studio. In early 1957 I cut "Who'll Be the Next One" and "Mule Skinner Blues" [Mercury #71066]. In the middle of that year we cut "I Cry" and "Do You Miss Me" [#71127]. And near the end of the year we did "Two Little Hearts" and "You've Always Won" [#71234] . . . among others.

Likewise, country singer Glenn Barber (1935–2008) credits Daily with transforming his career. After doing session work at Gold Star Studios as a teenage guitarist, his virgin attempt at recording under his own name was not for Starday, but it quickly landed him there. He recounts the evolution:

> I cut my first session as an artist with a song called "Ring around the Moon" and "You Took the Twinkle out of My Stars." It was also the song that got me on Starday Records with Pappy Daily. I first did this recording with some gentlemen by the name of Curt Peeples and Willie Jones, and we went over to Quinn's to record it.
>
> I had been at Quinn's earlier as a session guitar player. I was sixteen years old at the time we recorded that song with Bill. My brother was one year younger than me and was playing bass. It was a teenage band of guys in high school, and that's who played on the record. . . . The original was on Stampede Records, and we recorded that in late 1951 or early 1952. We recut the song later for Starday ["Ring around the Moon," #166, released in 1954].
>
> I recorded a song for Pappy called "Washed My Face in Ice Cold Water," which was the B-Side to "Ring around the Moon." . . . Starday

#249—"Shadow My Baby"/"Feeling No Pain"—received a *Billboard* mention on the 28th of July, 1956. Those two sides were my attempt at rockabilly for Starday. . . . The backup band on the record was some of my western swing band with Link Davis [sax] as a guest. Bucky Meadows, who played piano and guitar for many years for Willie Nelson, played piano on the song—and was only fourteen years old at the time. The drummer was Bill Kimbrough, and bass was Zane Compton. . . . Leon Thomas played steel. . . . Starday #214— "Ain't It Funny"/"Livin' High and Wide"—was also recorded with Bucky and the same guys.

Many Texas musicians laid the late-1950s foundation for the undiluted country music of Starday Records. It was a pure sound based on raw emotions and simple arrangements, and it was soon drawing fans nationwide— as well as the attention of the Nashville recording establishment. But one Southeast Texas singer in particular would uniquely personify it.

GEORGE JONES WAS BORN IN 1931 in Saratoga, a hamlet nestled in the Big Thicket region of the Lone Star State. When he was eleven years old, his family moved approximately thirty miles to the industrial boomtown of Beaumont. By 1943 Jones was strumming guitar and singing for tips on its streets, and from 1947 through 1951 he played various gigs in local honky-tonks. After a two-year stint in the marines, he returned to Beaumont and its nightclubs, one of which happened to be owned by the Starday cofounder Starnes, who signed him to the label.

Prior to the success Starday would find with Jones, it had already scored a hit with the seminal version of the classic country anthem "Y'All Come," written and performed by a Beaumont-area English teacher named Arlie Duff (1924–1996). Originally identified on the label as "You All Come" (#104, backed with "Poor Old Teacher"), that record unexpectedly rose to number seven on the country charts and won a 1953 BMI Music Award. Over the years so many country artists would cover this upbeat song that most fans today would never associate it with Arlie Duff or Starday. But those are the forces that collaboratively introduced this crowd-pleaser to the world. And in so doing, they had perhaps inspired Jones.

A story from promoter Slick Norris illustrates the point: "On March 9th, 1954, I went to Cook's Hoedown, which was the number one club in Houston, right downtown at Capitol and Smith. Me and my buddy went in there, and they had this little old band from Beaumont. It was George Jones." After setting the scene, Norris describes an epiphany: "There was something commercial about the way George picked that guitar. The first Starday hit was 'Y'All Come' by Arlie Duff. George picked guitar on the second turn-around on [his live performance of] that record, and I just said, 'Oh gosh!'"

By late 1954 Jones had recorded four Starday singles, all produced in the Starnes house in Beaumont. His first was "No Money in This Deal" backed with "You're in My Heart" (#130). However, neither it nor its sequel, "Play It Cool Man, Play It Cool" (#146), garnered much notice.

Sometime in 1955 Daily brought Jones to Houston for his first Gold Star Studios session. The result was a runaway hit called "Why Baby Why" (#202), cowritten by Jones and his boyhood pal Darrell Edwards. The record first entered the *Billboard* charts on October 29, 1955, and it stayed there for eighteen weeks, peaking at the number four spot. In the process it also revived the hit-making tradition at Gold Star Studios.

By the way, as writer Rich Kienzle makes clear in his liner notes essay for *The Essential George Jones*, "the song broke George out of obscurity, though not totally the way he (or Starday) would have liked." As sometimes happened in those days, this surprise hit by a newcomer was quickly seized upon, re-recorded, and rushed to release by someone else. In this case, "Red Sovine and Webb Pierce, both established stars, covered the song as a duet for Decca Records. Given their star status, their version became the Number 1 record."

Nevertheless, "Why Baby Why" signaled the arrival of Jones, and he subsequently recorded several other singles at the Gold Star facility engineered by Quinn. The biggest seller came in 1956 with the Jones-penned song "Just One More" (#264), peaking at number three. Among the others were "What Am I Worth" (#216, which went to number seven), "Ragged But Right," "Seasons of the Heart," "You Gotta Be My Baby" (#247), and a duet with Jeanette Hicks entitled "Yearning" (#279). At least two of those original Starday recordings were later released also on Mercury: "Just One More" (#71049) and "Yearning" (#71061). Moreover, a few other songs, such as "Don't Stop the Music" (#71029), were recorded at Gold Star and issued only on Mercury.

Jones and Daily thereafter staged sessions in Nashville. As an artist-producer team, they continued to collaborate through 1971, creating many other hit recordings. Supposedly it was the singer's 1969 marriage to Tammy Wynette that eventually led Jones away from Daily, for within a year Jones was making records with her producer, Billy Sherrill. Nevertheless, Daily and Jones had experienced a productive partnership for fifteen years, and they likely had a fairly close personal relationship. Sleepy LaBeef, a fellow musician, says:

> Pappy was great to all of us, but his main deal, you know, was "Thumper" [Jones]. Yeah, well back then he like adopted George and treated him almost like he was his son, you know. George always came first with Pappy. The rest of us had to line up, but George was quite a talent, and he still is. We all knew that George was the main man. Just like in Memphis, Carl Perkins and the others knew that Elvis was the main man there.

Jones, who has continued performing and recording in the twenty-first century, is now generally acknowledged (despite some highly publicized personal foibles) as one of the greatest singers in country music history. But back when nobody could have predicted that he would ever achieve that rarefied cultural status, he began establishing himself during those Gold Star sessions. Perhaps Daily's nurturing had something to do with that. Jones had found his own distinctive voice, and he had let it sing with a naturally flowing intensity of spirit. Though his style was still influenced by that of his idol Hank Williams, he was no longer merely imitating but creating something new.

However, sometimes a sequence of seemingly random circumstances can unexpectedly coalesce into a life-changing experience. Such was the case with the momentous recording session that yielded "Why Baby Why," as the memories of several studio insiders reveal.

In his *New Kommotion* interview, fellow Starday recording artist Eddie Noack explains the situation that led to the then-rare phenomenon of the featured singer double-voicing the song all by himself.

> George Jones wasn't selling anything on Starday to begin with. So they were cutting George [singing] with Sonny Burns to help him—stuff like "Heartbroken Me" [#165] and "What's Wrong [with] You" [#188]. And they were going to do a third one, and this was the biggest break George ever had [because] Sonny liked to drink, and he didn't show up for a Burns/Jones session, and you know, it was "Why Baby Why." Because Sonny did not turn up, George had to cut it on his own, and he overdubbed his own voice over it.

Thus, whether fans realized it or not, they were hearing the Jones voice harmonizing with itself on the catchy chorus of the song. Given that it was 1955, this technique was unusual, requiring some studio innovation.

Generally speaking, the technology that enables a singer to record a second vocal track, while wearing a pair of headphones and listening to prerecorded tracks of both the instrumentation and his own lead vocal, did not become common until the 1960s. To enable Jones to sing the background vocal part with himself on "Why Baby Why," Quinn would have had to set up a small speaker in the studio. He could then play the track back to Jones at a very low volume while the singer added his second vocalization. Meanwhile, Quinn could then record the original track plus the more recently performed second vocalization to a second tape recorder. Because the editing technology of "punch-ins" (or "drop-ins") was not yet established, Jones would have had to do all of his second vocal parts in a straight run-through of the song—after he and the band had already performed the complete song live in the studio as flawlessly as possible. Given the double-voicing effect achieved on "Why

Pappy Daily and George Jones,
publicity photo, 1963

Baby Why," its finished sound depended not only on Jones's flawless singing
with himself but also on innovative studio engineering by Quinn.

Glenn Barber, a regular Gold Star house musician at the time, offers other
details about the session that yielded this breakthrough record:

> One recording I remember was "Why Baby Why" by George Jones. When
> we did that session my little boy was in diapers, and my wife had him on her
> lap and was patting him on his butt to keep him quiet because there was no-

where to sit except in the studio itself. Herbie [Remington] was on steel and Tony Sepolio on fiddle. Doc Lewis played piano. . . . I also played on "Seasons of My Heart" [by Jones], and it was the same band as "Why Baby Why." We pretty much always had the same band on these sessions.

Despite the ultimate success of those first Jones recording sessions in Houston, musician Tony Sepolio reveals that it did not come easily. In an interview published by Andrew Brown in *Taking Off*, Sepolio recalls his role in and exasperated impressions of trying to collaborate with Jones:

"Why Baby Why." I got the band for him. He called me. It took him all day to make it. I'm not used to that. . . . Man, it took him all day to make the darn thing. He'd get drunk. . . . He went through a fifth of whiskey. He'd say, "Wait a minute, I forgot the chords," stop right in the middle of it. We'd start again, and then he'd say. "Ah, that's not the words." And I mean, I was up to here with him. Because when I was with [Jerry] Irby [bandleader of the Texas Ranchers], we'd make 'em boom-boom-boom. In one day, we made five 15-minute radio programs [transcriptions]. We might miss a note here or word there—we didn't care; we'd just keep going. And [on the "Why Baby Why" session] here's this idiot, man. Toward the end he'd say, "I forgot the words." We took a break about lunchtime. And [Jones] was going through his fifth of whiskey. And I told Lew [Frisby, bass player], "Hey, if we can't whip him, let's join him." So we went down to the corner and got us a six-pack of beer.

I got frustrated with him. I swore that I'd never record with him again—and I never have. I told Jones, "Man, don't ever call me again." We got paid union wages, but it wasn't worth it.

As such testimony makes clear, even in the early days, a Jones recording session could be a challenge for all involved. Steel guitar player Frank Juricek has his own recollections. "I remember a George session that took all night, 6 p.m. to 6 a.m., and we got only two songs done," he claims.

Yet, even in the midst of such proceedings, the Gold Star Studios founder Quinn tended to maintain his composure and eventually get the desired results. Consider this anecdote from musician Glenn Barber:

Bill was a great guy with a good sense of humor. I remember one early session with George Jones that wasn't going so well because he'd been drinking a bit too much. Bill finally came out and had a conference with all of us. He said, "Do you boys think we can do this on the next take?"

We all said, "Sure, we can do it."

George said, "I can sing it perfect. Let's do it and get out of here."

Bill said, "I don't want to put any pressure on you, but I only have one acetate dub left." So we cut it.

Building on Quinn's ability to achieve successful resolution of in-studio difficulties, Jones recorded several more tracks at Gold Star even after he had made the jump from Starday to Mercury Records. At least two of those tracks became 1957 hits: "Don't Stop the Music" (#71029) crested on the *Billboard* country charts at number ten, and "Too Much Water" (#71096) climbed as high as number thirteen.

It was not until Daily moved Jones's sessions to Nashville and made the 1959 Mercury recording of "White Lightning" (#71406), which rose all the way to number one on the charts, that the initial success of "Why Baby Why" and "Just One More" was surpassed. Although several takes on "White Lightning" (written by J. P. Richardson, better known as the Big Bopper) had previously been recorded at Gold Star, the later hit version was a product of the Nashville studio scene (including the presence of Hargus "Pig" Robbins on piano).

All in all, Jones released at least twenty-seven songs that were recorded at Gold Star Studios in the mid-1950s. (It is possible that other Jones songs were recorded there but never released, or they may have appeared without session credits on one or more of his early albums.) Though he would eventually become a legendary Nashville figure, this country singer from Beaumont launched his bid for stardom close to home in Houston. Accordingly, he—like the studio where he made "Why Baby Why"—is a key part of Texas music history.

ROCKABILLY DELIVERED A POWERFUL JOLT to much of the country music recording industry in the mid-1950s. Young white artists such as Bill Haley, Carl Perkins, and Jerry Lee Lewis—borrowing heavily from the African American–formed genre of electric blues—were speaking a new kind of musical language, one that drew simultaneously from country and early R&B. Across the nation, multitudes of white teens and young adults passionately liked what they heard and soon redefined, often to the angst of the older generation, popular tastes and standards for commercial success. By February of 1956, when Elvis Presley's "Heartbreak Hotel" became a number one hit, many country music producers were scurrying to react to this major shift in public opinion. Consider this anecdote from Starday rockabilly hit-maker Rudy Grayzell, as told to writer Dan Davidson: "I remember poor ol' Hank Locklin, man. We'd all moved on to rock 'n' roll, and on one show we did, he got up and did his straight country thing, and the kids let him have it with hotdogs and paper cups!"

But Daily had perhaps seen this change coming, and he had already re-corded several rock 'n' roll and rockabilly sides prior to Elvis's ascension in pop culture. Among the earliest Starday records in that vein were Sonny Fisher's "Rockin' Daddy" (#179) and "Hey Mama" (#190) and Sonny Burns's "A Real Cool Cat" (#209).

The swell of commercial interest in this fast-paced style of new music even prompted Daily and Jones to return to Gold Star Studios in early 1956 specifi-cally to record rockabilly. The results included a cover version of "Heartbreak Hotel" and a pair of original songs by Jones: "Rock It" and "How Come It." In May the last two titles were released as alternate sides of a Starday single (#240) under the rockabilly-inspired pseudonym Thumper Jones. Public re-sponse to this record was indifferent, prompting the producer-artist duo to focus thereafter solely on straight country music.

Yet by no means did Daily quit recording rockabilly. He just shifted his focus to more suitable artists on the Starday roster. Moreover, he would ex-pand that emphasis even more, within a couple of years, on his many Gold Star productions for D Records.

One of the most noteworthy Starday artists in the rockabilly genre was Rudy "Tutti" (Jimenez) Grayzell (b. 1933), a native of Saspamco, near San Antonio, Texas. Unlike many of his Starday peers, Grayzell did not make his first records at Gold Star Studios, for he had already cut his three singles for Abbott Records (where he sang in a traditional country style) back in 1953. While those records did not generate many sales, they were good enough to earn Grayzell guest appearances on both the *Grand Ole Opry* and the *Louisiana Hayride* radio programs. Grayzell, who was honing a more progressive rock-abilly-tinged sound, then signed with Capitol Records, which released three more singles (under the pseudonym Rudy Gray), but scored no hits.

Yet Grayzell was gaining attention—so much so that Elvis Presley, while touring in San Antonio, reportedly showed up at one of his gigs. Impressed by Grayzell's fiery on-stage presence, Presley offered him a job as his opening act, a role he served for approximately a year and a half. Presley allegedly also bestowed the "Tutti" nickname on the budding star.

Daily soon signed Grayzell to Starday Records. However, the first release, "The Moon Is Up (The Stars Are Out)" backed with "Day by Day" (#229, is-sued in March 1956), had used the regular Gold Star house band and thus conveyed a fairly traditional country sound, not rockabilly. Yet neither Grayzell nor Daily gave up, and shortly thereafter they recorded and released (in May 1956) a truly classic disc in the rockabilly mode, "Duck Tail" (#241, backed with "You're Gone").

With its title and lyrics referencing the ubiquitous hairstyle adopted by thousands of young American males as a symbol of cool rebellion, plus its fre-

Hank Locklin, inside Daily's Record Ranch, publicity photo, Houston, 1949

netic rockabilly groove, "Duck Tail" immediately climbed the regional charts, reaching the number seven position in Houston. Though Grayzell later denied any influence by the Carl Perkins hit with the signature line "Don't step on my blue suede shoes," his own breakthrough song had a similar hook in its repeated warning, "Don't mess with my duck tail." Davidson quotes Grayzell's explanation: "Most teenagers had ducktails in their hair and hell, so did I. I just kinda got the idea for the song from that." Writer John Tottenham offers further insight from Grayzell about the origins of the song: "Some girl was fooling with my ducktail one night . . . and it was making me mad—so I wrote about it. It seemed like a good idea at the time, and I guess a lot of other people thought so, too."

Perhaps the wild-eyed 1950s-era punk attitude that the song exudes was exaggerated by the conditions under which it was recorded at Gold Star Studios. Sleepy LaBeef recounts his impressions of that session:

> I was at the studio when Rudy Grayzell came in to record "Don't Mess with My Duck Tail." He and the band were not getting along well at all in the studio. Bill [Quinn] said, "Y'all have got to do something because y'all have got a lot of friction between you, and it ain't coming off." So Rudy called them all out back of the studio, and they had fisticuffs for what seemed like ten minutes. Then they came in and cut the song, and a few others.

The hit song established Grayzell's rock credibility, and he soon was touring and releasing follow-ups on Starday. The next single, issued in November 1956, featured the cut "You Hurt Me So" backed with "Jig-Ga-Lee-Ga" (#270). Following that, in 1957, Grayzell recorded perhaps his most frenzied rocker, the blunt call to debauchery entitled "Let's Get Wild." Coming as it did during the gradually evolving affiliation between Houston-based Starday and the Nashville-based branch of Mercury, this cut was ultimately released on both labels (#321 for the former and #71138 for the latter).

Though by the end of 1957 Grayzell would leave to record for other companies, he was arguably at his best during the dawning of rockabilly—when he was recording at Gold Star Studios for Daily, whom he continued to admire even after his departure. The Davidson article quotes Grayzell's assessment of the man who produced his biggest hit: "He was tremendous! A great man. Pappy stood behind me all through the Starday years. He told me, 'Rudy, you've got a message in there somewhere and we're gonna find it!'" As many rockabilly record collectors and aficionados would attest today, with the hit "Duck Tail," they surely did.

Yet Grayzell was not Daily's only Starday rockabilly sensation. Another was Sonny Fisher (1931–2005), originally from Chandler, Texas. At the time of his death at age 73 in Houston, he was memorialized by music writers not only nationwide but elsewhere, especially in western Europe, where he toured sporadically to wide acclaim between 1979 and 1993. Garth Cartwright, for instance, writing in *The Guardian,* proclaims him to be "one of America's pioneering rockabilly artists," and he notes, "when London's Ace Records reissued his 1956 recordings in 1979, he found himself proclaimed king of the rockabilly revival."

According to Fisher's own account, he paid for his first recording sessions out of his own pocket, a move that promptly led Starnes to recruit him to

Starday Records in early 1955. From Bill Millar's *New Kommotion* article, we get the story, in Fisher's words, of his first recordings at Gold Star Studios:

> There were two or three studios in Houston, but I think Gold Star, owned by Mr. Bill Quinn, was the cheapest. You could get hourly sessions done for a little demo record, and it wouldn't cost nothing at all. We paid for our own sessions and recorded "Rockin' Daddy," "Hold Me Baby," "Sneaky Pete," and "Hey Mama" at the first one. There wasn't much there except a little turntable behind the glass, one or two microphones, and egg boxes up on the wall. Quinn handled all the controls, and I paid him for the hiring of the studio. . . . When I came back to Quinn's for the second session [after signing with Starday], he'd installed a booth that I got into for the singing.

In the immediate aftermath of that first session, Fisher got the break he needed. He continues: "Quinn called Jack Starnes and told him there's a guy over here doing stuff like Elvis, and Starnes came over to hear us. That's how we got on Starday Records. Jack Starnes became my manager, and I signed a one-year contract with Pappy Daily."

Fisher's initial Starday releases were the four demo tracks that he had hired Quinn to record. "Rockin' Daddy" backed with "Hold Me Baby" (#179) came first and was a regional hit. Next was "Hey Mama" and "Sneaky Pete" (#190). These sides were followed later in 1955 by "I Can't Lose" backed with "Rockin' and Rollin'" (#207). In 1956 Starday issued "Little Red Wagon" backed with "Pink and Black" (#244).

Nonetheless, Fisher ultimately was unhappy with the label, so he got out when his contract expired. This move, however valid, may have derailed Fisher's career. Cartwright's posthumous tribute in *The Guardian* includes this account:

> When Starday presented Fisher with a royalty cheque for $126 at the end of 1955, he was so displeased by the sum he refused to re-sign with them. Attempting to set up his own record label and publishing company proved impossible for Fisher, and his band soon fell apart.

Fisher eventually migrated to different genres before abandoning the music business, only to see his career surprisingly revived by European fans over a decade later. Cartwright says of the post-Starday Fisher,

> In 1958 he began fronting an all-black band singing rhythm and blues. This was too radical a gesture for the South at the time, and Fisher was soon back playing country music. In 1965 he left the music industry, unaware that his

Starday 45s were now considered by connoisseurs as classic primal rockabilly.

When Soho's Ace Records market stall in London decided to set up as a label, they began with a ten-inch album featuring all of Fisher's Starday recordings. The success of the album not only launched Ace Records—now a leading force in reissues on this side of the Atlantic—but instigated a hugely popular rockabilly revival, and led to Fisher being brought to Europe for the first time.

Thus, though his Starday affiliation concluded on a sour note, Fisher reaped unexpected dividends years later—leading to several tours and recording opportunities in Europe. And the foundation for that success was laid in the sessions Quinn had engineered at his affordable studio facility.

DESPITE ITS CALCULATED FORAY into the rockabilly genre, Starday continued successfully recording country music at Gold Star Studios and discovering artists who, like Fisher, had come there on their own initiative to cut demos. One prime example is the singer Frankie Miller (b. 1931), whose Gold Star–produced demo disc would not pay off till a few years later. He recounts that experience:

> I first came to Gold Star Studios in 1951. I was visiting the studio and observing a session being recorded by Bill Quinn for a clarinet player named Hub Sutter, who had played with many of the big bands in the area, including Bob Wills and His Texas Playboys. Following Hub's session, I recorded a bunch of demos with just me and my guitar. I needed these demos to be able to talk to some record companies about signing me. Bill recorded me on a Magnacord tape recorder and then made me some dubs on acetate discs.
>
> I came back to record again in 1956 and did "Blackland Farmer" there. The song was released in 1959 on Starday Records [#424], but I recorded it in 1956 with Bill Quinn. The song went to number five on the country charts. The bass man was Hezzie Bryant, and the guitar man was real popular and recorded a bunch of his own records also at Gold Star; his name was Glenn Barber. My brother played the coconut shells that made the horse sounds on the record; his name was Norman Miller. I had a fiddle player on the session, and Jack Kennedy played piano. I made my career off that song. "True Blue" was the other side of the record.

When asked about the time gap between the studio recording of his signature hit and its Starday release, Miller is quick to blame the rockabilly phenomenon. He explains,

Well, guys like J. P. Richardson [Big Bopper] and Elvis Presley almost killed country music. I carried the tape around for two years and didn't play it to anyone because nobody was listening to country music anymore. Then one day I was in Nashville, and I was in Tommy Hill's office at Starday Records. Told him I had a country song, and he said, "Go get it for me."

I said, "C'mon, you don't want to hear a country song."

He said, "Yes, now go and get it." So I did, and he listened, and his eyes lit up, and he went right over to play it to Starday's president, Don Pierce, that same day. And I had a contract before I left Nashville.

That was in 1958, and the rest is history. I have a Gold Record from Starday for "Blackland Farmer," and I've seen it on fifteen or twenty different compilation CDs. . . . Don Pierce told me just a while ago that he had lost George Jones to Pappy Daily when Pappy left Starday—and that my record kind of saved the day for his business. . . . I played a big show in Houston with a bunch of rock 'n' roll cats, and I had the number one record in Houston on KILT Radio. I headlined the show with Roy Orbison and Ben E. King. This little old country boy did good.

Miller's Gold Star Studios memories include an account of Quinn's impromptu ingenuity in getting the desired sound effects within the room:

For "Blackland Farmer" Bill Quinn had me singing and playing guitar in a booth off to the side, much like you put drums in nowadays. My brother took a coconut and cut it in half and put them on the floor. Bill took a mic and put it down close to the floor, but the sound on the floor was too grainy and edgy. So we grabbed a pillow off the couch and put the coconuts on top of that. Sounded just like a horse walking through the room. He probably had about four mics out there recording. This was Bill's house studio.

Glenn Barber, the guitarist on that session, provides a theory about the commercial appeal of "Blackland Farmer" in an era when rockabilly was dominating the charts. He says,

There is a great story around why that song became a huge success in an era where country music was not very popular. Outside Houston is a place called Garner State Park [where] thousands of kids would go to have fun and dance and party with good supervision. The guy that ran the park had a big old concrete slab in the park with a jukebox in the middle of it. The kids would dance to whatever he had on it—and then would go out and buy those records. He happened to be a country music lover [so he stocked Miller's record], and "Blackland Farmer" was a song that the kids latched on to and started buying.

Miller followed up with several other Starday singles, including "Family Man" (#457), which charted as high as number seven in late 1959, and "Baby Rocked Her Dolly" (#496), which made it to number fifteen in 1960. That same year he won the *Cashbox* award for "Most Promising Country Artist"— an irony, given that none of his subsequent recordings (on Starday, United Artists, and elsewhere) did as well as those first Gold Star Studios–produced hits.

Among the many other notable Starday artists who recorded at Quinn's place was Benny Barnes (1936–1987). His "Poor Man's Riches" (#262) impressively soared to number two on the country charts in 1956. As Andrew Brown writes for the *Benny Barnes* compilation, "He had defied current trends and record industry wisdom by hitting with a hard country performance at a time when rock 'n' roll had threatened to consume everything in its path." The Beaumont native's first single for Starday had featured "Once Again" backed with "No Fault of Mine" (#236). But his second Starday release, "Poor Man's Riches," was the best-seller, and it was also reissued on Mercury (#71048). His last single for Starday, credited to Benny Barnes with the Echoes, was "You Gotta Pay" backed with "Heads You Win (Tails I Lose)" (#401). After that, like his friend George Jones, Barnes moved to Mercury. But he continued to be produced by Daily and, through 1959, make records at Gold Star Studios (for the Mercury, Dixie, and D labels).

Another Texas singer who came to Gold Star to record for Daily was Roger Miller (1936–1992), best known for later hits (such as "Dang Me" and "King of the Road") recorded elsewhere for other labels. In 1956 Jones had introduced the unproven Miller to Daily, leading to the production of several singles, including two issued on Starday: "Can't Stop Loving You" backed with "You're Forgetting Me" (#356) and "Playboy" backed with "Poor Little John" (#718). Other Daily-produced tracks by Miller were released on Mercury, including a reissue of "Poor Little John" with "My Pillow" (#71212). Quinn had engineered all of these.

The lineup of Gold Star staff musicians regularly used during its prime Starday era (1954 to 1957) included the following: Hal Harris, Eddie Eddings, Glenn Barber, or Cameron Hill on lead guitar; Ernie Hunter, Earl Caruthers, Joe "Red" Hayes, Kenneth "Little Red" Hayes, Tony Sepolio, or Clyde Brewer on fiddle; Herb Remington, Frank Juricek, Al Petty, or Buddy Doyle on steel guitar; Charles "Doc" Lewis or "Shorty" Byron on piano; Russell "Hezzie" Bryant, Ray "Shang" Kennedy, or J. T. "Tiny" Smith on bass; and Bill Kimbrough, Red Novak, or Darrell Newsome on drums. As Glenn Barber says, "It was a real who's who of Houston singers and musicians." Frank Juricek adds, "We always had great guitar players on our sessions. Quite often it was Hal Harris.

The Sun Downers (left to right, front row: Herb Remington, Clyde Brewer, Johnny Ragsdell, Frank Whiteside; back row: Red Novak on drums, Hezzie Bryant), at the Rice Hotel ballroom, Houston, 1950s

He started that plucking guitar stuff when it became the thing to do or the new sound in country records."

As for Hal Harris (1920–1992), he was a highly respected finger-picking guitarist who played on numerous Gold Star sessions. His aggressive guitar style shone brilliantly on many country and rockabilly recordings for Starday or D Records, including some credited to Jones, as well as others by Barnes, Barber, the Big Bopper, Link Davis, Eddie Noack, Ray Campi, Bob Doss, Sleepy LaBeef, Rock Rogers, and others.

By documenting and publicizing artists such as these during the mid-1950s, Starday ranks right up there with Quinn's previous Gold Star Records label in terms of historical significance. They both were early, influential, and unusually prolific independent Texas-based companies recording regional talent. Their respective catalogues are now cultural artifacts, a rich source of mid-twentieth-century roots music from the state's largest city.

As for Gold Star Studios, the numerous Daily-produced sessions there for Starday (and for its Mercury affiliation) provided what was surely Quinn's most important source of income from 1955 through 1959. However, he was still recording a variety of performers for other labels during this period. (For instance, in 1956 eventual country star Mickey Gilley made his first single there for Minor Records.) Yet the Quinn-Daily business relationship was crucial to the financial stability, and subsequent expansion, of the Gold Star enterprise, and it would continue even after Daily left Starday.

The Big Studio
Room Expansion

UST AS THE 1950S WERE A BOOM time for certain local independent record companies such as Starday, even more so were they a period of explosive expansion and prosperity in Houston proper. As Bob Allen writes, "All roads led to Houston in Southeast Texas in the early '50s. The teeming port metropolis was growing so rapidly from the spoils of the cattle, oil, and shipping industries that it was practically bursting at the seams." Given that context, perhaps it is not surprising that, even though scores of important records have been made there, Houston would rarely be considered a major recording center.

After all, Houston would never really develop or promote itself as such. By 1950 there was so much money being generated in the city's many business arenas that civic leaders and power brokers likely scoffed at the notion that recorded music could possibly be one of its prime exports. Perhaps unlike Nashville, the rapidly rising petrochemical capital of the nation did not really need the music business. At any rate, lacking any leadership or support from outside their decidedly eccentric ranks, the various studio proprietors, A&R producers, label owners, and musical forces never coalesced to create a collective identity for, or to promote, the Houston recording scene.

Nonetheless, it was a fertile and profitable era for some of the shrewdest of the independent music producers. And none was sharper than the Starday Records cofounder known by the paternal nickname. As Allen goes on to say, "If you came down the pike to Houston with music in your mind, the man to see was Harold W. 'Pappy' Daily . . . who had slowly built himself a small empire." Just as the Duke-Peacock owner Don Robey, despite the presence of many competitors, dominated the local recording of black talent in the 1950s, Daily prevailed over much of the white music scene. Their business pursuits surely stimulated the city's job market for engineers, songwriters, and musicians, as well as other investments in real property, equipment, and related services. But though they built impressive companies, neither Daily nor Robey could ultimately transform the role of music recording in Houston's overall economic development.

Nonetheless, for regular session players such as Clyde Brewer, the 1950s were a fine time to be working in the city. He says,

> Herbie [Remington] and I would get a call almost daily from either Quinn [of Gold Star Studios] or Holford [of ACA Studios] to cut a serious session for a record company or a vanity record for anyone wanting to ride the coattails of George [Jones], Benny [Barnes], or [Big] Bopper.

As far as the founder of Gold Star Studios was concerned, in the late 1950s things were going pretty well. In fact, from late 1958 to early '59, Quinn had constructed a large new recording studio of his own design. By expanding off the back and one side of his house (the ground floor of which remained a smaller studio), he had created a sizable and splendid sanctuary of sound. Since the bulk of the new building spilled over into the previously vacant side yard, it got its own entrance and street address, 5626 Brock, while the house number remained 5628.

In addition to the big studio room, the first floor of the new building also housed two bathrooms, an entrance foyer and reception office, the stairwell to the control room, and an engineer's office that led directly into the studio area. The exterior looked like a corrugated steel Quonset hut. The dimensions ran forty-eight feet long by fifty-three feet wide, with a ceiling height of twenty-two feet. The flooring was a type of hardwood parquet. The walls were covered with acoustic tiles and strategically placed heavy drapes that Quinn's wife had made. There were two vocal booths situated in the back corners below the large window, which signified the control room. In a highly unusual move, Quinn had installed the control room upstairs on the second-floor level, offering it an overhead view of the performance space below.

That control room ran twenty feet wide by sixteen feet deep, with a ceiling height of ten feet. Its wall surfaces and ceiling were covered with acoustic tiles. The floor was carpeted to reduce some of the sonic "liveness" caused by the huge window. Considering where Quinn had placed the stairway in relation to the new studio, it was a walk of many steps from the floor where the musicians performed up to the control console. However, because of the studio's unusually grand size, that elevated vantage point offered exceptional sightlines for the engineer.

Bill Quinn, at the gate to Gold Star Studios (with the "Big Room" expansion in the background), 1960 (photo by and courtesy of Chris Strachwitz)

The mixing console consisted of several Ampex MX-10 tube mixers ganged together. The first state-of-the-art machines that had been set up at Gold Star Studios in 1955 were Ampex 350 and 351 mono tape machines. The first multitrack machine, installed in 1960, was a three-track Ampex machine. In the mid-1960s it would be upgraded to an Ampex four-track that recorded on half-inch tape. Mixing was done first to a mono Ampex 350 quarter-inch machine and later in the mid-1960s to a quarter-inch Ampex 351 stereo machine.

There were also several smaller analog tape decks that were used to create the relatively new echo technology for vocal processing. Engineers had discovered that if you split the vocal signal off to a tape recorder that was rolling in record mode, and then brought that signal back from the playback head to the mixing board, you would have a slightly delayed signal which, used with discretion, could enhance the original vocal. This technique is often referred to as slap-back echo or delay, used frequently on early rockabilly, country, and rock 'n' roll records.

The control room monitors were JBL, and the studio had Altec A7 speakers. Outboard gear in the early 1960s consisted of some large passive equalizers, made by a company called Pulteq or custom designed. In 1964 Gold Star would add equalizers to the Ampex MX-10 and MX-35 mixers. The most common microphones in use at the time were the Neumann tube U-47 or U-67, various RCA ribbon microphones (like the DX-77 and DX-44), an Altec/Western Electric 634, and other smaller Electro Voice and Altec dynamic microphones.

Directly below the control room is where the reception area was located (and still is today). There was also an area that housed an acetate-cutting lathe (later replaced with a Gotham/Grampian lathe in 1965). That space is now the SugarHill Studios front entrance room.

The new studio and office space marked a significant upgrading of Quinn's Brock Street recording facility and the types of projects it could support. Though there was no concerted effort among other Houstonians, Quinn—with financial support from Daily and perhaps also from Robey—was doing his part to bring serious studio recording space and services to the city. Musician Clyde Brewer explains the visionary motivation for Quinn's expansion:

> Bill Quinn built the large studio big enough to be used for television shows and commercials, as well as to cater to the many Daily recording projects. . . . He built the new Gold Star studio to be used as a sound or TV stage, in the hopes that he would be able to do local video and audio production. I remember . . . comedian Jonathan Winters had come into Gold Star to do a TV commercial while he was on tour performing in Houston.

Musician Glenn Barber adds another insight: "Originally the reason he wanted a room that size was that he wanted to record high school and college marching bands in there, and also big orchestras and such. He was trying to bring in new business and create a new market."

Slick Norris says the strategy worked: "J. L. Patterson got in with Quinn in, like, 1963 and made his money cutting high school big bands." Another example is Ed Gerlach's Big Band, which recorded the album *The Big Band from Texas* (Dored Records) there in 1964, engineered by Walt Andrus. That seventeen-piece group, even with an extra singer, fitted easily into the new studio. Back when most recordings were done in relatively small rooms, engineering such a session in Houston would have been difficult. Thus, Quinn's ambitious expansion redefined the possibilities.

Nevertheless, despite its relatively grandiose scale and Quinn's desire to expand his clientele (which he did with some success), in the late 1950s and 1960s Gold Star Studios continued primarily to record blues, country, and rock bands or other small combos. Given Quinn's apparently low-key personality and working-class graciousness, his enlarged studio facility became a gathering place for many players in such groups. As Sleepy LaBeef put it during a 2004 tour of the building,

> It is like coming home. This place still has the same feel that it did when I recorded with Bill Quinn in the '50s and '60s. Bill Holford over at ACA was a great recording engineer, but Quinn was less formal, and Gold Star was a much better hangout for the musicians. Most of the players who came here to record in those years also felt like they were at home at Gold Star and [with] Quinn.

One of those who had accompanied LaBeef there on various sessions was musician Dean Needham, who recalls his first, awestruck impression of the place, circa 1963:

> I had been to studios before, but I had never seen anything like this before. It was this huge room with a plank wooden floor. Everybody else had egg-crate cartons on the walls and carpet on the floor. And I've never been in one since that looked like that big room here at Gold Star.

Precisely when Quinn started conducting recording sessions in the big room is not clear, but oral testimony suggests that it was in late 1958 or early '59. Norris says, "I cut my last record in the house studio in 1958. So I guess that the big room was built sometime after that; possibly in late spring or early summer of '58. . . . I never cut any records in that big room." LaBeef adds, "I recorded in both of Bill's studios; in the small place on the ground floor of his house and the big studio next door. He built the big studio in, like, 1959."

Glenn Barber concurs, "I think that big room was built in early 1959, and we were still doing sessions in the smaller studio while it was being built."

Then, to illustrate Quinn's prankish wit and down-home ingenuity—part of what made Gold Star Studios a cool place for many musicians perhaps—Barber relates the following anecdote:

> When they were building it, there was a young guy helping him do the construction. I think he was a musician. He was teasing and making fun of Quinn, [saying] "the old man" this and "the old man" that. [Saying] "He'll want this, and that's crazy."

True to his reputation for a calm demeanor, Quinn ignored the youth's insulting critiques—up to a point. Barber continues,

Bill was going to hang a speaker, and he was going to use a turnbuckle to adjust the angle of it as it hung. He didn't have any at first, but finally he found one that was all rusty and looked terrible. So the kid said, "So you aren't going to buy a new one, are you! You're going to use that one!"

Quinn said, "Come and hold on to this turnbuckle for me." He then pulled a can of silver spray paint from behind his back and painted the turnbuckle all the way down to the kid's wrist. Then he said, "Now that's pretty, ain't it?"

Despite such a capacity to humiliate an annoying hired hand, Quinn was evidently viewed by many of the musicians as a likable fellow. However, he was also often a curiosity. For example, Barber describes Quinn's typical approach to positioning musicians to record during a session.

Bill had a strange way of recording in that big room. He had a great big circle painted on the floor. It was a big black circle about twelve feet across. . . . He had a Telefunken tube mic hanging out over the middle of that circle. You'd go up in the control room, and he'd have this little Roberts tape recorder. It was a stereo machine, and he didn't have multiple tracks. He would set up the musicians in the circle, and he would move them around until he got it balanced the way he wanted. He would move the piano back and forth and the rhythm guitarist, and he had two isolation booths for the singer and background singers to sing in. He mixed as he went along on the session. He was a genius and very crude about what he did at the same time. But he cut hit after hit.

Again illustrating Quinn's mostly nonverbal manner for making a point, Barber recalls another encounter.

I remember one session where he called down from the booth and said, "Glenn, could you put a bit more treble on your guitar?"

Well, I didn't like a lot of treble, but I said, "Sure, I'll give you some more."

Finally he came down from the booth and said, "Where's your treble at?" So I pointed, and he turned it full on. He asked then, "Where's your bass?" And again I pointed. He turned it all the way off. That was the way he made me play.

He knew exactly what he wanted, and that's the way it was. A lot of times he would take a crude sound, something that was shrill and terrible, and make it something that the people wanted to hear.

Regarding Quinn's sound engineering skills, LaBeef adds these comments:

> Bill was a genius at the electronic stuff. He could take small equipment, things that seemed insignificant, and get a lot of sound out of it. He was the only one that I knew of that could compete with the sound coming out of the Sun Records Studio [in Memphis]. He had a lot of smarts and seemed to know what he wanted and how to get it out of the equipment that he had.

Even though Quinn's technical know-how was widely respected, his ability to pay for the expansion of his recording center was likely limited. Evidence suggests that Pappy Daily helped finance the remodeling. As previously cited, Ted Marek's 1957 article identifies Daily as a "co-owner" of Gold Star Studios. However, the precise nature of the Quinn-Daily business partnership remains a mystery. Until his retirement from the studio business in 1963, Quinn was the only officially acknowledged owner, judging from various business documents. But Daily's prolific level of production, first with Starday and later with D Records, made him Quinn's major client from 1955 through 1963.

Though by 1958 Daily was producing sessions in Nashville, he continued independently making records back in Houston, and Gold Star was obviously his studio of choice. By possibly paying for some of Quinn's expansion costs, Daily could have been protecting his own interests as a local label owner—and may have also been settling debts for previously rendered studio services. The result was a modernized facility with space enough to host any kind of session—and one at which Daily presumably carried clout concerning scheduling, rates, and related services. Norris opines, "With as much stuff that Pappy recorded at the house studio, he probably owed Quinn quite a bit of money. That might have been how Bill got the money to build that big room. I'd be more inclined to believe that it was pay-up time."

LaBeef concurs that Daily probably helped fund the renovation but believes that Daily's African American counterpart may have also been involved: "Pappy Daily contributed quite a bit to the building, as well as Don Robey. Robey had Duke, Peacock, and Back Beat and all those other labels. I'm pretty sure that Robey also contributed." If Robey were involved, however, it may have been retroactively. There is no evidence to suggest that Robey recorded at Gold Star before 1959—that is, before the big room was built. However, starting that very year Robey suddenly began to use Quinn's facility for many projects.

However he may have paid for it, Quinn's new studio appealed, in size and amenities, to label owners and musicians alike. By the time he was engineering sessions there, he had been in the record-making business about eighteen years. He had come a long way from the former Telephone Road grocery store building where he had launched the Quinn Recording Company—and from simply recording on the ground floor of his residence. As the 1950s ended, Quinn was—for the first time in his life—practicing his profession in a room originally created for that purpose.

SLEEPY LABEEF IS THE STAGE NAME of a musician who was born Thomas Paulsley LaBeff in 1935 near Smackover, Arkansas. After moving to Houston in 1954, he started performing on local stages. Eventually discovered and recorded by Daily, LaBeef became a regularly performing member of the *Houston Jamboree,* a popular Saturday night live radio show, where he joined an informal vocal quartet featuring George Jones, Sonny Burns, and Hal Harris. They sang old gospel songs recalled from their upbringing. With the six-foot, six-inch-tall LaBeef holding down the bass part, this quartet reportedly often closed the show to a standing ovation.

LaBeef spent much time at Quinn's Gold Star recording facility—both before and after the big room expansion. Here he explains how he came to know the place—and jammed with its founder.

> [After moving to Houston], I immediately went to visit the radio stations and recording studios to familiarize myself with the music of the city. I met radio personalities like Hal Harris, and of course he was a staff musician for Starday Records, and played on most all of their recordings. So I met Hal and went over to Gold Star to watch a few of the sessions, and I met Bill Quinn. . . .
>
> Bill was a musician also and played the organ. . . . One day I was over at the studio doing a few things . . . just me and my guitar. Bill left the control room and joined me on the organ. . . . It was the first time I ever heard of an engineer leaving the booth and playing on a session.

Performing in a style that drew from his country roots but also veered into rockabilly, LaBeef would go on to record at least thirty-three sides at Quinn's Gold Star Studios between 1957 and 1962 for various labels, including Dixie, Gulf, and Wayside. Daily first produced him for a May 1957 release on Starday (#292) featuring the songs "I'm Through" and "All Alone." This disc was reissued on the Mercury-Starday imprint (#71112), as was a follow-up single that offered the tracks "All the Time" and "Lonely" (#71179). Of the many songs LaBeef has recorded in his career, he is best known for his version of "Tore Up," which he recorded at Gold Star Studios in 1959 in the early days of the big room. It was originally released (under the name Tommy LaBeff) on Wayside Records (#1654), and it resurfaced later on the 1979 retrospective album *Early, Rare & Rockin' Sides* on the Baron label.

In February 1965, LaBeef returned to Gold Star Studios for a session paid for by the Nashville branch of prestigious Columbia Records, his new label. A Gold Star invoice shows it was a four-hour session that consumed two reels of tape. LaBeef explains how it came to pass.

Don Law Sr. [Columbia Records producer] came down to Houston and made the arrangements with Bill Quinn. . . . Mickey Gilley was visiting the studio during the session, and Kenny Rogers was playing upright bass with us. I had Wiley Barkdull on piano, and Dean Needham on one of the guitars, maybe lead guitar, Eddie Hamler on drums.

Bill Quinn did the engineering, and Don Law was A&R producer on the session. He had called me from Nashville, and I was working at the Wayside Lounge, which is just a few blocks away from the studio in Houston. Just before we went on stage, the waitress said, "Hey, Sleepy, you got a call from Nashville. Columbia Records wants to talk to you."

I said, "Yeah, I'll bet." Sure enough, it was Don Law. He said that he had set up studio time at Gold Star, and we went over and cut a few things. And I was with Columbia for four years. We recorded in the big studio, and Bill had some really fine equipment at that stage. I think we were recording on three tracks.

Of the Gold Star–produced records that initially launched his career, LaBeef says, "Those songs I did in '57 and '58 actually sold more the second time around in Europe than they had done in the States." Despite the fact that he recorded late in Daily's Starday tenure and soon departed, LaBeef remembers the label fondly. "We still receive royalty checks from the Daily family," he says. "Starday has paid better than every company I have ever been with."

Daily's involvement with Starday had always been a joint venture, ultimately shared in equal partnership with Don Pierce, who had moved the company to Nashville and linked it with the Mercury label. However, by July 1958, as writer Colin Escott puts it, "Mercury was dissatisfied with Starday because Pierce and Daily hadn't delivered much in the way of hits, and the deal between Pierce and Daily fell apart at the same time for reasons that have never become entirely clear."

So Daily got out, leaving Starday (as well as the Dixie label that he and Pierce had recently launched), and created yet another label with himself as the sole owner. Taking the initial letter of his family name, Daily proclaimed his new enterprise D Records. Based in Houston, it adds another chapter to the Gold Star Studios story.

Daily's Dominance
and D Records

IS IT MERELY A COINCIDENCE that the timing of Pappy Daily's creation of D Records corresponds with that of Bill Quinn's studio expansion? Probably not. It seems reasonable that Daily, going out on his own in a new Houston-based label venture, would make sure that he had sufficient studio space and upgraded equipment there to meet his needs. Given his previous success, especially with George Jones (whom he was continuing to produce for the Mercury label in Nashville), Daily understood the prevailing industry standards and technical requirements of a fully professional studio. The recent improvements at the Gold Star recording facility thus served his interests.

Whatever his level of investment in the expansion may have been, it was likely offset by the fact, as Daily knew, that he could record with Quinn more cheaply than anyone else could record in Nashville. For instance, writer Deke Dickerson quotes Daily's former Starday partner Don Pierce explaining why he chose first to record Roger Miller at Gold Star Studios in Houston: "Down there we could cut for five dollars per song per man. In Nashville, it was $41.25 per man per three-hour session."

As his prolific output suggests, Daily's strategy for D Records was to conduct lots of sessions, keep the costs down, secure the publishing rights, hope for a regional hit, and if he got one, lease it promptly to a major label, and collect the profits (without having to handle major distribution or promotion). As Colin Escott writes, "From the beginning, Pappy saw 'D' as an experimental label or a 'look-see' label as it was called then. . . . If anything looked likely to sell on a national basis, he would try to interest Mercury in picking up the master."

Given the pop cultural climate of 1958, the initial D Records releases offered an odd mix of traditional country and rock. However, Daily soon created another label, Dart, where he would increasingly channel most of the rock 'n' roll repertoire. Thus, the D label gradually evolved into what writer Kevin Coffey calls "a bastion of traditional country and honky-tonk against the double-barreled assault of rock 'n' roll and lush Nashville Sound country pop."

Like Starday before, both of Daily's new self-owned labels did a substantial amount of recording at Gold Star Studios. Most sessions featured artists living in or near Houston between 1958 and 1965. Ultimately, approximately 40 to 50 percent of the massive D Records catalogue was recorded with Quinn engineering and Daily or Gabe Tucker (D's vice president, 1915–2003) producing.

The first D Records national hit was "Talk to Me Lonesome Heart" (#1006), the flip side of "Changeable," both recorded by James O'Gwynn in June 1958. This classic country tearjerker reached number sixteen on the *Billboard* charts. Having first recorded for the Nucraft and Azalea labels, O'Gwynn had next released one single for Starday. However, with the subsequent dissolution of Daily's Starday interest, O'Gwynn was a free agent. He says, "I then signed with D Records in 1958. I had two hit records with D and made my debut on the Grand Ole Opry with the help of Jim Reeves. I then moved to Nashville in 1961." O'Gwynn's second D Records hit was "Blue Memories." Backed with "You Don't Want to Hold Me" (#1022), it peaked at number twenty-eight on the national charts.

Other notables in the early D Records–Gold Star Studios collaboration include Eddie Noack, who temporarily betrayed his country roots and cut the rockabilly sides "My Steady Dream" and "Can't Play Hookey" for the first D release (#1000). This record, perhaps an embarrassment to the country traditionalist Noack, was released under the pseudonym Tommy Wood. However, later in 1958 Noack did put a D single on the country charts, rising to number fourteen with "Have Blues Will Travel" (#1019), his biggest seller. He followed it up with country ballads such as "Don't Look Behind" (#1060) or loping shuffles such as "Walk 'Em Off" (#1037).

Glenn Barber, a Gold Star Studios regular and Starday alumnus, followed Daily to D Records too. In 1958 he cut his first D single, "Hello Sadness" backed with "Same Old Fool Tomorrow" (#1017). He then recorded numerous obscure classics, such as "Your Heart Don't Love" (#1069) and "New Girl in School" (#1098), all produced at Quinn's studio. "It is a strange thing," Barber says, "where a lot of the records I made for D, which didn't make it nationally, are the ones that I get asked about the most nowadays. I get questions from Europe all the time about those songs."

At Gold Star Studios in May 1959, Barber cut his D Records version of "Most Beautiful" (#1069), a track that he would later rerecord in Nashville and make a major hit. Barber recalls the session being produced "right after [Quinn] moved into the big room in the back." Working with the Gold Star house band, in 1960 Barber cut songs such as "The Window" ("a song about suicide," he says) and his own rockabilly-influenced composition "Another You" (#1128). Though none of his D singles made much commercial impact, Barber epitomizes the level of solid country talent that Daily featured on hundreds of recordings.

In addition to recording local country singers, Daily had other strategies. Having leased the rights from Quinn, D Records reissued the old Gold Star Records singles by the late Harry Choates. D Records also prospected for the elusive hit disc by crossing over into other genres. For example, Daily made a tentative foray into the burgeoning Hispanic market by recording artists such as Gaston Ponce Castellanos, who released "Que-Chula-Estas" backed with "Si-Yo-Te-Quiero" in early 1959 (#1038).

Daily sometimes gambled with novelty records spoofing current events with cornball humor—utilizing the technique of lifting one-line phrases from previously recorded songs and inserting them as responses to questions posed by a faux radio reporter. Ray Jackson's 1958 track "Texas-Alaska" (#1012) is one such example, a calculated attempt to capitalize on news of Alaska's pending admission to statehood in 1959, a federal decision that made Texas no longer the largest state in the nation. Seizing the opportunity to satirize this indignity from a Texan's perspective, Daily lifted one-liners and sampled vocals from other recordings to patch together this topical piece. The humor pretty much falls flat though, and as Escott points out, the main goal seems to have been to incorporate snippets of "as many of Pappy Daily's copyrights as could be squeezed into two-and-a-half minutes."

Often his ideas went nowhere, but Daily experimented relentlessly in hopes of producing another hit. Believing that such a phenomenon could not really be predicted, he elected to generate a large volume of singles of various types, trusting in the law of averages to occasionally reward his strategy. The deal he had worked out with Quinn granted him easy access and presumably economical rates for recording on a whim at Gold Star Studios. And just as he had hoped, sometimes he got lucky.

AMONG THE SCORES OF D RECORDS artists whom Daily produced at Gold Star Studios, one stands above all the rest in terms of both profits and fame. J. P. Richardson (1930–1959), better known as the Big Bopper, recorded "Chantilly Lace" (#1008) there in 1958, a massive hit then and an oldies radio staple for decades. Prior to that, in 1957, Richardson had made one Mercury-

Starday Records single for Daily, "Crazy Blues" backed with "Beggar to a King" (#71219), released under the name Jape Richardson. It did not do much, but "Chantilly Lace"—originally just a B-side filler song—unexpectedly soared to number six and stayed on the pop charts for twenty-five straight weeks. In a sign of significant cross-racial appeal, the song also spent fifteen weeks on the R&B charts, rising to number three. With the first hint of major success, Daily had leased it to Mercury Records, securing nationwide distribution and promotion.

Since then this certified Gold Record has become a multi-Platinum classic. Having recently achieved the "BMI Three Million Airplays" milestone, it is one of the most recognizable hits in rock 'n' roll history, and has graced the soundtracks of several films. *Texas Monthly* writers Jeff McCord and John Morthland rate it one of the one hundred best Texas songs. The most famous record in Daily's D Records and Starday career, it is also one of the biggest hits ever produced at Quinn's studio. The song spawned Richardson's only album, *Chantilly Lace* (Mercury #MG-20402), which was filled out with other singles recorded there.

In "Chantilly Lace" Richardson dramatizes a comic monologue (representing one end of a telephone conversation between an excitable young man and his girlfriend) before breaking into song for a sixteen-bar rock-shuffle chorus that is punctuated by his impassioned assertion of "that's what I like!" It is the cool-daddy Big Bopper persona, of course, that underlies the record's appeal, as Richardson exudes a cocky machismo that is clearly defenseless against his female antagonist's charms. But the deliciously raw-sounding backing band deserves its due too, as it lays down the rollicking groove over which Richardson's jive-talking character performs. Guitarist Glenn Barber provides a firsthand recollection of the Gold Star session that produced this unique single:

> I didn't play the lead on "Chantilly Lace." I played a kind of tic-tac guitar part over the bass line. The actual lead guitar player was Hal Harris. I'm fairly sure that Floyd Tillman played rhythm guitar on it. The sax was none other than Link Davis. I believe that Herb Remington played steel. The drummer was a guy named Bill Kimbrough. . . . Doc Lewis played piano.

According to well-circulated accounts, as well as testimony from one of the principals, Richardson had penned "Chantilly Lace" while riding in the backseat of a car with fellow Beaumont-area disc jockey Huey Meaux, traveling from Port Arthur to Houston for those first recording sessions at Gold Star Studios. Meaux confirms that Richardson scribbled the lyrics as an afterthought for the B-side to his novelty song "Purple People Eater Meets the

Witch Doctor." That latter, the main focus of the planned session, was an obvious attempt to capitalize on two current hits, "Witch Doctor" by David Seville and "Purple People Eater" by Sheb Wooley. That plan changed, however, when radio programmers chose to spin the B-side, and listeners enthusiastically responded.

That Gold Star session also marks Richardson's formal adoption of the "Big Bopper" persona. His D Records colleague, Eddie Noack, says in his *New Kommotion* interview,

> I was at that session. They got through, and J.P. said, "I don't know. I've been thinking about calling myself the Big Bopper, but I [have] done a number of commercials for the Big Yazoo [a lawn mower], and it's all over the South, so I might call myself the Big Yazoo."
>
> And Pappy said, "Well, I think the Big Bopper would be better."

Thus, an immortal nickname was born, like the hit single itself, rather casually.

Daily had ended up with the publishing rights not to the original A-side track that Richardson's manager (Bill Hall) hoped would be a hit but instead to that off-the-cuff B-side song. Noack goes on to explain:

> At the end of the "Chantilly Lace" session, Bill Hall—he denies it now but I was there—said, "What side do you want, Pappy?"
>
> They were going to split the sides [in terms of publishing rights]—and Pappy said, "Take your pick, kid." Bill Hall picked "Purple People Eater" for publishing, and Pappy had "Chantilly Lace."

When it became clear that "Chantilly Lace" had popular appeal, Daily began to promote it shrewdly. Colin Escott's essay in *The Complete D Singles Collection* quotes Bud Daily (Pappy's son) regarding a marketing ploy:

> Mercury wasn't interested in it . . . so dad put it on "D," and he had sold 25,000 in Texas before Mercury got interested. Sunshine Tucker [the company secretary] had a black lace party dress and she cut it up and pasted bits of it onto postcards, which were then mailed to dee-jays with a note saying "Please play 'Chantilly Lace.'"

Boosted by such efforts, the song rapidly gained momentum beyond Texas, and Mercury leased the rights to the record, boosting its status nationwide. According to their legal agreement, however, Daily was permitted to continue selling the D Records single in Texas.

Big Bopper, publicity
photo, 1958

Leasing a hit to a larger company was a key component of Daily's success in an industry that he—having risen through the ranks of jukebox owners and record distributors—well understood. As Noack says in *New Kommotion,*

> I [have] seen Pappy do this over and over. I didn't know too much about the record business back then, and I couldn't understand why Pappy leased the master to Mercury. He'd already sold 25 to 30,000 copies on D. He told me, "Hell kid, a million seller would break me—because the distributors won't pay me." This was very amazing to me because Pappy was a major distributor himself. . . . And if they wouldn't pay Pappy, who in the hell would they pay? But Pappy told me that the distributors have got to pay a major label like Mercury—because they were bound to keep coming out with hits.

Other mid-twentieth-century independent record business veterans confirm the wisdom of this counterintuitive business strategy. For instance, Meaux often alleged in conversation that distributors regularly cheated him on some of his most popular early recordings. He ultimately subscribed fully to Daily's notion that it was better to lease a potential hit to a larger label, and in the 1960s and '70s Meaux profitably did so with several of his Gold Star productions.

When Mercury issued "Chantilly Lace" nationwide, it also elevated Richardson's star status—so much so that by November 1958 he had resigned from Beaumont's KTRM radio station and devoted himself to performing full-time. This suddenly hot performer got booked on the top shows in pop music, including that fateful tour with fellow Texan and rock pioneer Buddy Holly (1936–1959), as well as the California teen sensation Ritchie Valens (1941–1959). A few months later, on February 3, 1959, they all died together in a plane crash in Iowa.

Although, as writer Alan Lee Haworth puts it in his "Big Bopper" essay, "most of his recordings were of novelty songs" and "his appeal was largely in his flamboyant stage performances," Richardson was also a talented songwriter. Though he did not record until the last two years of his short life, he is known to have composed at least thirty-eight songs, only twenty-one of which were recorded. Besides "Chantilly Lace," Richardson also scripted two number one hits performed on record by fellow Gold Star Studios alumni: "White Lightning" (sung by George Jones) and "Running Bear" (sung by Johnny Preston). Thus, on "the day the music died" (to quote Don McLean's famous line), we lost not only Holly, Valens, and the likable showman who had scored big with "Chantilly Lace." We also lost a clever wordsmith whose abbreviated legacy encompasses classic hits by three Southeast Texas singers.

Like both Jones and Richardson, the singer known as Johnny Preston hailed from the Beaumont area and recorded his first hit single at Gold Star Studios in Houston. A native of Port Arthur, his full name was John Preston Courville (b. 1939), and in early 1959 he was a direct beneficiary of the budding relationship between Richardson and Daily. Preston relates how he got started:

My group and I were playing around Southeast Texas and were well known to Bopper and his manager Bill Hall. One night at a club called the Twilight Club in Port Neches, Texas, he came and asked me to come and have a meeting at the radio station. The meeting resulted in an offer from the Bopper and Hall to record "Running Bear," which was written by the Bopper. I quickly accepted and a recording session was set up at Gold Star Studios. The Big

Bopper was signed to Pappy Daily's D Records, and Gold Star was the home recording facility for that label.

In mid-1958 on the first trip into Gold Star we recorded "Running Bear" and "My Heart Knows," a song I wrote. . . . My band did not participate in the recording session. They used the Gold Star Studios band, featuring Hal Harris on guitar and with Link Davis on the dominant tenor saxophone part. The session was engineered by Bill Quinn and was produced by the Big Bopper and Hall.

Preston's recollections of that session also reveal a noteworthy bit of trivia about the identity of the backing singers on his version of "Running Bear":

George [Jones] was in Beaumont and, being a good friend of the Bopper's, he [had] heard about the project and came with us. . . . The background vocalists performing the pseudo–Native American chanting [on the record] were none other than the Big Bopper, George Jones, Sleepy LaBeef, and Bill Hall.

Preston's treatment of Richardson's story-song "Running Bear," coming right on the heels of the smash hit "Chantilly Lace," was good enough to prompt Mercury Records to accept immediately Daily's offer of a lease agreement. So the D label did not issue this recording; like certain other Daily productions, it premiered as a Mercury single (#71474). Preston explains what transpired:

The single was released on Mercury Records through connections the Bopper and Pappy Daily already had with the label. The song entered the *Billboard* charts in September of 1959 and first peaked at number seventy, then fell off the charts for two to three weeks. Bill Hall then called me and said that a major jukebox operator in St. Louis [had] ordered fifteen thousand copies of the record for Midwest distribution, and the rest is history. The song reentered the *Billboard* pop charts . . . with a bullet and then went all the way to number one. "Running Bear" stayed at number one for nearly three weeks and to date has sold about three million copies.

As with "Chantilly Lace," this song's appeal reached across racially segregated marketing boundaries. As a result, "Running Bear" also rode the national R&B charts for thirteen weeks, peaking at number three. Together those two recordings made a lucrative windfall for Daily, who earned shares of their extensive profits not only on sales of discs issued by Mercury or D Records but also on the royalties paid to his Glad Music publishing concern.

Having recently completed his studio renovation, Quinn could take pride in Daily's success with this latest pair of hits, recordings that he himself had engineered. For his major client—and a possible business partner—to be reaping such rich rewards, it surely boded well for the newly expanded Gold Star Studios.

BUT NOT EVEN DAILY COULD ALWAYS JUDGE which songs and singers were destined for greatness. In the case of one particular D Records artist, Daily's usually astute business acumen failed him completely. Thus, he rejected a unique singer-songwriter-guitarist, a man who would later prove himself to be one of the greatest figures in Texas music history. Moreover, Daily also passed on issuing the first recorded version, made at Gold Star Studios, of one of that icon's most acclaimed compositions. We speak of Willie Nelson and his brilliant song "Nightlife."

Nonetheless, Nelson's relationship with D Records and Gold Star Studios was significant even before he recorded there in 1960. It was in Quinn's facility on December 18, 1959, that Claude Gray had recorded "Family Bible" backed with "Crying in the Night" for Daily's label (#1118), two songs written by the then relatively unknown Nelson. The classic "Family Bible" soon climbed as high as number seven on the *Billboard* country charts. Though a desperate Nelson, struggling to survive in Houston, had recently sold his publishing rights to that song, its success marked his professional debut as a writer of a certified country hit. It pointed toward the next phase of his storied career and encouraged him to develop more of his own material. As Joe Nick Patoski puts it in *Willie Nelson: An Epic Life,* "whatever royalties he'd lost by signing his rights away were balanced out by the word getting around that this Willie Nelson fella knew how to write songs."

Born in Abbott, Texas, in 1933, Nelson had mainly been performing or working as a radio disc jockey in Waco, San Antonio, and Fort Worth before coming to Houston in 1959. He had already signed with D Records before leaving Fort Worth, and it was there that he had recorded his first inconsequential single for the label, "Man with the Blues" backed with "The Storm Has Just Begun" (#1084).

The decision to move to Houston was motivated by Nelson's desire to advance his career as both a performer and a writer. As Patoski says, Nelson reasoned "if he was closer to the home office, maybe he would get more attention from D Records and Glad Music." Arriving in the city with little money and a family to support, Nelson gigged with local bands such as Larry Butler's Sunset Playboys and worked for a while on the country radio station KRCT. One of his fellow musicians at the time, Wiley Barkdull (b. 1927), recalls the scene—and his own regrets about not recognizing Nelson's genius at the time:

One night I was playing with Link Davis, and [Nelson] sat in with us. He was a good-looking young man with a great voice, but he had the weirdest timing on his guitar and phrasing, and it was really hard to follow him. That night at the end of the show he came to me and told me that he had been playing my Hickory [label] records up in Dallas and wanted to form a band with me. I didn't know who he was, but he sure knew me.

At the time I had a day job, and I was playing five nights a week, and I was working two TV shows a week. I was also doing five weekly radio shows, so I told him, "Man, I don't have time to start a band." At that time I didn't know that Willie had "Family Bible" in his back pocket and wanted somebody to help him. . . . I let that one slip by me.

Not long after that, on March 11, 1960, Nelson entered Gold Star Studios to record his first sessions with Quinn. The resulting D Records single (#1131), his second, featured his own songs "Misery Mansion" and "What a Way to Live." The supporting musicians included bandleader Paul Buskirk on guitar, Ozzie Middleton on pedal steel, Darold Raley and Clyde Brewer on fiddles, Dean Reynolds on bass, and Al Hagy on drums. In Patoski's opinion, "Both songs were head and shoulders above his D sessions in Fort Worth, a reflection of the musicianship behind him, the recording facility, and Willie's developing talents." Thus, though this record was not a commercial hit, it likely elevated Nelson's consciousness of what he could achieve in the recording studio.

But before that D Records single was released, and just a few weeks after his initial session at Gold Star, Nelson returned to Quinn's big room to record again, and this time he experienced a breakthrough epiphany. Using three of the members of the previous session band—Buskirk, Reynolds, and Hagy—plus Bob Whitford on piano, Herb Remington on steel guitar, and Dick Shannon on vibraphone and saxophone, Nelson performed two more of his own recent compositions, "Rainy Day Blues" and "Night Life."

As Patoski indicates, the former song "showed Willie had chops as a guitarist." But it was the musical results on the latter that triggered a career-changing moment for the artist. Patoski continues,

"Night Life" was from another realm. Mature, deep, and thoughtful, the slow, yearning blues had been put together in his head during long drives across Houston. At Gold Star, he was surrounded by musicians who could articulate his musical thoughts. He sang the words with confident phrasing that had never been heard on any previous recording he'd done. . . .

"It was a level above what we had been doing," Willie said of the session.

Willie Nelson, 2008 (photo by and courtesy of Gina R. Miller)

Now if Daily's discernment on such matters had been impeccable, that inspired performance by Nelson and the band might have yielded yet another D Records hit. But Daily reportedly despised "Night Life," dismissing it gruffly as not "country" enough and refusing to issue it.

As a result, the disgruntled Nelson and his studio bandleader Buskirk conspired to abscond with the tape, which they paid to have mastered at Bill Holford's ACA Studios, and then on their own they released "Nite Life" (with the indicated change of spelling in the title) on the tiny Rx label under the name Paul Buskirk and His Little Men featuring Hugh Nelson. Only a small number of copies were ever pressed, and, backed by no strategy for promotion or distribution, that recording all but disappeared without notice. In fact, though Nelson would obviously record new versions of "Night Life" over subsequent years, that original treatment from his Gold Star sessions would not be released under his own name until 2002, when it was included among *The Complete D Singles Collection* CD boxed sets issued by Bear Family Records in Germany.

Though he would later become famous for recordings made elsewhere (and would record for a SugarHill Studios project in 2008), Willie Nelson may well have first realized his aptitude for greatness during those 1960 sessions for D Records at Gold Star Studios.

THROUGH THE EARLY 1960S D RECORDS continued to use Quinn's Gold Star Studios to document a wide range of Houston-based artists. Representative examples include Johnny Nelms, who waxed "Old Broken Heart" and "I've Never Had the Blues" in February 1961 (#1178); Perk Williams, who cut "What More" and "Are You Trying to Tell Me Goodbye" that same month (#1182); Herb Remington, who made "Fiddleshoe" and "Soft Shoe Slide" in March 1961 (#1186); Link Davis, who recorded "Come Dance with Me" and "Five Miles from Town" that same month (#1191); and Al Dean doing "I Need No Chains" and "A Girl at the Bar" in May 1961 (#1192).

While the prolific D Records was continuing to produce new singles, in May of 1961 Daily also convinced Mercury Records to lease and reissue a 1958 Benny Barnes performance originally recorded at Gold Star—the single "Yearning" (#71806). This decision paid off nicely, for the salvaged recording (of a song written by Eddie Eddings and George Jones) soon became another *Billboard* country chart hit, rising as high as the number twenty-two spot.

Over the next few years D Records remained in operation, but its success waned. Revolutionary changes in musical tastes concerning artists and repertoire were largely responsible perhaps, as Daily never fully accepted the hegemony of rock 'n' roll, and he had nothing but disdain for the hippie types who were starting to dominate the genre. Though he would stay active with his publishing company and other concerns, he gradually ceased his involvement in D Records productions around 1965. By that time he was in his sixties and probably inclined to enjoy the proceeds of his many profitable years in the music business (though he continued to produce George Jones records in Nashville through February 1971). However, in the twenty-first century his grandson, Wes Daily, would revive the label name for his own productions of new recordings of Texas country music.

Similarly inching toward retirement was Quinn, Daily's favorite Houston studio owner. Following his long run of engineering sessions for Daily and others, by 1963 he was reducing his role in studio operations, where he would eventually serve only as landlord before ultimately selling and entrusting the Gold Star legacy to new ownership. As musician Glenn Barber sums it up, "Bill recorded in that big room for a few years and then retired in the early '60s and leased the place to J. L. Patterson and lived in his house next door. He would come over pretty often and watch things but didn't have much to do with anything."

An era was passing in Texas and beyond—that wild time in the mid-twentieth century when the first generation of maverick studio owners and old-school independent record producers such as Quinn and Daily could collaborate with young talent and limited budgets in hopes of making a hit.

Little Labels

BLUES, COUNTRY, AND SHARKS

WHILE THE HUNDREDS OF SESSIONS produced by Pappy Daily had dominated much of the Gold Star Studios schedule during the late 1950s and early '60s, proprietor Bill Quinn certainly did have other clients. Some of those were small label owners trying to replicate the commercial success that Daily had achieved with Starday and D Records. Others were individuals, bands, or loose affiliations of people collaborating on a common music project—representing a widening diversity of genres. Some may have even been con artists playing the so-called "song-sharking" game. And of course, there were also various high school or college marching or stage bands, which utilized the big room expansion. Whichever the case, for many musicians who came to Gold Star Studios to record during this era, it was an initiation experience—the first time they ever cut studio tracks. Some of those performers went on to establish famous careers in music.

Of all the record company owners who rented Quinn's space and services, the only one who could rival Daily's clout was the African American mogul Don Robey. He owned five Houston-based labels between 1949 and 1973—and his Gold Star Studios connection is explored more fully in Chapter 11. Most of the rest had far less success. Yet even among those, there were several historically significant recordings.

For instance, one aspiring independent record company owner was the musician Henry Hayes (b. 1924). Though he had a distinguished thirty-year career as an educator in public schools, Hayes also recorded on many Houston sessions, usually performing on saxophone, with his own band. The resulting singles were released on various labels, including Quinn's old Gold Star imprint, as well as Savoy, Peacock, Mercury, and others.

Quinn had engineered Hayes's very first session as a bandleader, staged at the original Telephone Road site in 1947 or '48—that is, right around the time that Quinn had started recording black men playing the blues. The result was a 78 rpm Gold Star Records single (#633) offering two Hayes originals, "Bowlegged Angeline" and "Baby Girl Blues," with the performance credited simply to Henry Hayes and His Band. On some of the subsequent recordings for other labels, Hayes led his group (billed variously as the Four Kings, the Rhythm Kings, or the Henry Hayes Orchestra) as the backing ensemble for his protégé, piano-playing vocalist Elmore Nixon (1933–1973), or other singers.

However, Hayes truly made his mark on recording history when he and a partner, M. L. Young, launched their own "look-see" label, Kangaroo Records. In Roger Wood's book *Down in Houston: Bayou City Blues,* Hayes sums up their start:

> A friend of mine . . . was also a music teacher, . . . So we decided that we was going to put our funds together and start a little record label. . . . And the idea was to put out records on different talent, build 'em up, get some company interested, and then get a lease with them. . . . Kangaroo Records, that was my idea, Kangaroo Records—because it jumped!

Because Gold Star Studios was well established, relatively inexpensive, already familiar to Hayes, and close to the Third Ward (where he and most of his musicians resided), it was a natural site for those Kangaroo Records sessions. And Quinn was manning the booth when Hayes went there in the spring of 1958 to make the first recordings of two postwar masters of Texas blues guitar, Albert Collins (1932–1993) and Joe Hughes (1937–2003).

Those sessions yielded the debut singles for both artists, issued by Kangaroo Records on 45 rpm discs: "The Freeze" (#103) backed with "Collins Shuffle" (#104) by Albert Collins and His Rhythm Rockers, as well as "I Can't Go On This Way" (#105) backed with "Make Me Dance Little Ant" (#106) by Joe Hughes and His Orchestra. The Hughes record was reviewed in *Billboard* magazine in June 1959, but remains an obscurity to all but the most informed fans (who often cite it nonetheless as "Ants in My Pants"). Today its main import lies in its status as the earliest recording by an ultimately widely admired blues artist—as London-based writer Paul Wadey puts it, "a favourite amongst European audiences."

On the other hand, "The Freeze," a magical instrumental groove, soon became a regional hit that even reportedly inspired a local dance craze. Moreover, it served as Collins's signature tune throughout the rest of his career, which would escalate to international blues superstardom by his final decade. Its potency also triggered a succession of various other cold-themed metaphors that Collins would employ to define his guitar playing—what he called "ice picking"—including later album titles such as *Iceman, Frostbite, Cold Snap, Deep Freeze,* and *Don't Lose Your Cool,* to cite only a few. Today "The Freeze" is generally considered a modern blues electric guitar classic.

But according to both Hayes and Hughes, the presence of Collins at that session was a fluke. The only plan for that day was to record Hughes and a local female vocal group, the Dolls. However, as Hughes was preparing to depart for the scheduled morning studio session, he realized in a panic that he had left his only guitar at Shady's Playhouse, a Third Ward club where he gigged each night. When he raced to that venue only to find it locked and empty, he turned to his friend Collins, who then resided less than a block away. As Hughes puts it in another interview from *Down in Houston,* "So I had Albert go out there with me, and that's how 'The Freeze' got cut, by accident. I went by there and got his guitar and took him to the studio."

Hayes, in the same book, picks up the story from there:

See, I was the producer in the studio . . . and Albert came along with Joe Hughes . . . So the piano player that used to play with Albert told me, "Man, Albert has a number he's playing out at the clubs—boy, people are going wild about it! Man, you've got to hear that number."

So Albert came out that day, so when we got through recording the others, I told him, I say, "Albert, I heard about this number 'Freeze.' . . . A lot of people [have] been going wild for it in the clubs. . . . They've been telling me about it, and you haven't recorded it with anybody. Do you want to record it with me?"

He said, "I guess so." . . .

We'd never rehearsed on it or anything. So I say, "Well, okay, you start it off, and when you get ready for me to come in on the tenor [saxophone], let me know. Just bow your head, and I'll come in." . . . And the first time, he came in, played with the drummer and the rhythm behind him and everything, and then after he played it, told me to come in on the saxophone. Then he came back and played another chorus and played it out.

And the man [Quinn] that was over the studio shouted, "Whoa, that's a hit!" [Laughs] The first time down! And that's how I recorded Albert Collins.

Hoping to emulate Daily's model of success, Hayes planned to capitalize on the fervent initial reaction to this release by enticing a major label into a lease agreement. However, before he could do so, that plan fell through. When the local mogul Robey observed the frenzy over "The Freeze," he quickly recorded a blatant cover version performed by guitarist Fenton Robinson (1935–1997) and his band. Robey rushed to issue it on his Duke label (#190),

Albert Collins, publicity photo (by Benny Joseph), early 1960s

backed with another instrumental titled "Double Freeze." Years later Collins recorded "The Freeze" again elsewhere. But as for the original track of that song, Hayes bitterly asserts that Robey "just killed that record"—and with it, the Kangaroo label's best chance for a breakthrough hit.

Of the six songs recorded by Hayes on that fateful first session as a Kangaroo Records producer, two by the Dolls were issued first (#101/102), followed by a pair from Collins and then the two from Hughes. The next two releases, credited to Henry Hayes and Orchestra, featured the songs "Two Big Feet" and "Call of the Kangaroo" (#107/108) and "It Takes Money" and "Stop Smackin' That Wax" (#109/110). The final Kangaroo release was by Little Joey Farr performing two Christmas songs, "I Want a Big White Cadillac for Christmas" and "Rock 'n' Roll Santa" (#111/112).

Though Hayes would remain active as a session player and bandleader into the 1990s, he soon gave up on his Kangaroo Records experiment, convinced that Robey's powerful influence over radio DJs, record distributors, and the black Houston music scene in general would make further efforts futile. But thanks to his relationship with Quinn and Gold Star Studios, as well as that unforeseen chance to record Collins's original articulation of "The Freeze," Hayes had made music history, if not much money, with his little label that "jumped."

Conversely, Quinn's late-1950s affiliation with Kangaroo Records only added to his already impressive legacy as one of the most important sound engineers ever to document Texas blues, especially as performed by postwar African American singers and guitarists in Houston. Having recorded seminal figures such as Lightnin' Hopkins, Lil' Son Jackson, and others in his original studio in the late 1940s, Quinn brilliantly (even if unknowingly) accentuated his behind-the-scenes role in blues history by also being the first to engineer sessions for Collins and Hughes, their worthy successors. In the span of ten or eleven years, Quinn thus made some of the most relevant recordings for tracing the evolution of Houston blues guitar.

Sometimes he did so on debut recordings that were unfortunately never released or even pressed. Such was the case with yet another stalwart of the Texas blues guitar sound, Pete Mayes (1938–2008). Playing in a style heavily influenced by his role model T-Bone Walker (1910–1975), with whom he first performed on stage at the age of sixteen, Mayes worked with numerous other blues giants from the mid-1950s into the start of the twenty-first century. Some of those who used his talents on stage include Big Joe Turner (1911–1985), Lowell Fulsom (1921–1999), Percy Mayfield (1920–1984), Junior Parker (1932–1971), and Bill Doggett (1916–1996). Moreover, Mayes recorded as a session player with numerous groups over the years, and he released his own W. C. Handy Award–nominated album, *For Pete's Sake,* on the Austin-based Antone's label in 1998.

Yet like his good friend Hughes (with whom he collaborated on the album *Texas Blues Party, Vol. 2,* issued in 1998 by the European-based Wolf Records), Mayes first recorded at Gold Star Studios under the technical supervision of its founder, Quinn. That virgin experience occurred in 1960, and Mayes would not return to the site again until 2006, when he recorded tracks with the Calvin Owens Blues Orchestra for the album *Houston Is the Place to Be.*

Here Mayes recounts how that inaugural 1960 session came to be and his memories of the place:

> We were playing for Van Bevil [at the venue called Van's Ballroom], and he thought we were great and offered to pay for us to go into the studio to record a 45. My close friend Percy Mayfield, who lived in Louisiana, was hanging around and offered his services for free to coproduce the project with me. So in either June or July—I know it was then because it was stinkin' hot outside and it was great to be in a big air-conditioned studio—we went over to Gold Star. Big old room with a hardwood floor and high ceilings. We got a great sound with my band. Van paid for the session, and we cut a song called "I'll Tell the World" and an instrumental track.

Over forty years later, Mayes has no regrets about making that recording and says that he learned a lot from both Mayfield and Quinn. "I don't know why, but we never got to release it," he says, "and nobody knows where the master tapes or any of the acetate dubs went. . . . It was a great experience, but I wish we still had that master!"

Though few people probably ever got to hear that Mayes recording, the fact that it existed—even if only briefly—underscores again the crucial role that Quinn and Gold Star Studios played in documenting African American blues players in the South's largest city.

Similarly, Quinn's studio was involved in recording tenor saxophonist and jazz bandleader Arnett Cobb (1918–1989). Though in the 1940s he had moved to (and recorded in) New York as a member of Lionel Hampton's band, Cobb never lost sight of his Texas blues roots. Writer Keith Shadwick aptly characterizes Cobb's style as marked by "blues phraseology and wild swoops and hollers." As further evidence, in 1984 Cobb shared a Grammy Award for best traditional blues performance for his collaboration with B. B. King (b. 1925) on the MCA album *Blues 'n' Jazz*.

In mid-1963, while home from the East Coast, Cobb brought a band of like-minded musicians into Gold Star Studios to record. Included in the group was special guest Don Wilkerson (1932–1986), a tenor saxophonist best known for his own recordings on the prestigious Blue Note label, as well as for his acclaimed work on stage and on recordings with Ray Charles (1930–2004). Together Cobb and Wilkerson delivered a full session of musical improvisation. As far as we know, this was the only time these two artists ever played together in a studio-recording situation. The supporting players included Duke Barker on drums, Paul Schmitt on piano, Buel Niedlinger on bass, and Cleon Grant on percussion. The results were preserved on a tape that was archived at the studio and only recently discovered. Though material from that session has not been released for public consumption, the primary heir to the Cobb estate has been exploring options for issuing it as an album.

Based on the conversations (captured on tape) between the players and the technicians, we infer that this project was self-produced by Cobb. That may explain why it was not released, for not only did Cobb maintain a busy schedule of professional work nationwide and abroad (including numerous recording sessions for other producers), he also suffered a series of health problems that could have caused him to shelve this project.

This intriguing reel of tape features about a dozen different tunes, with multiple takes of some numbers, as well as some busted takes and intervening studio chatter. To hear Cobb and Wilkerson trading solos is remarkable, and the sonic quality of the recording is excellent for that time. We hope that someday soon it will be made available on CD, but as for now, it remains an unpublished yet valuable cultural artifact from Gold Star Studios.

OF THE NUMEROUS SMALL START-UP labels that recorded at Gold Star Studios in the late 1950s, if they were not focused (like Kangaroo Records) on blues, they were most likely to be doing country or pop. One of the most unusual of the country-based labels was Sarg Records. Founded by a former U.S. Army Air Corps sergeant named Charlie Fitch (1918–2006), the company was based in Luling, Texas, located approximately 140 miles west of Houston. There he operated the Luling Phonograph and Record Store, which also served as the headquarters for his jukebox business. As Andrew Brown has documented in the richly detailed book that accompanies *The Sarg Records Anthology*, Fitch ultimately released 150 singles over a span of twenty-five years, producing his first session in December of 1953 and the bulk of his catalogue by 1965. In so doing, as Brown puts it, Fitch "single-handedly ensured that at least a portion of the music of South Texas at mid-century would be preserved, and the musicians themselves remembered."

Some of those regional musicians who made their recording debuts on Fitch's label would subsequently become famous stars elsewhere. Perhaps the best example is Willie Nelson, who did his first work as a studio guitarist for a pair of two-sided Sarg recordings by Dave Isbell and the Mission City Playboys in August 1954 (#108 and 109). This session was produced at Houston's ACA Studios and engineered by Bill Holford, Quinn's friendly cross-town rival. Of course, Nelson would finally record under his own name a few years later when he joined the D Records roster, which led him to Gold Star Studios.

Another figure who got started with Sarg was the almost equally legendary Texas musician Doug Sahm (1941–1999)—who would later come to Gold Star Studios to record (for another label) with his band, the Sir Douglas Quintet. But Sahm had been, as described by James Head in *The Handbook of Texas Music,* "a musical prodigy who . . . was singing on the radio by the age of five, and was so gifted that he could play the fiddle, steel guitar, and mandolin by the time he was eight years old." With that background, Sahm made his studio debut at age thirteen on a Sarg single (#113) issued under the name Little Doug. That 1955 track, like much of the Sarg catalogue, was also recorded at ACA Studios.

Of the Sarg-controlled tracks recorded by Quinn at Gold Star Studios, some had actually been leased as finished masters from Nucraft Records, whose owner Boyd Leisy was in the process of shutting down. Among those were recordings by Link Davis, Floyd Tillman, Johnny Nelms, James O'Gwynn, Coye Wilcox, and Sonny Burns. From that bulk acquisition, Sarg actually issued only two records as new singles: Link Davis's "Cockroach" backed with "Big Houston" (#136) and Floyd Tillman's "Baby, I Just Want You" and "Save a Little for Me" (#137). Unbeknownst to Fitch, however, two of those four tracks had already been released on Western Records: "Big Houston" (#1073) and "Save a Little for Me" (#1072)—a surprise that perhaps prompted him to withhold the other titles.

Apart from those Leisy recordings, Sarg staged its own Gold Star sessions that led to several releases in 1956, including three discs by Al Parsons and the Country Store Boys (#140, 147, and 154), plus others by Johnny Carroll (#144), Al Urban (#148), and Dick Fagan (#155). In 1958 and 1960 Al Urban returned to Gold Star Studios to record additional sides for Sarg (#158 and 174).

Though the Sarg label never scored a hit record, it produced sonic documents of historical value. Moreover, the fact that the majority of the Sarg sessions occurred in Houston speaks again to the professional reputations of those two important early Texas recording engineers, Holford and Quinn, and their respective studios, ACA and Gold Star.

For Quinn, such renown meant that he was regularly dealing with musically minded entrepreneurs such as Fitch or Henry Hayes, men with big ideas and minimal funding who nonetheless wanted quality sound engineering on the recordings they produced.

On the other hand, there were also guys such as Dan Mechura, the owner of Houston-based Allstar Records. That label operated from 1953 to 1966, issuing many legitimate recordings but also perhaps dabbling in the less than reputable business known in common music business parlance as "song (or song-poem) sharking."

That practice involved advertising for and otherwise recruiting gullibly optimistic amateurs who believed they had scripted words (as lyrics or poetry) worthy of being set to music and immortalized on record. The typical scam required the flattered victim (whose ego had been pumped up by repeated declarations that his work was simply brilliant) to pay an exorbitant amount of money in advance to the shark-producer. These funds ostensibly went to hire a composer/arranger to create the musical setting for the words, as well as to pay studio musicians and one or more singers to perform the song at a recording session arranged by the shark-producer—and to cover the costs (all of which were inflated) of renting the studio and engineering, mastering, pressing, distributing, and promoting the record.

Of course, most of the money actually ended up in the shark's pockets. To cover himself he not only overcharged the naïve client but pressed only a small number of copies of the disc (just enough to appease the customer's desire for some complimentary samples and to have a few to send out). He then mailed copies to a trade magazine for possible review and to a local radio station or two—the better to foster the illusion that the record was truly being promoted. Meanwhile, he claimed to be distributing it widely and shopping it to major labels in hopes of a lease agreement and national hit. In reality, of course, he would sit on his client's investment, feigning surprise and regret that demand for the record never materialized.

The most notorious song-sharks were the blatant criminals who made no attempt at legitimacy, seeking only to victimize. However, historically there has been another class of song-sharks comprising producers who earnestly may have sought to record good talent and cultivate hits—but who also occasionally made some easy money by taking advantage of would-be writers who possessed more cash than common sense.

Others have made well-documented allegations that the founder of Allstar Records, Mechura, may have been involved in such operations. We turn again to Andrew Brown—this time to his essay about Allstar published on the American Song-Poem Music Archives website. Brown writes,

> Allstar Records, a quasi-song-poem label with a slightly more plausible claim to legitimacy than most of its song-sharking peers, was the brainchild of Houston country musician/"singer" Daniel James Mechura. The ambitious Mechura started out as the front man of a local outfit, the Sun Valley Playboys, enjoying one release on the Starday label (which they paid for themselves) in 1955. By that time, Dan had discovered the seedy underworld of songwriters' clubs and, sensing an opportunity ripe for exploitation, soon began doing business as president of "The Folk Writers Co-Operative Association," generously offering "every songwriter the help which is necessary to succeed in this competitive field," as stated in one sales pitch. A record label of their own was the logical outgrowth of this "co-op."

That label turned out to be Allstar, which issued many records credited to a variety of obscure figures, such as Cowboy Blair (whose Allstar recording of "Top of Your List" actually includes the credit "A Gold Star Recording" on the printed label). But Brown makes it clear that Mechura's company did actually operate, at least in part, like a genuine record label. That is, regardless of whether he engaged in song-sharking or not, Mechura actively did seek to record and promote true musical talent. Brown continues,

> Allstar issued "legitimate" commercially-oriented records right alongside their song-poem efforts. . . . Throughout the label's life, Mechura was able to recruit established, professional country singers well-known in Texas—not faceless studio hacks, but guys with proven track records and recording careers.

Among the respected musicians who made records with Allstar were Eddie Noack, Link Davis, Johnny Bush, and local favorite Smilin' Jerry Jericho, to name a few.

Another was Wiley Barkdull, a seasoned piano player and singer who had first recorded elsewhere for the Hickory label in 1956 but who also was long familiar with Gold Star Studios. He recalls the scene at a couple of Allstar sessions, with special emphasis on Quinn's efforts to adapt to get the best possible sound:

> The records I did for Allstar were done in that big room in '61 and '62. . . . [Quinn] set us up in a circle over by the piano, with it just over to the side of us. The recordings had quite a bit of echo in that big room. We cut "Tear Down This Wall" and "These Old Arms" [#7222]. . . .
>
> I did a session after that with Link Davis. . . . Bill had made some changes and had these partitions that he put around us. He created these phony walls on wheels, kind of like baffles. He was using those partitions to cut down on the amount of natural echo that was being recorded.

The Allstar catalogue contains hundred of titles, some of which may well have been only amateurish song-poem product of little merit. But because it also includes efforts by serious musicians such as Barkdull (who ultimately recorded at least five singles for the label), it too is part of the Gold Star legacy in Texas music history.

Into the '60s and
Quinn's Last Sessions

NUMEROUS OTHER NOTEWORTHY young artists recorded at Gold Star Studios in the early 1960s—an era when popular music was rapidly changing and Bill Quinn was in the final phase of his remarkable career.

Gene Thomas (b. 1938) scored a hit with the product of his very first session. That song, "Sometime," recorded and mastered by Quinn, was released on Venus Records (#1439) in 1961. After proving itself first regionally, the soulful ballad was leased and reissued by the major label United Artists (#338). "Sometime" debuted nationally in late October 1961 and peaked at number fifty-three on the *Billboard* pop charts. Thomas returned to Gold Star Studios in 1962 to cut the tracks "Mysteries of Love" and "That's What You Are to Me" for Venus (#1443). Later the Texas native moved to Nashville, where he worked as a songwriter and recorded successfully for other labels.

Country singer Mel Douglas launched his career with a Gold Star Studios–produced record. Though he would go on to cut other tunes, he would never top the acclaim directed at his 1961 track called "Cadillac Boogie," issued on SAN Records (#1506). Douglas recalls how that hit came to be:

> Troy Caldwell, he had the lyrics for "Cadillac Boogie" and "Since You Walked Away." I straightened up the lyrics and added the music. Man, I was nineteen, maybe twenty, at the time. . . . We came over to Gold Star and laid them down. That was back in 1961, and it was my first recording ever. . . . We put the single on Troy Caldwell's label, SAN Records. The record then got taken over to the Dailys. . . . They distributed it, and I got to meet Pappy and Don Daily, and Gabe Tucker and his wife Sunshine [all of D Records]. They were all great people. They helped make that record take off regionally. KNUZ

[radio station] played that record every hour on the hour. I joined with Gene Thomas, Roy Head, and others who were making the circuit playing the teen shows.

In 1962 Douglas returned to make his second single, "Dream Girl" backed with "Forever My Darling," for the Gulf label (#1630/1631), which Quinn had briefly revived around this time. He continues,

> "There Must Be a Way" and "Pounding Heart" . . . was my third single and was recorded right here at Gold Star. It was done on the 19th of January 1963. That single was my first real big session because we had five horns on it. I also wrote both of those songs, and the record was released on the Tamel label [#11]. . . . J. L. Patterson was the engineer who recorded and mixed that single.
>
> In late 1964 or early 1965 I cut my fourth single here at Gold Star. The songs were "My Lonely Girl" and "Box Lunch." They were released on the Dream label (#101).

One of the relatively few female singers to record at Gold Star in this era was Mary McCoy, who worked with producer Huey Meaux. In 1960, Mary McCoy and the Cyclones recorded two songs there: "Deep Elem Blues" and "Breaking Up Is the Thing to Do." The resulting single on JIN Records (#140), a South Louisiana–based label, was a minor hit on the local scene.

Louisiana artists had long figured into the facility's history. But under Meaux's influence, a new breed of Louisiana singer, performing a style called swamp pop, came to Gold Star to record. Involving a fusion of New Orleans R&B with country, early rock, and certain Cajun or Creole influences, this music was intensely popular during its heyday along the upper Gulf Coast.

One of the swamp-pop stars to record at Gold Star was Rod Bernard, who had previously scored a 1959 national hit with "This Should Go On Forever" on the Argo label (#5327). Then, after a stall in his career, he attempted a comeback on Meaux's Teardrop label. He says,

> I was a success and a failure by the time I was twenty. After a while when nobody wanted me, I called Huey, and he said, "Come to Houston and let's record." . . . It was like '63 or '64. And he would have a band record the track before I even got there, and then I would go to Gold Star and cut the vocal, often late at night.

Although Bernard never replicated his earlier success, his swamp pop added another spice to the rich musical gumbo percolating at Gold Star

Studios. Along with the roots music sounds that Quinn already knew well, new styles of popular music were taking shape. Whatever Quinn may have thought of them, Gold Star played a key role in documenting them for posterity. And one rare album cut there in 1963 provides an especially remarkable example of how the times truly were changing.

IN EARLY-1960S HOUSTON, there was an unusually fecund scene for independent singer-songwriters. It comprised a subculture of young Texans who identified both with the old-style blues and traditional country music, as well as with certain aesthetics of the gradually emerging folk-rock movement. Some of the figures who cultivated their talents there were Mickey Newbury (1940–2002), Guy Clark (b. 1940), K. T. Oslin (b. 1941), and Townes Van Zandt (1944–1997)—soon followed by Rodney Crowell (b. 1950), Lucinda Williams (b. 1953), Nanci Griffith (b. 1954), Steve Earle (b. 1955), and Lyle Lovett (b. 1957). But scores of other local enthusiasts were also syncretizing variant strands of music and laboring poetically for the sake of the song.

One of the most popular places where Houston singer-songwriters would congregate and perform was a folk club called the Jester Lounge, located on the corner of Bammel Lane and Philfall Street. Jon Jones, a regular at the now-defunct establishment, provides this orientation:

> The Jester itself was kind of the first folk venue in Houston. . . . It was a little tiny club with a small stage and no sound system at the beginning. Then Mac Webster, the owner, expanded the club after it became a hot venue. But there were still lines of people, through the parking lot onto Westheimer [Road], waiting to get in to the club. . . . It was the place to play back in those days. Even the Kingston Trio played there after their shows at the Shamrock. Also the [New] Christy Minstrels played the Jester quite a bit. Janis Joplin often came to the club, but somehow she never got to perform on that stage.

Though the vibrant scene at the Jester Lounge nurtured itself with nationally touring acts, it was more likely, on any given night, to feature homegrown talent. It also held Sunday-afternoon hootenannies, offering an open mic to anyone who wanted to perform a song. In part, what made this place special was its policy of readily booking older African American players such as Lightnin' Hopkins right along with younger white folks such as Van Zandt.

But what made the Jester absolutely unique was the fact that its management and some of its regular performers decided in 1963 to self-produce a record album showcasing its potent racially integrated mix of local performers. To do so, they went to Gold Star Studios.

Thanks to that LP album project, several important artists got their first professional recording experience, including Clark, who performed "Cotton Mill Girls." Another rookie who would go on to a major career was Oslin (though she was credited in those days simply as Kay, not K. T.). Including the iconic Hopkins (who delivered the blues standard "Trouble in Mind"), fourteen different artists were featured. Among those were Vivian and Scott Holtzman, who performed solo on separate tracks. Other highlighted singers were Arthur Hodges (who contributed two tracks), Frank Davis (who performed also on a duet with Oslin), Sarah Wiggins, Alex Martin, Jim Gunn, Jenny Bell Dean (backed on one of her two contributions by the Dradeaux Sisters), and the duo billed as Ken and Judy.

Though it is most commonly referred to as simply "the Jester album," the actual title is *Look, It's Us!* On the cover, beneath that exclamation, is an arrow pointing down to a group photograph (credited to Gary Wallace) of the participants. Judging from the heavy black drapes in the background of the interior space where this assemblage is posed, it seems probable that the shot was taken in the big room at Gold Star Studios. Nationally renowned folklorist John A. Lomax Jr. contributed the liner notes, in which he describes the Jester Lounge as a "folk music mecca."

Frank Davis, a regular performer at the Jester Lounge, made his recording debut on *Look, It's Us!* He later became a successful recording engineer himself. Davis offers these recollections:

[Gold Star engineer] Dan Puskar was a really neat guy of Polish descent. He had all kinds of wonderful innovations for recording. We were recording on a three-track half-inch tape machine made by Ampex. . . . Bill Quinn was not around for these sessions. Dan pretty much did it all by himself. And of course, the sessions were all pretty late at night. There were lots of little sessions recorded over a couple of weeks. . . .

The sessions were orchestrated very well. There were several large groups and a bunch of individuals, and everybody got equal time. Everyone accompanied themselves, and there were no extra musicians on the gig. . . .

There was a neat thing that Dan did while he was recording me. When I performed on stages around town, most of them were thin plywood, and I would tap my foot near the base of the mic stand and get some extra percussion. Dan set up a board for me to sit on and play and to tap my foot on— and put a mic underneath it. It was really great and added a nice touch to the sound of the recording. Basically he built a small platform for me to sit on—a foot or so above the floor of the studio.

Clark, one of the most revered Texas-born songwriters of our time, worked in the early 1960s as art director for Houston's CBS-affiliated television station, KHOU. He had then just begun hanging out in folk clubs and composing his own songs. Though he would ultimately settle in Nashville, his Houston years were a key time in his prolific career. As his booking agent Keith Case puts it in an online profile,

> Moving to Houston, Clark began his career during the "folk scare" of the 1960s. Fascinated by Texas blues legends like Mance Lipscomb and Lightnin' Hopkins and steeped in the cultural sauce piquante of his border state, he played traditional folk tunes on the same Austin-Houston club circuit as Townes Van Zandt and Jerry Jeff Walker. . . . Eventually, Clark would draw on these roots to firebrand his own fiddle-friendly and bluesy folk music, see it embraced as country, and emerge as a songwriting icon for connoisseurs of the art.

Clark shares with us his memories of the genesis and execution of the Jester album project:

> This was my first recording in a studio, for sure. I believe that this was also K. T. Oslin's first recording as well. We were all playing this folk joint called the Jester, and Scott and Vivian Holtzman felt that we should make a record, and most of us had never made a record before. We all felt that it would be exciting and interesting to do this. I remember that everybody who participated in the record came to the studio, and we recorded in shifts. Those that weren't recording were sitting around listening to the others.

Though the Jester album was never widely distributed, this unusual LP highlights the generally underappreciated vibrancy of the Houston folk scene in the early 1960s—and makes yet another case for the historical significance of Gold Star Studios.

BACK IN THE 1950S GOLD STAR STUDIOS—especially via its affiliation with Pappy Daily's Starday, D, and Dart labels—had played an important Texas role in the rockabilly revolution. But by the early years of the next decade, the genre commonly called rock was rapidly changing. For many in the younger generation, the formerly cool rockabilly sound and persona were now considered antiquated. Gone were the greasers with the ducktail haircuts and their countrified mannerisms. Instead, more record-buying youth were identifying with a style that overtly embraced the influence of postmodern urban black music, particularly R&B, and rejected the hillbilly connotations. That movement would accelerate under the influence of the so-called British Invasion bands. But American rock and pop were already evolving in new directions, and several Gold Star Studios productions provide evidence of that trend.

The Jades, in front of Gold Star Studios, 1961

A group billed as C.L. and the Pictures were an early white R&B-inspired Texas rock band. The original lineup featured C. L. Weldon on vocals, Charlie Broyles on guitar, Trent Poole on drums, Leroy Rodriguez on bass, and two sax players, Leo Grimaldo and Glenn Spreen. While the group's biggest hit, "I'm Asking for Forgiveness," was recorded at ACA Studios, they also recorded some classic blue-eyed soul tracks at Gold Star Studios, songs such as "Smacksie Part II," "I'm Sorry," and "For the Sake of Love."

As for that last song, Poole relates that it came to them from an impeccable source, the black Creole musician Clarence Garlow (1911–1986), best known for his 1949 hit "Bon Ton Roula," recorded in Houston on the Macy's label. Poole explains how he interacted with Garlow to buy the rights to new material:

He was an old guy who wrote songs, and people bought them from him. . . .
I was working with Huey P. Meaux and Steve Tyrell in the early '60s. . . .
And I would go . . . to this old garage apartment and knock on the door, and this guy would hear me and say, "Hold on a minute." Then the door would open, but I couldn't see in. He'd just hold the door and say, "You got fifty dollars?"—because they always sent me with a fifty-dollar bill.

I'd say, "I got the money." . . . Then he'd shut the door, and I'd hear him rummaging around in there for a bit. Then he'd come back to the door and hand me a song written on a paper bag like you get your groceries in.

So he wrote us a song . . . called "For the Sake of Love," and we recorded it at Gold Star with an engineer by the name of Dan Puskar. We were nineteen and twenty years old. Dan was like thirty-five and an accomplished musician, and he helped us with the song. It was the only record we made that became popular on Houston radio stations, KYOK and KCOH.

Getting airplay on those two prominent African American–oriented stations represented new ground for a white rock group in Houston at the time—a situation that later led to some confusion. Poole continues, "The song became big in Houston, and we were invited to come play live at the radio stations. When we showed up, they discovered we were white guys and Latinos. It was a bit awkward at first, but they finally warmed up to us, and we played all afternoon."

While C.L. and the Pictures never achieved much fame beyond the region, several of their musicians did so as individuals. One of those was session horn player Luis (aka Louis) Gasca (b. 1940), who launched his recording career at Gold Star Studios but later achieved national stature in the music industry, recording with a diverse range of superstars, ranging from Janis Joplin to Count Basie to Van Morrison to Carlos Santana to Brasil '66 to Mongo Santamaria, and many others. This trumpeter went on to establish himself not only as a versatile session musician but also as a jazz composer and band conductor.

Somewhat similarly, during the nascent phase of his recording career, the artist now known as Mark James ventured into Gold Star Studios. A native Houstonian born Francis Zambon (1940), he recorded his first song, "Jive Note," there in 1959 for the Vamalco label (#503). By 1960 he had changed his professional name. At Gold Star he also made an early demo recording of one of his compositions, "Suspicious Minds," which would later become a hit for Elvis Presley, as would a song cowritten by James called "Always on My Mind." Another singer from Houston, B. J. Thomas (b. 1942), would earn a Gold Record Award in 1968 with James's composition "Hooked on a Feeling," which hit again in 1974 via an eccentric cover version by the Swedish group Blue Suede.

Today James owns Music Row Studio in Nashville and resides in Santa Monica, California. He provides an insightful recollection of Gold Star Studios at the time of his recording-industry initiation:

I had singles mastered at Gold Star because Quinn was a good mastering engineer. I also played guitar on a bunch of things at the studio. On my own recordings, I was moving back and forth between the studios, mostly at Bill Holford's [ACA Studios]. Quinn's studio was busier than Holford's because of Pappy's involvement, so it was easier for me to get in over at Holford's.

. . . When I was seventeen or eighteen I went in [to Gold Star] and cut that instrumental "Jive Note" and put a vocal song on the other side. When it went to number one in Houston, I realized then at an early age that maybe I could really do this.

Another major music business figure to emerge from this time and place was Steve Bilao, a guy who grew up literally around the corner from Francis Zambon in southeast Houston. However, like his childhood friend, Bilao soon changed his Italian surname. Since then this vocalist, songwriter, producer, and industry mogul has been known as Steve Tyrell.

Tyrell's fame today extends in multiple directions in the Los Angeles–based entertainment industry, including roles as a singer or songwriter for a number of films, plus productions for Dionne Warwick, Ray Charles, Diana Ross, Burt Bacharach, Stevie Wonder, Bette Midler, Rod Stewart, Linda Ronstadt, and many others. Moreover, in more recent years he has recorded several successful albums as a singer of jazz and pop standards. But Tyrell got started in music recording at Gold Star Studios—during his tenure as the second singer in C.L. and the Pictures.

Some of Tyrell's bandmates in the Pictures also migrated to entertainment centers to forge their own careers. Trent Poole became a successful studio drummer in Los Angeles. Sax man Glenn Spreen first attended the Juilliard School of Music in New York, and then moved to Nashville and became a record producer. He also wrote the string arrangements for Elvis Presley's recording of "Suspicious Minds," as well as for Johnny Mathis's "Chances Are."

Tyrell was also involved in producing Joyce Webb (b. 1940), a popular local singer who later served a ten-year stint as featured vocalist with the Houston Pops Orchestra. Having made her first recordings for the Austin-based Domino's label at age 17, Webb also cut 45 rpm singles for various other record companies nationwide, including Ric Tic, Golden World, Warner Brothers, Probe-ABC, Columbia, Lee-Roy, and Epic. In Houston she frequently did sessions as a backup singer at Gold Star Studios, working there first when Quinn was chief engineer and later with successors such as Walt Andrus, Bert Frilot, Doyle Jones, and Jim Duff. She also recorded there with producer Tyrell in the 1960s on the single "I Sang a Rainbow," released on Warner Brothers Records (#7048).

Among other young talent that graduated, in a sense, from early '60s sessions at Gold Star Studios to become part of the national musical industry were two acclaimed drummers: Willie Ornelas and Tony Braunagel.

After relocating to Los Angeles, Ornelas became one of its premiere session and touring musicians. His studio work has included sessions with

Dionne Warwick, Ray Charles, Tom Jones, Dolly Parton, José Feliciano, Andy Williams, Dean Martin, David Foster, Larry Carlton, Bill Champlain, Al Jarreau, and others. He has also worked in television, contributing to soundtracks for shows such as *Hill Street Blues, LA Law, Magnum PI, NYPD Blue, Greatest American Hero, White Shadow, Boston Public, The King of Queens, Law and Order, The Love Boat,* and others.

Yet the impressive Ornelas résumé begins with session work back in his hometown. He relates,

> The first session I ever did was in the big studio at Gold Star. It was probably in 1961, and Bill Quinn was the engineer. He was an older gentleman who just generally told us what to do, and we did it—because we were idiots. It was a group called Cecil and Anne. We had a hit record in Houston back then, called "You Wrote This Letter," and it was the first group I ever played with. . . . It was for a local label that Lelan Rogers had at the time, called Sabra Records [#520].

Soon, however, Ornelas bid farewell to Texas. "I left Houston in 1966 for the first time and went on tour with B. J. Thomas," he says. They appeared together on the teen-music-oriented TV show called *Where the Action Is,* setting the stage for the long and productive career that Ornelas has fashioned for himself on the West Coast.

Though he gigged throughout Texas for much of his early career, Ornelas's childhood friend and fellow drummer Tony Braunagel eventually ended up in Los Angeles too. His album session credits include work with Bonnie Raitt, Rickie Lee Jones, Johnny Nash, Dionne Warwick, and others—as well as production of a 2006 project by Eric Burdon. He too did demos and session work at Gold Star Studios before setting off on the major phase of his career.

Another R&B-influenced rocker with a Gold Star pedigree is Jerry LaCroix, an extraordinary vocalist and tenor sax player from Beaumont. Though he is best known for his roles with Edgar Winter's White Trash, the legendary Gulf Coast bar band the Boogie Kings, or the famous group Blood, Sweat, and Tears, LaCroix recorded some obscure but powerful records at Gold Star Studios in the 1960s.

LaCroix's initial work there yielded the 1961 single "Band Doll," credited to Jerry and the Dominoes on Meaux's Teardrop Records. Next, under the pseudonym Jerry "Count" Jackson, he recorded "Falling in Love" for Meaux, released on Vee-Jay Records (#563). Later, the Boogie Kings, featuring Jerry LaCroix and G. G. Shin on vocals, recorded there, again for Meaux. At that point LaCroix's talents propelled him to higher-profile gigs beyond Southeast Texas. But approximately thirty years later, LaCroix returned to the Houston studio where he had cut his first tracks to record the 1999 CD *Better Days* with Jerry Lightfoot (1951–2006).

Other prominent musicians who passed through the studios in the early 1960s include Johnny "Rabbit" Bundrick, who eventually played keyboards for the Who. Another was Snuffy Walden, a guitarist who later appeared on hit tracks by Stevie Wonder, Heart, and REO Speedwagon—and received a 2004 Emmy Award for his music on the hit TV show *West Wing*.

However, of the many artists who first recorded at Gold Star and went on to make successful careers in music, some did so without leaving Houston. Instead, they became stalwarts of the local scene. Guitarist and bassist Rock Romano (sometimes billed as Dr. Rockit) has led his own band and played with scores of other highly regarded regional groups. Since 1988 he has also owned and operated his own studio, called the Red Shack.

Romano's career path began, like so many others, in Quinn's Brock Street facility. He recollects the scene:

> My earliest memories of Gold Star Studios were probably between late 1961 and early 1963. . . . We were all grouped in a circle around one big fat mic, possibly a U-47, hanging down from the ceiling. The singer was standing closer to the mic than the rest of us. Then when the sax player needed to take his solo, he'd run up under the mic, and then he'd back up from the mic.

Romano's exposure to this now quaint method for group recording perhaps laid the foundation for his ultimate vocation. As a Houston-based studio owner and engineer, every time he positions the mics today for a group performance or mixes overdubs created in isolation, he follows—consciously or not—a path first blazed by Quinn.

Perhaps the youngest of all the artists who first recorded at Gold Star Studios in the early 1960s were the Champagne Brothers. That band was a regionally successful white R&B-pop group, originally from South Louisiana, composed of male siblings, managed and promoted by their parents.

Don Champagne relates his childhood experiences as a Gold Star Studios recording artist:

> We moved to Houston when I was nine and started playing gigs full-time. . . . I was about ten years old the first time I ever came over here to record . . . in 1961. We had signed a contract with Huey P. Meaux, and he put us on his Typhoon label and then later on his Teardrop label. We would be playing a gig in town and he would call up and say, "Y'all come to the studio as soon as you are through." Charles, my brother, who was the lead singer, would be warmed up, and Huey would say, "What do you want to cut?" Or he would

have a specific song in mind and kind of lead us through it. Another guy who was involved in the production was Steve Tyrell. . . . Many times after we'd rehearsed it a bit we would get the finished track on the first take. After we were done, later they would add strings and voices to the recording. It was amazing to us, what they sounded like after they were done.

We did "It's Raining"/"Robin" [Typhoon #2003], "Stranger to You"/"Chickawawa" [Typhoon #2002], and one called "Let's Live"/"I'll Run Away, Far Away" [Teardrop #3042]. "Stranger to You" went to number one in the areas around Houston and in East Texas and Louisiana. The success of that record and some of the others guaranteed us a great deal of work.

The Champagne Brothers recorded numerous other 45 rpm singles released on several regional labels. In their prime, they were major players on the upper–Gulf Coast pop music scene—as evidenced by a chart from KOLE radio for September 4, 1963, which ranks their song "Stranger to You" as number one. At the height of their popularity, they also toured the region as the opening act for national stars such as the Righteous Brothers, the Everly Brothers, and the Four Seasons.

With groups like the Champagne Brothers, time was ushering fresh players onto the studio floor to sing and play into those suspended mics. And for the founder and chief engineer, time was pointing out the door.

IN JULY OF 1963 BILL QUINN partially retired, leasing his Gold Star Studios to an entrepreneur named J. L. Patterson, who had already been involved on some projects there. Patterson had worked as a franchised agent for a company called Century Records, a California-based label that specialized in custom record pressings for high school and college marching bands. Given its booming population and numerous colleges and universities, Houston was an ideal location for Patterson. His control of the studio offered additional ways for him to capitalize on what he already knew—and soon would learn—about the recording business.

Based on the paperwork available in the SugarHill archives, it is possible to piece together a partial view of Patterson's evolving role in the daily operations. For example, we have a Gold Star receipt dated August 14, 1964, that shows J. L. Patterson as lessee and Doyle Jones as engineer. Two invoices from December 22, 1964, show Patterson actually engineering separate sessions for recordings by Lightnin' Hopkins and Floyd Tillman. We also have a February 2, 1965, document from the JLP Corporation, dba Gold Star Recording Company, with the names of Patterson and Jones included as key members of the group.

Meanwhile, as Patterson took over, Quinn and his wife continued to reside nearby. Who knows what it was like for Quinn to cease running the studio while still living on site? Maybe he was simply relieved to be free of the responsibilities he had voluntarily shouldered in building his business. But we think that perhaps he also sometimes missed it.

As a musician who was working in the studio from 1961 through 1965—an era overlapping the founder's transition out of the control booth and into retirement—Mel Douglas observed Quinn in the last stage of his involvement with studio operations. When queried about his memories of the man, Douglas evokes a striking image:

> Bill Quinn was an older man. He was nicely dressed and had fairly long gray hair. He was a real pleasant and outgoing guy. He reminded me of one of those older actors, like Jimmy Stewart. I was real impressed with the way he did things. It seemed like he tried to accommodate everyone who asked him for things. He was always talking and friendly, even when he was cutting me the acetate dubs after the session was over.

This description of Quinn in the twilight of his career suggests a professional who clearly loved his work and the environment in which he did it. In retrospect, part of Quinn's achievement is that he practically invented this job and this workspace for himself. It is perhaps no wonder that he may have seemed so satisfied and fulfilled as he practiced his well-honed craft.

After all, this mild-mannered yet defiantly self-reliant maverick had learned almost everything he knew about sound recording technology entirely on his own—no training or mentorship. Since leaving that carnival company back in 1939, this husband and father had remained successfully self-employed, dependent solely on his own ingenuity and vision, a good provider. He had designed and expanded the very studios in which he had daily worked—structures that were literally an extension of his family's home. When it came to trusting one's instincts and endeavoring to be true to them, he seems to have got it right.

Duke-Peacock

THE GOLD STAR CONNECTION

THE SIGNIFICANCE OF Houston-born music magnate Don Robey in postwar independent recording history, previously documented in various books and articles, is immense. However, few if any writers have noted that Robey conducted numerous recording sessions at Gold Star Studios. This fact challenges the common (and false) assumption that Robey recorded mainly in the studio that he had constructed inside his office building in 1954. For the better informed, it contrasts with the generalized knowledge that Robey utilized ACA Studios for many Houston recordings. Nonetheless, Robey's role as the first nationally prominent African American record-label boss is also part of Gold Star Studios history.

As the proprietor of Peacock Records, founded in 1949, Robey had launched several stars of urban blues and early R&B—influential performers such as Clarence "Gatemouth" Brown (1924–2005) and Willie Mae "Big Mama" Thornton (1926–1984)—as well as gospel stalwarts such as the Original Five Blind Boys, Bells of Joy, Dixie Hummingbirds, and Mighty Clouds of Joy. As the owner also of Duke Records, acquired in 1952 from David James Mattis, Robey forged a fusion of its original Memphis sound with fresh talent from Texas. That move triggered a succession of hit recordings by Bobby "Blue" Bland (b. 1930), Johnny Ace (b. John Alexander, 1929–1955), Junior Parker, Roscoe Gordon (1928–2002), and many others. As the creator of other labels—Sure Shot, Back Beat, and Song Bird—Robey introduced hit-making artists such as Joe Hinton (1929–1968), O. V. Wright (1939–1980), and Roy Head (b. 1941) to popular culture. And Robey did it all in or near his home neighborhood of the Fifth Ward.

His base of operation was located at 2809 Erastus Street in what is now an inconspicuous rectangular building covered in whitewashed stucco. Today its only distinguishing architectural feature is a wing-shaped protrusion, pointing skyward, above the front door. From 1945 through most of 1953, this unusual protuberance carried a neon sign that spelled out "Bronze Peacock" and outlined an image of the namesake bird. That establishment—a nightclub featuring live jazz orchestras on stage, fine dining in the main room, and a reputation for high-stakes gaming opportunities in the back—was so impressive in its time that Johnny Ace biographer James M. Salem refers to it as "Las Vegas in Houston." The Bronze Peacock too was owned by Robey, and along with his Buffalo Booking Agency, it had been his primary focus until he entered the record business.

Today the Bronze Peacock is remembered as one of the finest African-American-owned-and-operated entertainment venues in the mid-twentieth-century South. But in 1953, four years after cutting his first recordings, Robey closed it, concentrating thereafter on his record labels and their affiliated artists. He then remodeled the nightclub structure, transforming it into his corporate headquarters. Within another year he had commissioned the building of a recording studio there too. Given the phenomenal success of his first two labels, Robey's amalgamation of operations has often been referred to as Duke-Peacock, or sometimes simply as Peacock. Thus, that Erastus Street property has often been called, misleadingly, the Peacock studio. Yet Robey's robust achievement depended almost entirely on hits produced elsewhere.

When Robey retired in 1973 and sold his music business holdings to ABC/Dunhill Records, that deal encompassed five record labels, a catalogue of close to 2,700 song copyrights (which he had typically purchased outright from cash-starved songwriters), approximately 2,000 unreleased masters, and contracts with over one hundred artists. Yet his success as a capitalist (whose medium just happened to be music recording) should not overshadow his impact on cultural history. For example, Jerry Zolten, in his book *Great God A'mighty!: The Dixie Hummingbirds,* acknowledges that "Robey signed some of the most important artists in African-American blues, rhythm and blues, and gospel, making Peacock a prime force in the business of recording American roots music." Moreover, in the *Handbook of Texas Online* Ruth K. Sullivan writes of Robey, "Although controversial because of his shrewd business practices and dealings with artists, he is credited with substantially influencing the development of Texas blues by finding and recording blues artists." Indeed, hundreds of people—instrumentalists, singers, songwriters, arrangers—were part of the collective creative process that ultimately made Duke-Peacock so profitable, and Robey provided a way to showcase their talents.

The potent artistry cultivated during Robey's twenty-four-year reign particularly invigorated the Houston blues scene. Even in the early twenty-first century, its most distinctive characteristics are vitally linked to Robey's empire, particularly as defined by the polished arrangements of his primary A&R man, trumpeter Joe Scott (1924–1979).

As is most thoroughly documented in the book *Duke/Peacock Records* by Galen Gart and Roy C. Ames, Robey actually conducted the majority of his Houston recording sessions at ACA Studios under the technical supervision of its founder Bill Holford. In fact, Gart and Ames call Robey "ACA's best customer." However, even in the early stages of that business relationship, Gold Star Studios was peripherally involved. As Gart and Ames also acknowledge, after paying for recording sessions at ACA, "Robey would indicate which of the numbers on a given date he wished to have mastered for release. Holford would then send the final selections on to Bill Quinn's Gold Star facility (or to various other places around the country) for processing." Thus, almost from the start of his hit-making endeavors, Robey's product was dependent in part on Quinn's expertise.

After using ACA Studios almost exclusively for Houston sessions during his first five years, in April of 1954 Robey hired Holford to design and install a recording studio within the Duke-Peacock office complex. Many people have assumed that Robey produced his recordings there, but that was only rarely the case. As quoted by Gart and Ames, Holford himself indicates otherwise: "He built that basically as a rehearsal studio. . . . Although some gospel sessions were cut there, the soul and pop groups mainly rehearsed there and then cut the finished recordings elsewhere." A quick scan of the discographical data for top artists such as Bland or Parker reveals that "elsewhere" could have been out of town or another studio in Houston. Holford adds, "By that time, many of them [the Duke-Peacock stars] were on the road almost continuously. When Robey was ready to record a session, he'd hire a studio in whatever city they happened to be in."

Evelyn Johnson, Robey's longtime office manager, indicates in Roger Wood's *Down in Houston* that the Erastus Street in-house recording studio was mainly used to make demos of new songs. These tapes were then often sent out to touring artists to provide aural orientation to new material that Scott or others had developed in the demo studio. Then, when Robey booked them into a studio session on the road, they could efficiently perform the track the way the home-based arranger had envisioned it.

Nonetheless, a large share of Robey's recordings continued to take place in Houston—and if not at ACA, then often at Gold Star Studios.

OF ALL THE ARTISTS WHOM ROBEY recorded, his most enduring success came with Bobby "Blue" Bland. Between 1957 and 1972, his prime years with

Bobby "Blue" Bland, publicity photo, mid-1960s

Robey, the singer placed hits on the *Billboard* R&B charts an amazing forty-five times. Thirty-three of those tunes crossed over to register on the pop charts too, with four making it into the Top 40. Since then, Bland has remained intensely popular, touring widely and releasing scores of albums on other labels. In the Rock and Roll Hall of Fame's induction proclamation, Bland is credited with achieving "a definitive union of Southern blues and soul." This iconic singer, too, is part of the Gold Star Studios story.

Because Robey and Johnson kept Bland frequently on tour, many of his recordings for the Duke label were made at studios in Nashville, Chicago, or Los Angeles. But there were still many done in Houston, dating as far back as 1952, mostly at ACA. However, by 1963, Robey also had begun to use the big room at Gold Star Studios to record various artists, including Bland.

Bland came there initially in 1965 to record the Duke single "I'm Too Far Gone (to Turn Around)" backed with "If You Could Read My Mind" (#393). The A-side went to number eight on the *Billboard* R&B charts and crossed over to register at number sixty-two on its Hot 100 pop listings. Some time later, Bland returned to Gold Star for a session that yielded another single: "Back in the Same Old Bag Again" and "I Ain't Myself Anymore" (#412).

In terms of popularity and record sales, Bland's closest Duke rival was the harmonica-playing singer known as Junior Parker. This Mississippi native (born Herman Parker Jr.) had signed with the label in 1953 and scored his first hit with "Next Time You See Me" (#164), recorded in Houston in May 1956. From the mid-1950s into the '60s Parker and Bland frequently toured together, sharing the same band and road manager, in a package show billed as "Blues Consolidated."

On January 23, 1963, Parker recorded "Walking the Floor over You" at Gold Star Studios. However, that track was not released until 1965 when Duke issued it as a single backing "Goodbye Little Girl" (#398).

One of the musicians who toured with Bland and Parker and played on many of Bland's classic Duke tracks was trumpeter Melvin Jackson. Noting that Jackson appears on nine of the sixteen tracks documented on the 1998-issued Bland CD *Greatest Hits Volume One: The Duke Recordings* (MCAD #11783) should establish his credentials. There his brassy tones are heard, often in tandem with those emanating from Joe Scott, on the original versions of songs such as "Cry Cry Cry" (#327), "I Pity the Fool" (#332), and "Turn On Your Love Light" (#344). As Jackson says, "I was on the road with Bobby Bland from 1959 all the way through 1987, and I was his bandleader for about twenty of those years. So if we were in Houston recording, I was with him." Jackson also appears on the classic 1974 album *Together Again for the First Time . . . Live* by B. B. King and Bland (MCAD #4160). Reflecting on his life in music, Jackson recounts various memories of recording at Gold Star Studios:

> Whenever we were in Houston, we would record demos over at the studio on Erastus Street where [Robey] kept his offices. If there was a real recording session, we would go over to Gold Star to do it. . . . Some of the musicians I remember working with were Johnny Brown, Wayne Bennett, and Clarence Hollimon on guitar. Drummers were John Starks and Harold Portier. Joe Scott was the man who created the big horn sound for blues bands. Our band playing with Bland and Parker was the hottest band in Houston.

As for Robey's reasons for renting studio space elsewhere even though he owned his own facility, it seems likely that he deferred to the superior equipment, sound rooms, and engineering staffs offered by established recording companies. In particular, he might not have wanted to invest in necessary upgrading, especially during the transition from mono to multitrack recording.

Whatever the case, Gold Star invoices from 1964 to 1968 confirm that Robey frequently staged his sessions there.

Veteran engineer Doyle Jones (1928–2006), who started working there in 1965, says, "Duke and Peacock did a hell of a lot of recording while I was at Gold Star. I remember sessions with Buddy Ace and Junior Parker and many others." Though he reports that Robey rarely visited, Jones adds, "One of his [producers] was always there, either Gil Capel or Joe Scott."

Jones had replaced the engineer who handled the earliest known Duke-Peacock sessions at Gold Star—Walt Andrus, who had been hired when J. L. Patterson leased the facility from Quinn in 1963. Before departing to build his own studio, Andrus specialized in custom recordings and pressings, particularly for Duke-Peacock. In addition to sessions with Bland and Parker, Andrus also recorded tracks by other Robey artists, such as Joe Hinton, the Mighty Clouds of Joy, and Ernie K-Doe (1936–2001).

As for determining precisely when Robey started to use Gold Star, the paper trail is incomplete. One source suggests that it could have been earlier than 1963, but no corroboration has been established. "We talked a lot there in the studio," musician Sleepy LaBeef says of Robey. "He would lease the studio sometimes for a day, and sometimes for a whole week." Because he recalls Robey being there during Quinn's studio expansion project, LaBeef insists, "The time period that Robey was there was from 1959 on. He was there at the studios a lot, and he and Bill Quinn got along real good. They kind of believed in each other."

Trumpeter Calvin Owens (1929–2008) did Duke-Peacock session work and served as A&R man during a couple of stints. Owens says that such assignments brought him to Gold Star for the first time in 1962 and that he worked on recordings for Parker as well as K-Doe with a variety of engineers, including Dan Puskar, Bert Frilot, and Andrus.

Meanwhile, jazz drummer Bubbha Thomas also worked lots of sessions for the Duke-Peacock concern, including its Back Beat and Sure Shot imprints. Starting in 1963, he gigged as part of a studio unit that featured guitarist Clarence Hollimon (1937–2000) and bassist Lawrence Evans. "Clarence, Lawrence, and I played on sessions for Buddy Ace, the Mighty Clouds of Joy, the Loving Sisters, O. V. Wright, and others," he says. "Early on, sessions were being done at Bill Holford's ACA Studios, but then quite a number of the sessions were moved over to Gold Star." Thomas's earliest session credits there include Verna Rae Clay's "He Loves Me, He Loves Me Not," released on Sure Shot (#5001) in October 1963, and Bobby Williams's "Play a Sad Song" and "Try Love" on Sure Shot (#5003), issued in May 1964.

Leo O'Neil, trombonist and arranger, says, "The earliest I remember being at Gold Star was maybe 1964. I remember working with a lot of Don Robey's artists back in those days. They had great writers and arrangers . . . so my job was to work with those guys and get the arrangements written out correctly."

O'Neil's assessment of the quality of the arrangers is almost universally shared. For instance, ACA Studios owner Holford, quoted in Gart and Ames, says of Robey, "First, he hired good arrangers. Every part was ready when the session started." Gold Star staff engineer Doyle Jones adds,

> The one thing that I remember the most about Don Robey's outfit was the two A&R men that came over during the sessions. One was an older gentleman named Wilmer Shakesnider, and the other was a real famous guy, Joe Scott. I was real impressed with those two guys. They always handled the sessions very well, and almost every session was productive.

Musician Melvin Jackson says that his first Duke-Peacock session at Gold Star took place "in a gigantic room that was like being in a Quonset hut." In a subsequent period that he estimates to have been "between 1965 and 1968," he worked there "in a smaller room [a studio addition,] and it had a gold star in the floor." He also remembers recording a Bland session engineered by Robert Evans "in the early '70s, after Huey Meaux bought [and renamed] the studio."

A Fifth Ward native, ace guitarist Clarence Green (1934–1997) not only worked on Duke-Peacock sessions at Gold Star Studios backing others but also recorded there as a front man with his own group. As Gart and Ames point out, "Often he and another guitarist, Clarence Hollimon, would team in the studio to lay down background tracks for artists such as Junior Parker, Bobby Bland, Joe Hinton, O. V. Wright and others." Impressed with Green's instrumental skills, and aware of his fervent popularity on local stages, Robey financed a 1966 session for Clarence Green and the Rhythmaires. The result, issued on Duke (#399), was the single "Keep a Workin'" and "I Saw You Last Night." Robey later released another—"I'm Wonderin'" and "What Y'all Waiting on Me"—on Duke (#410). Meanwhile, Green and his band remained a vital presence on the Houston scene for the rest of his life. And while his affiliation as a front man for one of Robey's labels was short-lived, Green's string-bending blues often evoked the classic Duke-Peacock sound.

BEYOND THE DUKE AND PEACOCK LABELS, Robey also reaped big dividends, especially in the 1960s, from the Back Beat imprint that he created in 1957. Back Beat became the Texas home for a more progressive style of music that would ultimately be known as soul, and it is part of the Gold Star story too.

Robey found Back Beat success with the exquisite soul singer Joe Hinton— but not right away. In 1959 the Duke-Peacock owner had recruited the young vocalist from a gospel group, the Spirit of Memphis Quartet, which was then recording for Peacock. For the first few years, Hinton's solo career foundered, but in 1963 he broke through with the minor Back Beat hit "You Know It Ain't Right" (#537). Shortly thereafter Hinton came to Gold Star Studios, presumably for the first time, to cut another Back Beat single featuring "There's No In Between" and "Better to Give Than Receive" (#539). The latter track also ranked on the *Billboard* R&B charts, besides receiving the "hot" designation in its pop listings for October 12, 1963.

However, the Back Beat song for which Hinton will always be remembered is the Willie Nelson–penned classic "Funny (How Time Slips Away)" (#541), and it too was recorded at Gold Star. Like so many of Nelson's prime compositions (such as "Crazy," which was first a hit for Patsy Cline), this number was not initially linked in public consciousness to the man who wrote it. In fact, Texas country singer Billy Walker had introduced it to predominantly white audiences with his 1961 rendition, which went to number twenty-three on *Billboard*'s country charts. But when Hinton, an African American, cut his own hit interpretation of the dramatic ballad, it changed the whole dynamic of Nelson's potential as a songwriter. That recording established Nelson's first major success as a crossover songwriter—that is, someone whose material could appeal to artists and audiences of sharply contrasting demographics. Accordingly, it represents a key moment in pop cultural history.

Hinton's recording of "Funny (How Time Slips Away)" peaked at number thirteen on the pop charts in August of 1964, making it Robey's biggest Back Beat hit up to that date. Apart from Hinton's fine singing and Nelson's eloquent writing, the arrangement and instrumentation were also superb, a key element in making this recording a masterpiece of well-crafted sound. Owens remembers Scott and Capel working on the distinctive arrangement back at the Erastus Street studio. Later, when the song was actually recorded at Gold Star, with Walt Andrus engineering, Owens played trumpet and led the horn section.

The Back Beat version opens with a flourish of trumpets. Horns then coo harmoniously in the background as Hinton suavely articulates the opening line—"Well, hello there. My, it's been a long, long time." They punctuate the first verse with a brassy blast of passion on the turnaround. Obbligato guitar lines spun seamlessly by Hollimon distinguish the second verse, and the horns gracefully emerge with more prominent embellishments in response to the singer on the third. As the musical tension builds toward conclusion, Hinton's over-the-top falsetto climbs even higher, wavering brilliantly at the climax.

Robey brought Hinton back to Gold Star Studios at least one more time that year. The resulting Back Beat single, "I Want a Little Girl" and "True

Joe Hinton, publicity photo
(by Benny Joseph), early 1960s

Love" (#545), charted in both the R&B and pop categories of *Billboard*. With this new hit, coming on the heels of "Funny," Hinton had put Back Beat in the 1965 national spotlight. But that very same year, one of his label mates would score an even bigger hit.

Robey's achievement was clearly dependent in part on the genius of his A&R staff—producers such as Scott, Don Carter, and Jimmy Duncan. Scott, in particular, was his most valuable man, an in-house employee with a salaried position. But given the wide scope of Robey's five-label empire, the owner also often called on other independent producers to find prospective talent and songs. Moreover, by the 1960s Robey racially integrated his operations by also working with white producers such as Charlie Booth and Huey Meaux—an affiliation that led to Robey's most successful single ever, a 1965 hit cowritten and performed by Roy Head.

Both Booth and Meaux were involved in bringing Head to Robey's attention. As a producer Booth had previously produced one bona fide regional hit with the single "Down on Bending Knees" by the singer and guitarist Johnny Copeland (1937–1997), released on Booth's own label, Golden Eagle (#101). That track too—the first by another of Houston's great African American blues performers—had been recorded at Gold Star Studios in 1963, and invoices show that Booth frequently produced his own sessions there between 1960 and 1967. But neither he nor Meaux posed any threat to a big wheel such as Robey, whose acumen and achievement they generally admired. As Copeland says in Bill Dahl's liner notes for *The Johnny Copeland Collection,* "All of us, we were all feelin' in the wind. Huey was a barber. Charlie Booth, he was a recording artist. We didn't really have a lot of knowledge about the business. Not as much knowledge as Mr. Robey."

Booth claims to have met Robey during a high-stakes game of craps without realizing at first who he was. Afterwards, and shocked to have learned his identity, Booth says (as quoted by Gart and Ames), "I told him I was a producer, and he said he was interested, especially in some of my white soul groups for his Back Beat label." That invitation led to Booth and Meaux introducing Robey to the dynamic singer Roy Head and his band the Traits, which laid the foundation for the recording that would become the Back Beat label's all-time best-seller, "Treat Her Right" (#546). *Texas Monthly* writers Jeff McCord and John Morthland rank that track among the hundred best Texas songs ever recorded. It also, of course, is one of the most successful recordings ever produced at Gold Star Studios.

Roy Head and the Traits were a crowd-pleasing band of rowdy young white musicians based in San Marcos and working the Central Texas nightclub circuit. While much of their musical orientation had evolved from country and rock, their signature song is generally considered pure R&B—what Ron

Wynn in the *All Music Guide to Rock* accurately describes as "one of the great pieces of uptempo soul in the mid '60s." Writing in the *Austin Chronicle,* Margaret Moser adds,

> "Treat Her Right" defied genre and lured those who heard its siren call. Written by Roy Head and Gene Kurtz, the song swaggered with an elastic rhythm bolstered by the punch of brass . . . and its double-entendre lyrics promised heaven "if you practice my method just as hard as you can." With twelve bars and three chords, "Treat Her Right" delivered heaven in 125 seconds flat.

The Gold Star session that produced this classic disc is documented on invoice #19411 for June 6, 1965. The lineup for the Traits on this recording included Gene Kurtz (electric bass), Gerry Gibson (drums), Johnny Clark (lead guitar), Frank Miller (rhythm guitar), Dickie Martin (trumpet), Doug Shertz (tenor sax), with Head on vocals and flamboyant dance moves. The engineer, Doyle Jones, has vivid memories of that date, including his take on a previous instance of the interracial tensions that Head's affiliation with Robey's label could sometimes trigger. He says,

> Charlie Booth had sold the rights to Roy Head and the Traits to Don Robey prior to them coming in to record at the studios. Don sent Roy and the band in to record with one of his guys in charge of the session. Well, the black and the white [guys] couldn't exactly get it together, and it was a fiasco; what it was, was a damn mess. I think that we might have spent thirty hours over a period of a few days trying to get something recorded.
>
> Well, everybody gave up, and about a week later Roy called and booked a session. We did it on a rainy Sunday, June 6, 1965, and it was the first time I ever got a tip at a recording session. It really embarrassed me because I knew that Roy was selling insurance, and I knew that I wouldn't give him ten dollars [the amount of the tip] for the whole session. Turns out that three of the four songs from that session made the charts and, of course, "Treat Her Right" was a monster hit.

As Jones indicates, the race-tinged uneasiness could have permanently derailed the whole project. Moreover, that first studio experience foreshadowed the tensions that Head would sometimes experience, after "Treat Her Right" became popular, when he appeared at venues in which most of the patrons expected him to be black. In Moser's article Head recounts one particularly influential incident and how he overcame it, backed in this case by African American musicians:

There was a black disc-jockey convention in Houston, at one of the biggest black clubs in the country. Robey didn't want me to go on stage, didn't want people to know I was white. . . . A couple [of] folks said, "You need to let him play 'cause there'll be a problem if we don't." When I went on stage, the place went silent. "Oh, God," I thought. "I gotta do something now." Joe Scott's band backed me—Bobby "Blue" Bland's band—and after I got started, they were high-fiving, throwing hats in the air. The next day "Treat Her Right" was played all over the United States by black stations.

The R&B market enthusiastically embraced the song, which eventually peaked at number one on the *Billboard* charts for that genre. But it also zoomed up the pop charts simultaneously, where it rose to the number two position—and stayed there for eight straight weeks. Only the strength of the Beatles (who commandeered the top slot first with "Help," followed immediately by "Yesterday") kept this Back Beat single from scoring the ultimate honor in the pop category too.

Since 1965 the song has been recorded by all manner of major artists, from Otis Redding to Mae West to the Box Tops (with Alex Chilton on vocals) to Jerry Lee Lewis to Barbara Mandrell to Johnny Thunders (ex–New York Dolls) to George Thorogood to Los Straitjackets with Mark Lindsay (of Paul Revere and the Raiders fame) on vocals. There are live versions by Bruce Springsteen, Bon Jovi, Neil Diamond, and the Tragically Hip, among others.

As Jones previously noted, Head and his band had recorded four tracks on the session that yielded "Treat Her Right," and two of the remaining three cracked the *Billboard* charts too. "The Apple of My Eye" (#555) peaked at number thirty-two, and Head's cover of the Willie Dixon blues "My Babe" (#560) registered at number ninety-nine. Though the original Traits soon broke up, Head continued to record for Back Beat using the Duke-Peacock studio band (billed nonetheless as the Traits). In 1966 Head returned to Gold Star Studios to record a single featuring "Wigglin' and Gigglin'" (#563), soon followed by "To Make a Big Man Cry" (#571). Both of those records charted respectably just outside the Hot 100.

The great vocalist O. V. Wright scored yet another classic Back Beat hit in 1965 with "You're Gonna Make Me Cry" (#548), also recorded at Gold Star Studios. It was the first national Top Ten single by this electrifying performer, considered by many among the greatest deep-soul singers of all time. Backed with "Monkey Dog," it peaked at number six on *Billboard*'s R&B charts, while also crossing over into the pop realm's Hot 100. At Gold Star Wright also cut Back Beat singles such as "Poor Boy" and "I'm in Your Corner" (#551), "I Don't Want to Sit Down" and "Can't Find True Love" (#544), plus "Gone for Good" and "How Long Baby" (#558).

With artists such as Wright, Hinton, and Head, Robey helped define mid-1960s soul music from a Texas perspective. That in so doing he also used the engineers and facilities of Gold Star Studios is further evidence of the unique role that this recording complex has played in music history.

A FEW OF THE HIT RECORDS MADE at Gold Star Studios by artists linked to Robey ended up being released on labels that he did not control. A prime example of that seemingly unlikely scenario is the song "Think," written and performed by Jimmy McCracklin (b. 1921). Released in 1965 on the California-based Imperial Records (#66129), it went to number seven on the R&B charts and number ninety-five in the pop category. Its status as a classic would be confirmed years later by its inclusion on the multidisc compilation *Mean Old World: The Blues from 1940 to 1994,* issued by the Smithsonian Institution— though the liner notes by Lawrence Hoffman mistakenly identify Los Angeles as the song's recording site. Yet "Think" was actually recorded independently by McCracklin in Houston, where he made use of both Robey's in-house studio on Erastus Street and the Gold Star facility across town.

Though born in St. Louis, McCracklin was a California resident and a proponent of the West Coast blues sound for the entire second half of the twentieth century. After launching his recording career with Globe in 1945, he went on to issue other singles and albums on numerous labels nationwide, including Modern, Atlantic, Swing Time, Checker, Mercury, and many others—as well as Robey's Peacock brand. That arrangement had evolved during a two-week special engagement featuring McCracklin (along with Big Mama Thornton, Billy Wright, and Marie Adams) at the Bronze Peacock nightclub in 1952. McCracklin's first Peacock single, issued later that year, offered the minor hit "My Days Are Limited" (#1605). Peacock released four other McCracklin singles over the next few years, but by 1954 he had moved on to another company.

However, McCracklin continued to perform periodically in Houston, a regular stop on his tours across the South. Though his formal ties with Robey's label were broken, McCracklin evidently maintained a friendship with the A&R man Scott, which likely led to McCracklin recording one of his most famous songs in Houston. "I had an agent in New York who was booking me in Houston all the time. So I was in your area a lot," McCracklin explains. "The song 'Think' just came to me one day, and I wanted to record it."

Being in Houston as he was at the time, McCracklin turned to his former associates at Duke-Peacock to bring his plan to fruition. Someone there, presumably Scott, facilitated McCracklin's initial use of the office-building studio. Whatever arrangements may have been made to garner Robey's approval of this plan are unclear. But the wheeler-dealer label boss, via his commonly evoked alias, did receive publishing credit as cowriter of "Think"—and hence a half-share of the composer royalties in perpetuity. As is widely known (and covered in more detail in Wood's *Down in Houston*), after being criticized for claiming writer's credit for countless songs that he had simply purchased outright from others, Robey had adopted the pseudonym Deadric Malone (based on a combination of his own middle name and his wife's maiden name— often abbreviated in credits as D. Malone) to use in such situations, which for Robey were numerous indeed. He thereafter still received the lucrative royalty payments but avoided some of the public embarrassment (for allegedly taking advantage of desperate artists by buying and publishing their songs without acknowledging their role as the actual creators). Because "D. Malone" appears with McCracklin's name in the songwriting credits on this Imperial Records disc, we infer that Robey perhaps permitted the traveling blues musician to make use of the Duke-Peacock studio and ace producer in exchange for a piece of the songwriting action. Gambler that he was (by his own self-description), Robey had to like the odds. After all, assuming no other sessions were scheduled at the time, he would have nothing to lose for allowing McCracklin into his studio; however, if the song proved to be a hit (as it did), Robey could earn some fat and easy royalty checks—what musicians of his era often called "mailbox money."

McCracklin continues the story, explaining also how Gold Star Studios came to be involved:

> We started the recording over at Robey's studio in his building, with Joe Scott producing. But Joe wasn't happy with some of the playing, and he went over to your studio [Gold Star] and replaced some of the music behind my voice. . . . I used my own road band on the [first] recording of that song. The other song we did was . . . "Steppin' Up in Class." I recorded those sides for Imperial Records. . . . "Think" was a Gold Record for me.

Among the studio musicians whom Scott employed to rerecord the selected instrumentation for overdubbing was the drummer Bubbha Thomas. The engineer for that session was Frilot, who handled the mixing as well. As for his role on the track, Thomas says, "The reason I got the Jimmy McCracklin thing was because they really liked my backbeat. Robey would say, 'You tell that damn drummer'—me—'to play that same backbeat he used on the O. V. [Wright] session last week!'"

McCracklin adds, "I think that we might have done maybe four other songs during that time period." In fact, he staged several additional sessions specifically at Gold Star Studios in 1965. We have three invoices made out to Imperial Records for Jimmy McCracklin for that same year: a recording session on April 21, a mixing session on April 26, and then twelve straight hours of recording and mixing on September 28. In the company vault we also have a safety master of six untitled tracks labeled as "Jimmy McCracklin/Imperial Records." Such artifacts are physical reminders of the sometimes surprising, multifaceted history of Gold Star Studios.

WHILE ROBEY'S RECORDING CONGLOMERATE scored big with secular music, it was also deeply involved in the production of gospel recordings. As a result, some of the greatest performers in that genre came from across the nation to record in Houston. In a few cases, they are known to have done sessions at Gold Star Studios too.

For instance, the Sunset Travelers—who originally had featured the singer Wright—indeed traveled, several times, from Memphis to Houston to record. They came twice in 1961 alone, producing at least fifteen sides at those sessions. Where they recorded (and whether at one or two studios) is not documented. But in October of 1964 the Sunset Travelers are known to have returned to Houston for sessions at Gold Star Studios. They recorded eleven tracks there—some of which appear on the group's Peacock Records LP entitled *On Jesus' Program* (#122).

Even nonreligious music fans are likely to know of the Mighty Clouds of Joy. Writing in *All Music Guide*, Jason Ankeny calls them "gospel's preeminent group," adding that they "carried the torch for the traditional quartet vocal style" even while "pioneering a distinctively funky sound." Formed in Los Angeles in 1955, they signed with Peacock Records in 1960 (which was already home to several gospel supergroups). There they made a large number of best-selling gospel singles and albums for Robey's company. In particular, we know that their 1965 single "I'll Go" (#3025) was recorded at Gold Star Studios, and it was reportedly a mainstay of *Billboard*'s "Hot Spiritual Singles" chart for that year. Likewise, their 1965 album, *A Bright Side*, was a top-seller, and much of it was recorded at Gold Star (featuring veteran session players such as Thomas, Hollimon, and Evans).

Though gospel music had never been the primary focus of Quinn's studio, it had been recorded there on many sessions in the 1950s—typically by white country singers with cagy producers who sensed that old-time Christian numbers on the B-sides might help sell records. But the Duke-Peacock connection distinguished Gold Star Studios as a recording site for some of the biggest groups in the history of black gospel.

Similarly, though African Americans had recorded at Quinn's facility since the late 1940s, the Duke-Peacock connection signified also a changing dynamic in terms of race relations. Given Robey's self-confident demeanor and obvious financial success, as well as his tendency to employ brilliant fellow African Americans (such as Johnson or Scott) in key positions of authority, blacks took on increasingly high-profile roles among the studio's clientele. In some cases, the blacks were now the bosses exploiting and promoting the talents of whites—and marketing music (such as Head's "Treat Her Right") that appealed to both groups. Writer Tim Brooks notes "the significant socioeconomic and cultural contributions Robey made to the industry and to the convergence of black and white popular music," and then sums up a key fact: "He was a rare breed, a black man succeeding in a white man's business, in the South, at a time when that was not encouraged."

In part because of Robey's involvement with studios such as ACA and Gold Star, scores of blacks and whites—musicians, engineers, managers, producers, songwriters, staff members, and such—worked together in close proximity. For some, it was perhaps the first time to experience a racially integrated professional environment. And despite whatever frictions may have occasionally transpired, some of them, at least sometimes, collaborated creatively in ways that were rare in Texas at the time.

Producer and songwriter Flery Versay provides his own insight on the matter:

> I arrived in Houston with my partner Robert Staunton in 1967. We came from LA via Motown Records. Robert had written to Don Robey of Duke and Peacock Records. He asked us to come down to Houston to be staff songwriters, and I wound up being head of A&R for a couple of years, around 1966 and 1967. . . .
>
> I am glad that I got to work with a lot of white cats in the late '60s. Race relations were a big deal if you listened to the media. They made it out to be a lot worse than it really was. In the entertainment business, everybody pretty much got along. And I'm glad that my experience made that possible.

Of course, Robey's business sense was focused on making money, not necessarily making racial harmony. But because he needed, and could pay for, the services and facilities that an experienced studio such as ACA or Gold Star could offer, Robey nonetheless may have inadvertently stimulated racial integration in the 1960s recording scene in Houston, the largest city in the South.

Whatever his motive, as an entrepreneur Robey had blazed new trails. Even the cantankerous "Gatemouth" Brown, the first artist he ever recorded, had to admire what Robey had achieved—a feat that until the mid-1960s had yet to be matched. Brown, as quoted in Gart and Ames, offers this assessment: "He pulled off something in America that no one else ever pulled off [before]. We had the only world-renowned black recording company, the biggest."

The Duke-Peacock story is thus unique. Moreover, the fact that it includes Gold Star Studios adds yet another dimension to that site's claim to a special status of its own.

12

The HSP Corporation
Experiment Begins

BY 1965 J. L. PATTERSON, who was leasing Gold Star Studios from the retired Bill Quinn, had developed a concept that, he hoped, would give him and his partners in the facility unprecedented control of the regional recording market—and make lots of money. Patterson essentially convinced several previous competitors and independent contractors to join forces with him under a single corporate umbrella. This larger company's staff thus comprised many of the best recording engineers from the Houston-Beaumont area. Most prominent in this partnership was Bill Holford of ACA Studios, one of Houston's most reputable recording companies. By coupling ACA's business and staff with Gold Star's, this new hybrid corporation was primed to dominate the recording services industry in and beyond the state's largest city. It was called the HSP Corporation, based on the initial letter of each founding officer's surname. Formed on May 1, 1965, it supplanted Patterson's previous JLP Corporation as the organization operating Gold Star Studios. And for a while, it worked out very well.

Its principals were (in H-S-P sequence) Holford (vice president/director), Louis Stevenson (president/director), and Patterson (secretary/treasurer). Ultimately there were several other people involved too, including former Sun Records engineer Jack Clement and producer Bill Hall, previously of the Gulf Coast Recording Company in Beaumont. Engineers included Doyle Jones, Hank Poole, Bert Frilot, Bob Lurie, Gaylan Shelby, and others.

By this time, engineer Walt Andrus had left to create his own recording company. By late 1965 Huey Meaux, a former regular Gold Star client, would be gone too, as he elected to build his own studio, called Recording Services, in nearby Pasadena. However, he would make some serious Gold Star history before departing, and eventually he would return.

For a while, Patterson's newly formed corporation operated as ACA/Gold Star Recording Company, based at the original Gold Star Studios on Brock Street. Though the HSP Corporation would ultimately fail as a business partnership, during its tenure in charge of Gold Star, that already historic facility continued to host important hit-making sessions in a wide range of genres.

Despite issues of mismanagement and mistrust that would ultimately dissolve HSP, the company employed outstanding sound engineers. One of the best, who would eventually depart in disgust to form his own studio, was Jones. He had started working for Patterson in August 1964. As an inside observer during the corporate transition from JLP to HSP, Jones offers this summary of the evolution of the company:

> Patterson was a clever guy. He started the JLP Corporation, which included me in some great plan to corner the market on all the recording in Houston. . . . At first it also included Jack Clement and Bill Hall from Beaumont and Louis Stevenson and Bob Lurie, who had come from owning a studio in Paris, France. It was successful enough at the beginning for Patterson to expand the company and rename it the HSP Corporation. That is when he added Bill Holford and Bert Frilot. For about a year we were the busiest studio anybody had ever seen. . . . J.L. had cornered the market on all the best engineers in Houston, and there was almost nowhere else to go, except for maybe Walt Andrus's studio over on Broadway. If J.L. hadn't been such a crook, the sky was the limit as far as what might have been.

Stevenson, the president, was an investor who also served as resident studio technician, mastering engineer, and disc cutter. (During this time period the studio still cut its own acetates on the Gotham/Grampian lathe.) Stevenson played a key role in modifying and repairing studio equipment during the HSP era. Bob Lurie, already an excellent engineer, became one of the resident disc-cutters too. He brought with him a Steinway grand piano and installed it in the big studio.

Because Patterson's vision for HSP required it to be staffed with numerous engineers and do a high volume of business, he expanded the Gold Star facility. In 1964 Patterson had commissioned Jack Clement (b. 1931) to design a recording room as part of a major studio expansion. Upon completion, this new building, connected to the front of the big studio room, housed the "gold star" room, so called because of the emblem installed on the studio floor. The structural addition also encompassed two new acoustic reverb chambers, plus the old front entryway to the studio complex.

Studio B ran twenty-one feet long by twenty feet wide, with a seventeen-foot-high ceiling. The walls were covered in common acoustic tiles and strategically placed rectangular panels made of a cloth-covered absorbent material that reduced room echoes. The ceiling was T-grid with acoustic tiles. The floor was a thick, light-gray-colored linoleum tile with the aforementioned emblem placed slightly off center.

The adjoining control room measured twenty feet long by twelve feet wide, with a thirteen-foot-high ceiling. It was long and narrow, with the shorter side facing into the studio. The linoleum floor was raised nearly eighteen inches above the ground to allow cable troughs to run underfoot. The walls were acoustic tiles except for a corkboard surface (for extra absorbency) on the back wall behind the engineer's seat.

The designer, Clement, has excelled in recording, publishing, and writing American music for over fifty years—and was already well established in the industry when he started working with Patterson in 1964. As an engineer, for instance, Clement had previously recorded Jerry Lee Lewis, Johnny Cash, and other icons at Sun Records in Memphis. Later, following his stint in Houston, he would produce Charley Pride and establish his own hit-making studio in Nashville. There he would record albums for singers Townes Van Zandt and Waylon Jennings, among many others. Scores of artists—from Hank Snow to Dolly Parton to Tom Jones—have covered his songs.

Here Clement recalls his introduction to Patterson and Gold Star Studios:

My first memories of the place were when J. L. Patterson asked me to come over and visit. There was only one studio at the time; it was the big one in the back. He asked me to help him build a second studio.

It started when I moved to Beaumont and built . . . Gulf Coast Recording Studios. I partnered with Bill Hall. We both had equipment, and we moved it into that new studio. I recorded B. J. Thomas a couple of times and also worked with Don Robey a bit.

Then one day Patterson came along. At the time I owned all this gear and was thinking about moving back to Nashville. He talked me into moving to Houston. So we cut all the gear loose and moved to Houston in late 1964.

Patterson had the big fine room in the back, but he wanted a second room. I designed and built it from the ground up—footings, foundations, and everything. It was a well-built building. I did the layout and the acoustics inside as well. Then we put in these two echo chambers. . . .

My concepts for the Gold Star studio were that I wanted it good and "dead" with very controllable sound. . . . I would deaden the walls and be able to move reflective partitions in to change the sound and tune it up when I wanted to. The walls were a cloth covering with fiberglass insulation behind it. The cloth would have had about nine inches of fiberglass behind it. This went from the ceiling down to about three feet from the floor. There was a wood border all around the studio from the floor up to the three-foot level, and that was a sort of a bass trap that ran around the room. My approach to designing a studio is to make it good for the musicians to hear each other. I would start with it fairly dead and then tune it up as I would go. That studio I built in Houston was solid. We put these pylons in the ground every so-many feet; it should not have moved at all.

The control room had a gang of four-channel Ampex mixers chained together and fed an Ampex four-track one-half-inch machine and a one-quarter-inch mono machine and maybe a stereo deck also. . . . They had a lot of good mics: all the Neumann tube mics and RCA ribbons and some Altec dynamics. . . .

I brought all my clients from Beaumont to work there. I remember recording Mickey Newbury at Gold Star, one of the first clients of the new studio I had just built.

As for the reason his tenure at Gold Star Studios did not last longer, Clement offers this cryptic analysis:

J.L. was a very interesting character, and I didn't want to get in too deep with him. He had a lot of wild ideas. His main thing was this burglar alarm system called Vandalarm. It worked on sound, and apparently it was reliable, and he sold a bunch of them. That's how he got his money. . . . After a while I decided to move back to Nashville and took my equipment back with me.

While Clement's time at Gold Star Studios was limited, it was significant. First, he brought impressive music-establishment credentials to the enterprise. Before his arrival, the self-taught Quinn had designed and installed every facet of this recording facility. Clement's work on the 1964 expansion project infused the complex with a fresh professional perspective. Moreover, Clement literally changed the size, shape, and quality of the facility, and many of his modifications remain intact and in use today. But his quick departure, bolstered by his observations about Patterson (whom he depicts as motivated by money, not music), suggests that he sensed that something was not right with HSP.

Jones soon came to a similar conclusion about Patterson. Jones says, "When I came over to work in late 1964, the gold star room was about a week away from completion." Thus, he worked mainly in the new, state-of-the-art location. But given the conditions under which he would leave Gold Star Studios, he has no nostalgia for the site. "I have not set foot in the building since that time," he explains. "The whole experience with J. L. Patterson's running of those studios left me with a very bad taste in my mouth."

Another engineer, Hank Poole, had originally worked at Houston's KILT radio before taking a position at ACA Studios. Thus, with the HSP consolidation, Poole moved to Gold Star Studios. He says,

I came over to Gold Star when the two Bills, Quinn and Holford, merged. I guess they figured between them they would have a lock on it. I think that J. L. Patterson was in trouble financially and tried to put the ACA/Gold Star concept together, and figured that the two of them could do real well together. . . .

We cut loose all the equipment from Fannin Street [ACA's mid-Sixties location] and moved over to Brock Street and put the gear into the big studio in the back of the building. . . .

Eventually Bill Holford left and moved back over to Fannin. . . . But we sure turned out some mighty stuff in the time that we were there.

While the people employed there generally concur on the high quality of the new studio equipment and design, the HSP Corporation lasted little more than a year.

SOME OF THE MOST HISTORICALLY SIGNIFICANT Gold Star Studios recordings to occur during the HSP regime featured Clifton Chenier (1925–1987). Though he had cut 1950s-era singles elsewhere for labels such as Elko and Specialty, his first Gold Star sessions changed his life and added a zesty new influence to the American musical vocabulary. Chenier and producer Chris Strachwitz (b. 1931) launched their long-term affiliation there. And those Gold Star Studios recordings became the primary medium by which Arhoolie Records introduced the future King of Zydeco to popular consciousness.

As Cub Koda says of zydeco in *All Music Guide,* "Chenier may not have invented the form—an accordion-driven, blues-inspired variant of Cajun music played for dancing—but he single-handedly helped give it shape and defined the form as we know it today." While Chenier and the black Creole music that he personifies came from southwest Louisiana, Houston has played a key role in its evolution, as documented extensively in Roger Wood's book *Texas Zydeco.* During the prime of his career, Chenier resided in the Frenchtown section of the city's Fifth Ward, and it was there that Strachwitz first heard him perform—the very night before their first Gold Star Studios session.

The California-based producer was introduced to Chenier by Lightnin' Hopkins, who had been the focal point of Strachwitz's first field trip to Houston in 1959. Later Hopkins had started recording for the Arhoolie label. During his early visits to Houston, Strachwitz had also witnessed firsthand the vibrant black Creole music scene. As he told writer Barbara Schultz in a *Mix* magazine interview,

I caught some of the early zydeco people who were just beginning to kick into gear in Houston at that time. This was in '60, and nobody had ever heard of this stuff except in these few beer joints down there. I was lucky to meet up with this fellow Mack McCormick, who lived in Houston and was not only trying to be Lightnin' Hopkins' manager, but he also knew a lot about the scene, the ethnic music in Houston.

In 1961 Strachwitz and the influential McCormick (who had coined the now-standard spelling of the word *zydeco* in 1959) made field recordings of various black Creoles performing a primitive strain of this strange music at Houston venues. But it was not until 1964, when Hopkins suggested that Strachwitz accompany him to hear his "cousin" perform, that the producer would experience Chenier. As Strachwitz relates in Wood's *Down in Houston:*

> So he took me over to this little beer joint in Houston in an area they call Frenchtown. And here was this black man with a huge accordion on his chest and playing the most unbelievable low-down blues I'd ever heard in my life—and singing it in this bizarre French patois! . . . So as soon as Lightnin' introduced me, Clifton said, "Oh, you're a record man. I want to make a record tomorrow."

Strachwitz explains the situation further in the Schultz article: "He hadn't had a single in some years, so he figured any white guy that's in the record business, that must be it. I finally agreed. We went over to Bill Quinn's studio on February 8, 1964."

From our own 2003 interview with Strachwitz, the story continues:

> Yeah, but what showed up the next day was not only Clifton and his drummer [the duo Strachwitz had previously seen], but he brought the whole damn band! And he said, "You know, Chris, that old French stuff isn't hitting. I've got to make rock 'n' roll records."
>
> I said, "Well, I don't know. What I heard last night knocked me out." . . . Anyway, he had a drummer and a guitar player and an electric bass man and a piano player. . . . Thank goodness, the bass literally didn't work because the whole damn paper on the cone of the bass speaker had come off. And the guitar player's amp started smoking. So we were down to piano, accordion, and drums. We were getting closer [to the desired sound], except for the repertoire. He didn't want to do that French stuff, so we did "Ay Ai Ai" and "Why Did You Go Last Night." That was his first single for Arhoolie Records [#45-506]. The engineer on that session was a guy named J. L. Patterson, and he wasn't very good, but the record sounded okay.

Clifton Chenier, Houston, 1965 (photo by and courtesy of Chris Strachwitz)

The next year Strachwitz returned to Gold Star Studios to produce a full album of Chenier tracks. Incidentally, two months earlier, he had also recorded Hopkins there with Lurie engineering. But for the May 11, 1965, session with Chenier, Jones engineered—with the retired Quinn looking on. Following his initial Gold Star session with the disappointing Patterson, Strachwitz was pleased to work with Lurie and Jones, commenting especially on the latter's ability to record drums and bass effectively.

That 1965 album session yielded the Arhoolie LP *Louisiana Blues and Zydeco* (#1024), which introduced thousands of far-removed fans to this Gulf Coast musical hybrid. Most of the tracks were also issued on 45 rpm singles—in deference to the jukebox market and radio. In the Schultz article, Strachwitz explains that after taping one particularly potent number, on which Chenier was accompanied only on rubboard and drums, he received some insider advice: "Bill Quinn, who was standing behind me, said, 'Chris, that's going to sell down here; it's got that sound.'" The veteran Quinn was right, for that track, "Louisiana Blues" (#509), became the closest thing to a hit single that Arhoolie had ever released. Strachwitz had improvised that simple song title when he could not translate Chenier's French phrasing. As he tells Schultz, "If we had put the French name on there, the jockeys probably wouldn't have played it. But this way, they put it on, and the first note just killed you. You just heard that unbelievable low-down song, and it doesn't really matter which language he's singing in."

Two tracks from *Louisiana Blues and Zydeco* and two from Chenier's first Gold Star session appeared on the 2003 Arhoolie CD *The Best of Clifton Chenier* (#474). Of the fourteen studio-recorded songs on that retrospective compilation (three others were taped live in concert), ten were made in Houston. Of those, eight were products of Gold Star Studios—the earliest tracks, the ones that first established Chenier as a force in roots-music recording.

TWO MAJOR ARTISTS, both of whom had launched their recording careers earlier at Gold Star, returned during its HSP phase: country singer George Jones and blues master Albert Collins.

When Jones visited the refurbished facility in 1965, it had been eight years since his last session there. For Jones to record again at the relatively humble site of his first hit, after having earned his place by then among the Nashville country music elite, was a notable exception to the norm. But though he was mainly based in Tennessee, he was still working with Pappy Daily, the Houston man who had made him a star. The 1965 Gold Star session occurred after Patterson had handled a live recording project for Jones and Daily at the Houston country music venue Dancetown USA. The tape of that concert was then brought back to the studios, mixed, and delivered to Glad Music, Daily's company.

That arrangement likely set the stage for Jones's return to Gold Star Studios. Two months later, on March 31, Doyle Jones (no relation) engineered a session there featuring George Jones singing duets with Johnny Paycheck (1938–2003), perhaps an experiment based on Daily's recent success with Jones in the duet format. This project was for the Musicor label, which the A&R man Daily partly owned.

Having been Jones's mentor from the start, Daily had brought him to Musicor in 1964 too. As cowriters Mike Callahan, Dave Edwards, and Patrice Eyries point out in "The Musicor Records Story," Daily and Jones almost immediately scored several hits that revived the label—in part by producing a series of duets, released throughout 1965, between Jones and Gene Pitney, Musicor's only previous star.

Given those results, it seems likely that Daily was angling for another hit duet by pairing Jones with Paycheck. However, no recordings from that session seem to have been issued. A few years later Paycheck, as lead singer of the group billed as the Jones Boys, would perform again in that role with Jones on a 1970 hit single. Moreover, in 1980 Paycheck and Jones would join forces to make an all-duets album for Epic Records. Thus, that 1965 Jones-Paycheck session at Gold Star Studios may not have yielded much itself, but it perhaps laid the foundation for subsequent collaborations between the two singers.

Like Jones, who had cut his initial hit there in 1955, the blues star Collins revisited Gold Star Studios during the HSP era. Though much had changed, it was the same site where in 1958 the rookie guitarist had recorded his original version of "The Freeze."

Collins returned in April 1965 for at least two sessions, both engineered by Doyle Jones. The producer was Bill Hall (1929–1983), Clement's partner in the previously mentioned Beaumont studio. Hall too was familiar with Gold Star, having been there when the Big Bopper (whom he had managed and coproduced) cut "Chantilly Lace," as well as when Johnny Preston recorded "Running Bear," among various other occasions.

Hall had also elsewhere previously recorded several singles by Collins, most of which were issued on one of his Beaumont-based labels, Hall-Way or Hall Records, or on TCF. As Andrew Brown explains in e-mail correspondence with the authors, the TCF company was a subsidiary owned by the famous movie studio Twentieth Century Fox (hence, the initials), which evidently had made a licensing arrangement with Hall to supply masters. The resulting discs were released either on TCF or under a combined TCF-Hall logo.

Hall had produced Collins's 1962 hit, "Frosty," issued on his namesake imprint (#1920). That number, a hot-selling single, reappeared in 1965 on the first Collins LP, a compilation of Hall-produced recordings. The album was originally titled *The Cool Sounds of Albert Collins,* issued by TCF-Hall (#8002). In 1969, after Bob Hite (of the California-based band Canned Heat) had introduced Collins to white audiences, those album tracks were licensed to Blue Thumb Records and reissued on LP as *Truckin' with Albert Collins* (BT-8). In 1991 that album resurfaced on CD, issued by MCA (#10423).

Given that background, we surmise that Hall's purpose in recording Collins at Gold Star in April 1965 may have been to create the additional tracks he needed to fill out that debut album, which was released later that same year. Of the twelve tracks comprising that record (and its subsequent reissues under alternate titles), nine had previously been released on singles for Hall Records or TCF. However, three numbers—"Kool Aide," "Shiver 'n' Shake," and "Icy Blue"—were evidently new recordings, as there is no documentation of their existing before they showed up on *The Cool Sounds of Albert Collins.*

If Hall did produce those three mystery tracks during the April 1965 sessions, then the significance of Gold Star Studios in relation to Collins takes on a new dimension. For not only is it the site where Henry Hayes recorded Collins's first single; it may also be where Hall recorded one-quarter of the tracks featured on his debut album.

IN ADDITION TO THOSE IN THE BLUES, country, and zydeco genres, numerous artists were recording pop or rock during the HSP phase of operations. In this regard, producer Ray Rush was an important client. In 1964 and '65 he self-financed sessions at Gold Star on at least nineteen separate occasions, each documented by a separate invoice issued in his name. Additionally, there are numerous invoices identifying Rush as producer on sessions bankrolled by other clients: Hickory Records, Zenith Productions, and D. W. Martin.

Rush had moved from West Texas to Houston around 1961, seeking to advance his career in the music business. Within a few years he was deeply involved there in recording a variety of regional artists—including the first hit by B. J. Thomas. As for his frequent sessions at Gold Star then, he says, "Bill Quinn was around but wasn't doing any sessions. He was a really nice guy. The engineers I worked with the most were Doyle Jones and Bert Frilot."

Among the artists Rush produced there was a band called the Triumphs. They scored a regional hit for Joed Records with "Garner State Park" backed with "On the Loose" (#117). By the time the group's second and third singles were released (#118, #119), their name had changed to B. J. Thomas and the Triumphs, foreshadowing the pop stardom that lay ahead for the lead singer. Rush recounts the phenomenon:

> "Garner State Park" was a huge local hit for B. J. Thomas. It was recorded on the 5th of April 1965. I remember that the song stayed at number one in Houston for at least a month, if not longer. I also remember that it sold a lot of records locally, and that was why it was picked up and rereleased on Hickory in 1966.

One of the original members of the Triumphs, Don Drachenberg, shares his memories of the band and the session that produced their most-well-known recording:

> We recorded "Garner State Park" at Gold Star. . . . Our engineer was Doyle Jones. B. J. Thomas was in the band from 1959 to 1966. We both sang on "Garner State Park." Tim Griffith was the lead guitarist. Bass was played by Tom Griffith. Fred Carney played keyboards. Drums were played by Teddy Mensick, and we also had two horn players—but all they did on that cut was sing background vocals: Gary Koeppen, trumpet, and Denny Zatyka, sax.

In less than a year Thomas had gone solo and released his debut album. Drachenberg explains:

> B. J. left the band in March of 1966. Huey [Meaux] and Charlie Booth then recorded some sides at Gold Star and some in New York. They took those

and the best cuts from the Pasadena sessions and turned that into B. J.'s first album for Scepter, *Tomorrow Never Comes.*

That album included a remake of the Hank Williams tune "I'm So Lonesome I Could Cry," which unexpectedly soared to number eight on the pop charts, catapulting the young Houston singer into the national spotlight.

One of the musicians who played on Thomas's debut album was Aubrey Tucker—a composer, arranger, trombonist, and music educator who had earlier worked with various jazz luminaries. He had started doing freelance session work at Gold Star Studios in 1964, first for radio commercials as well as for country, rock, and pop producers. Regarding *Tomorrow Never Comes,* Tucker recalls,

> It pretty much launched his career. A lot of people have forgotten about this record. There were a lot of members of the Houston Symphony used on that album. It was a big orchestral recording. The sessions that I was on for this album were done [at Gold Star], not over at Huey's studio in Pasadena.

Within a couple of years, hit songs such as "Hooked on a Feeling," "Raindrops Keep Falling on My Head," and "I Just Can't Help Believing" had made B. J. Thomas a major force in pop music. But Thomas's first modest achievement as a recording artist, the one that powered him toward prominence, came from those early Gold Star sessions.

In the mid-1960s various other bands or individuals, looking to achieve a breakthrough as Thomas had, made recordings there at a frenetic pace. Singer-songwriter Gaylan Latimer came there first in early 1965 to record with the Dawgs, which he fronted under the stage name Gaylan Ladd. Meaux produced the session, yielding the single "Shy" backed with "Won't You Cry for Me" (two Latimer originals) on Pic 1 Records (#119).

In mid-1965 Meaux booked time in Gold Star's Studio A for three days of recording with essentially the same personnel. ACA/Gold Star invoices indicate sessions occurred in April and June, with Jones engineering.

Having used compositions by band member Robert Sharpe as well as by Latimer, the crafty Meaux refashioned the group's persona, billing them as Bob and Gaylan on singles such as "Don't Go in My Room, Girl" on the Ventura label (#722) or others on his Pacemaker imprint. Latimer provides the rationale for that change:

> Bob and Gaylan and our band had a very English mop-top or Mersey-beat look to it. . . . Together with Huey we then worked on a concept and convinced Epic Records that Bobby Sharpe was from Dover, England. And [then we] had a major deal signed with the company. Epic was all set to put a huge

investment into the band when, for some inexplicable reason, Bobby leaked to the Houston news media that he really wasn't from England. That was the kiss of death for the project because the deal hinged on this Texas/English band being able to compete with the Beatles and the English invasion of the American charts.

Meaux had sought to convey an image appealing to fans enthralled by the latest phenomenon in pop music, then at its height. This is an example of a deceptive marketing strategy that Meaux would later similarly employ to rechristen Doug Sahm's band as the Sir Douglas Quintet.

In August 1965 Steve Tyrell produced a session for an artist named Chuck Jackson, which was billed to Stan Greenberg of Scepter-Wand Records from New York City. Meanwhile, in a matter of just a few months (and for singles issued on a variety of labels), Meaux also produced artists such as Warren Storm, T. K. Hulin, the Sir Douglas Quintet, Doty Roy, Barbara Lynn, Joe Barry, Johnny Copeland, Ray Frushay, Johnny Williams, Joey Long, and Ivory Joe Hunter—who collectively represent almost any regional subgenre that might have viably struck pop gold.

But apart from Meaux there were plenty of other producers renting time and expertise from Gold Star Studios during this era. For example, Jimmy Duncan was a Houston songwriter and singer, very much in the mold of Pat Boone, who had founded Cue Records around 1955 and later a label called Cinderella Records. He wrote "My Special Angel," a hit recorded by Bobby Helms for Decca Records in 1957. Duncan also wrote "Echoes of Time," which would be recorded by the Houston psychedelic rock band Lemon Fog in 1967. Later Duncan built his own studio complex, called Soundville, in southwest Houston. When it failed a few years later, Holford purchased it as the new home of ACA Studios.

But Duncan had first recorded at Gold Star Studios as early as 1956, when he cut two Cue sides, and he came back frequently during the HSP days. From July 1964 through July 1965, he and his various production companies staged at least fifty-three Gold Star recording sessions. Andrus had engineered approximately the first third of those, and Jones handled the rest. Archived documents show Duncan booked Gold Star sessions also for the blues artist Clarence "Gatemouth" Brown, the white R&B singer Jesse Langford, the pop vocalist Jimmy Henderson, a duo called Cathy and Joe, as well as for himself and others.

There were other self-produced projects by artists hoping to break through on their own. For instance, in 1965 country singer Mickey Gilley visited the studios at least eight times to record demos or masters, including the songs "I Miss You So" and "Lotta Loving," which were later released on Astro Records

left to right: Huey Meaux, Doyle Jones, and the Dawgs, at Gold Star Studios, 1965
(photo courtesy of Gaylan Latimer, third from right)

(#106). Gilley says, "Doyle Jones engineered those for me over at Gold Star. About six months later we did another session, and the songs that we did were 'If I Didn't Have a Dime' and a B-side. . . . released on Astro [#110] in 1966."

Meanwhile, the Houston-based producer Steve Poncio came to Gold Star Studios at least six times between May 1965 and September 1966 for recording, mixing, and mastering on blues or rock artists such as Don Cherry, Joe Hughes, Jimmy "T-99" Nelson, Piano Slim, Joe Medwick, and C.L. and the Pictures.

Not all of the clients were pop bands, however. In early November 1965, members of the Houston Symphony Orchestra returned to Gold Star Studios to record. This project, produced by Dr. Paul Carlin, featured selected orchestra musicians grouped in a smaller ensemble, conducted by Dick Anthony, performing with a special all-star choir comprising some of the best religious singers from the region. The result was a contemporary gospel album titled *What Manner Love*. It featured the singer Jerry Wayne Bernard with music written by Bill Harvey and others and arrangements by Dick Anthony. Lurie staged, recorded, mixed, and mastered the album over the course of four days. This sort of project underscores again the importance of the Quinn-designed big studio room in the Gold Star legacy.

But regardless of the quality of the facility and the artists it recorded, like any business Gold Star Studios required competent, honest management to succeed in the long run. And the HSP Corporation run was not very long. Though its tenure marked a particularly productive era in terms of numbers and types of sessions, there was trouble ahead. Legal issues resulting in serious charges against Patterson would soon surface, threatening to destroy the whole enterprise forever. Some members of the corporation had seen it coming and got out before the situation deteriorated. Others lingered there through HSP's demise. And a few, like the engineer Jones, simply got themselves fired. He says,

> I recorded a lot of great sessions at that studio: Roy Head, the Sir Douglas Quintet, the Pozo Seco Singers, a bunch of Duke and Peacock Records artists. I worked a lot with Huey P. Meaux, Charlie Booth, and Don Robey's people, like Joe Scott and Wilmer Shakesnider. . . . But it didn't work in the long run. Jack [Clement] and Bill Hall pulled out and went to Nashville.
>
> . . . I got fired because I had differences with Patterson. I thought he was a thief and told him so, and that ended my involvement with the studio. Bill Holford and Bert [Frilot] pulled out just a couple of months after I left. . . .
>
> I quickly got tired of the scams that J. L. Patterson was running and not getting paid for my work.

Yet before this obviously bitter ending, Jones and others had a little more history to make.

13

A House of Rock,
Despite the Muck

THE HSP CORPORATION REMAINED intact for less than a full year, dissolving as key members and unhappy employees gradually pulled out. But during its brief existence, its operations included the making of hundreds of recordings at Gold Star Studios, and some of those are undeniably historic. Despite the ill will generated among insiders by J. L. Patterson's emerging reputation for bad checks, half truths, and scheming opportunism, HSP's strong start and an especially propitious regional music scene fueled an explosion of new business that kept Gold Star Studios functioning. HSP had begun with a large engineering staff, so it took a while for Patterson's antics to deplete the whole roster. In the meantime, groups such as the Sir Douglas Quintet and the 13th Floor Elevators, among others, used the facility to forge fundamental tracks. No matter how much bad management may have sullied the company, a new breed of clientele was clamoring to make records, some of which would become classics.

Jeff Millar's *Houston Post* article from September 1965 provides a view of Gold Star Studios at essentially the halfway point of the HSP era. In recounting the recent national success of locally produced artists (such as Roy Head, whose "Treat Her Right" is cited as having already sold some 300,000 copies), Millar focuses on ACA/Gold Star Studios as Houston's main house of hits, lauding its size and reputation. In particular, Millar quotes the company's vice president/general manager and engineer, Bill Holford, who notes that—along with many sessions for pop music groups, commercials, and high school bands and orchestras—he had recorded six tracks there for the Kingston Trio a few months earlier.

An accompanying photograph depicts Mickey Gilley's band recording in Studio B with Holford at the controls. Millar says the studio has so much work that it operates approximately eighteen hours per day. Ultimately, Holford explains the company's bottom line: "We charge $32 an hour for our recording services. Figure three hours to cut two songs, both sides of a [45 rpm] record. There's a little more time needed for re-mixing and mastering. Each acetate master is $10. The average recording session runs around $110." This description covers the minimum starting point for making a record—a process that would yield a single tape and one acetate master. For the cycle to come to fruition, that master would then have to be pressed to make sufficient copies to send to DJs and retailers, entailing additional expenses. Yet the ACA/Gold Star Studios prices for recording, remixing, and mastering were quite reasonable for the time, suggesting that economical rates may have fueled the prolific level of recording activity.

As previously noted, producer Huey Meaux paid to use the studio frequently through August 1965, when he moved to his own facility for a while. Perhaps his decision to depart was triggered by HSP's plan to monopolize local recording services. Creating his own studio may have been Meaux's defiant assertion of independence, his unwillingness to have his projects controlled by the likes of Patterson. Whatever the case, before leaving, Meaux staged some of the sessions most important to the legacy of Gold Star Studios, featuring a group that he had dubbed the Sir Douglas Quintet.

Meaux's concept in naming that band is well known in Texas music folklore. Given the intense public appetite for mid-1960s English rock groups performing music based on American blues and R&B, Meaux decided that Sahm could be the catalyst for a grand scheme. As Gary Hartman writes in *The History of Texas Music,*

> Hoping to capitalize on the popularity of the British Invasion, Meaux apparently selected the name Sir Douglas Quintet because it sounded "English," and he encouraged Sahm and the others to wear the "mod" clothing and hairstyles of their British counterparts. They may have looked much like the popular British bands of the day (despite the fact that two members of Sahm's group were Mexican American), but the Sir Douglas Quintet's music clearly reflected the band's eclectic Texas-based musical background.

Prior to that group's first session at Gold Star Studios, Sahm had been pestering Meaux to record him for at least a year. However, Meaux was busy producing and promoting hits with artists such as Barbara Lynn or Dale and Grace. But when Beatlemania began to alter the pop cultural landscape, Meaux brainstormed a new tactic. He reportedly called Sahm, told him to grow his hair long, assemble a band, and write a song with a Cajun two-step beat—a sound echoed in the familiar conjunto music of Sahm's hometown, San Antonio.

On January 14, 1965, in Studio A of the Gold Star Studios complex, the Sir Douglas Quintet recorded a track that married Gulf Coast R&B, a Cajun-conjunto backbeat, and elements inspired by "She's a Woman" by the Beatles. The result was "She's About a Mover"—which ranks as the all-time number one recording in Jeff McCord and John Morthland's *Texas Monthly* analysis of the greatest Texas songs. It was originally released on Tribe Records, one of Meaux's labels, backed with "We'll Take Our Last Walk Tonight" (#8308). The record went to number thirteen on the U.S. pop charts and did equally well in the United Kingdom. In so doing it launched not just a band but a sound. Propelled distinctly by Augie Meyers's pumping groove on Farfisa organ (evoking a Tejano accordionist accompanying a *bajo sexto*), that sound fused disparate influences and foreshadowed the substantial musical cross-pollination that Sahm and Meyers would later cultivate with other bands (including the Texas Tornados supergroup they would form in the 1990s with Freddy Fender and Flaco Jimenez).

The session that produced "She's About a Mover" was clearly a break-through moment in Texas music history. Jones, one of the original HSP engineers, recorded it on a three-track machine with Ampex tape. He shares these memories:

> It was a very smooth and organized session with no problems. . . . Huey mastered it right after we finished mixing it, and he worked with Bob Lurie on that. Doug and Augie Meyers were good people to work with. After we recorded it, I never imagined that it would become a hit record or have the cult status that it has to this day. I did notice that it was something totally different. As a matter of fact, it was even different from the English sound that was prevalent in those days.

The Sir Douglas Quintet and Meaux also recorded numerous other songs at Gold Star in 1965. Invoices show they also taped "In Time" and "Wine Wine Wine" on that inaugural session. On February 23, they returned to cut "The Tracker," "Please Just Say So," "We'll Never Tell," "In the Pines," and "Bill Bailey." On April 12, they did "Working Jam," "Bacon Fat," "You Got Me Hurtin'," and "The Rains Came." Then on August 9, they made "It's a Man Down There," "Isabella," and another title that is indecipherable on the invoice. "The Rains Came" (backed with the dance-themed number "Bacon Fat" on the 45 rpm single) went to number thirty-one on the charts in early 1966.

In his book *All Over the Map: True Heroes of Texas Music*, Michael Corcoran devotes a chapter called "The Genre Conqueror" to the legacy of Doug Sahm. Describing him as "fluent in every style of Texas music, from blues and conjunto to Cajun, honky-tonk, and psychedelic rock," Corcoran mourns the 1999

Sir Douglas Quintet, publicity photo, 1965

death of the man who "gave the Austin music scene its soul." He also quotes this astute assessment by Joe Nick Patoski: "When you look back on the true originators, the real pioneers of Texas music, there are four main guys: Bob Wills, Willie Nelson, T-Bone Walker, and Doug Sahm." Like Nelson, who had recorded his first version of "Night Life" there in 1959, the innovative Sahm is thus a big part of the Gold Star Studios story.

ANOTHER IMPORTANT BATCH of Jones-engineered recordings involved a folk-pop group from Corpus Christi called the Pozo Seco Singers—the trio that propelled famous country singer-songwriter Don Williams (b. 1939) into the national spotlight. The Spanish phrase "pozo seco" translates literally as "dry well," yet these singers found success in their recording debut at Gold Star Studios. That effort produced a 1965 hit single that stayed on the *Billboard* pop charts for fifty-four straight weeks and led to a multiple-album deal with Columbia Records.

In addition to Williams, the lineup featured Susan Taylor and Lofton Kline; all members sang and played guitar. Their hit recording of "Time," originally released on Edmark Records, attracted major label interest—and became the title track of their debut album in 1966. Working with producer Paul Butts (himself a folksinger and guitarist), the Pozo Seco Singers recorded "Time" at Gold Star Studios on May 23, 1965. Jones remembers it well:

> That was one of the few records that I was the engineer on that I thought actually had a chance to be a hit. . . . I was real impressed with Paul Butts, and also Don Williams. Don back in those days sounded a lot like Johnny Cash. They were all fine people and excellent singers and musicians. . . . Susan Taylor was the lead vocalist on "Time." . . . I know that we recorded the song "heads up" [live in the studio, with no overdubs].

Founding member Taylor (who is still active today as a folksinger known as Taylor Pie) offers her recollections of the song, the session that made it famous, and the deal with Columbia Records:

> Michael Merchant, who wrote the song, played bass on the session. Mike and I had a folk group when he was a senior at Miller High School. He went off to Penn State, and when he came back home after the first semester, he played me this song that he had written called "Time." I freaked when I first heard it, and I asked him to teach it to me right away. He had written the song around this cool guitar lick. Well, I learned it immediately, and . . . went over and played it to the other guys in Pozo, Lofton Kline and Don Williams. . . .
>
> So we headed over to ACA/Gold Star to record two sides for Edmark Records. . . . Don's song, "Hello Blues and Down the Road I Go," was to be the A-side of the record, and "Time" was to be the B-side. . . . I think the whole thing took three hours. We came out of there with two songs mastered and ready to go and press records. . . .
>
> Edmark Records was out of Port Aransas, and Paul Butts had something to do with them. When we formed Pozo Seco, Paul became our manager and helped organize the deal with Edmark. He backed out of the picture when

Albert Grossman [1926–1986, most famous for managing Bob Dylan] came and signed the group. We put the record out and started getting airplay all around Texas. But the DJs flipped the record over and started playing "Time" instead. . . . The song became a regional hit. It started in Corpus . . . made it over to San Antonio, then Houston and Dallas, and it charted everywhere that was playing it.

Following the reception the single was getting in Texas, the group got the kind of lucky break that every would-be star dreams of. Taylor continues,

A guy named Joe Mansfield, who worked PR for Columbia in San Antonio, heard it. He got a copy of it and took off for New York to a meeting of Columbia's national PR guys and played it to everybody. They all liked it, and when they found out that it was busting out all over Texas, they contacted us.

We signed and not much happened. . . . All of a sudden in February of 1966 they contacted us and told us that in six days we were going on a seven-day tour of the West Coast because the song had hit number one in Los Angeles. . . . Right after L.A. it went to number one in Chicago, and then as it fell there, it went number one in Boston. You have to get all the numbers in at the same time to crack the Top Ten in *Billboard.* We never got any higher than number forty-seven in *Billboard,* but the song stayed in the Top 100 for something like fifty-four weeks. The song had an amazing ride.

The Pozo Seco Singers immediately capitalized on their hit single with two albums on Columbia, *Time* and *I Can Make It with You,* released in 1966 and '67, respectively. The title track of the latter also charted in the Top 40. When Kline left the group, Williams and Taylor retained the Pozo name on a follow-up LP in 1968 called *Shades of Time.* In the 1970s Williams would reemerge as an extremely popular solo artist and Nashville-based songwriter. Yet as with many others before him, his professional recording career first took off in a Houston studio called Gold Star.

GIVEN THE TYPES OF RECORDINGS commonly produced there, the folk-pop sound represented by the Pozo Seco Singers was somewhat of an anomaly for Gold Star. But in September 1965 singer Kenny Rogers (b. 1937), a native Houstonian, booked two days to record and mix some tracks that fit that mold, albeit with a slightly rockier edge. Listening to the Bob Lurie–engineered safety-copy tape from our vaults, we believe that these recordings may represent Rogers's early concept for his vocal group the First Edition, in this case with backing on drums, upright bass, and guitar.

Meanwhile, straight-ahead rock and pop were more commonly recorded at Gold Star during this era. For every Sir Douglas Quintet, of course, there

Pozo Seco Singers, publicity photo, 1965

were scores of Texas bands trying in vain to replicate its production of a big hit. Rock Romano was part of that bustling rock scene and recorded twice in Studio B with the group called Six Pents. "One [session] was with Doyle Jones, and the other with Bert Frilot," he recalls. "We recorded a song called 'Good to You,' which was produced by Gordon Bynum, who would go on to produce the 13th Floor Elevators."

That seminal psychedelic rock band looms large in Gold Star Studios lore. The Elevators' most significant work there would occur in 1968 after their record company purchased the studio, but in June 1966 the original members first used the facility to produce some demos. Personnel on that session included Roky Erickson on vocals and guitar, Stacy Sutherland on guitar, John Ike Walton on drums, Ronnie Leatherman on bass, and Tommy Hall on amplified jug. Based on the limited documentation, not much else can be determined beyond the song titles they recorded: "You Gotta Take That Girl," "Before You Accuse Me," "You Can't Hurt Me Anymore," and "Splash 1." As fans will note, that last song resurfaces on the debut album, *The Psychedelic Sounds of the 13th Floor Elevators,* which would be recorded in Dallas in October 1966, a few months later. Thus, this Gold Star session marks one of the Elevators' first studio experiences.

But more typical of the mid-1960s rock roster at Gold Star was the pop-flavored style highlighted by small local labels such as Jamel Records. Owned by Charlie Jamel, it booked Gold Star sessions between April 1965 and January 1966 for a short-lived group led by Buddy Wright—first referred to as the Wright 5 and later as the Wright Sounds. They cut five songs there, engineered by Bert Frilot and Lurie, with mastering by Louis Stevenson. Band member David Russell recalls the process:

> We started [recording] at one a.m. following our gig that night, and the rest of the horn players, a group of about five or six players, arrived at two-thirty after their gigs. . . . I think it was about five a.m. when we laid down the vocals to those songs. We did all that recording in the smaller studio with the gold star in the floor.
>
> I came back the following Saturday to record the instrumental lead. . . . The Hammond B3 organ resided in that bigger studio, and that's where we added the parts. The song was then mixed back in the smaller studio, and then discs were made to take to the radio stations.

In March 1966 Neal Ford and the Fanatics recorded the song "All I Have to Do Is Dream" at Gold Star with Frilot at the controls. The song would become a regional hit and top the charts in Houston.

In 1966 Billy Gibbons, who would later achieve fame and fortune fronting ZZ Top, made two appearances at Gold Star with producer Steve Ames. Both times Gibbons recorded a song called "99th Floor," first with his group the Coachmen. That session, according to invoices, occurred on April 22, 1966, and was engineered by Lurie. Gibbons paid for it himself, in cash. A month later Gibbons had reorganized his band, named it the Moving Sidewalks, and returned to Gold Star to record "99th Floor" again, this time with Frilot at the controls. According to Ames, neither of these versions got it right, so the band recorded it yet again—but elsewhere.

Despite the fact that the vinyl version of "99th Floor" (which became number one in Houston) was not recorded at Gold Star, a master tape of the earliest attempt lives in the tape vault at SugarHill Studios. The Coachmen version marks Ames's first effort as a producer and possibly the earliest studio recording by Gibbons—making both of these important figures part of Gold Star history too.

By the mid-1960s the clientele came from increasingly varied backgrounds. For instance, on June 6, 1965, a group called the Dinos recorded three songs in a Gold Star session engineered by Holford. Two of those songs—"This Is My Story" and "Baby Come On In"—were released as a single on Van Records (#03265). The Dinos were a Hispanic bilingual pop and doo-wop vocal group led by Abraham Quintanilla. He later would father the ill-fated Tejano-pop queen known as Selena (1971–1995), who started her career with a revived version of the family band known as Selena y Los Dinos. Moreover, in 1983 she would record her earliest demos, performing with a family band, at the same (but renamed) site.

True to its founder's original vision, Gold Star Studios has always recorded country music too—even during the rise of pop-rock. For instance, drummer and singer Johnny Bush revisited the site in early 1966 to record gospel music with George Jones. He recounts how that came to pass:

> I was living in Nashville. Willie [Nelson] and I were off the road for a couple of weeks, and George Jones's band called and asked if I could fill in. Willie said, "Go ahead and do it. We're off for a while." So I joined up with them in Houston, and our first gig was a recording session right back at Gold Star.

Meanwhile, in addition to its various music projects, during the HSP era Gold Star Studios significantly elevated its local profile in relation to electronic advertising. In fact, some of the most ubiquitous clients during this time were advertising agencies—more than double the number the studio was handling before Patterson had persuaded Holford and Stevenson to consolidate with him in a new corporation. A review of the invoices shows it recorded ads for companies as diverse as Humble Oil (the predecessor of Exxon), Houston Natural Gas, Dentler Potato Chips, O.J.'s Beauty Lotion, and Star Furniture. As trombonist Aubrey Tucker reminds us, such work often meant easy gigs for session musicians. "I did a major jingle here that Leo O'Neil arranged for a big ad company, and the client was Shell Oil Company," he says. "I remember that well because of the residual checks that I received for a number of years—because the ad ran for a long time."

GIVEN THE INCREASED REVENUES from advertising as well as the large numbers of regular sessions it was handling, one might assume that Gold Star Studios was flush with cash by 1966. It may have been, but somehow Patterson sometimes failed to pay his engineers or fulfill other obligations.

Where did the money go? After repeatedly raising that question themselves, after waiting for delayed compensation only to see the promised settlement again be postponed with a new set of excuses, the key staff members departed. By March of 1966 Holford was gone. Likewise, ace engineer Jones got out, soon followed by Frilot. They all resurrected their own businesses, leaving Patterson with the Gold Star property lease and a stack of unpaid bills.

On a website devoted to the memory of Frilot (1939–1999), writer Larry Benicewicz quotes the famous Louisiana record producer Eddie Shuler's opinion of the erstwhile HSP employee: "He was as honest as the day is long—someone you could always trust. And that's saying a lot in this nasty racket I'm in." Having come over with Holford in the ACA/Gold Star merger, during his brief time at the Gold Star site Frilot conducted sessions for Roy Head, B. J. Thomas, Kenny Rogers, and various others. However, as Benicewicz notes, because Patterson "had a penchant for writing bad checks," after eight months the likable engineer, "having had his share of being stiffed by his new boss, abruptly vacated the premises."

The mucky payroll situation over which Patterson presided ultimately killed the HSP Corporation, but it did not immediately end Patterson's tenure at Gold Star Studios, which he still controlled as the lessee to the property. And for a while, even after Quinn sold the facility to new ownership, Patterson was still around.

Meanwhile, this change in the executive administration and staff was reflected by a physical alteration within the structure. Just after Holford pulled out, the control room for the big studio was moved downstairs—probably in March or April of 1966.

Stevenson and Patterson had built the new downstairs control room about fifteen months after Studio B was created. It was a virtual duplicate of the original control room upstairs, although a bit smaller, and located directly below it. It was fourteen feet long by thirteen feet wide, with a ten-foot-high ceiling. The floor was raised about eighteen inches to allow cable-trough access and provide a good view of the big studio. Like the other control room, it had acoustic wall tiles, a dropped ceiling with acoustic tiles, and a linoleum floor. Meanwhile, the abandoned space upstairs was converted into an office. At some point after that, Stevenson departed too.

Although Lurie would remain a bit longer, the end of HSP meant that Patterson had to hire new personnel to keep operating. Somehow he would pull it off, and Gold Star Studios continued to function—despite the expanding ranks of disillusioned former associates—as one of the most active and significant recording sites in Texas.

14

The HSP Aftermath and
a New Direction

FOLLOWING THE DISSOLUTION of the HSP Corporation in 1966, Gold Star Studios nonetheless remained as one of the primary recording companies in Houston, a status signified in part by its impressively large advertisement in the local Yellow Pages directory. In November 1966 that big ad caught the attention of new Houston resident Jim Duff, who would soon find himself employed there—and unwittingly embroiled in controversies generated by J. L. Patterson's increasingly aberrant management practices. On the other hand, Duff would also get to record some classic tracks during the next phase of Gold Star operations.

Duff, who had some previous background in recording, had arrived from Florida in August, first finding work in the furniture business. A few months later, having seen the Gold Star ad in the Yellow Pages, he called to inquire about employment possibilities and, to his surprise, was offered an immediate interview for a part-time engineer position. When Duff visited the facility, his audition took place in a four-track room with an enormous twenty-channel tube console designed by Louis Stevenson. Duff had never seen a soundboard that large, but he got the job.

Following the interview he was told that many hit records had been made at Gold Star Studios and that the complex was now owned by a thirty-seven-year-old Texas "millionaire" named J. L. Patterson. Whether or not Patterson rightfully possessed a million dollars, he did not actually own the facility; he was leasing it from the increasingly reclusive Bill Quinn, who still resided next door. That first day Duff also met the two full-time engineers, Gaylan Shelby and Bob Lurie, as well as the new studio manager, Don Travis (aka "Cadet Don," a persona he had adopted as a local children's television show host).

Within two days of Duff's start there, Shelby quit in a dispute with Patterson over nonpayment of engineer fees. That schism created a full-time opening for the new employee, but it also made him uneasy. He soon discovered too that Lurie was frustrated with Patterson, but Duff initially ascribed that to the fact that Lurie's classical music background may not have meshed well with the staples of Gold Star recording: country, blues, rock, and pop.

Nevertheless, remaining for the most part uninformed about any behind-the-scenes troubles, Duff plunged into his work. "One of my first sessions at Gold Star was an album for Utah Carl in late 1966, and I think he paid for it himself," Duff says. "I also remember doing albums for Chris Strachwitz of Arhoolie Records on Clifton Chenier, and on Gatemouth Brown for manager/producer Roy Ames." Soon, however, he found himself pulled into an entirely different kind of project.

Near the start of 1967, the Houston Symphony Orchestra initiated plans for Gold Star to make a remote recording. Guest conductor Andre Previn (who later returned in a full-time role) wanted to record a rehearsal so that he and the composer could evaluate the progress of a major new work. That piece was *Elegy for Strings* by John Williams, who later scored grand soundtracks for films such as *Star Wars*. As the assistant to Lurie, Duff gamely loaded up studio gear, transported it to the spacious Jones Hall in downtown Houston, and installed it for the session.

The recording was successful, and Previn and Williams soon visited Gold Star Studios to mix and edit—taking all the tapes, including outtakes, with them when finished. In a few days they scheduled a second remote recording session. However, during the brief interval between those two sessions, Duff had witnessed another angry resignation when Lurie suddenly packed his gear and left for New York—which he had incessantly been threatening to do. The last holdover from the HSP era, and like all the engineers before him, Lurie was reportedly dissatisfied with Patterson's handling of remuneration. In fairness, we note Duff's report that Lurie had also frequently expressed his disdain for living in Texas.

Having absorbed some of Lurie's recording techniques, Duff promptly found himself promoted to chief engineer and working solo with the orchestra. He says he scrutinized Previn's every gesture, bringing up the relevant microphones as the maestro pointed to sections during the trial takes. Somehow Duff pulled it off, as well as the subsequent mixing and editing session with Previn and Williams. Though he could not read a note of the music on pages that Previn often pointed to in their discussions, he had the ears and technical savvy to engineer a successful on-location symphony recording.

By the way, in 1965 the Houston Symphony Orchestra (then directed by Ezra Rachlin) had previously visited Gold Star Studios to record *Texas Suite,* a piece by composer David Guion, commissioned by Ima Hogg. Lurie had engineered that project in the big studio room. But Duff's more recent recordings represented something altogether new for Gold Star—that is, going out to record large orchestras in live performance at public venues. Thus, Duff inadvertently helped start a tradition that has continued to date (with the Houston Symphony Orchestra, Houston Grand Opera, Shepherd School Symphony of Rice University, Orchestra X, Symphony of Southeast Texas in Beaumont, International Festival-Institute at Round Top, and others).

But Duff, like each of his predecessors, soon realized that his pay was falling into arrears. As the sole remaining engineer, he decided to confront the alleged millionaire owner, whom he had yet to meet. However, the smooth-talking Patterson convinced Duff that his fears were groundless and all debts would soon be covered. He even persuaded Duff to accept the title of general manager. As Duff explains, "Cadet Don was real frustrated trying to manage a studio with the engineers all preparing to leave. That's what I found when I first got here. He really didn't know how to go about managing a studio, and I eventually took over from him."

Meanwhile, the new administrator first hired another engineer, Dennis Trocmet. "He was a real intelligent guy," Duff says. "All the younger kids that came in to record really liked him, especially because he was a young guy—couldn't have been more than twenty-four or twenty-five years old." Before long, however, Trocmet was killed in a motorcycle accident. "I'd say that he worked at the studio for about a year, from early 1967 into early 1968," Duff adds.

Duff had independently begun investigating the music scene in the Houston, Beaumont, and Port Arthur areas—hoping to conceive a new plan for promoting Gold Star. Impressed by the large number of successful music artists based in the region, he wondered why the major trade publications had seldom taken note of this hotbed of recording activity. In an attempt to rectify that situation, Duff decided to contact other studio companies and develop a strategy for collectively attracting more attention from the national media.

Ignorant of recent Gold Star Studios history, Duff first called on Bill Holford of ACA Studios, Doyle Jones of Jones Recording, and Walt Andrus of Andrus Studios—whom he perceived to be Gold Star's three main competitors in Houston. Of course, Duff had no idea that these established engineers had had any previous affiliation with Gold Star, Patterson, or each other. Thus, when he naïvely introduced himself to them by referencing his employer, his polite queries were abruptly dismissed. Baffled by what he took to be rude, close-minded behavior, Duff turned his attention to upgrading the studio and rebuilding its business—which had obviously suffered from the HSP fiasco and the defection of clients to competitors.

Duff had learned that Jones and Andrus were moving from four-track to eight-track recording while Gold Star lagged behind. Unable to convince Patterson to invest immediately in new technology, Duff's counterstrategy was to mail an attractive brochure to former customers announcing changes in management and policy, and a new economical custom-record deal. His initiative helped. "After I put out that brochure about the studio, we started getting pretty busy," Duff recalls. "Then when Gabe Tucker [a Pappy Daily associate] found out that I was running the studio over here, he started coming back to Gold Star. After that a bunch of his people also came over to record with me."

During Duff's tenure only the smaller studio room was in full operation. The big studio room was used mainly for storage—and lacked equipment, Duff reports. By that time, some gear may have already been repossessed from Patterson, or some may have belonged to Holford, who rightfully would have taken it with him. Duff says,

> J.L. was leasing gear from three different leasing companies—and was constantly writing hot checks to all of them. I remember a day when all three leasing companies turned up to repo the equipment. He also sold his accounts receivables to three different companies. One day a guy showed up with two bounced checks and a truck to pick up the equipment. We called up over at Vandalarm [another Patterson company], and he came running over and took the guy out to lunch at Benihana's, took the two cold checks back, and wrote a new hot check to cover the first two and another payment. I said to him after the guy left, "J.L., you can't write him that check. We don't have enough in the studio account to cover that much." He mumbled quietly, "Oh, don't worry about it." That was always his answer.

Bewildered, Duff nonetheless worked on in the one available studio, which despite some older technology remained well stocked for making records. The control room featured the Stevenson-designed mixer, which comprised four Ampex M35 mixers slaved together with pan pots and high- and low-pass filters. The multitrack deck was an Ampex 350 four-track machine. The mix decks were an Ampex 350 mono recorder and an Ampex 351 stereo machine. There were also some Pulteq tube equalizers and Fairchild tube compressors. Microphones included Neumann U-67s, Neumann U-47s, an AKG C-12, and RCA DX-77s and 74 Juniors.

With this gear Duff threw himself into recording music, leaving business affairs to Patterson and hoping for the best. Given some of the exciting projects he would soon engineer—such as an album featuring Lightnin' Hopkins jamming with members of the 13th Floor Elevators—Duff's enthusiasm for the work helped to counterbalance his other concerns, at least for a while.

DUFF'S GOLD STAR EXPERIENCE concentrated mainly on recording country music, blues, and especially the explosion of late-Sixties garage bands experimenting with new directions in rock.

As for his work with country singers, Duff had first cut tracks with Utah Carl, the hillbilly-singer persona of Carl Beach, who was from Galveston. Duff also recorded one of the earliest sessions by Texas-born singer Gene Watson (b. 1943), who Duff notes "would eventually go on to have a pretty big career in the country music world." Additionally he recorded two tracks by Richie Moreland, as well as more sessions with Mary McCoy, including a duet with Jimmy Copland on a song he had cowritten with Sonny Hall, "Somewhere There's Someone." It and "Kiss and Make Up" were issued together as a single on Tonka Records. McCoy also cut another Hall composition, "Ring on My Finger," for Tonka Records. Working with McCoy introduced Duff to some of the key supporting players in the local country scene at the time, including Frenchie Burke, Herb Remington, and Clyde Brewer—as well as to Hall himself.

Duff did not actually record, but helped shape Hall's production of, the album *Portraits of Floyd Tillman*. As Duff explains, "They cut the album at Ray Doggett's studio, but Sonny was not satisfied with the final mix, so he brought it to me to enhance it a little, cut the master acetate, and to get the albums pressed."

Gold Star Studios would also remain a fertile site for blues recording throughout the 1960s. In the 1971 book *Nothing but the Blues*, edited by Mike Leadbitter, for instance, Bruce Bastin writes about doing research in Houston from May to July 1966. He recounts meeting Clifton Chenier, Elmore Nixon, and Lightnin' Hopkins—and being invited to a recording session:

> I called Elmore the next day to be told he was off to the Gold Star studios to record with Lightnin'. Lightnin' then came to the phone and suggested that I come on down. The session was held to make a promotional tape for a young Negro singer names Jimmy Ray Williams. . . . Lightnin' was on guitar. Also accompanying was Elmore on piano and his cousin Robert "Red" Ingram on drums. . . . Elmore said they'd (he and Lightnin') recorded about two weeks ago. Lightnin' later said that he is contracted to go to Gold Star studios, the tapes are then mailed to the contacts and he gets paid by post; a rather hygienic way of recording, which may account for the mass of Prestige [Records] material [issued on LPs]. . . . Bill Quinn, he stated, still owned the Gold Star studios, lived next door to it, but nowadays leased it out.

This report from a European blues researcher provides a fairly objective snapshot of the close relationships that artists such as Hopkins and Nixon maintained with Gold Star Studios—where both of them had recorded often over the years. Though it slightly pre-dates Duff's arrival on the scene, it suggests the kind of blues milieu in which he would soon be immersed.

Another major blues artist who returned for one last session at Gold Star Studios was former Duke star Junior Parker. Having broken with Robey in 1966, Parker signed with Mercury Records. On June 13, 1967, during Duff's tenure, Mercury funded a mixing and editing session for Parker's "I Can't Put My Finger on It" (Mercury 72699), which peaked at number forty-eight on the *Billboard* R&B charts in late August.

But the blues player Johnny Winter (b. 1944) was one of Duff's most frequent clients. Duff recalls that on many occasions (which generally went undocumented in liner notes) Winter played guitar as a supporting musician on blues or R&B sessions at the studio. However, Winter also recorded at Gold Star Studios as a featured artist.

The album *Birds Can't Row Boats*, released on LP in 1988 on Relix Records (#2034), contained a number of tracks recorded at different studios in Houston and Beaumont between 1965 and 1968. Two cuts came from Gold Star, both engineered by Duff. One of those, "Take My Choice," included Texas blues singer Calvin "Loudmouth" Johnson. The other, "Tramp," recorded when Winter served briefly as leader of the Traits in 1967, was previously released on 45 rpm disc by Universal Records. However, the session pairing Winter and Johnson set the stage for another Gold Star project.

In mid-1967, Roy Ames of Home Cooking Records produced an album featuring Winter and Johnson, also engineered by Duff. Ames writes in the liner notes,

> In 1967 Johnny Winter told me he'd love to record an album with a genuine down-home bluesman. Albums were less popular than they are now; usually we cut only four or five songs at a session and would release the best two on a 45. One of my previous records featured a real down-home bluesman, Calvin "Loudmouth" Johnson, growling "I got a lien on your body, I got a mortgage on your soul" over a slow grinding beat that had brought the record some success. Johnny listened to the 45 and halfway through lifted up the needle to exclaim, "That's it. Let's do it." The tracks for this album were recorded on May 17, 1967. We used Calvin's band with Johnny on lead guitar. Loudmouth couldn't help but be impressed with Johnny, blurting out at various times while the recordings were in progress his enthusiasm for Johnny's playing. After the session Loudmouth told me, "I never heard a white boy could play the guitar like that!"

Originally recorded for Home Cooking Records, the album *Blues to the Bone* has since been reissued on CD on various labels, including Collectables

(#0675) and Relix Records (#2054), and most recently under the title *Raw to the Bone* on Thunder and Sky Ranch Records (#724384008727).

On projects such as these, Duff was introduced to recording Texas blues at a time when it was reaching across the generation gap and the racial divide to appeal to new fans. He would find other such opportunities in the near future, but most of his sessions involved recording groups of young white men who, inspired by the late-1960s cultural revolution, were redefining the possibilities of rock.

EVEN BEFORE THE PSYCHEDELIC ROCK record label International Artists bought Gold Star Studios in 1968, lots of Texas garage bands were recording there, and many of those were embracing a hazy ethos of surrealism, experimentalism, and altered states of consciousness as the twisting path to new musical forms.

One of the most sought-after psychedelic rock singles in Houston music history, for instance, is a song called "Wake Me Up Girl" by the Continental Five. Though never a big seller in initial release, copies command large dollars at record auctions. Little is known about the band except that they were from the LaMarque/Texas City area (southeast of Houston) and recorded at Gold Star Studios in the summer of 1967, with Duff engineering. "Wake Me Up Girl" was written by Karl Horn, whose name appears on a Gold Star invoice as the person who paid for the recording, mixing, and pressing of one hundred 45 rpm records (issued on the band's eponymous label). A second pressing came later, producing more copies for a label called Radel. To date, only two of the first batch of discs—pressed on the purple Continental label—have surfaced. The original four-track recording resides in the tape vault at SugarHill Studios.

A better-known band of this ilk that recorded at Gold Star was the original Bad Seeds (not to be confused with the postpunk group of the same name formed by Australian Nick Cave in the 1980s). As Bruce Eder and Richie Unterberger assert in *All Music Guide,* "The Bad Seeds were the first rock group of note to come out of Corpus Christi, Texas, itself a hotbed of garage-rock activity during the middle/late 1960s." The Bad Seeds comprised Rod Prince (guitar), Mike Taylor (guitar and vocals), Henry Edgington (bass), and Bobby Donaho (drums). The band was signed to J-Beck Productions, an important label for late-Sixties Texas rock owned by Jack Salyers and Carl Becker.

Having first recorded in Corpus Christi, in early 1966 the Bad Seeds came to Houston for a four-and-a-half-hour session engineered by Lurie. It yielded one of their most acclaimed releases, "All Night Long" backed with "Sick and Tired" for J-Beck (#1004). When the group broke up in late 1966, Prince later joined the rising psychedelic ensemble called Bubble Puppy, which too would record at Gold Star. But as Eder and Unterberger point out about the Bad Seeds,

> They stayed together long enough to record three singles during 1966, of which two, "A Taste of the Same"/"I'm a King Bee" and "All Night Long"/"Sick and Tired," are unabashed classics of blues-based garage-punk, three of them originals by Taylor (who wrote most of their originals) or Prince. . . . The band's sound was the raunchy Rolling Stones–influenced garage-punk typical of Texas rock groups in the mid-'60s.

Becker produced the Bad Seeds. "My earliest memories of Gold Star Studios would have to be in late 1966. Those first sessions would have been the Bad Seeds and Tony Joe White," he says. In addition to the Bad Seeds tracks, Becker recalls cutting at least four other songs, featuring the Louisiana-born swamp-rock singer White (b. 1943, best known for his 1969 hit "Polk Salad Annie"). Becker adds, "the backup band on those singles was the Bad Seeds." But because they "weren't the greatest singers," Becker says he and Duff "buried their parts in reverb from those live chambers in the hallway."

Original Bad Seeds member Taylor (who incidentally is the brother of Pozo Seco's Susan Taylor) describes the studio environment at the time:

> Back in the Gold Star days I remember the control room as being very stark: linoleum floors, white sheetrock walls, white acoustic ceiling tiles, speakers hanging from the ceiling, machines on the side wall, the small board with the huge black knobs, and a couple of chairs. There was no furniture to speak of and not much else to break up the starkness of the area. I think we were recording on four tracks. . . . They were mixing down to mono and stereo. Then over next to an unused control room was a cutting lathe, and Duff went over there to prepare an acetate copy of the finished tape master.

Though short-lived, the Bad Seeds made music highly favored among certain aficionados of primal rock. Their studio recordings have been reissued on various compilation CDs, including one called *Texas Battle of the Bands* (Collectables, 1995). Of the twelve tracks on that disc, half feature the Bad Seeds and half present Zakary Thaks, another Corpus Christi group that mined a similar vein. But Zakary Thaks, despite its also brief existence, would be a seminal ancestor of the Texas garage-punk subculture.

Consider that critic Richie Unterberger (in his *All Music Guide* profile) refers to Zakary Thaks as "one of the best garage bands of the '60s, and one of the best teenage rock groups of all time." Bruce Eder (in his review of the

The Bad Seeds, publicity photo, 1966

aforementioned CD) calls Zakary Thaks "an undeservedly overlooked group, at least as worthy of respect for their music as the Thirteenth Floor Elevators." Given the globally established cultlike following that still deifies the Elevators four decades after their demise, that is high praise indeed. So who was Zakary Thaks?

The original lineup featured Chris Gerniottis on vocals (fifteen years old on the first recordings), John Lopez on lead guitar, Pete Stinson on rhythm guitar, Stan Moore on drums, and Rex Gregory on bass. Gregory says,

We took our musical cues from the more hard-rocking bands from England—like the Kinks, Rolling Stones, Pretty Things, and the Yardbirds.

. . . Our first single, released in 1966—"Bad Girl," with the cover of a Kinks song, "I Need You," on the B-side—was recorded in a small one-track studio in McAllen, Texas. Both sides of that record got tremendous airplay, and national distribution was picked up by Mercury Records.

Our second single on J-Beck Records, "Face to Face" and "Weekday Blues," was done at Gold Star. . . . "Face to Face" was number one in Corpus Christi for about a month, and it went to number one in San Antonio and Austin for a couple of weeks. It also went high up the charts in Houston. . . . We recorded a couple of more songs on that session also, and one of them was "Won't Come Back."

As with the Bad Seeds, the band's Gold Star sessions were produced by Becker and engineered by Duff. In certain Texas cities in 1967 "Face to Face" shared Top Five ranking with songs by the Rolling Stones, the Beatles, and other heavyweights.

"The Zakary Thaks were my hottest act," says Becker. "We were way ahead of our time with that band. We were using controlled feedback on that record." Unterberger also notes the power of that sound, particularly how "the group added a thick dollop of Texas raunch to their fuzzy, distorted guitars and hell-bent energy." But he adds, "Most importantly, they were first-rate songwriters."

As for that strange band name, according to Beverly Paterson, writing in the liner notes to a CD compilation of Zakary Thaks recordings, the choice was motivated by its connotation of British exotica. She quotes Gerniottis as saying, "Somebody saw it somewhere in a magazine and it sounded different. And it also sounded English, which was perfect since we were all heavily into the whole British Invasion thing."

Later, Zakary Thaks also issued recordings on the Cee-Bee label and the band's own imprint, Thak Records. Their success even attracted the entrepreneurial attention of Duke-Peacock boss Don Robey and music promoter Huey Meaux, who lured the group back to Gold Star Studios to cut more tracks for possible release on Robey's Back Beat label. Gregory recalls one such case:

I remember one session when [Meaux] brought us to Houston. . . . Bobby "Blue" Bland was here also. He was staying at the [same] hotel with his little entourage and was also recording at Gold Star. . . .

The session that we did was produced by Andre Williams for Don Robey, who was also working in the studio with Bobby Bland. . . . One of

Zakary Thaks, 1966

the engineers was Jim Duff and also a guy named Fred Carroll, later on. . . .
Apparently none of the songs that we recorded for Back Beat were ever released, and there were at least three or four finished songs.

Though the band broke up and re-formed several times between 1968 and
1972, the prime phase for Zakary Thaks was 1966 to 1968—a period that covers the evolution from its garage-punk roots into experimental psychedelia.
After the first breakup Gerniottis also recorded in Houston with the similarly inclined group Liberty Bell, and some of those tracks were overdubbed
and mastered at Gold Star Studios too. "Look for Tomorrow" ended up as an
A-side on a Back Beat single.

Zakary Thaks was at Gold Star both before and after a new partnership
would take over studio operations. The band roster was fluctuating too. Thus,
we find a June 1968 International Artists invoice made out to Stan Moore for
a lengthy recording and mixing session for Zakary Thaks, engineered by Fred
Carroll. Featuring only Lopez, Gregory, and Moore in the power-trio format,

that date produced several songs. Among these are some of the most vividly psychedelic Thaks tracks, including "Green Crystal Ties" and "My Door."

Gold Star Studios served as the recording base for various other notable rock bands in the 1960s, including Leo and the Prophets, the Minutemen, and Yesterday's Obsession. Duff recorded Yesterday's Obsession for the Pacemaker Records single "Complicated Mind" and "The Phycle" (#262). Not much is known about the band, but its music intrigues. As Brett Koshkin describes it in his *Houston Press* blog: "A heavy-handed organ chugging along with soft vocals and some really interesting swirling guitars, 'The Phycle' is a true psychedelic work of audible art from Houston. Released in 1966, this single 45 stands as the solitary release by yet another one of Huey P. Meaux's mystery groups."

Meanwhile, an independent rock label named Orbit Records staged numerous sessions at Gold Star, all engineered by Duff, between mid-1967 and early 1968. Among the results are the Rebellers doing "The New Generation" and "Common People" (#1114) and the Nomads doing "Three O'clock Merriam Webster Time" and "Situations" (#1121). The Nomads, featuring singer Brian Collins, were also produced by Duff.

BY EARLY 1968 THE RETIRED GOLD STAR STUDIOS owner Quinn was looking to divest himself of his holdings. For the first time since he had hung a microphone in the downstairs room of his house, somebody else would own the recording site that he had founded. Quinn's age was surely a factor in his decision, but we suspect that dealing with Patterson was growing as tiresome for him as it was for Duff and others. Summing up his view of Patterson, Duff points to certain behaviors that speak for themselves:

> I remember that during the negotiations to sell the studio to International Artists, J.L. was constantly carrying things out of the building, saying that these things were personal possessions and not part of the sale. One day I was sitting in the control room with Bill Dillard [the buyer], and J.L. came in to disconnect a piece of gear, and Dillard said, "If you so much as take one more wire out of here, the deal is off, and I mean now, immediately." He turned to me and said, "Don't let him take one more thing out of this building."
>
> So Dillard goes out, gets a huge new lock, and puts it on the door. Quinn comes over and sees the new lock and says, "If you are putting a lock on the door, I'm going to put a new lock on there also." J.L. then puts one of his locks on the door. So the damn front door had three locks on it, and they all had to give me keys so I could get in the door.

It was a surrealistically distrustful time for the parties involved in the pending transaction. Duff adds, however, that "J.L. had no problems getting through the three locks and could get in within a minute anytime he wanted to. He would get anything he wanted."

Despite the tensions, Patterson would continue to be marginally involved with the studio into its next regime. But he had serious legal problems of his own brewing, some of which would eventually result in felony convictions and imprisonment. Thus, the imminent sale of Gold Star to International Artists pleased Duff. After all, he was the key engineer before and after this transition, a survivor, and it signified a resurrection for him. Along with new owners and staff, it would bring a different identity and new priorities as the late 1960s unfolded.

International Artists Record Company

THE PSYCHEDELIC BUSINESS PLAN

IN ITS HAZY INCEPTION, A HOUSTON company called International Artists was just another start-up independent record label with little experience and no interest in acquiring or operating a recording studio complex. Yet through a series of odd deals and maneuvers, orchestrated in part by J. L. Patterson, this corporation would become the first rightful owner of the Gold Star facility in the post-Quinn era. It would maintain that status for about two years, 1968 to 1970, before declaring bankruptcy, losing the studio it had renamed, and getting out of the music business altogether.

Founded in 1965 as the International Artists Producing Corporation (IA), the company actively produced recordings for five years, issuing twelve albums by eight different bands and forty-two singles encompassing even more. That catalogue includes seminal tracks of late-1960s American rock music. As the cowriters Mike Callahan, Dave Edwards, and Patrice Eyries sum it up, "International Artists was an innovative label, releasing both early 'psychedelic' music and also proto-industrial rock many years before that became a genre in vogue. From today's viewpoint, they might also be classified as garage bands or even early punk rock."

The label's first big draw was the Austin band called the 13th Floor Elevators, which accounted for four of the twelve IA albums and its first hit single. That song, "You're Gonna Miss Me," featured a fast-paced groove and the primal, passionate vocalizing of Roky Erickson (b. 1947). It flirted with the *Billboard* Top 50 in the fall of 1966. Inspired by that modest success, IA soon built its small but impressive catalogue by signing the avant-garde group Red Krayola, the progressive rockers Bubble Puppy, and other groundbreaking experimental bands of the moment, as well as one vintage bluesman, Lightnin' Hopkins.

In so doing, IA was the unlikely vinyl vanguard of a cultural revolution that arguably sprang first from Texas. The esteemed critic Chet Flippo, for one, makes the case that musical psychedelia originated in Texas, asserting that "The Elevators pre-dated and anticipated almost everything the San Francisco bands did." As the dominant musical force on the IA label, the Elevators largely defined the company, which would follow the band's arc of ascent and demise—seemingly mirroring its confusion along the way.

Understanding the next phase of Gold Star Studios history requires insight into both the Elevators and the whole IA corporate venture—the kind of company it was and how it came to possess and utilize the property at 5626 Brock Street. For starters, consider Flippo's further observation:

> The Elevators and their record company are one of the strangest couples in music history. International Artists was a strange, faceless Houston company that, quite obviously, didn't know the first thing about music and, consequently, would sign anybody. The Elevators, as IA's first act, were a virtual baptism of fire for the company. Neither the band nor the record company had any idea what the other was up to, but both were sure they were onto a good thing.

On the other hand, consider this opinion from Mayo Thompson, the leader of Red Krayola, which recorded two albums with the company:

> In its brief history, IA managed to help Houston's emergent musical and social forces to consolidate. They had recorded the 13th Floor Elevators, Red Krayola, Lost and Found, Golden Dawn, Endle St. Cloud, Bubble Puppy, Dave Allen, and tapped Houston's blues roots by recording an album with Lightnin' Hopkins. They provided real production access for musical expression in Houston. And, for a time, they promoted a semicoherent set of formal and informal attitudes in a sphere of international production. With the solidity provided by IA, Houston's underground had begun with some cohesion. Although it didn't sweep all before it, it did manage to earn a place in the history of that period.

So who was IA? Four men had founded the International Artists record label in 1965: Bill Dillard, Noble Ginther Jr., Ken Skinner, and Lester Martin. Skinner, whom writer Paul Drummond describes as "a music business hustler and publisher," apparently was the catalyst for creating the label. Prior to IA's inception, Skinner had already created Tapier Music (the publishing company that IA would use for its duration) and done some local recording production. Martin, in partnership with former Gold Star Studios engineer

Doyle Jones, co-owned the Jones and Martin Recording Studios and the Astro Records label. Dillard, a lawyer, would maintain an office at the studio site. As the president, he was the most involved in company affairs. Ginther, also an attorney, was a relatively silent partner, rarely appearing at sessions.

Dillard had become part of the organization because of a prior legal controversy with Patterson, the Gold Star facility lessee. That situation ultimately led to IA buying the studio property in early 1968—and getting further entangled with Patterson in the process. Dillard explains how it began:

> The way I got involved in the business was . . . Ken Skinner and my law partner [Ginther] met at a party or somewhere, and Skinner wanted to sue J. L. Patterson. I didn't know Patterson or Skinner. I didn't want to get involved, but finally Noble came back to me and said, "You know, Skinner is willing to pay a retainer," and so forth. So I represented him for about six months.

While details of that case remain unexplained, it led somehow to Dillard and Ginther joining the organization in 1965. Dillard continues,

> Then we signed up the Elevators. Skinner told me about them. Told me that their music was trash and so forth, but for some reason a lot of people were after them. . . . Skinner wanted me to help him get the record company started. Working with him, I got hooked on the business. Anyone who said we were doing it as a tax write-off is lying. We got a little spin on the local radio stations for the Elevators, and their record began to sell—the "You're Gonna Miss Me" single. We were trying to get it started all over the country. Finally, Skinner—he knew a little about the business—said, "We need a good national promotion man. I know one in California. . . . Lelan Rogers." So Lelan joined up. . . .

Rogers, a native Houstonian a generation older than the scruffy youngsters in the band, would go on to produce their first two albums—and to become, fairly or not, a target of vilification by some. However, as quoted by music critic Jim DeRogatis, Rogers once declared, "I didn't produce them, I baby-sat them."

As for IA's acquisition of Gold Star Studios, Dillard says,

> Doyle Jones, we had used him [to engineer recording sessions]. We used Walt Andrus. And there was a third [studio] called Gold Star. That's the one we bought later—because we couldn't work with the other two. Bill Quinn was the guy that owned it at the time. . . . but J. L. Patterson came to us and said he'd bought it, and he wanted to sell it to us—and get involved with us

in the record business. Anyway, Patterson told us that he owned that studio. But, knowing Patterson, he might have just leased it until he made the deal, and then bought it. [Laughter] He sold it to us. We bought it. . . . Patterson had told us that he owned Gold Star, so we bought it from him. We had no intention of doing business with him outside of buying the studio.

As soon as we'd signed the papers, he said, "I got a few personal things here I want to pick up." So he brought a pickup truck and loaded it up with his "personal" stuff. Quinn came over—he was living next door—and introduced himself. I'd never met him. Anyway, he asked me how long I'd known Patterson. . . . He said, "He'll be scraping the paint off the walls unless you stop him. You won't have anything left."

Nevertheless, the IA principals somehow fell under Patterson's spell—and, incredibly, became his partners. Without being privy to the particulars, we surmise that Patterson played up his status as the president of Data Industries, Inc., to convince them to align with him in some new scheme.

At any rate, here is Dillard's explanation:

Anyway, Patterson was a hustler. He was interested in the law firm because Ginther was wealthy, you know. He started hanging around. . . . At that time [late 1968], we had bought Skinner and Martin out. It was just me and Noble, really. We had it fifty-fifty. Patterson said that if we'd give him a third of our stock, enough to take it public, he'd go to New York and raise $100,000. We had about $40,000 that we owed, so we took him up on it, and he came back and said he had it. I never did see the money—I don't know whether he got it or not. But he got on the board. . . . What Patterson wanted me to do was to come to Data Industries as executive vice president, and help him with that as well as International Artists.

Unfortunately for Dillard and Ginther, Patterson's already troubled involvement with Data Industries would soon enough become IA's problem too.

Meanwhile, Dillard says Patterson was always angling for ways to extract cash from IA, such as insinuating himself as the middleman for an alleged bribery scheme involving distant, unseen grafters. "When Patterson came back from New York, he said he'd talked to somebody who told him we never would get a number one record or get a spin in L.A. or New York until we made a deal with the Mafia," Dillard claims. Patterson also made expenditures replacing the very equipment that he had recently removed as "personal property." "Patterson had decided that he was going to spend most of that $100,000 jazzing up the studio," Dillard says. "We didn't have a studio anymore, because he had wrecked it."

For the first time since Quinn had folded his Gold Star Records label to concentrate solely on studio ownership, the company that owned the facility also owned the record label that mainly used it; they were one and the same. Unfortunately, IA proved inept at running both. Marilyn von Steiger, the IA secretary following the acquisition, claims, "Ray Rush was the only person in the whole building who knew anything about the music business."

Rush produced albums by the Elevators and Bubble Puppy, among others, at the recently rechristened International Artists Studios. He recalls how the Gold Star founder responded to having acid rockers and counterculture types on site. "Quinn was living in his house and never hung out when we were around. He was old school and thought we were rude and obnoxious," he says. "He headed into his house and closed the door when he saw us coming."

Rush had encountered IA after independently producing two singles by a duo billed as Frankie and Johnny (actually K. T. Oslin and Scott Holtzman). "IA wanted to lease the records from me, and that's how I came to be first associated with the label," he says. "It did okay, but it is what got me involved with Dillard and Ginther."

As for Patterson's role in actual studio operations, both Rush and von Steiger assert that he was rarely on site. "J. L. Patterson was what I called an investor in the company," Rush explains. "There was Bill, Lelan, Noble, and whoever else we could get to invest in the company."

They managed to stay afloat through 1970.

THE 13TH FLOOR ELEVATORS WERE the trailblazing psychedelic rock band in terms of the timing of their debut, instrumental innovations, philosophical underpinnings, stream of consciousness experimentalism, and intensity of performances. From the quirkiness of LSD guru Tommy Hall's wobbly tones on the electric jug to the cascading wail of high-pitched rhymes spewing forth from Erickson, from Stacy Sutherland's mind-bending guitar licks to the grinding groove conjured by the rhythm section (originally bassist Bennie Thurman and drummer John Ike Walton), they were unique. Though the band broke up in 1968, today their recordings still attract a devoted and evolving coterie of fans worldwide.

Their first album, *The Psychedelic Sounds of the 13th Floor Elevators*, recorded in Dallas, had introduced their potent sound in 1966. They followed up in 1967 with their masterpiece album *Easter Everywhere*, recorded in Houston at Andrus's studio. The next year, their label company having acquired its own recording facility, they started working there on what would become *Bull of the Woods*, their final album.

The Elevators had first come to Gold Star Studios in June 1966 for a demo session pre-dating their debut LP. When they came back in January 1968—this time with Danny Thomas on drums and Dan Galindo on bass—the Gold Star name would soon be gone. They recorded one song "Never Another," then abruptly aborted the session and Galindo exited the band.

Shortly thereafter on January 30, 1968, IA completed the purchase and renamed the facility International Artists Studios. Vivian Holtzman reported that transaction in her February 4th "Nowsounds" column and quotes Rogers saying that the Elevators would soon record there, followed by the Red Krayola and the Blox, as well as Lightnin' Hopkins.

On February 7, 1968, the Elevators returned to resume work on the new album, tentatively titled *Beauty and the Beast*. However, producer Rogers had decided to quit the company, so Rush took over. He says, "I did quite a bit of work with the 13th Floor Elevators. Producing them was not difficult because they really had an excellent knowledge of what they were about and what their limitations were." The engineers on the various Elevators sessions at IA Studios were Jim Duff, Fred Carroll, or Hank Poole, depending on the date. The sessions continued frequently through February and into March. Then two more were documented in April, and the last session was May 3rd.

That the album took so long to record is not surprising, given that this troubled band, particularly its lead singer, was in crisis. Duff remembers recording three songs for the Elevators—"Livin' On," "Scarlet and Gold," and "May the Circle Remain Unbroken"—and witnessing a brawl between Erickson and Hall. Duff recounts the scene:

> Roky was about to begin vocals on the new material. Prior to vocal sessions Roky always had the studio cleared and recorded with no one present except the engineer and the gray cat. Tommy Hall insisted on remaining and wanted to coach Roky through his new song. At this point Roky went on a tirade . . . and proceeded to wrestle him to the floor—beating him soundly. Then he grabbed a guitar and was about to brain him with it when Duke Davis and I pulled Roky off Tommy.

The once brotherly band was fracturing—due, no doubt, to creative differences, rampant drug abuse, and the well-documented psychological problems Erickson was starting to experience. As Michael Hall puts it in *Texas Monthly*, during those sessions, "Roky was in and out of clarity." Hall also quotes the blunt assessment of the Elevators' original bassist Ronnie Leatherman, who had quit the band in 1967 but, following Galindo's departure, filled in on the final studio album: "He was a vegetable." Dorian Lynskey, writing in *The Guardian*, sums up the dominant view of the aftermath:

What Erickson became famous for was losing his mind. In 1969, he pleaded insanity over a drugs charge and spent three years in a Texas mental institution, from which he emerged somewhere south of normal . . . a befuddled wreck, burbling about aliens and demons.

Whatever the cause of Erickson's mental disarray—LSD, schizophrenia, the trauma of being institutionalized, or some combination of the three—he became . . . a tragic totem of the relationship between drugs, music and madness.

By early May, Erickson's mental breakdown was so severe that IA gave up hope of resurrecting its strongest-selling band to date. With an unfinished LP, IA decided in July to take a collection of previously scrapped studio tracks, overdub them with fake applause, and release the results on an album with the blatantly misleading title *Live*. Carroll engineered that project, and the bulk of the work was done on a single day, July 8th. This infamous LP was released later in August. Rush says, "The *Live* Elevators album was Bill Dillard's idea, to make catalogue. I had to sell that stuff to distributors, and, of course, they were not stupid. I would ship to the distributors and most of them came back."

Meanwhile, the tapes for the new studio album remained momentarily on the shelf at IA Studios. Thomas, the drummer for those tracks, sums up the scenario:

Beauty and the Beast was the next project we worked on, and it was never finished as that album. We got started on the album, and then all hell broke out. Roky went into a mental institution. Eventually Tommy broke Roky out of the institution by taking the door off its hinges. They came by the studio on their way to California.

The last thing we did as a band was "May the Circle Remain Unbroken." . . . We would go into the studio and camp out for three or four days in a row, and go through a number of engineers. One guy would start nodding off, and he'd call in the next guy and so forth. They were Jim, Fred, and Hank Poole; those were our guys. Fred Carroll did a masterful job of putting "May the Circle" together because we were just sitting around and jamming; we were hitting and missing a lot. I was playing a beat with my thumbs on the back of an acoustic guitar. Fred came running in and miked me up. Stacy was sitting on a stool. Roky was playing organ and singing. You know, we weren't even set up, and they came running in and miked everything up—because it looked like the last time we might be together. . . .

"Livin' On" was done for *Beauty and the Beast*. I [and] Flery Versay, who was an arranger from Motown working for Don Robey of Duke and Peacock

Roky Erickson, early 1970s (photo by and courtesy of Doug Hanners)

Records, . . . did the horn parts for that with three members of the Houston Symphony . . . also "Never Another." . . . The Symphony players came down to the studio after a concert one night, and we did that recording at about two in the morning.

When IA decided to finish *Beauty and the Beast,* it was renamed *Bull of the Woods.* We had to call Ronnie Leatherman back to play bass, because Danny Galindo had split by then. The rest were works in progress and had to be finished. The original sessions for what was to be named *Beauty and the Beast* produced seven songs. They were all finished before Tommy and Roky split. They are as follows: "Livin' On," "I Don't Ever Want to Come Down," "Never Another," "Wait for My Love," "Dr. Doom," "Fire in My Bones," and "May the Circle Remain Unbroken." The rest were works in progress and had to be finished.

Sutherland later regrouped the remaining members to finish off the LP, with Carroll and Poole engineering. *Bull of the Woods,* the fourth and last album by the 13th Floor Elevators, was released in December 1968.

The IA session sheet for August 14–15, 1969, shows that Erickson was booked for solo recordings. Biographer Paul Drummond says, "Roky demoed some new material at Gold Star Studios" on July 25 and August 14. But the Elevators were no more. Erickson remains a legendary figure, not only in rock music history but in studio folklore.

For example, I recall Beth Thornton, who worked in the IA office, recounting the day Erickson entered the building with a Band-Aid in the middle of his forehead. She said that when she quizzed him about it, he informed her that it was to cover his "third eye."

Mike Taylor, from the Bad Seeds, recalls another incident:

> Engineer Jim Duff went off to pick up Roky and bring him to the studio. He arrived back without him and told us they were on their way back when the police stopped them. Roky was wearing an Abraham Lincoln stovepipe hat and had a Band-Aid on his forehead. The police were talking to him and he wouldn't answer them at first, but then he peeled off the Band-Aid, which was covering a drawing of an eyeball. He said, "Officer you'll have to speak into my eye." They took Roky away for evaluation or something and let Jim go.

Even though fewer than half of their recordings were done there, the 13th Floor Elevators are a key part of the history of the former Gold Star Studios. It is the place where they made those early 1966 demo tracks—and the place where, with the numerous 1968 sessions for *Bull of the Woods,* they cut their last tracks. During the brief interval they became the greatest Texas rock band of their time, pioneers of the psychedelic subgenre, and mythic. Their visionary cohesion, though tragically brief, still resonates with musicians and fans today.

FORMED BY YOUNG INTELLECTUALS with ties to the University of St. Thomas in Houston, the Red Krayola are sometimes described as a "literate band," but that phrase misleads. With their avid experimentation with atonal music and their somewhat dada-inspired approach to recording sounds from various sources, they were pioneers of minimalist performance art and psychedelic noise rock, the latter best exemplified by tracks labeled "Free Form Freakouts," interspersed among the other tracks, on their debut album.

That 1967 disc, *Parable of the Arable Land,* was the second LP issued by IA. Recorded in Houston at Andrus's studio, it offered music more aligned with that of postmodern composers such as John Cage or Karl Heinz Stockhausen than with traditional rock. "If the Red Crayola had gone to New York instead of California," writes Chet Flippo, "they might have ended up as the Velvet Underground."

On the first LP, the spelling "Crayola" was used, but since that orthography denoted a trademarked name, they had to change it. Hence, the second

LP, *God Bless the Red Krayola and All Who Sail with It,* established the artsy ensemble's ultimate signifier. It was recorded in 1968 at IA's newly acquired studios. The group originally comprised Mayo Thompson (b. 1944) on vocals and guitar, Steve Cunningham on bass, and Rick Barthelme (b. 1943) on drums. Tommy Smith replaced Barthelme before the second album.

Duff recalls engineering studio sessions for the Red Krayola.

> They were very normal-looking, intelligent college students, but what they referred to as their "music" would make a basket case of a middle-aged, boozing recording engineer. . . .
>
> One night they brought about forty people into the studio with pots and pans and a motorcycle. In order to find out what this conglomeration was going to do to my equipment, not to mention my ears, I asked them to demonstrate what was going to happen so that I could prepare microphone placement and get a level. They started the motorcycle, and everyone was beating on the pots and pans. I saw one man standing right in the middle of this noise who did not have a pot or pan. When I checked to see what he was doing, I broke up. He was standing there, as serious as any symphony musician, striking two matchsticks together.

Duff let the tape roll and documented the phenomenon as best as he could. Before long, though, Carroll would take over for the final engineering.

Band founder Thompson (who later joined Pere Ubu and performed in other collaborations—sometimes as Red Krayola) recalls those 1968 recording sessions.

> My first album was mixed mono; the second, done at Gold Star, was mixed in stereo. . . . We did our first album at Walt Andrus's studio, and then International Artists acquired—and I do not know what that means—Gold Star Studios. . . . Lelan Rogers was already gone. So we were kind of cut loose to produce ourselves. We sat in the studio one, two, three nights in a row experimenting with [Duff]. We did this over a period of a few weeks, and we recorded about twenty tunes.

As for the record label and studio space that Red Krayola was sharing with IA's most famous band, Thompson says,

> The Elevators were still around at the time; it was before Roky . . . was institutionalized. . . .
>
> The big studio in the back was used for meetings, and the Elevators and other bands would rehearse [there], and they also used it for storage. In fact,

I remember the Elevators trying out a new bass player back there once while we were recording. . . . Duke Davis and Roky just sitting in the back jamming and learning all the Elevators' tunes.

Consonant with their reputation for experimentalism and using nonmusical sounds, Red Krayola approached the former Gold Star building as an opportunity to explore. "Everything we wanted to do could be done in the [smaller] studio," Thompson says. "It had a big black curtain that went down one side of the room so you could change the acoustics if you needed to." Then he adds,

I guess that we had the funniest use of the Gold Star reverb chambers. One night we just decided to do something funny in the chambers. So we went to a 7-11 store and got a whole bunch of those little paper bags. . . . So we had a whole stack of these things, and we opened up the chamber and crawled in there. We put a guitar in one corner, then we started blowing up the bags with air, and then we popped them, wadded them up, and threw them at the guitar. We recorded the whole process and used it in a song called "The Shirt." We added some tracks to that, but it was basically the song.

I think we were the only guys at the time—except for the engineers who moved mics around in them—who ever saw the insides of the reverb chamber. The studio had a spring reverb and a plate reverb in those days, but we had the live chambers. If you asked the engineer for a longer reverb time, he would disappear for a few minutes and then come back, and it would be done.

You can hear the results of this experiment and other odd tracks they produced on site on *God Bless the Red Krayola and All Who Sail with It*. Its twenty mostly fragmentary "songs" (featuring cryptic titles such as "Ravi Shankar: Parachutist" and "Dirth of Tilth") include one called "Listen to This," which runs all of eight seconds, features a spoken introduction (the title phrase), and comprises a single note. A peculiar sonic document, more acoustic than its heavily electric predecessor, this album would be the group's final release before they disbanded and Thompson pursued other projects.

Yet the historic studio would also figure into the next phase of his career, for there he discovered his potential as a producer. Thompson explains,

I cut John David Bartlett's first demos at Gold Star for IA as a producer. They were the first to place that kernel of an idea in my mind. And I did go on to produce a lot of records in England later. John David was the first session that I did where it was not my own band or my own project.

Today Red Krayola, however the name might be spelled, are revered by some, derided by others, and unknown to most. However, they undeniably made unprecedented recordings that forced listeners to examine cultural assumptions about musicality. Writing in *Oxford American,* the band's first drummer, now famous as the novelist Fredrick Barthelme, sums up the ethos that informed their undertakings:

> Because we couldn't play all that well, we had to do something else, something more interesting, and since we were art-inclined, we went that route, leaning on every possible art idea at every turn. Soon we were making "free music," playing long improvised pieces heavily invested in feedback, random acts of auditory aggression, utterances of all kinds. We began to have big ideas about ways to listen to music, and what "music" was.

Meanwhile, having failed to profit much from the Red Krayola's two LPs, the IA administration was refocusing its priorities. Though the late-1960s youth-culture marketplace was rapidly changing, IA needed something like a hit single—the proven formula for success in the industry—to revitalize the company.

IA found its momentary commercial salvation in a Texas progressive rock quartet that reportedly found the inspiration for its name in Aldous Huxley's *Brave New World:* the Bubble Puppy. Originally based in San Antonio and then Austin, this band featured vocalist-guitarist Rod Prince backed by guitarist Todd Potter, bassist Roy Cox, and drummer Dave Fore. When they signed with IA, the group moved to Houston. At its studio there, they recorded tracks that became IA's highest-charting single and its only Top 200 album.

Potter explains how the group came to IA—and the consequences:

> In 1968 we ventured to Houston to play at the Love Street Light Circus [psychedelic nightclub]. . . . International Artists discovered us in that room.
>
> IA was home to the Elevators, the Red Krayola, and several other Texas psychedelic groups. Unfortunately, the label's legendary roster was inversely proportional to both its business acumen and its treatment of the artists. They waved the contract in front of us, and the Elevators were saying, "Don't do it." It was our first exposure to a record deal, and we just went for it. In hindsight, I don't know that it was the worst thing we could've done. Given our style, it's possible that major labels would've passed us over. I think this was a label that was willing to take a chance on this style of music.
>
> We moved to Houston, to a house not far from Gold Star, and holed up in the studios with a producer named Ray Rush. He was a West Texas veteran who'd worked with Buddy Holly and Roy Orbison. We combined a progressive rock time signature with a crunchy, dive-bombing guitar riff.

The Bubble Puppy's big single "Hot Smoke and Sassafras" hit number fourteen on the *Billboard* singles charts and earned a Gold Record award. As for the song's title, Potter says,

> We composed the song in the studio. We went home after playing the song, and we needed some words. We were watching *The Beverly Hillbillies* on TV. Granny was berating Jethro for something, and she goes, "Hot smoke and sassafras, Jethro! Can't you do anything right?" That's where it came from.

Released in December of 1968, the song got heavy rotation on rock radio, first in Texas and soon nationwide. By the spring of 1969 the group was lip-synching its hit on *American Bandstand*.

Poole engineered the Bubble Puppy sessions. He says,

> I recorded "Hot Smoke and Sassafras" for the Bubble Puppy, and then the album *A Gathering of Promises*. That band was way ahead of their time, and that album had a great '60s sound to it. We didn't use any booths on the recording. We had everybody out in the open, and we had David Fore, the drummer, over in one corner. Rod Prince and Todd Potter, the two guitar players, were real talents in that band. Roy Cox was sort of the manager, a major songwriter, and he played bass in the group. A lot of people said we had one of the best sounds of that era. The Beatles were killing everybody back in those days with that incredible songwriting team, but many people said that *A Gathering of Promises* had a better sound than the Beatles or anybody else. I am very proud of that album. Everything was cut live at one time, except the vocals and hand claps.
>
> We were using an Ampex MM-1600 sixteen-track machine. The board we were using was six of these Ampex M10 tube mixers that had been modified with some low- and high-pass filters, and had a patch panel added. . . . We had three mixers for the left channel and three for the right. . . . We had to do a lot of patching to use the sixteen tracks. . . . It was a bit primitive, but it sure sounded good.

Unfortunately, despite the fine studio work and the opportunity to open concerts for major touring bands such as the Who, the Bubble Puppy could not replicate the success of that first brilliant album.

According to Prince's "The Tale of Bubble Puppy 1966–1972," the problems were rooted in IA's ineptitude, particularly its decision not to lease the hit single to a major label (supposedly the Beatles' Apple imprint was interested) and its dismissal of producer Rush.

For his part, Rush says, "Working with the Bubble Puppy and their album *A Gathering of Promises* was definitely a highlight of my time at IA."

Bubble Puppy, publicity photo, 1968

Prince writes, "Ray Rush was very much the fifth member. Awesome production skills, adept at pulling the true song from one's brain. The loss of Ray was the final blow—there was nothing left at IA musically, and the Puppy WAS music."

GENERALLY SPEAKING, IA EMBITTERED many of the artists it signed to contract. The beleaguered company is often accused of having mismanaged marketing, production, and especially money. The norm seems to have been for artists to be put on a small weekly cash allowance (as an advance against future earnings), which some say never increased (no matter how many records sold) and sometimes failed to materialize. However, Dillard, IA's president, steadfastly disagrees: "It's ridiculous. There's no truth to it. They got a lot more than their royalties."

Given the rift between labor and management over such issues, as well as the spirit of the age, the musicians came together and creatively staged a protest. Singer-songwriter John David Bartlett sets the scene:

In mid-to-late 1968 the Bubble Puppy were in-studio, working. The re-formed 13th Floor Elevators were in finishing the *Bull of the Woods* album. A number of the other bands were also waiting their turn to work on their albums. They [IA] were way behind on paying everybody or giving advances. Nobody had gotten any money for weeks. Everyone was broke and hungry, and they wanted us to record some more. So all the musicians got together and went to management and told them that they had this idea for an IA supergroup that would record an a cappella vocal song—that we wanted to record and they could release it as a supergroup single. Management got all excited and set up the session. We had worked up the chorus of the song, and it was a repeating chant of "hamburger-hamburger-hamburger-hamburger." And then various singers would go "I needa" or "we all needa." Management didn't think it was too funny, but . . . they got the message.

The Lost and Found, previously known locally as the Misfits, were another esoteric psychedelic rock band that signed with IA—reportedly following their involvement in a drug bust that put them in need of legal representation. Lead guitarist Jimmy Frost has claimed that a retainer for IA attorney services was factored into their contract. The band, which included Peter Black on guitar and vocals and James Harrell on bass, with various drummers, recorded two singles and one album, *Everybody's Here,* for the IA label. The second IA single was "When Will You Come Through" and "Professor Black," engineered and produced by Carroll. Following an exhausting tour across the South, which IA claimed was a financial loss, the band quit in a pay dispute.

Another IA artist was Sterling Damon, actually a stage name of singer-songwriter Mel Douglas. "They changed my name to Sterling Damon because of the British Invasion and the psychedelic rock movement," he says. Though he recalls recording enough material at IA sessions to make an album, the company issued only one Damon single (#108), featuring "Rejected" and "My Last Letter."

The aforementioned Bartlett had come to IA in 1967 because his high school English teacher was the mother of Red Krayola's Thompson. "Mayo and I became friends, and Mayo introduced me to the art scene, and also to the executives at International Artists," Bartlett says. He provides an insider's account of IA operations:

IA owned two houses [where] they would put their bands up while they were in town to record. . . . They would send a van to pick up the bands and bring them to the studio. They would arrive at the building, head into the studios, and were told, "Play music, make a record, now!"

The big studio in the back of the building was closed and used for storage—and as a hangout for the musicians who were waiting their turn to record. . . . IA was storing hundreds of boxes of records in there. We often threw records at each other and at the walls while we were hanging out in there. . . . We'd sleep on top of those boxes—there were so many of them. . . . It was pretty strange.

Given such an environment—and not only the schism between labor and management, but also the gap between young hippies and older business-men—IA might have seemed to some of the musicians to be a microcosm of all that was wrong with a corrupt establishment.

THE FORMER GOLD STAR STUDIOS had been a key site for recording Texas blues, epitomized by Lightnin' Hopkins, almost since its inception. During IA's bizarre proprietorship, Hopkins returned to jam with some members of the 13th Floor Elevators. These sessions broke racial barriers and generational obstacles simultaneously, uniting the elder Hopkins with the latest cohort of longhaired youth to form the rhythm section of the primordial psychedelic rock group.

The most recent drummer for the Elevators, Danny Thomas, explains how it came to be:

The Elevators were friendly with all the other popular acts around and hung out with Johnny Winter, and Billy Gibbons, and also with a lot of the black musicians in the area. . . . I got to play drums on the Lightnin' Hopkins album for IA. I can thank Lelan for that. Duke Davis played bass on that record. He was our [first] replacement for Danny Galindo when he left the band.

There was a harmonica player that was a friend of Lightnin's, named Billy Bizor. We would pick him up for the sessions. . . . He was a legendary harp player in his day. Snuffy Waldron also played piano on some of those songs. . . . The engineers on the Lightnin' album were Jim Duff and Fred Carroll.

Duff provides additional context for these sessions—and an anecdote involving two of the Beatles:

Lightnin' would do an album for almost anybody for six hundred dollars. He wouldn't sign a contract with anyone. I recorded part of the album that he did for International Artists that Lelan Rogers produced.

Mansel Rubenstein . . . was managing him at the time of the IA album. We were cutting the session, and . . . my receptionist . . . called me and said, "Mansel is on the phone and wants to talk to Lightnin'."

So I said he was in a session, but she insisted I talk to him. So I got on the phone and he said, "Jim, I've got to talk to him."

I said, "You know how he is about being bothered while he [is] in a recording session."

Mansel said, "You've got to go and get him because Paul McCartney and John Lennon are in Houston, and Lightnin's their hero. They saw him when he was over in London, and they're in Houston and want to talk to him."

So I went and got him and said, "Mansel really needs to talk to you, and it's real important that you talk to him because some very special people want to see you."

So he gets on the phone and says, "I ain't got time to mess with those fools"—and hangs up the phone! He didn't care about anything except cutting those tracks and making his money.

Assuming the veracity of this account, imagine what might have transpired, under more welcoming circumstances, if Hopkins, Lennon, McCartney, and part of the Elevators had all met—and in a recording studio.

But the fusion of Hopkins's old-school blues with the Elevators' vibe is intriguing enough on its own, and it definitely happened. The result was the sixth IA LP, *Free Form Patterns,* a disc reissued on CD under the same title on various labels (Collectables, Charly, Fuel 2000), but also titled as *Reflections* on the Bellaire label.

The two strikingly different LP covers IA used for this album suggest its dual nature and cross-cultural significance. One fit the traditional mode, featuring a photograph of Hopkins in a white suit, dark shirt with open collar, gold chain around the neck, and Panama hat perched cockily on the side of his head. The graphics are simple, with Hopkins's name in all capital letters printed in a vertical line, running from bottom to top, on the left side and the album title imposed in slightly off-kilter horizontal fashion across the top. However, the alternative cover, for the same album, evokes the psychedelic poster art of the era. Against a black background, with lots of squiggly line drawings in red bordering the bottom and top, the album title emerges in wavy asymmetrical block lettering squeezed around the borders of an oblong shape, inside which the artist's name appears in oddly formed block lettering in partial shades of red, white, and sky blue.

Bartlett, one of the youngest IA hippies, relates his behind-the-scenes role in the Hopkins sessions: "When they recorded the *Free Form Patterns* LP, . . . IA got me a fake ID, and my job was to go pick up a bottle of Scotch every day, then go pick up Lightnin' and bring him over to the studio. I sat through all of those sessions because I was his gofer."

Duff, who engineered about half the tracks, indicates that the Elevators members were absent for those—but that another famous Texas blues guitarist also participated:

> It was strange to do a blues album in the middle of all that psychedelia. I think Lelan did that album for his own personal satisfaction. I don't know if they included any of the talking on the IA album [see the Fuel 2000 reissue]. Between songs Lelan would interview him. . . . The band that I was recording were all his own musicians and were all black—except for Johnny Winter, who was playing lead guitar. . . . He was often in the studio doing session work. One day after IA had taken over the building, he came in to talk to Dillard and to ask to be signed to the label. . . . Dillard asked me about Winter, and I told him, "You are crazy if you don't sign him! He is a great musician." . . . Well, Dillard didn't listen to me, and he let Johnny go.

Though IA passed on Winter, the guitar slinger soon signed with Columbia Records and became a national star. But the Hopkins recording project forever links IA with Texas blues. Whatever its flaws, IA's experimental nature supported a project that could not have been produced at many places elsewhere in Texas in 1968—another milestone in the heritage of a unique recording facility.

WHILE IA HAD ITS CORPORATE HANDS full producing its own artists, its studio was still a viable commercial facility booking independent projects, and various other producers made use of it as the 1960s came to an end and the corporation stumbled toward bankruptcy. For example, Chris Strachwitz of Arhoolie Records returned on November 6, 1969, to record tracks for the Clifton Chenier album called *King of the Bayous.* Duff engineered, in what may have been his last session before leaving IA.

Cassell Webb, now an established singer and producer in England, was in the Houston late-1960s rock group called the Children. She sums up a local musician's view of the IA Studios environment in this era:

> I remember so many occasions when there were jam sessions going on at Gold Star, people would just arrive totally spontaneously and quite often they would be recorded. . . . I was on the second Red Krayola album. . . . Janis [Joplin] definitely went to Gold Star several times because I saw her at parties in the building, and she participated in some of the jam sessions.

Kenny Cordray, a former member of the Children, acknowledges the festive fun that often prevailed there during free time, but he says it rarely carried over to the recording process:

Even though we were hippies, there was a certain sense of order to the sessions. Everything was real straight. You had a certain time for the session. It was all business. I don't recall there being too much of a party atmosphere. It was real serious; you were in a real recording studio trying to make a record.

But Cordray makes it clear that, from a player's perspective, this recording facility was a cool place to be:

Most musicians in Houston loved the vibe or the great attitude at the studio. The most famous thing about this studio was the reverb chamber—and that the studios were a great place where guys got stoned and hid out. That sound was unique to many hit records recorded there in the mid-to-late Sixties. . . . This studio always got great guitar tones.

However, in assuming ownership of the historic Gold Star property, IA had again miscalculated, for what was intended to be a valuable asset ultimately only hastened the company's failure.

16

Disillusioned Dissolution

JUST A FEW YEARS AFTER J. L. PATTERSON had first proposed that he join IA and raise funds for a stock offering, the U.S. Court of Appeals, Second Circuit, would review and uphold the conviction in a case in which Patterson testified about participating in stock fraud. We quote from the first paragraph of the summary findings of *United States of America, Appellee, v. M. Perry Grant and Service Securities, Inc., Appellants,* decided May 25, 1972:

> The evidence presented at trial established that Grant, operating through Service, a securities broker dealer, and in conjunction with J. L. Patterson, the president of Data Industries Corporation of Texas, Inc. ("Data"), and others, defrauded public investors in connection with an offering of a new issue of Data stock.

Elsewhere in this document Patterson is defined as "a co-conspirator but not a defendant" because "he had agreed to cooperate with the government in the prosecution of this case." It also establishes that the criminal conspiracy began in December 1968 and the defrauding carried over through 1969. This period closely corresponds to that of IA's acquisition and first year of operation of the former Gold Star Studios. Patterson's stock fraud included manipulating the apparently clueless IA principals to entrust him with handling a move into the corporate stock market.

Determining how much IA suffered financially because of Patterson's nefarious actions is not easy. But the many problems the company experienced in its last two years of existence were insurmountably exacerbated, if not solely caused, by Patterson's court-proven ability to mislead investors. Hence, IA's ownership of the former Gold Star Studios contributed directly to its downfall via the consequent affiliation with Patterson.

"When IA acquired Data Industries, it was the beginning of the end of IA," says producer Ray Rush. What had started off merely as a record label company and then expanded into studio ownership eventually morphed a third and fatal time. By the summer of 1969, following a merger of IA with the Patterson-controlled Data Industries, the new conglomeration had purchased a Nashville company called Southern Plastics, the home of an independent record-pressing plant. IA took control of operations and began pressing its own products there too. Bill Dillard had even moved his office there. Making such a big acquisition required hefty financing, payment of which eventually came due. That was perhaps the final trigger in causing IA to crash. It was the inevitable outcome of a wild flight that—with Patterson navigating for the novice pilots—had been doomed from the start.

"Well, the bank called in the loans. And we didn't have the cash to pay them," explains Dillard. "We would have made it, even filing for bankruptcy. We went down because of the IRS. If we hadn't filed bankruptcy, they wouldn't have shown up."

Rush offers his take on the managerial disarray that had precipitated the downfall:

> Dillard hired me to be in charge of A&R and staff producer. Back then I was trying to record the Elevators, the Bubble Puppy, about ten other acts, run the record label, and collect money, and all that on the phones, and it wasn't working so well. So Dillard had brought in Fred Carroll. Fred was a very talented man and a good producer.
>
> The main blame in the whole IA debacle can be leveled again at Patterson. When he joined up, his main thing was to get rid of me. . . . But to Dillard's credit, he wouldn't have any of that.

While Rush eventually left the company, Carroll survived at the tumultuous IA Studios almost till the end. In 1970 he produced two of the last few singles to be released on the label: "She Wears It Like a Badge" backed with "Laughter" by Endle St. Cloud (#139) and "Ginger" backed with "Country Life" by Ginger Valley (#142). Thereafter, Carroll voluntarily departed.

Compounding the personnel and financing issues that threatened the organization, under recent management the quality of the recording equipment had diminished and IA lagged behind in adapting to new technologies. A clever teenager named Kurt Linhof became the last recording engineer to be hired by IA (he was also the bassist for the rock group the Children). He provides his rookie insights on the matter:

The management attempted to modernize the facility on a shoestring budget but was never able to complete the operation. We were never able to get the new custom-built twenty-four-channel console designed by freelancer Dennis Bledsoe to completely work. The modular design channel strips and master modules were purchased from Los Angeles. Dennis Bledsoe designed the chassis and motherboard that the purchased modules would fit into. . . . Only nine tracks were in operation because the moment a tenth module was installed, the entire mixing console went into wild and crazy oscillations due to a huge number of ground loops. Eventually IA brought in a couple of technicians from Los Angeles. The best that they were able to do was get eleven channels working.

With things going wrong on all fronts, and most bills going unpaid, Linhof actually became an indispensable employee, the only person left who could handle recordings. Thus, he was able to remain employed on site through the end—one of "the only people getting any money out of the cash-strapped company," he says.

Linhof also witnessed a late change in administration that seemed to indicate, in his opinion, questionable judgment. "While I was there, the IA executives installed Dale Hawkins [the writer of the song "Suzie Q"] as the new president of International Artists," he reports. "But Hawkins rarely ever visited the facility."

The last act to be signed to IA was a vocal rock group called Denim, and Linhof engineered its studio debut. Denim recorded only a few tracks of cover songs—one of which, a treatment of "Suite: Judy Blue Eyes" by Crosby, Stills, and Nash, actually garnered local radio airplay and got national attention via an article in the July 7, 1970, issue of *Billboard*. Linhof says, "I was nineteen, and I got a credit on the cover of *Billboard* as a production engineer. 'Producer'! Can you imagine? I was nineteen, and I'd been riding the knobs for all of two weeks."

Thus, even while the IA Corporation was hurtling toward demise, positive things were happening for Linhof. Paul Clagett, a member of Denim, says of him, "He was a good guy who helped us with harmonies and such." As one of the final IA bands to record, Denim soon discovered its new label was not going to survive. "We met a band named Ginger Valley who told us some stuff about IA not being honest, a bunch of crooks, et cetera," Clagett recalls. "After a period of almost a year we were able to get out of the contract with IA due to the fact that we were never able to do any more recording."

Eventually the bankruptcy proceedings and subsequent IRS-related investigation caused IA Studios to cease operations and leave the property in dormancy. When the legal dust later settled, it no longer belonged to any of the former IA principals. As Dillard explains, "The attorneys got the studio as part of their fee for representing us in the bankruptcy. And they in turn sold it to Huey P. Meaux."

Linhof's final duty as the sole remaining employee of International Artists Studios was to assist agents from the bankruptcy court in shutting down the building and padlocking the doors.

The IA bankruptcy and subsequent loss of the property engulfed also the Quinn family house—the place where Gold Star Studios had been founded. For most of the 1960s, Quinn had resided nearby while Patterson leased the studio facility, concocting deals and partnerships that finally brought it all into disgrace. By 1971 Quinn was eventually forced to vacate his longtime home at 5628 Brock Street, as it was legally part of the property seized by the lawyers. He died elsewhere in Houston just a few years later.

AS A FINAL PIECE OF EVIDENCE from the public record regarding Patterson's character, we note that in a separate and unrelated case, the U.S. Court of Appeals, Fifth Circuit, in March 1976 affirmed his conviction on three felony counts of wire fraud and acknowledged his role in various other crimes. (See *United States of America, Plaintiff-Appellee, v. J. L. Patterson, Jr., Defendant-Appellant.*) He was thereafter sentenced to prison.

17

Meaux Moves In,
SugarHill Ascends

THE FAILED INTERNATIONAL ARTISTS Producing Corporation went into receivership in August 1971. By late fall, the record producer Huey Meaux, recently released from prison himself, acquired the former Gold Star Studios via bankruptcy auction. Having paid the attorneys' fees, he received the land, building, and any remaining contents.

Meaux was already quite familiar with the Gold Star facility, having been there during sessions for "Chantilly Lace," "She's About a Mover," and many other hits. But after the Patterson regime had emerged, Meaux departed. Always a shrewd observer, he perhaps had distrusted Patterson from the start. Following Meaux's term in the state penitentiary for violating the Mann Act (by driving a prostitute across state lines to a Nashville convention), he was looking to make a fresh start in the record business. And now that this piece of real estate was up for grabs—and at a bargain price—Meaux was keen to return on his own terms.

Songwriter-musician Gaylan Latimer recalls how the timing of the IA bankruptcy meshed with Meaux's schedule:

> I remember driving around Houston with Meaux looking for a new location for a studio in late 1971. We stopped by Gold Star and discovered that nothing was going on. The studio was partially torn up, and the gold star [emblem] had been covered up with carpet. Huey made a mental note that it wouldn't be long before this studio could be acquired. Not long after that, International Artists went bankrupt and the property was for sale. Huey immediately took action and acquired the studios.

The Meaux era first brought a new moniker for the place, SugarHill Studios—a phrase that appealed to Meaux's fancy, inspired by a street name in southwest Houston. Besides, as he often pointed out, it did not evoke any particular music genre and thus would leave the future of the enterprise open to any potential type of production.

As the next step in revitalizing the place, Meaux took the big studio room in the back (recently used as warehouse space) and converted it into offices. He also transformed its dormant control room into his personal office. Thus, SugarHill would begin producing recordings only in the smaller studio. However, the new proprietor soon realized that he would require a second studio room to maintain a balance between his own in-house recording projects and the other cash-paying business that he needed to attract to stay afloat financially.

In February 1973 Meaux hired the necessary workers and remodeled the interior of Bill Quinn's attached house (the original Gold Star studio space). They gutted the structure and removed the upstairs flooring, leaving in place the load-bearing wooden beams, then sealed and soundproofed all window openings. This shell then was refashioned into new studio space. They constructed also a two-story addition, connected to the front of the house, in which they built a large control room and, above it, a tape vault. The dimensions for the main studio room were twenty-eight feet long by twenty-eight feet wide, with a twenty-two-foot-high ceiling—the largest such facility in Houston at the time.

Adjacent to the primary recording space, there were four isolation booths of varying sizes, plus a drum chamber. Red carpet covered the floor, and acoustic tiles adorned the ceiling. The wall surfaces featured red burlap, stuffed from behind with fiberglass insulation. The room's interior décor conveyed a rustic Mexican hacienda theme.

This newly designated Studio B had the largest control room in town, stocked with the custom-designed tube board with Audiotronics modules and the sixteen-track Ampex MM-1000 that came with the property. Meaux also purchased and installed one sixteen-track Scully tape recorder and a used Ampex 440 eight-track machine.

Musician Mike Taylor, of the Bad Seeds, talks about his employment during the earliest days of the new company:

> I actually worked for Huey P. Meaux for about a year and a half just after he bought Gold Star and renamed it SugarHill. The console that we used in Studio A was an old Spectrasonics board that he bought used from a guy called "The Chief" in Philadelphia. . . . It was just him and me and no one else. I believe it was late 1971 or early 1972 when I started.

With Taylor as the only resident employee early on, Meaux relied on various freelancers and subcontractors to fulfill his goals. One of those was Hank Lam, an audio, video, and repair technician. He says of Meaux,

He wanted me to do some repair work . . . on the board and the Scully sixteen-track. He had a lot of equipment, and quite a bit of it was not working at the time. He had a lot of people working at building stuff but no repair staff. When I first walked into the building, Studio B wasn't in operation, and Quinn's old house was standing unused. Only the gold star room was operational. . . .

In Studio B, after Huey converted it in early 1973, he had the custom-built tube board that probably was left over from the IA days. It had a bunch of tube modules . . . in a badly designed custom frame . . . [with] voltage rails, like train tracks, under the board. I spent quite a few days fixing it. . . . The speakers in the A room were Altec 604Es with mastering lab crossovers driven by Altec power amps. In the B room the speakers were Altec A-10s, also with an Altec power amp.

By early 1973, Meaux had hired a British engineer named Roger Harris, wooing him to Houston from a freelance position at a famous Alabama studio. Harris says,

I first came to the USA and went to Muscle Shoals Studio, and they gave me a little job. Then one day Huey called his old partner-in-crime Jimmy Masters, the chief engineer. . . . So they recommended me to Huey, and he said, "Come on down to Houston, brother. . . . I got a house for you, a studio, and a salary. I'll take care of you." . . .

Sure enough, he had everything all set up for me, and put me to work right away. When I arrived, he had Studio A and Studio B. . . . Studio A was sixteen tracks with that great Scully machine and a board. . . . Huey had a great [Teletronix] LA-2A compressor that sounded incredible. We ran everything through it, especially vocals. I ran bass through it, and it made the bass and all of the instruments just jump out at you. The old Scully sixteen-track machine was the best ever. It sounded fantastic, like analog with Dolby SR.

Through his various expenditures on the property, equipment, and personnel, Meaux had refurbished the old Gold Star facility and positioned SugarHill for success. As the '70s unfolded, the return on his investment would be huge.

PRIOR TO EMBARKING ON HIS SUGARHILL enterprise, Meaux had already established himself as a savvy record producer and promoter. But by the time he sold SugarHill in 1986, he had been involved, directly or indirectly, in the production of approximately fifty singles or albums that earned Gold Record awards. Together with Pappy Daily and Don Robey, Meaux helped put Houston on the musical map of the world.

Though his personal proclivities would lead to multiple prison terms and ultimately public disgrace, the fact remains that Meaux played a major role in creating some of postwar America's favorite records. Writing in *Texas Monthly* after Meaux's 1996 arrest, Joe Nick Patoski bluntly acknowledges the man's crimes and double life but also calls him "a musical wizard—the man behind more hits made in Texas and Louisiana in the last half of the twentieth century than anyone else."

Meaux's first notable achievement as a producer had come with the 1959 hit "Breaking Up Is Hard to Do" by a singer billed as Jivin' Gene (Gene Bourgeois). Over the next few years and with a variety of different singers, Meaux scored again and again, producing records such as "You'll Lose a Good Thing" by Barbara Lynn, "I'm a Fool to Care" by Joe Barry, and "I'm Leaving It Up to You" by Dale and Grace. "The reason why I had so many hits," Meaux explained to Patoski, "was that around this part of the country you've got a different kind of people every hundred miles—Czech, Mexican, Cajun, black." And certainly a multicultural dimension imbues the long list of artists who made hit records with Meaux. For someone with the right song and the right voice for it, regardless of ethnicity or gender, he controlled a pipeline to the big time.

Meaux was one of the few independent outsiders who could do consistent commerce with Nashville or New York without becoming part of their respective music-industry establishments. Most of his earliest hits were recorded in Louisiana, but from about 1962 on, Houston was his base of operations. There, often at Gold Star Studios, he developed a reputation for canny production instincts—and taking whatever financial advantage he could in any transaction.

Former studio engineer Jim Duff offers this profile:

> Huey was a Cajun, originally from Louisiana, with a manner of talking that defied any form of the English language that I had ever heard. His distinctly Southern-accented voice spouted a vocabulary that was a mixture of Cajun and black jive, laced with more than a little of his own homespun philosophical idioms and four-letter words.

As did Duff, many folks found Meaux's colorful persona to be engaging, and there are numerous testimonials regarding his humor and capacity for generosity. Even some artists who may have been financially outwitted by Meaux profess to care for him on a personal level. As Roy Head puts it, "You know, when it comes to the business of music, I love Huey and I hate him. He is what he is and will always be my brother and my friend."

Doug Sahm—whose Sir Douglas Quintet was named, produced, and promoted by Meaux—visited SugarHill Studios several times during Meaux's ownership. Sometimes he came to record, but often seemingly just to see someone for whom he obviously had a deep affection. Sahm's longtime collaborator Augie Meyers has been known to joke in retrospect about Meaux's one-sided contracts and dubious accounting practices, but he also claims a depth of friendship that belies oversimplified characterizations of the man as a con artist.

Apart from any fraternal feelings between Meaux and others, what almost universally garners musicians' respect for the man was his ability to pinpoint the right elements for crafting a hit. As Duff says,

> Huey had the knack for knowing what might be a hit record if the circumstances were correct. Generally his detractors were either jealous producers who failed to have hits, or exceptionally jaded or stupid musicians who thought that the world owed them a living. Huey produced, leased, or sold many hit records and artists to the major labels and gave many singers a chance to make it into the big leagues.

An unsigned "Producer's Profile" article in a 1969 issue of *Cashbox* magazine describes Meaux as a music business figure worthy of emulation and quotes him explaining the keys to his success:

> Huey's approach to producing might serve as a guideline for young producers. . . . "The thing that makes a hit record is the promotion behind it. Number two is the material. Number three is the producer, and number four is the singer. I think the man behind the desk who's handling the promotion is the hit-maker. The song is way more important than any singer. If the song is right, it doesn't matter who sings it. Anybody can have a hit with a good piece of material. . . . Songs have to be about reality, about the simple things, about the hound dog stretching by the split-rail fence, about the things we walk over, the things we miss, the things that are the beautiful part of living."

Regardless of his many flaws, when it came to grasping how words and music can touch human beings and motivate them to buy records, Meaux knew far more than most. And by the time he had completed renovations at SugarHill Studios, he was ready to put that knowledge to work.

ORIGINALLY AS A REPAIR AND MAINTENANCE technician and later as a studio engineer, Lam witnessed the initial phase of activity at Meaux's refurbished facility. "There were plenty of recordings going on," he reports. "Huey had people skillfully trying to make hit records." Among the artists Lam worked with in the early '70s were country star Freddy Fender (1937–2006), the Gulf Coast blues-rocker Marcia Ball (b. 1949) with her original group Freda and the

Firedogs, and the prolific blues and R&B songwriter-musician Oscar Perry (1943–2004).

Lam explains that Meaux did not focus so much on discovering artists who had the right material as on generating hit-worthy material via in-house composers, including Perry. Lam says,

> I worked quite a bit with Oscar Perry. Oscar would come and lay down these hellacious instrumental tracks, and then he would have all these different lyricists come up with melodies and put down vocals. They would try to make hit records out of these tracks. Huey certainly had a wealth of talent around him in those days.

Meaux eventually employed a large songwriting staff. He was not only searching for that special song to match with a particular performer. Having signed the writers to publishing contracts with his own company, the boss would also benefit from royalties a hit song generated. Like Daily and Robey before him, Meaux understood that a sizable share of the profits for a success-fully marketed record ultimately went to the publisher. By the time Meaux sold SugarHill Studios, his hedonistic lifestyle and other financial commit-ments were likely funded almost entirely with income generated by his song-publishing interests.

According to an archived office document, one of the earliest recording sessions at the newly acquired studios was also perhaps the most unlikely. It was engineered and produced by Meaux himself, before his new technical staff had been hired, and it featured the Jamaican progressive reggae artist known as Burning Spear (Winston Rodney, b. 1948). Intrigued as we are by this revelation, we have no other information about this session. However, it shows that Meaux's SugarHill would attract performers from a diverse array of genres.

But as in its previous incarnations, this studio complex would also remain a base for blues and gospel recording. Under Meaux's ownership, Robey's various Houston-based labels resumed their relationship with the facility, and his associates were among the first paying customers at SugarHill Studios. For instance, invoice #101, dated October 13, 1972, is a bill to Pilgrim Outlets, a gospel group on Robey's Song Bird label. Invoice #102 appeared four days later, made out to Bobby Bland, Robey's biggest star on Duke.

Between December 30, 1972, and January 10, 1973, there were thirteen other invoices issued for Bland, with another six coming in May 1973. This was the very month that Robey sold all of his music holdings to ABC/Dunhill, so perhaps these sessions were part of the deal. We also have a copy of a bud-get request, made in February 1973 by producer Robert Evans, to cut eight sides featuring Bobby Bland in May at SugarHill—a request which came from Duke Records and went to ABC/Dunhill. So while Robey was negotiating the sale of his companies, he continued recording at SugarHill. February and March of 1973 also brought sessions with other Robey artists, including Eugene Williams, Bobby Carter, and Willie Banks, as well as gospel groups such as the Smiling Jubilaires, Gospel Chariots, Simaires, and Ziontones.

This high level of commercial activity perhaps helped Robey demonstrate to the prospective corporate buyer that his labels were still actively producing records. We infer also that Bland's massive amount of recording just prior to the completion of the sale likely produced tracks used on at least one subsequently released album. For instance, several track titles listed on invoices later reappear on Bland's first ABC/Dunhill LP, titled *His California Album,* including "I Don't Want to Be Right," "This Time I'm Gone for Good," "Going Down Slow," and "Right Place at the Right Time."

As for Meaux's own projects, one of his more obscure but fascinating artists in the early '70s was the singer known as Little Royal (b. Royal Torrance), an emotive soul singer who released one album. A generation later, several rap artists, most prominently Ice T, would sample some of those tracks on their own productions. Between 1972 and 1974 Meaux recorded lots of Little Royal material. Two of his singles on Meaux's Tri-Us label charted in the R&B category and were distributed by Starday. "Jealous" (#912) went to number fifteen in May 1972 and was the title track for his only album, released by King Records in a presumed deal with Meaux (and reissued on CD by the Japanese label P-Vine in 2007). Later, the single "I'm Glad to Do It" (#916) registered at number eighty-eight on the charts. Tri-Us issued several others: "I'll Come Crawling"/"You'll Lose a Good Thing" (#913), "I Surrender"/"Soul Train" (#915), and "Don't Want Nobody Standing over Me"/"Keep on Pushing Your Luck" (#917).

Gaylan Latimer became a staff songwriter for Meaux "under an assumed name, Emery Capel," he says. "This was so I could also be an ASCAP affiliate. Under that name I wrote some songs that were recorded at SugarHill for Bobby Bland and Peggy Scott." But during this time Latimer was also a member of a group called Heather Black, which recorded a live album that was overdubbed and mixed at SugarHill in late 1972. It was subsequently released on another Meaux label, Double Bayou Records.

Roger Harris recalls other SugarHill sessions he engineered:

My first real session was with Floyd Tillman, some great country music, and he was a great old guy. . . . I did sessions with Sonny Rae and Fancy, a husband and wife combo. I did a lot of recording with Oscar Perry. . . . I did sessions with Bobby Byrd from James Brown's band. . . . also Freddy Fender.

Pat Brady, another studio engineer, offers insight about the Austin-Houston connection that was nurtured by SugarHill:

A band from Austin that I worked with was Freda and the Firedogs, alias Marcia Ball and her band. Actually we recorded a lot of bands from Austin because the scene there was just beginning, and Houston was still the place to do serious recording. You could tell that she had "it" then, and she still has it now. . . . Her musicians were just spirited, fun-loving, high-energy guys, and they were good.

One of those musicians was Bobby Earl Smith, now an attorney in Austin. He explains the scenario that brought them to SugarHill in 1973 and '74:

Freda and the Firedogs had become a very popular band in Austin and around Texas. John Reed was the guitar player in the band. David Cook was steel and electric guitar and also accordion. I played bass. Freda was, of course, Marcia Ball, the vocalist and piano player.

We met Huey P. Meaux through Doug Sahm, who was a tireless promoter of Freda and the Firedogs. . . . We started to back him up quite a bit and be the opening act at concerts. He started sitting in with us every so often. Doug started telling us about Huey.

Doug was on Atlantic Records when we formed the band. Jerry Wexler had signed Doug, and he'd signed Willie Nelson. He also offered us a contract. . . . We screwed around for quite a while, thinking we could get something better, and eventually signed nothing. Marcia has often said that this incident set her career back quite a number of years. After that mess Doug said, "Well, I've been talking to Huey, and he is interested." Doug said, "Huey is real groovy."

Huey called my wife early one day and turned his Cajun charm on her and eventually got us to agree to come and do a demo. He knew about the aborted Atlantic contract from both Doug and Wexler. . . . We were cautious about Wexler, so of course, we would be cautious about Huey. But we cut a demo there. . . . We recorded a master at the studio.

We also backed up Floyd Tillman on an album for Huey. . . . We didn't do the whole album, but we did a bunch of the songs on that Tillman record. We did one cut with Doug Sahm in the same period . . . called "Hot Tomato Man" [issued as a single on Meaux's Crazy Cajun label, #2004].

Harris adds to the memories of this phase of studio operations:

I remember doing a remix of a Barbara Lynn song, "Lose a Good Thing," which he put out on his Crazy Cajun label. That was one of my first sessions ever for Huey. I think the tape was from Cosimo's Studio in New Orleans. Then I did some work with Tommy McLain. . . .

I did a lot of work with Sonny Landreth. . . . There was some really good music there. "She Left Me a Mule to Ride" was the first song on the tape we created. It was a whole demo album that we did for Warner Brothers Records . . . in 1974. Sonny is an incredible talent and player, especially on slide dobro, [but] Warner never signed Sonny. I think that Huey might have asked too much on the contract or some other screwup.

As for those Landreth sessions, we note that much of the material described by Harris was later released on CD as one of the numerous "Crazy Cajun" compilations issued in 1999 by the UK-based Edsel Records.

That series encompassed over thirty separate CDs, each featuring one of the many artists whom Meaux recorded in the 1960s and '70s (including Oscar Perry, the Sir Douglas Quintet, Barbara Lynn, Clifton Chenier, Frenchie Burke, and various others). The series was made possible when Meaux's accountants leased the rights to a large quantity of master tapes from his vault to Edsel in order to raise funds to settle Meaux's debts following his 1996 arrest and incarceration. The Crazy Cajun series is laden with hundreds of tracks recorded at SugarHill Studios—and thus are valuable historical documents of a time, a place, and the many sounds of Meaux's productions.

AFTER APPROXIMATELY ONE YEAR OF WORKING for Meaux, Harris departed. Brady, who had arrived in March 1974, took over most of his projects and set about improving on equipment maintenance. He describes that experience and offers additional information about the studio:

> When I got here the boards in both studios were noisy, and it was real hard to get a clean take on tape. . . . It took me a while to track everything down. Despite the few problems, the sound of the equipment and the studios were first-rate. The guys before me were like mix engineers, and they weren't good at maintenance.
>
> The other engineers that were hanging out here were Crash Collins and Robert Evans. . . . The studio had basically lost its edge because it was so badly maintained. But with better maintenance things improved quickly.
>
> Studio A was totally dead [soundwise] in those days. The green burlap was Huey's idea. It was five rows of acoustic insulation over the brick, and then chicken wire, and the burlap over that. So if you poked the burlap you'd feel the chicken wire holding the insulation against the wall.
>
> My take on this building is that it was well built and designed. The walls are divorced from the floor. If you go down to the bare walls and look at where they meet the floor, you're going to see a couple rows of that black tar

paper, so that there's really insulation between the concrete floor and the walls. The walls . . . are double rows of concrete block filled with sand. Those double thick walls did a great job of keeping the outside sounds from coming in. The green burlap all over the walls meant that nowhere in the room did you have any flutter echoes, and the room was reasonably dead. Thus, when you had bands . . . who all wanted to play in the same room together, if the room was live, you would be in big trouble to get any kind of isolation on individual instruments. The little booths in the back of the room also helped a bit, especially the small one with the Leslie speaker cabinet in it.

Although already possessing technical expertise that he brought to his job, Brady learned much more about production and mixing from his new employer. We close this chapter with his memories of the role Meaux played in getting the right sound:

> Huey was always in on the critical parts of sessions, vocals and mixing. He would sit next to me, to my right, and he had a big old rolling chair, and he would be, like, leaning back in it, and you never knew what he was thinking, but, boy, that little wheel was just turning all the time.
>
> What he was listening for was quite different to what we engineers were trying to achieve. . . . Huey set the tone for all mixing. I mean, from the moment I sat down to mix a tape, he said, "You're doing it all wrong." I was bringing up instruments and sound, kind of getting a half-ass low end. But he said, "The first thing you're going to do is you're going to stick that big bass drum in there—boom, boom—and I want to see those needles come up to here, you know." And he'd be fattening it up and just getting a nice big low thump at the bottom, but also a nice little pop at the top end of the thump at the bottom. Then he'd bring up the bass guitar, match it to the kick drum so they had somewhat equal weight, dead center, and then he'd start bringing in the snare and the toms and the cymbals. He'd always do his drums and his bass and get all that established. From that moment on, we would start adding piano. . . . The vocals were last, always. We'd start putting in the rhythm instruments and then the leads. You'd think of it like you were building a house, foundation up to the top with vocal, or maybe, like a pyramid.
>
> So Roger [Harris], Crash, and myself—we all learned from the best, Huey himself. That's why when you hear his old records they had more bass and more drum sounds than most records of that era. They were just fat and easy to dance to, and you have got to remember, most radios in cars were little six-inch speakers, and you had to fatten stuff up to sound good in them. Motown Records understood that concept. . . . and so did Huey Meaux.

The Freddy Fender
Phenomenon

O CCASIONALLY THE BIGGEST BREAKTHROUGHS come by sheer accident. At first, no matter how diligently or intelligently an artist, a producer, and others may have worked, their efforts may have just fallen flat. But then, rarely, and only for the lucky ones, something unplanned and unforeseen happens, and—eureka! A new pathway, a new energy, a new previously unnoticed possibility is suddenly there.

An important change in American popular music history occurred in 1975 when the Country Music Association bestowed its prestigious "Single of the Year" award on a certain recording produced by Huey Meaux at his SugarHill Studios. Sung by Freddy Fender, a Mexican American from South Texas, that single was unprecedented in ways that signified a cultural shift. The song was the very first release ever to be number one simultaneously on both the country and the pop charts, a remarkable achievement. But more to the point, it was the first bilingual song ever to register on the country charts. Its mainstream success was a true phenomenon.

That best-seller, "Before the Next Teardrop Falls," earned Gold and Platinum Record Awards—and anchored the first Platinum country album ever. *Billboard* magazine named its singer the 1975 "Male Vocalist of the Year," regardless of genre. Given that kind of adulation, it is no wonder that critical opinion has generally acclaimed Meaux's genius in getting Fender to sing part of a country ballad in Spanish.

However, as good as Meaux often was at cracking the code for crafting a hit, this groundbreaking vocal interpretation may well have been triggered by a fortuitous fluke.

Enter the scene, compliments of the eyewitness testimony of recording engineer Pat Brady, who starts by describing the instrumental track over which Fender would reluctantly sing:

> "Teardrop" originally came from Nashville, and the sixteen-track reel I worked on had the original tracks from the Nashville tape transferred to it. We then erased all except the drums, bass, and keyboards. It was written by Vivian Keith and Ben Peters, who have had a lot of hits.
>
> Freddy had written a whole bunch of songs and was not really happy about the way Huey was forcing certain songs [by others] down his throat. Freddy listened to a run-through of the track, but he didn't want to do that one, and we were doing lots of other songs at the time. It's just that Huey had a knack of dropping things on people—I mean, just surprising them a bit. And he insisted that we go ahead and do the song right away.
>
> So as Freddy listened to it for the second time, he started making notes [of the lyrics] on a big yellow pad, and when he got done, he put it out on a music stand in the A Studio. So I set up one of our U-67s, or maybe it was the U-47 [vintage Neumann microphones]. Then we started doing vocals.

However, as Brady goes on to describe, they did a couple of takes, and then a propitious accident occurred:

> But on one take, he didn't remember the words. . . . He dropped the yellow sheet on the floor at the end of the first verse. And before he had time to reach down and pick it up, the second verse came around—and that's when he did it in Spanish. When the instrumental break came, he was able to reach down and pick up the lyrics, and he finished the bridge in English. Huey sat bolt upright when that happened and said, "Let's keep that!" . . . So we left the Spanish verse, just like it was from that one take.

Thus, though Meaux has often been depicted as having brilliantly coaxed Fender into singing part of this song in Spanish, random chance and linguistic improvisation may have been at play.

Of course, Meaux did recognize the power of Fender's reinterpretation of the original lyrics—the beauty of his organic, effortless, and ultimately transcendent blending of the two languages of his heritage. Moreover, Meaux evidently did so at the very moment that he first heard it. As they say in the industry, the man had good ears.

But after Fender had taped the vocal track for what would prove to be his life-changing hit single, there was yet one other unplanned moment, another improvised idea that would infuse this masterpiece recording with a crucial element of sonic texture. One of the other SugarHill staff engineers, Roger Harris, explains how during a subsequent meal break, fortuity struck yet again:

> "Before the Next Teardrop Falls" was . . . on eight-track. So we dubbed the reel over to the sixteen-track, and then we went to lunch at a Mexican restaurant across town. We brought back to the studio the little band from the restaurant. And for a case of Tecate beer, they overdubbed accordion and Mexican guitars on the song. This changed the complexion of the song.

That spontaneous decision, presumably made by Meaux, to incorporate authentic Mexican-style instrumentation gave the song its crowning grace. Though nobody had possessed the strategic insight to prepare in advance for it, given the surprising developments during Fender's previous vocal session, it complemented his performance perfectly.

Genius is sometimes simply a matter of making the connections at hand, combining readily available components in an innovative way. Over the course of putting together Fender's original recording of "Before the Next Teardrop Falls," the singer and the producer had trusted their instincts and created something beautiful and unique. But during the actual studio production, and for a good while thereafter, they had little reason to believe that they had intuitively built a megahit.

Meaux had originally received the song from a friend, producer Shelby Singleton from Nashville. Singleton said he believed that this composition could be a bona fide hit, but that no one in Nashville, where it had been previously recorded by various singers, could do it justice. He then suggested that one of Meaux's "characters" might be able to do the job. As Singleton explains, "'Teardrop' was written by two of our staff writers. The Freddy Fender recording was the thirty-fifth recording of the song. The song made the bottom of the charts each time it was released, but never was a big hit till the Freddy recording."

By the time they produced their definitive version of the song at SugarHill Studios, Meaux and Fender had already been collaborating in vain for a couple of years, trying to resurrect Fender's career—which had been launched back in the 1950s when, known as "El Bebop Kid," he was playing rock 'n' roll and doing Spanish-language covers of Elvis Presley songs. Based on the fervent recommendation of Doug Sahm, who as a teen had idolized Fender after seeing him perform at a San Antonio drive-in movie theater, Meaux had sought out the singer. In 1972 he found him washing cars in Corpus Christi. A week later Meaux signed him to his Crazy Cajun label. They tried several new angles in search of '70s success, including even reggae. Harris says that shortly before the "Teardrop" session, he engineered "an album for Freddy Fender, thirteen or fourteen songs. . . . Huey had gone to Jamaica and brought back an eight-track reel of reggae rhythm tracks that we transferred to the sixteen-track. We then added Freddy's voice to them." But the results of that album—and their partnership in general thus far—had been mediocre at best, leading to some artist-producer tensions.

Thus, when Meaux played the "Teardrop" demo and urged the singer to give it a try, Fender had bristled and asserted his distaste for doing a country song. Meaux's persistence and manipulation eventually led to Fender desultorily scribbling the lyrics and cutting some tracks to appease the producer. But the magic that transformed that session depended on Fender dropping his page of notes and improvising a verse in his people's language.

"I have always felt that the Spanish that Huey and Freddy put in the song was the main reason it became a big hit," says Singleton. As for his motivation, beyond support for his own staff songwriters, for offering the song to another producer, Singleton adds, "At the time Huey was struggling, and I wanted to help him as a friend, so I gave him the tracks."

Thus, through a series of atypical circumstances, one of the biggest records of the mid-1970s came to be. Not only was the single well received nationwide, but so was the subsequently released album of the same name, which spawned even more hits. Brady offers this account of its success:

> It was actually the number four record [album] of all in 1975 in sales . . . and I mean he's up there with Elton John and some of the other pop stars of that year—the fourth-largest-selling album of that year! And that was a shock to me when I found out that it was that big. Prior to coming to Houston I had worked PR for CBS Records for about five years, so I knew a bit about the music business. The album sold like crazy. . . . It was the first country album to be certified Platinum, which was quite a milestone. I'm not sure they made a big deal out of it at the time here in Houston, but it was something in *Billboard*.

Based on the success of the "Before the Next Teardrop Falls" single, Meaux had placed Fender's identically titled debut album on a major label, ABC/Dot. According to *Nashville City Beat* magazine, by the end of that year it had already sold 650,000 copies in the LP format and another 450,000 on cassettes. Since then it has sold millions more, right into the MP3 era.

Thanks to the tip from Sahm, who later formed the Grammy Award–winning Texas Tornados supergroup with Fender and others, Meaux had achieved the biggest hit record of his career. Though he had changed the site's name from Gold Star to SugarHill, Meaux had also produced it in the same Houston studio where, almost ten years earlier, he had recorded the Sir Douglas Quintet's "She's About a Mover," the big break in Sahm's storied career.

But the success of the Fender recording did not come right away. Meaux first vigorously shopped the master tape to a variety of larger labels, only to be repeatedly rebuffed. Finally, still believing in the magic of that taped moment, he issued the recording himself on his Crazy Cajun label, paired with "Waiting for Your Love" as the B-side (#2002). Then, given his limited distribution network and his inability to match the major labels' well-funded promotional efforts, Meaux personally committed to getting the record heard. Brady picks up the story:

> Huey then hit the road with a ton of records in the trunk of his car. He also took with him a bunch of cash and allegedly a bunch of not-so-legitimate drugs to use as incentive for the disc jockeys at the many country music radio stations out in the Texas countryside to play the record. Whatever the methods used, Huey got them to play the record. As they say, the rest is history.

As Meaux was fond of pointing out, promotion was the key that made a record a hit, and with "Teardrop" he had proven it yet again.

But ultimately, no matter how much push a producer or a DJ might give, the fickle public had to respond. And in 1975, when Americans of various generations, ethnic backgrounds, and musical tastes heard Fender's exquisite tenor articulating this dual-language heart ballad, millions of them connected with it—making it one of the greatest recordings ever produced at the oldest continuously operating studio in Texas.

SIX MONTHS AFTER "TEARDROP" had climbed the charts, Meaux released a new version of one of Fender's older songs, originally recorded in 1959—the swamp-pop classic "Wasted Days and Wasted Nights." This single quickly claimed the number one slot on the country charts, duplicating its predecessor's achievement. It also made the Top Ten on the pop charts, cresting at number eight. "Wasted Days" solidified Fender's status as an established star, and, paired with the previous hit ballad, it showcased his versatility as a singer.

It would be followed by even more astounding success. As John Morthland notes in *Texas Monthly*, "From January 1975 to the end of 1977, Freddy had twelve straight Top 20 country hits, nine of them in the Top 10, four reaching number one."

Another SugarHill engineer, Mickey Moody, relates his memories of the sessions that produced Fender's second round of hits:

My first recordings with Freddy included "Wasted Days and Wasted Nights." That electric harpsichord solo was Bruce Ewen. Randy Cornor played guitar. Donny King was on bass. Dahrell Norris played drums. I put at least three rhythm guitars on it, and Tracey Balin did the background vocals. That song was recorded from the ground up [as opposed to being based on a preexisting instrumental track].

Given Fender's previous nationwide hit, "Wasted Days" bypassed Meaux's little Crazy Cajun imprint and was released right away on the high-profile major label ABC/Dot Records (#17558).

The subsequent third-in-a-row number one country single for Fender, "Secret Love," was released near the end of 1975 on ABC/Dot. This composition, by the Hollywood songwriting team of Sammy Fain and Paul Francis Webster, was already an oldie, having won the Oscar Award for Best Original Film Song for its interpretation by Doris Day in *Calamity Jane*. Released also as a Day single, the song had hit number one on the pop charts in 1954—and thereafter was covered by various singers. But nobody had sung it the way Fender did in his SugarHill session, where taking his cue from the "Teardrop" success, he made a point to sing one verse in Spanish. In addition to achieving first place in the country rankings, that record also made the pop charts, peaking at number twenty. Moody says that this one "was also totally recorded from scratch here at the studio with members of the Houston Symphony on strings." The poignant ballad received lush accompaniment, and Cornor provided some tasteful guitar embellishment. In fact, Cornor's work on several Fender records led him to a contract, as an artist in his own right, with ABC/ Dot Records.

Moody tells how he had come to be affiliated with the studio where he first worked with Fender:

> I was producing a group called the Cate Brothers. Tom Noonan—from the record company that I was leasing their album to—suggested adding voices and horns to their record. Then he asked me if I knew Huey Meaux. I was not familiar with him. But I said, "If you think we need to add those things, set it up."
>
> Meaux called me about a week later and asked me when I could bring the masters. They were on four-track; he wanted to transfer them to eight-track and do his work on them. That thrilled me because I had only heard vague tales about eight-track machines existing. So I brought them down, and we went from there on to other projects and talked about production and started working together.

left to right: Huey Meaux, Leo O'Neil, and Mickey Moody, at SugarHill Studios, 1976

He asked me to come down to Houston and take over the engineering department at SugarHill. I was happy to do it, especially after I had found out about some of the credits that he had.

In April of 1976 Asylum Records released a single called "Union Man" and an eponymous album from the Arkansas-based Cate Brothers. Although formally produced and mixed by Steve Cropper in Memphis, Moody actually engineered some parts of the recordings at SugarHill. Moreover, he and Meaux shared the publishing rights for both sides of the single and eight songs from the album. Moody comments, "The first hit record we worked on was the Cates. I did vocal overdubs here at SugarHill on that record."

Around the time of the Cate Brothers releases, Fender had a new album out on ABC/Dot Records, called *Rockin' Country,* and the first single released was an old Hank Williams nugget, "I Can't Help It."

The fourth of Fender's SugarHill-produced number one hit records came with a distinguished pedigree. Back in 1962 Meaux had scored a crossover hit with the song "You'll Lose a Good Thing," written and performed by Barbara Lynn (though Meaux secured the official songwriting credit, and hence royalties, for himself). That song, originally recorded in New Orleans and released on the Jamie label (#1220), had topped the national R&B charts and soared as high as number eight on the pop charts for Lynn, making it one of Meaux's early big successes. It also demonstrated his uncanny ability to find hit songs and unusual artists such as Lynn, who was probably the first left-handed female R&B guitarist ever to have a hit record.

Approximately fourteen years later Meaux's production of Fender's crooning cover of her signature song not only topped the country charts but also made the pop Top 40, registering highest at number thirty-two.

Leo O'Neil, a veteran of previous work at Gold Star Studios, returned to SugarHill to perform on that session and others. He says,

> Huey brought me back here in late '76 or early '77. I remember Huey playing "Teardrop" to me over the telephone. When I came back to SugarHill, I used to keep a Mellotron [polyphonic keyboard] in Studio A and would play lots of string parts on it for the sessions. The first song I ever played on for Freddy was . . . "You'll Lose a Good Thing." The players on that record were my band. Evan Arredondo played bass, Louis Broussard played drums, Eddie Nation played guitar, and I played piano.

Meanwhile, O'Neil did string arrangements and keyboard overdubbing for various other Fender songs, and his group backed the singer again on "Talk to Me." That song, which hit number thirteen on the country charts for Fender, was a remake of the 1958 R&B hit (sung by Little Willie John) that had been popularly covered again in 1963 by Fender's fellow South Texan, Sunny Ozuna.

Starting in early 1975, musician Don Michael "Red" Young also played on sessions for Fender and other artists at SugarHill. It happened as a result of Young's role in a Fort Worth–based band called the Ham Brothers. He says,

> We came down to Houston often to work on projects for Mickey [Moody]. My first trip down was with Bill Ham and Bruce Ewen to work on an album for Freddy. Some of those cuts wound up on his *Before the Next Teardrop Falls* album. We would come down for a week and work on Freddy's stuff, the Ham Brothers album, and other tracks. . . .
>
> One of my primary jobs was arranging vocal parts. The studio had this chick singer named Tracey Balin, and she would do all the harmony parts on the records. Originally she lived in Florida, and they would fly her in. . . . We would wind up working on twenty-five or thirty songs over the course of a few days.

Musician Gaylan Latimer, a former member of the Dawgs, had recorded for Meaux earlier in his career in the duo Bob and Gaylan. By the 1970s, however, he was working regularly at SugarHill as an in-house songwriter and occasional session player. He comments on the facility's level of activity during the peak of the Fender phenomenon:

> In 1976, following the success of Freddy Fender, Huey signed a large number of writers to publishing contracts to write for Freddy and his other artists. Back in the space that had been the original big studio, Huey set up a number of long tables and had as many as a dozen writers working on song ideas. Oscar Perry, Danny Epps, Doak Walker, myself, and a number of others were being paid between fifty and seventy-five dollars a week to just come in and write. Huey would give us ideas and then turn us loose. . . .
>
> During this time period both studios were working hard. In the B Studio, Mickey Moody was cutting tracks for Freddy Fender, Donny King, Tracey Balin, and other artists. . . . It was in 1977 that Freddy cut my song, "Think about Me." It was on the ABC/Dot album *If You Don't Love Me* (#2090), and in November of that year it peaked at number eighteen on the *Billboard* country charts.

Young adds, "Huey had a bunch of songwriters hanging around and cutting demos continually—guys like Lee Emerson, Gaylan Latimer, Oscar Perry, Danny Epps, and some other guys." Meaux sought to craft more hits not only for Fender but also for other artists whom he was producing. Maintaining a songwriting staff contractually obligated to his publishing company was a key part of the process. And though Fender would continue to make numerous other recordings that sold well, Meaux kept prospecting in search of another star.

THE FIRST HALF OF 1976 WAS A PROLIFIC TIME for SugarHill Studios. A new Kinky Friedman album was in the works for ABC/Dunhill Records. Sahm was recording an album for ABC/Dot. Balin, a background vocalist on many Fender recordings, was making her own new recordings. Sherri Jerrico had just finished a Crazy Cajun single called "A Friend of Yours and Mine." Donny King had recently recorded "Wake Me Gently" (written by Beth Thornton, Meaux's executive secretary) for Warner Brothers Records. The former bassist with the Jimi Hendrix Experience, Noel Redding, was recording a new album for RCA Records. Singer-songwriter Lee Emerson recorded a song called "Gospel Truth (Telling It Like It Is)." John Stuckey and the Magic Cowboy Band recorded a single with Jerry Jeff Walker: "Grandma's Love" and "Moonlight Mailman."

Brady recalls other SugarHill recordings of that time:

Donny King recorded a version of the old Cookie and the Cupcakes hit "Mathilda." Huey leased it to Warner Brothers Records, and it charted on *Billboard* country and went as high as number twenty. We also did a version of another old song, "I'm a Fool to Care," . . . [which] charted [at number seventy-two].

Donny King . . . had been part of Bob Wills' Texas Playboys. "Mathilda" was recorded in a style you would pretty much expect from a Wills side-man—some excellent swing. Huey released the record on his American Plaboy label [#1983] for distribution through the Southwest. . . . Andy Wickham, head of Warner's Country A&R, snapped it up and released it—and an album produced by Meaux.

Meaux pursued a new direction via an ongoing western swing revival, which had been triggered in part by two exceptional Austin-based neotradi-tionalist bands: Asleep at the Wheel (which would later record independently at SugarHill) and Alvin Crow and the Pleasant Valley Boys. In 1975 Crow recorded a single for Meaux's Crazy Cajun label, "Retirement Run" backed with "Country Ways" (#2001). The Pleasant Valley Boys featured a number of prominent talents, including Bobby Earl Smith on rhythm guitar and Herb Steiner on steel. But the record made little impact. Crow claims that was be-cause Meaux was distracted from promoting it. "When Freddy Fender hit big," he explains, "quite a number of the artists that Huey signed fell by the wayside."

However, Meaux continued to record numerous artists. One from his home state was Tommy McLain, who says,

I first met Huey P. Meaux [in 1965] when he took [my recording of "Sweet Dreams"] and promoted it all over the country and helped break it in Philadelphia. . . . I wrote the B-side, "I Need You So," and it was later record-ed by Freddy Fender. I recorded nine or ten albums with Huey and some of it has come out on Edsel Records in Europe. . . .

"Jukebox Songs" was one of my regional hits from SugarHill. I recorded that with my two boys, Barry Lynn and Chad McLain. Barry played drums and Chad played guitar also on "Baby Dolls." *The Backwoods Bayou Adventure* album was picked up by CBS and released in Canada and Europe.

McLain also recorded a Crazy Cajun LP with Fender during this phase titled *Friends in Show Business*. Looking back, McLain says,

Recording at SugarHill with Huey was the best. The engineers were terrific, and so were the musicians. If he needed special players, he would fly them in. Otherwise, they were the best from Texas and Louisiana. The recording sessions there were like nowhere else. It was the big time, and it was going on! Huey knew about the music business, and he had a great spirit about him. He was a great father-figure in the music business.

Warren Storm, another swamp-pop singer, reviews his experience at Meaux's studio:

I first came to SugarHill in 1965, when it was called Gold Star, and recorded a few things for Huey back then. In the 1970s we must have recorded at least a hundred masters. He must have released at least twenty or twenty-five singles. The first actual album was that record we did for CBS/Starflite in 1978. We had several releases on Huey's subsidiary Starflite. . . . That European label, Edsel, put out a CD called *King of the Dance Halls*. . . . One of the 45s that got good regional airplay was "King of the Dance Halls." "Things Have Gone to Pieces" made some noise on *Billboard*. . . . I did a lot of country out there and some swamp pop. I also did some blues.

But of all the SugarHill productions that Meaux would bankroll with his Fender-windfall profits, perhaps the most personally satisfying, if not profitable, resulted in a new album and two singles by Sahm. That LP, called *Texas Rock for Country Rollers,* credited on the cover to Sir Doug and the Texas Tornados, is an obscure 1976 gem. In addition to Sahm's performance on lead vocals, guitar, piano, and fiddle, this ten-track set features musical back-up from Augie Meyers, Atwood Allen, Harry Hess, Jack Barber, and George Rains. Produced by Meaux, the album was engineered by Moody, who also performed on acoustic guitar. Like Fender's recent smash hit *Teardrop* LP, this one was released on ABC/Dot, as were the two singles. The latter featured "Cowboy Peyton Place" and "I Love the Way You Love" (#17656), as well as "Cryin' Inside Sometimes" backed with "I'm Missing You" (#17674), all of which appear also on the LP.

Through this album project, not only was Meaux reconnecting with a protégé but also perhaps repaying Sahm for recommending Fender—advice that had yielded huge rewards for both of Sahm's old friends. Meaux also reunited Sahm and Fender in the recording studio—producing tracks for the Crazy Cajun LP *Re-Union of the Cosmic Brothers* (#1013).

THE CASH FLOW GENERATED by the Fender phenomenon encouraged Meaux to invest in more studio equipment. By adding new technology to the inventory of vintage tube equalizers, compressors, and microphones already there, the studio would appeal to a wider range of clients.

Doug Sahm and Freddy Fender, 1975

At the time of the upgrade, the tape machines had been a Scully with six-teen-, four-, and two-track decks, and an Ampex 440 eight-track that ran one-inch tape. There were also two tube EMT 140 plate reverbs housed up above the control room in the tape vault. Studio B had a Fairchild multispring reverb. Control room monitors were Altec 604E speakers with Master Lab crossovers and a matching Altec power amp. Studio monitors were Altec A-10s.

Moody, the chief engineer, provides this overview of the changes in the studio's hardware situation at the time:

> Most of my early recordings were done in Studio A. Until we got the MCI tape recorders and Auditronics boards, the serious recording was done in A. Demo sessions and a lot of experimentation with gear were done in the B Studio, which had a lot of old gear. We wound up buying two of everything for the studios. Eventually we had two boards, two MCI sixteen-track ma-chines, two sixteen-channel Dolby A racks, four MCI two-track machines with Dolby A as well. Following the arrival of the new equipment, I moved over to Studio B to do the main recording. The new gear began arriving in very early 1976, and we did the B room first.

As part of the remodeling, Studio B's control room was walled in sheetrock covered in red burlap. The floor was carpeted and a wooden railing installed around the raised section of flooring. Meaux modified the other control room too, covering most of the acoustic tile walls with cedar wood paneling or cork tiles. He also installed a sloping false ceiling lined with absorbent baffles.

Lines ran from the plate reverbs so that both studios would have access to them. The reverb chamber closer to the smaller control room was dedicated primarily to its use. The other chamber was wired to Studio B. Sixteen lines ran between the two studios connecting the two consoles together, for use in the event of a very large recording project. As early as 1973, equalized phone lines had been installed in the Studio B control room closet so that live broadcasts to radio could be readily engineered.

In late 1978, directly behind Studio B Meaux built an air-conditioned warehouse, space that he would later lease from new owners. Having started a label called Starflite and secured a 1979 distribution deal with CBS Records, Meaux used the warehouse for shipping and receiving of products.

The Starflite label launched with three artists—Fender, Storm, and McLain—who were featured in a huge coming-out concert at Mickey Gilley's famous nightclub and broadcast on local radio. Earlier in the evening Meaux had hosted a cocktail party/dinner at the Galleria Plaza Hotel for key media personnel and a number of visiting record executives.

With such big deals being negotiated and new opportunities abounding, Meaux gradually participated less in studio production. "Huey wasn't one for hanging around in those days," says Latimer. "He would pop in and give his blessings and go back to whatever he was doing. In the '60s he would hang in there with us, but not in the latter part of the '70s. He was busy doing other things."

By that point, "Huey was an armchair producer," says Moody. "A lot of the time he was in the office taking care of the business or running Freddy's career . . . involved in the process—but not sitting in the studio for ten to twelve hours a day."

Given the affluence that he had achieved as a result of Fender's success, Meaux could now afford to hire others to man the studio productions. In less than a decade, he had transformed himself from recently paroled ex-con to a struggling studio owner/producer to high-profile music magnate. Trusting his wheeler-dealer instincts and good ears, Meaux had turned his life around, financially speaking at least.

But beyond that, Meaux had also resurrected the music business reputation and hit-making tradition of the oldest recording studio in the state.

19

The Later '70s and Early '80s

Y THE LATER 1970S HUEY MEAUX and SugarHill Studios were famous nationwide, and several notable bands or musicians from beyond the region trekked there to record. Some of them came because of connections they had made with Meaux, some to perform for live radio broadcast, some to handle a task while touring, and some to utilize the facility's vintage equipment. Regardless of their motivations, there was an upsurge in the number of visitors who ventured to SugarHill.

In October 1973 the California rock group Little Feat came to Houston for two concerts at Liberty Hall. At SugarHill Studios they also staged a four-song set (which lasted about twenty-five minutes) for live broadcast on KPFT-FM radio. In addition to founding guitarist and singer Lowell George (1945–1979), the classic lineup of Paul Barrere, Bill Payne, Richie Hayward, Sam Clayton, and Kenny Gradney performed. The set they delivered is a dazzling display of surrealistic rock and R&B, preserved on a reel of one-inch eight-track tape in the studio vault. The songs are "China White," "Somebody's Leaving Tonight," "Dixie Chicken," and "Tripe Face Boogie." Roger Harris engineered, and the recording quality is superb. Little Feat thus helped inaugurate the live-broadcast relationship between SugarHill and KPFT that flourished throughout the 1970s and has continued, in various forms, to the present.

We wish we had archived tape to document the studio's complete history, but some known sessions remain mysterious. "I was also the engineer on the Ted Nugent and the Amboy Dukes recordings done here. I don't know if any of that material ever got released," says Mickey Moody. We do have confirmation, through Nugent's management company, that the bombastic rocker (b. 1948) recorded at SugarHill in the '70s. Moody adds, "A lot of times they would record, and then when we were completely done, they would take the reels with them, and that's the last that we would hear about it."

Even more surprising, the eclectic pop-rock composer, singer, multi-instrumentalist, and producer Todd Rundgren (b. 1948) recorded at SugarHill in late 1975 and early 1976. Like much of his acclaimed studio work, these sessions reportedly involved Rundgren playing most of the instruments and doing all the vocals himself. Some of the results can be found on his 1976 album *Faithful*. Of this unique project Stephen Thomas Erlewine writes,

> Presumably *Faithful* celebrates the past and the future by juxtaposing a side of original pop material with a side of covers. Actually "covers" isn't accurate—the six oldies that comprise the entirety of side one are re-creations, with Rundgren "faithfully" replicating the sound and feel of the Yardbirds . . . Bob Dylan . . . Jimi Hendrix . . . Beach Boys . . . and the Beatles. . . . It's remarkable how close Rundgren comes to duplicating the very feel of the originals.

Pat Brady, one of the studio engineers, explains why Rundgren had traveled to Houston to cut these tracks:

> One of the reasons he wanted to come down here is because we had a working Telefunken U-47 [microphone], and by that time they had stopped making them, and they were rare gems. It was a mic you could only find in certain studios. Anyway, he came here for that mic and all the other tube gear that we had here. The original songs he was rerecording were all done on tube gear, and we had a lot of it. . . .
>
> Todd was recording material that came out on his *Faithful* album. He did that Beach Boys hit "Good Vibrations" here. He did re-creations of different groups, and he did them really well. . . . He brought a number of reels that weren't finished that he finished here, and in some cases he was doing whole new songs. Mickey Moody handled whatever engineering Todd didn't do himself.

Moody adds, "I know that some of what we worked on wound up on the album *Faithful*. At the same time we cut a lot of tracks that were not finished here. . . . I know he was totally happy with what he did here and took the tapes back to the Northeast for more work."

Staff songwriter and musician Gaylan Latimer provides additional insights: "Every so often Huey would tell me to tell all the guys that the building was off-limits for a couple of days, and Todd would have been one of those times."

During the same era, Texas-based acts were still frequently using the facility, of course. And in 1975 one of the hottest Austin ensembles was the posthippie western swing revivalist group known as Asleep at the Wheel. This Ray Benson–led band was coming off a successful album release on Capitol Records when it recorded two tracks at SugarHill for the 1976 follow-up release. That effort, *Wheelin' and Dealin',* would earn spots on both the country and pop LP charts and, like its predecessor, would yield three hit singles and receive a Grammy Award nomination.

Benson recorded both SugarHill tracks with his Wheel lineup of the moment: Chris O'Connell, Floyd Domino, Tony Garnier, Scott Hennige, Danny Levin, Bill Mabry, Lucky Oceans, and Leroy Preston. One of the hits they made there, "Miles and Miles of Texas," remains a signature number for the band today. In his "Artist's Song Notes" commentary for *Lone Star Music,* Benson explains the background of this classic track:

> In 1974, Tommy Allsup and I went over to Hank Thompson's publishing company to see if they had any old tunes we might want to do. We turned up this gem, "Miles and Miles of Texas," which was a demo from around 1950. It had never been recorded . . . so we cut it in Houston, TX for our album, *Wheelin' and Dealin'.* Since then it has become a Texas standard and a song forever associated with Asleep at the Wheel. A tip of the ole Stetson to Diana Johnston and the late Tommy Camfield for writing this great ode to the Lone Star State!

The special guest guitarist on the SugarHill recording of "Miles and Miles" was Bucky Meadows.

During the same session Asleep at the Wheel also taped "They Raided the Joint," an album track. This blues boogie featured guest appearances by the venerable jazz saxophonist Arnett Cobb and the former Bob Wills sideman and fiddler/mandolinist extraordinaire Johnny Gimble, as well as additional sax work by Link Davis Jr. Moody says, "I engineered, and production was handled by committee."

Of the many diverse SugarHill productions, the weirdest involved Kinky Friedman and His Texas Jewboys in 1976. Over a series of days, they cut several tracks for the album *Lasso from El Paso,* coproduced by Meaux. As David Lonergan writes in *St. James Encyclopedia of Pop Culture,* "Friedman achieved his musical high-water mark with an album on the Epic label, *Lasso from El Paso.* (The song was originally titled 'Asshole from El Paso,' a parody of Merle Haggard's 'Okie from Muskogee,' but Epic required a title change before issuing the record.)" On parts of the album recorded elsewhere (including a live concert performance), Friedman (b. 1944) featured guests such as Bob Dylan,

Eric Clapton, and Ringo Starr. Musicians on the SugarHill tracks, along with Friedman, included Jim Atkinson, Tom Culpepper, Bill Ham, Brian Clarke, Terry Danko, Ira Wilkes, and Major Boles.

Moody recalls those sessions:

> The album we did for Kinky . . . only problems we had were his people. He had a hard-core bunch of followers that went everywhere with him. When people in Houston heard he was making an album at SugarHill, tons of people showed up wanting to hang out. It was a real hassle to keep them under control while we were trying to record. Even the mayor's wife wanted to hang out during the recording, and we had to organize security. Except for that, we all had a hot time making the record.

The former bassist from the Jimi Hendrix Experience, British musician Noel Redding (1945–2003), also recorded at SugarHill Studios in 1976. Both Brady and Moody handled engineering duties at various sessions, staged over three weeks, cutting tracks for Redding's *Blowin'* album, his second for RCA Records. "The album rocked harder than its predecessor," William Ruhlmann writes, "and, recorded largely in the US, seemed to have more of an American, on-the-road feel." "There were six or seven guys in the band," Brady says. "And these guys were really happy, jolly, drunken guys. . . . It was a kind of loose session that lasted a long time."

CLOSER TO HOME, NEW ORLEANS PIANIST and vocalist Mac Rebennack (b. 1940), better known by his stage name Dr. John, also cut an album at SugarHill during this phase of operations. This blues, funk, and R&B arranger, producer, and musician had been a friend of Meaux's since the early 1960s. In 1973 Dr. John had achieved major pop stardom with the Allen Toussaint–produced LP *In the Right Place*. However, by the later '70s his career was stalled. During this time he came to Houston and recorded, perhaps adding to older unreleased tracks Meaux already had on tape. Ultimately at least seventeen tracks were completed at SugarHill Studios by 1977, engineered by Moody.

They evidently all remained unreleased until the Edsel label (England) issued *Dr. John: The Crazy Cajun Recordings* in 1999. Then in 2000 the same tracks were licensed also to Demon Music Group (England), which reissued them under the title *Hoodoo: The Collection*.

Along with Dr. John on piano and vocals, these recordings also featured late-Seventies SugarHill Studios mainstays such as keyboardist Leo O'Neil, drummer Dahrell Norris, bassist Ira Wilkes, three different guitarists (including Moody), and backing vocals by the Merlene Singers. O'Neil adds, "I would write arrangements for Mac [Dr. John]. Huey and Mac were good friends, and

Huey had him record all kinds of songs on piano and vocal, and then bass, drums, and other instruments were added later."

Pop singer and former teen actor Rick Nelson (1940–1985) was also a Meaux acquaintance and reportedly performed anonymously on guitar on numerous SugarHill Studios sessions in the late 1970s. He was part of a behind-the-scenes crew of top-rate players that Meaux sometimes hired. So was James Burton—famous for his guitar work on recordings by Elvis Presley, Merle Haggard, and others. Moody recalls, "Ricky was a good friend of Huey's, as was James. Ricky did a lot of recording of his own music, and we used him as a guitar player and backup singer. James played in Ricky's band and would do sessions for us whenever he was in Houston."

It was an exceptionally busy time at SugarHill Studios. Musician Gordon Payne even recalls Waylon Jennings, with whom he was touring, coming there to do "voice-overs for *The Dukes of Hazzard* TV show."

By the late 1970s Meaux had raised the profile of SugarHill Studios in a way that attracted many nonlocal stars and new types of business.

NEVERTHELESS, THE RENAISSANCE at SugarHill Studios also impacted the local music scene profoundly. For one, it provided a place of employment for songwriters, arrangers, and session musicians. Also, it hosted recording sessions for various artists living in the area at the time—including future star Lucinda Williams.

Latimer describes the SugarHill environment in those days:

> While the hits were being cut in Studio B, a group of musicians and songwriters and I were busy in the gold star room cutting demos of all the songs that had been written by the staff writers. Musicians on the demo sessions were Billy Block or Robbie Parrish on drums, Rick Robertson on bass, the various songwriters playing guitar, and Leo on keyboards. Huey paid us twenty-five dollars a day to come in and record demos. One day we would record all of the songs I had written recently. The next day we would do Danny Epps's songs, and then the next day it would be Oscar Perry's, and so on. The building was absolutely hopping, and it was wild times. It was a real free time. We would go in and cut and play songs all day long.

Guitarist Kenny Cordray adds, "I remember coming in one morning at 10 a.m. and—literally did twelve to fifteen songs' worth of guitar tracks and solos—not leaving until well after dark." He also opines that engaging in this expedited process, though exhausting, was good training. He points out, "Gaylan was one of the better writers in Houston and benefited by having all of this recording done."

However, Houston-based musicians such as Latimer and Cordray also used SugarHill Studios to record some of their own projects. By 1978 they had re-formed the group called Heather Black with some new members. They then recorded what Latimer calls a "rock 'n' roll album with a jazz influence," but it never got released. "We had horn players like Kirk Whalum and Larry Slazak on the record. Huey wouldn't have anything to do with it; he didn't like it, or understand it," Latimer says. "It wasn't rock-pop with verse, hook, and out. It was complex music, and Huey didn't get off to that stuff."

During this time, Latimer introduced Meaux to a Texas singer (born Chris Geppert, 1951) who would go on to achieve major pop stardom under his stage name, winning five Grammy Awards for his 1979 debut album on a major label. Latimer reports,

> Quite a few members of Heather Black eventually left and joined up with Chris Geppert and formed the Christopher Cross Band. I brought Chris to Huey as a possible artist for Huey's label, and Huey authorized a demo session in 1977. . . . Huey decided not to sign Christopher Cross, and just shortly after this session, the band signed with Warner Brothers Records, and "Sail Away" took Chris to a hit record.

Given the amount of traffic through the studio doors in those days, it is no wonder that Meaux might have erred occasionally in evaluating a prospect. They were plentiful and often impressive. Brady recalls,

> Jerry Jeff Walker would come in with a friend named Big John Stuckey. John owned a tattoo parlor and was a big ol' Texas boy, huge guy. . . . We never formally recorded him, but I always put two mics on him, one on guitar and one on vocal. I recorded him straight through the board and went to the two-track machine. . . . He would do songs that would literally bring tears to our eyes because they were so tender.

Brady also speaks highly of a local country-rock group he recorded, called Dogtooth Violet. "This was a great band and I severely loved these guys: Bob Oldrieve, Joe Lindley, and Marty Smith," he says. "This was some of the best folk-rock that I had ever heard." Band cofounder Oldrieve tells how they came to record at SugarHill:

> We were playing at a club on Main Street called Papa Feelgood's. Huey P. Meaux came out to see us and heard us. He liked the band and wanted us to come in the studio and do some demos. . . . Shortly after doing this session, he approached us with a record deal. We thought about signing with him,

and we knew that anybody who had success from Houston had gone through him. But we turned him down.

Oldrieve goes on to express his regrets at declining Meaux's offer to produce a real record, and within a few years the group had disbanded to pursue other projects.

As the 1970s were ending, one of the hottest folk-rock groups in the region was called St. Elmo's Fire. One of the singers was Connie Mims. "Everybody told us that we should make a record. I think we came to SugarHill because it was SugarHill. The studio was having hit records, and everybody knew that," she says. Craig Calvert, St. Elmo's Fire singer-songwriter-guitarist, adds, "SugarHill came with a great rep, and already had a lot of success under its belt. . . . We wanted to entice record companies into signing us, and we needed something on tape to do that."

In 1977 Crazy Cajun Records issued a Meaux-produced album by Doak Snead called *Think of Me Sometime* (#1096). But Meaux was simultaneously looking to exploit the Tejano music scene in some fashion. In 1977 he recorded the Latin Breed, breaking ground in the San Antonio–based vanguard of the highly produced, modernized Tejano sound. The resulting album on the BGO label, *A New Horizon* (#1143), was coproduced by Meaux and bandleader/saxophonist Gilbert Escobedo. The lead singer of the group, Adalberto Gallegos (b. 1956), also recorded a solo album at SugarHill during the same time. Called *La Voz de Adalberto Gallegos,* it was released on the GCP label (#144) and coproduced by Meaux and Gallegos. Moody engineered both projects.

But of all the area artists who recorded at SugarHill Studios in this era, perhaps the most noteworthy was the singer-songwriter Lucinda Williams, an intermittent resident of Houston during much of the 1970s and early '80s. In 1980 she went to SugarHill to record the eleven tracks for *Happy Woman Blues,* her first album of original material.

Years later, following the Grammy Award for her 1998 album *Car Wheels on a Gravel Road,* Williams became a major star on the alternative country scene. By 2001, *Time* magazine even declared her "America's best songwriter." But in the late '70s Williams was relatively unknown beyond the nurturing environs of places like the Houston acoustic folk music club called Anderson Fair. In 1978, after sending a demo tape to Moses Asch of Folkways Records in New York City, she had gone to Jackson, Mississippi, to record her first album, which comprised covers of folk and blues standards. In 1979 it was released to little notice on the Folkways imprint.

Back in Houston, Williams next worked at SugarHill on *Happy Woman Blues,* her debut recording as a songwriter. During April, May, and June of

1980, she coproduced it with Mickey White, while Moody engineered. The supporting cast of musicians includes White and Moody, plus Rex Bell, Andre Matthews, Ira Wilkes, and Malcolm Smith. The album was originally released on a Folkways LP (#31067) later that year, and then reissued on CD by Smithsonian Folkways in 1990.

As Steve Huey writes for *Allmusic.com*, "As her first album of original compositions, it was an important step forward, and although it was much more bound by the dictates of tradition than her genre-hopping later work, her talent was already in evidence." Former *Houston Press* music editor John Nova Lomax notes, however, that "the languid, drawling voice" for which Williams is famous was already present, as were "the poetic and geographical imagery and memorable melodies, the keen eye for telling details, the chronicles of the faulty attempts lovers make to meld minds as well as bodies." Nonetheless, the album sold poorly, and Williams would remain relatively obscure for a while.

As with the public's general indifference to *Happy Woman Blues* in 1980, the legacy of SugarHill Studios has frequently been overlooked in the annals of music history. But in retrospect we see that greatness sometimes takes time and perspective to appreciate.

Meaux's Final Phase

BY 1984 THE FLOW OF PROFITS from Huey Meaux–produced hits had slackened to a trickle. Most members of the engineering staff, including the recently added Lonnie Wright, were gone or professionally engaged only sporadically at SugarHill Studios. The recording equipment there had not been updated since the 1970s, and poor maintenance had caused quality control to decline. Moreover, the building had yet to recover fully from the major damage it had sustained from Hurricane Alicia in August 1983.

That storm had spawned numerous tornadoes, one of which ripped a huge hole in the roof of Studio B. Insurance coverage eventually provided funds to replace the roof—but not before the studio and control room had been thoroughly soaked and exposed to weeks of extreme humidity. Numerous valuable microphones and the piano were badly damaged. The burlap walls were drenched and eventually covered in funky mildew. The flood line, approximately six to eight inches high, indicated that equipment on the floor had sat in dirty water. Consequently, even after the roof was repaired, the room was effectively closed because of technical issues and the stench of rotting burlap and carpet.

Unfortunately, there was not a lot of activity going on in the other studio room either. Most of Meaux's original client base had left, and he was no longer producing many recordings. By then Meaux was perhaps out of touch with music trends, and the prospects for him finding another hit-maker were bleak.

So in 1984 Meaux decided to put the studio complex up for sale, a move that would bring me to the front entrance of SugarHill Studios (which then faced Brock Street) and into a new and major phase of my professional life.

By late 1984 I had resigned my position at ACA Studios. My ACA mentor and boss, Bill Holford, was retiring, a decision triggered by the pending expiration of a sweetheart lease he had negotiated upon selling the building back in 1978. Having not previously been told of his plans, I was shocked—and suddenly found myself looking for employment at other recording facilities in Houston.

When I had learned that Meaux was selling his studio company, I proposed instead to take over all recording operations and let him remain as owner. Particularly because I was in a position to transfer my ACA client base, Meaux was receptive to the idea. We reached an agreement, and in October 1984 I moved my gear and office to SugarHill Studios.

After my quick orientation to the historic complex, SugarHill resumed recording in what was now Studio A, the old room with the gold star embedded in the floor. The larger, newer studio and control room were initially off-limits because of the flood damage and lingering aftereffects. However, it soon became apparent that the smaller studio was insufficient for certain sessions. Many of the tube mics and vintage gear that were catalogued on the studio inventory were missing. Some Pulteq tube equalizers and Teletronix LA-2A compressors did later emerge, having been stashed clumsily in the warehouse, coated with dust and debris. But it would take extensive rewiring to prepare the studio for the anticipated influx of new clients.

Fortunately, one of the rock bands that made the transition with me from ACA to SugarHill included guys with construction expertise. So we traded their labor and skills for future studio time and went to work to restore Studio B. Over a period of three months we resealed the walls, dismantled two of the small booths, recarpeted the floor, and replaced or tested the wiring. We reequipped and rewired the reverb chambers with speakers and amps found stored in the warehouse. We hung the main set of large control-room monitors, Altec 604Es, from beams in the ceiling, which improved the listening quality for the engineers and provided a full view of the studio through the wide window. We removed all excess gear and furniture from the control room and enhanced the lighting.

Meanwhile, the piano, Hammond B3 organ, Fender Rhodes, and other keyboards were all moved back into Studio B, along with all the best outboard gear and machines. At that point, we shut down Studio A except for dubbing and rehearsals.

As the rebirth of SugarHill Studios proceeded, mixing was done on an Auditronics 501 console. The multitrack deck was an MCI JH-16 series sixteen-track machine that ran two-inch tape. I discovered Dolby A racks in both studios for the multitrack and mixing decks and upgraded them with DBX cards. Mix-down decks were one-quarter-inch MCI JH-110 two-track machines. Along with the rewired and reequipped acoustic reverb chambers in the hallway, the EMT plates and Lexicon digital processors provided reverb. I also installed racks of personal effects units. Monitoring was done on Altec 604E speakers utilizing the Auratone sound cubes.

In addition to physically restoring the facility, I brought with me clients who would help to reenergize the place. Among them in particular were many of the alternative-rock bands from the local scene, including Really Red, the Mydolls, the Recipients, and Culturcide (which featured Dan Workman on guitar). There were a number of power-pop or pop-rock groups too, such as Rick Tangle and the Squares, the Voices, and Private Numbers.

Workman, my future business partner, was introduced to the new era at SugarHill via an editing project for Culturcide's *Tacky Souvenirs* LP. "All of the songs were carefully edited on one-quarter-inch analog tape, long before Pro-Tools or any digital editing systems," he says. "All these little pieces of tape [were] hanging carefully along the sides of the MCI tape deck."

Working often with bands on projects such as these, the studio company soon regained its equilibrium. Yet the roster of clients remained somewhat diverse.

For instance, country singer Johnny Bush recalls a 1985 SugarHill session timed to coincide with, celebrate, and—most obviously—profit from the Texas sesquicentennial anniversary in 1986. Bush says,

> Huey Meaux and Don Daily produced an album [packaged] in the shape of Texas, with some memorabilia [depicted] on the cover—like Travis' last letter from the Alamo and other important documents. The record featured Bob Wills, Willie [Nelson], myself, Tanya Tucker, Billy Walker, Freddy Fender, and several others. The tracks were already cut, and all I had to do was sing. I did two songs that were real nice western swing arrangements.... "A Little Bit of Everything in Texas," originally by Ernest Tubb, and ... "I Got Texas in My Soul."

In addition to the occasional country music project, SugarHill regained its groove as a choice locale for blues recordings. One of the mainstays in the 1980s was the Gulf Coast guitarist and singer Bert Wills. Though grounded in Texas blues, Wills has also mastered styles such as country, rock, and in particular the surf-rock subgenre—and led regionally popular bands such as the Cryin' Shames and the Country Cadillacs. Wills, who would record several albums at SugarHill, describes his earliest memories of the place:

> I do remember coming into the studios when Huey owned it back in the 1970s. I didn't know him real well, and he was a very high-profile business-man back in the day. The engineer I worked with was Mickey Moody, and

I was called in to play guitar and harmonica on a number of sessions for [producer] Roy Ames. I was finishing guitar tracks for some pretty famous guys who had gotten tired of his [Ames's] allegedly bad business dealings. They had quit in the middle or near the end of these album projects, and Roy had a number of unfinished tracks. I had a reputation for being able to copy other guitar styles very convincingly [so] . . . I helped complete them. I was well paid for it, but never realized what was going on till very much later in the game. Most of these records were being put out in Europe.

However, not all the major clients at the time were bands or artists. For instance, one that followed me to SugarHill was Merrbach Record Service, a square-dance music supply company. Norman Merrbach and Johnny Wyckoff were at the studio every six weeks, almost without fail, to record another half-dozen new tracks for the many callers who staged square dances around the state. To make these recordings they used top studio musicians such as Louis Broussard, Jake Willemaine, Randy Cornor, Steve Snoe, Robbie Springfield, and others.

Challenge Records also moved to SugarHill. It was an independent label that I had previously formed with Art Gottschalk, Tom Littman, Cliff Atherton, and John D. Evans (aka singer Johnny Cantrell). Challenge Records issued singles by Kay Rives, Roy Clayborne, the Voices, Johnny Cantrell, Susan Watson, Chet Daniels, and Anthony Arnt. All of them had begun their recording projects at ACA Studios and then moved with me to SugarHill to finish them. Based particularly on the success of the Kay Rives single, which had registered on the *Cashbox* country charts, the small company discussed a merger with a Las Vegas–based concern, but when that deal died, Challenge Records folded.

Nonetheless, SugarHill Studios was attracting new business too. Among the recordings of note done in this time period was an album titled *Scenes from "Shir ha Shirim"* featuring classical composer Mario Davidovsky on CRI Records (#530), produced by Art Gottschalk and George Burt. The ensemble was conducted by Larry Livingston and featured world-famous violinist Sergiu Luca.

Another project was the mixing of a new LP for Little Joe y La Familia, led by Joe Hernandez (b. 1940). As Texas music historian Gary Hartman writes, "Hernandez is often considered the 'father' of modern Tejano music," and in 1992 he would be the first artist ever to win a Grammy Award for that genre. Back in 1984, Hernandez had recorded the album *Renunciacion* (featuring the hit song "Cuatro Caminos") at his own studio in Temple, Texas, but he brought it to SugarHill for mixing. Hernandez was already friends with Meaux, who had made some of Little Joe's earliest recordings.

Prominent session drummer Robbie Parrish recalls an unusual SugarHill undertaking from this time:

> I remember a major recording project for a New Zealand country singer by the name of Jody Vaughn. She won female vocalist of the year in New Zealand and Australia in the mid-1980s and went to Nashville to seek her fame and fortune. They sent her to Huey because she was unusual, and he had been the King of unusual and different singers. . . . I played drums on two albums for Jody and enough tracks for a third album. The first album was released only in New Zealand and featured a guitar player from there named Gray Bartlett and our own Randy Cornor. Paul English played keyboards, and bass was Gene Kurtz. The second album, which was also released here, was called *Kiwi Country* [Challenge Records].

We also recorded an R&B singer and songwriter named William Burton Gaar and his partner George Hollinshead from Baton Rouge, Louisiana. They recorded over an album's worth of material, with Gaar and Meaux producing. Several Gaar-written singles were released on the Crazy Cajun label, including "(If You Can't Put Out the Fire) Don't Fan the Flame" backed with "Sugar Roll Blues" (#2072), "You Go Crazy All Alone" and "Two Timed" (#2092), and "Teardrops from Heaven" with "After All These Years" (#2097). Meaux then signed Gaar as a country artist to a Mercury/Polygram subsidiary called Smash Records in Nashville. The first single on Smash, cowritten by Gaar and Meaux, featured "Somewhere between Mama's and Daddy's" (#884-828-7). Its follow-up release was "I'm Gonna Rise Up through These Ashes." However, at that time the Mercury/Polygram company underwent an executive shake-up, and Gaar was soon dropped from the label before any real success was realized.

One of the strangest pop successes of 1985 occurred with the zydeco artist known as Rockin' Sidney (Sidney Semien, 1938–1998). Sidney brought his then-regional hit "Don't Mess with My Toot Toot" to Meaux, who orchestrated a deal with CBS Records to release it nationally. Defying expectations, that single became so popular with diverse audiences that it earned a Platinum Record award as well as a Grammy. Meaux then encouraged Sidney to record a proper follow-up at SugarHill, but the artist was disinclined to do so—another lost opportunity perhaps.

Yet Meaux was reengaging more fully in the music business, apparently stimulated by his marginal involvement in another national hit. Turning back to his home state, Meaux then brought in Tommy McLain, T. K. Hulin, and Warren Storm to record a flurry of singles for his Crazy Cajun label. Among the results were McLain's "I'll Change My Style Crazy Baby" backed with "They'll All Call Me Daddy" (#2083) and "Louisiana People" with "Roses Don't Grow Here Anymore" (#2087). With his band Smoke, Hulin released "You've Been Bad" and "She's Got a Love Hold on Me" (#2082). Storm cut "The Rains Came" and "You Need Someone Who'll Be Mean to You" (#2093). Meaux was likely hoping to cash in on the so-called Cajun Renaissance of the mid-1980s, a time when interest in South Louisiana food and music heightened nationwide.

As part of this same effort, Meaux also produced new recordings by singer Jim Olivier (1951–2008), a Louisiana cultural icon best known as the host of the long-running bilingual Cajun television program *Passe Partout*. Olivier explains,

> I met Huey through swamp-pop legend Rod Bernard and visited the studio several times with many of the artists from Louisiana that Huey was recording. I was programming everyone else's music on my television program; why not my own? Huey invited me to record at SugarHill. From that point we did four more albums, all recorded there. 1981: *Sings the Cajun Way* [Swallow Records LP-6044]. 1982: *Let's Keep It Cajun* [Swallow Records LP-6048]. 1985: *La Musique de Jim Olivier* [Swallow Records LP-6059]. 1987: *Good Hearted Man*.

During this era, Olivier recorded a single with Rockin' Sidney for Lanor Records (#597), also produced at SugarHill.

Finally, I had the privilege of engineering a session with country singer Benny Barnes (1936–1987), just a year before he passed away. Barnes had first recorded at Gold Star Studios in 1956, under the direction of Pappy Daily for Starday Records. Some thirty years later Meaux, who had produced a Barnes album for Crazy Cajun in the 1970s, asked Olivier to bring Barnes back to the studio. From the tape archives they selected a couple of instrumental backing tracks, and Barnes sang over them to create his final single: "Foolin' Myself" backed with "You're Telling Me Lies" on Crazy Cajun (#2089). Olivier adds this detail:

> For that session I brought with me one of the greatest fiddle players of our generation, Rufus Thibodeaux. He began his career with Bob Wills. He played with George Jones and many other greats, including Willie Nelson. In that time period he was touring and recording with the great Neil Young. I was happy to be able to have Rufus in on the last Benny Barnes record at SugarHill.

In retrospect, that 1986 Barnes session now seems laden with symbolic import. For not only was it the final studio performance by one of the great yet relatively unknown country singers from Southeast Texas; it was also one of Meaux's last productions as the actual owner of SugarHill Studios. Both men had created their most impressive professional successes at that studio site. Yet, in different ways, it was time for both to move on—and for the facility itself to evolve in a new direction.

Not long after the Barnes session, Meaux announced that he was looking for a buyer for the whole property. He indicated that he was quitting the studio business but intended to maintain his personal offices in the building (an arrangement to be negotiated with the buyer).

This development arose concurrently with my ongoing discussions with Gottschalk and others regarding a proposal to start a classical record label. As part of that plan, I had also been considering investing in additional remote recording equipment. Suddenly, with Meaux's news, several divergent opportunities seemed to coalesce at once.

Modern Music (Ad)Ventures

IN 1986, APPROXIMATELY FOURTEEN YEARS after assuming ownership, Huey Meaux sold the entire property called SugarHill Studios (the building, land, equipment, and name) to a newly formed company named Modern Music Ventures (MMV). As part of this deal, Meaux was permitted to maintain offices and warehouse space in the building until his designated retirement date in 1995.

However, he essentially semiretired right away. One of the last music-business transactions Meaux handled was the 1989 major label record deal for Beaumont-born country singer Mark Chestnut. Increasingly reclusive, Meaux had no involvement in running the studios.

MMV was actually an umbrella corporation that encompassed the recently purchased SugarHill Recording Studios, SugarHill Sound (devoted to recording advertising jingles), Musica Moderna Management, the Discos MM record label, three publishing companies, and the Foundation for Modern Music. The primary owners of MMV were Berry Bowen, David Lummis, Barry Leavitt, and Art Gottschalk, its first business manager. Meanwhile, David Thompson assumed the role of studio manager, and I formally became the chief engineer, with Rod Thibault serving as maintenance technician.

Almost immediately MMV invested in a major remodeling and upgrading of Studio B. Heavy industrial carpet and painted sheetrock replaced the old burlap-covered walls. In the booths the burlap surfaces were covered in chicken wire and retextured. We raised the drum booth floor about a foot and filled the space below with sand to enhance sound isolation. The drum booth walls were double-sheetrocked and then carpeted, and the roof was covered and sealed properly. The drum booth windows were double-glassed. We improved the lighting in the studio and brightened the color scheme to suggest a tropical Latin flavor. The control room was remodeled in a gray and black industrial look with carpeted walls and floors, plus new ceiling tiles. The two small booths on the right side of the studio were converted into partial isolation space for the seven-foot Yamaha G7 grand piano.

MMV purchased an Otari MX-90II twenty-four-track two-inch tape machine and an additional eight tracks of DBX noise reduction to complement the vintage Auditronics 501 console. Fortunately we discovered some vintage Pulteq, Teletronix, UREI, and Fairchild gear stored in the warehouse—then refurbished and utilized it. We installed new effects racks and moved various unneeded but valuable tape decks to the smaller studio, which remained mostly unused for the moment.

This project accomplished Studio B's first major overhaul since 1973. The 1984 work had simply repaired the hurricane damage and got the room working again. Given the reclaimed glory of the larger studio room, MMV renamed SugarHill's two studios, designating the recently refurbished space as Studio A and the smaller room, then used for rehearsals and dubbing, as Studio B (reversing Meaux's nomenclature).

The MMV subsidiary Foundation for Modern Music existed to promote the recording of classical music by contemporary composers—and its projects were among the first recordings made in the new era. With Bowen (the first MMV president) executive producing, the Foundation recorded artists such as the Continuum Percussion Quartet, Thomas Bacon, and Sergio de los Cobos.

Another MMV-financed recording documented a live 1987 concert by jazz saxophonist Arnett Cobb performing with trumpeter Dizzy Gillespie and vocalist Jewel Brown at Houston's Wortham Theater. We hired the Dallas-based Omega Audio mobile truck to handle the off-site recording. The microphone selected for Cobb's saxophone was a Neumann tube U-67, possibly one of the very mics used on his early-1960s recordings at Gold Star Studios. Gillespie's trumpet was rigged with an RCA DX-77 ribbon mic. Back at SugarHill Studios I mixed the album, which was produced by Thompson and Gottschalk plus Steve Williams of the Jazz Heritage Society of Texas. In 1988 Fantasy Records issued it as *Show Time* (#9659), Cobb's last major recording.

Around this time, R&B saxophone veteran Grady Gaines (b. 1934) and his band, the Texas Upsetters, came to SugarHill to record the album *Full Gain,* released in 1988 by Black Top Records (#1041). Gaines was a living link to music history, having played early on with Little Richard, James Brown, Sam Cooke, Otis Redding, and many others. Black Top producer Hammond Scott (b. 1950) had brought Gaines out of semiretirement for this project, which reintroduced him to new audiences. In addition to Gaines's regular band— which included former Duke-Peacock pianist and vocalist Teddy Reynolds (1931–1998) and singer Big Robert Smith (1939–2006)—these sessions featured special guest guitarists Roy Gaines (b. 1937) and Clarence Hollimon, as well as singer Joe Medwick (1933–1992). This ensemble represented an all-star roster of Houston African American blues and R&B musicians, many of whom had previous connections to the facility. (For example, Reynolds had recorded there with Bobby Bland and Junior Parker during the Gold Star era.)

Using engineers from the New Orleans–based Black Top label and SugarHill, we recorded the marathon sessions, the last of which ran for thirty-seven hours straight. About a month later I engineered the backing horn section overdubs, with Scott in attendance as producer. The result was a critically acclaimed album, which writer Bill Dahl praises on *Allmusic.com* as "a veritable Houston blues mother-lode."

By 1988 MMV had replaced the old Auditronics console with a Neotek IIIC, which served as SugarHill's flagship gear until early 2000. After selling off some now superfluous equipment, we purchased and installed new DBX noise reduction units and outboard effects units. We made a deal with Manley Labs to trade one of our plate reverbs for the rebuilding of the primary and backup electronics of the remaining EMT 140 tube plate reverb. The studio added a pair of Yamaha NS-10M near-field monitors and a pair of Tannoy 6.5 near-field monitors to the Altec 604E speakers and Auratone sound cubes— all hooked up to a selector switch. Around this time, MMV also purchased a beautiful, white Pearl Birch–series six-piece drum set for Studio A, complete with all the accoutrements.

Meanwhile, Thompson had secured a new and unusual client for SugarHill: Galveston Island Outdoor Musicals (GIOM), then based at the Mary Moody Northern Amphitheater adjacent to Galveston Island State Park. Relying on taped instrumentation, GIOM staged several Broadway-style musicals each summer in its open-air amphitheater. GIOM's previous backing tracks had been custom-recorded in England, but they were expensive to produce. So SugarHill assembled a small orchestra of local musicians who could record the necessary scores in a more timely and economical fashion. Starting in 1987 and continuing well into the '90s, in conjunction with the GIOM music directors, we produced new instrumental soundtracks for popular productions such as *Oklahoma!* and *Hello Dolly.*

Another new direction involved SugarHill Sound, a company that produced advertising jingles. Working with marketing agent Jane Witt, between 1987 and 1992 we created numerous radio and television spots, primarily but not exclusively for the Hispanic market—including the local affiliate of the Spanish-language television network Telemundo.

Thus, by expanding beyond Meaux's previous focus on producing potential hit singles or albums, MMV established a more stable and diversified foundation for its business.

Yet SugarHill remained a comfortable recording base for scores of local or regional musicians working on their own projects. One example is David Beebe, the founder of various pop-rock groups such as El Orbits and Banana Blender Surprise. Music critic Christopher Gray describes the latter as "a sugar-crazed combination of Chuck Berry, the Meters, and Fabulous Thunderbirds." Beebe says, "Banana Blender Surprise came to SugarHill in December of 1989, with [engineer] Steve Lanphier in the gold star room with the old Auditronics 501 console," cutting tracks for their 1990 debut album *Check Please*. Country singer Kelly Schoppa illustrates another case, having started recording at SugarHill in 1986 and producing part or all of three albums there within a few years: *Two Steps Away, Yesterday and Today*, and *Home Is Where the Heart Is*.

But given the changing demographics among record buyers in Texas and nationwide, coupled with the rise of a new sound, a different type of regional band soon dominated SugarHill's productions of hit records.

THE LEGACY OF GOLD STAR/SUGARHILL STUDIOS has included Spanish-language songs since the late 1940s, when founder Bill Quinn recorded Conjunto de Maxie Granados performing "Flora Perdida" for his Gold Star label (#401). Pappy Daily had dabbled briefly in the regional Hispanic market too in the 1950s, but it was not until Meaux's production of Freddy Fender's bilingual hits that such projects became even somewhat common at SugarHill. However, by the late 1980s and the '90s, Tejano music, which energized folk-style Mexican conjunto with elements of contemporary pop, had developed as a major subgenre with a huge fan base. As a result, many of the best-selling recordings produced at SugarHill during this era came from Latinos.

MMV first capitalized on the growing Tejano music scene via discussions with Bob Grever of Cara Records, an established independent recording and publishing company based in San Antonio, the home of Tex-Mex culture. One of Cara's major artists was La Mafia, one of the most prominent Tejano groups. But Grever had recently signed a new band, called Xelencia, comprising several ex-members of La Mafia plus singer David DeAnda. In an unconventional move, this group had recorded its first two songs in Nashville, utilizing country music studios and personnel to create a different, relatively progressive sound that was not commonly found in San Antonio recording facilities. Grever was therefore interested in recording next at SugarHill. The historic facility possessed the proper country music credentials and a reputation for quality studio work, yet was cheaper than Nashville and much closer to home.

In late 1988 Grever first brought Xelencia to SugarHill Studios to record tracks for the 1989 album *Ni Por Mil Puñados De Oro* on the Cara Records/

CBS label. It earned our first of many Gold Record Awards for Tejano music. Since then, Xelencia has recorded nearly a dozen albums at SugarHill.

Our successful marriage of Tejano and country sounds prompted Grever to bring others there, including the young star singer Emilio Navaira (b. 1962). We cut all the tracks for Navaira's 1990 album *Sensaciones,* released on CBS Discos International. That record produced at least three hit singles, quickly going Gold and then Platinum.

Around the same time, Grever brought in the young Tejano-outlaw group called La Fiebre. Fresh off a major hit single recorded elsewhere, the initial SugarHill sessions for La Fiebre yielded the album *Out of Control* for CBS Discos International and another Gold Record.

Those projects led to sessions with the established country singer Johnny Rodriguez (b. 1951). Hoping to cash in on the surging Tejano music industry, in 1990 Capitol Records commissioned him to record a mostly Spanish-language album called *Coming Home.* Producer Bob Gallarza assembled top-notch musicians and cut some tracks in San Antonio and others at SugarHill, where we also engineered most of Rodriguez's vocals and the brass overdubs.

Meanwhile, La Fiebre returned to SugarHill in 1991 to record vocals for the album *No Cure* for release on the Capitol/EMI Latin imprint, another Gold Record award winner.

Gallarza came back next to produce a solo album for Adalberto Gallegos, the former lead singer of the pioneer 1970s hit-making Tejano group, the Latin Breed. That record, issued by CBS Discos International, was called *Me Nace.*

Eventually Grever sold his label to Capitol/EMI Latin, also based in San Antonio. Thereafter, our many subsequent recordings by Emilio Navaira, Xelencia, and La Fiebre were for that label with Grever producing.

This outburst of Tejano recording activity also stimulated Discos MM, MMV's independent record label, which was initially distributed by Polygram. Its premiere recordings, all made at SugarHill, featured two groups: the Jerry Rodriguez and Mercedes album *Rebelde* and the Rick Gonzalez and the Choice debut *La Primera Vez.* However, Polygram soon divested itself of its Latin division, so Discos MM made another distribution agreement with Capitol/EMI Latin. Both albums were reissued, and Rodriguez scored a regional hit with a dance track called "El Pinguino." Rodriguez followed up with the album *No Somos Criminales,* and Gonzalez with *Por Ti.*

Discos MM also produced the vocalist Elsa Garcia, who debuted with the well-received album *Simplemente.* But Garcia's follow-up album, *Ni Mas, Ni Menos,* was even more popular, earning a Gold Record award. In February 1994, its title-track single peaked at number eight on the Latin category in *Billboard.* The album reached number forty-two on the Latin charts too. At this time, *Billboard* did not recognize Tejano music as a category unto itself. Hence, all music by Spanish-speaking performers directed at Hispanic audiences was grouped together as "Latin." There was no distinction recognized among styles as diverse as South American pop and Dominican salsa and Tejano. Thus, Garcia's achievement in cracking the Top 10 was even more substantial than it might first appear.

Concurrent with SugarHill's production of Tejano hits, MMV sought to establish itself in the burgeoning Spanish-language rock movement. Thus, MMV signed a Houston-based Latino rock band called the Basics, fronted by singer Lupe Olivarez and guitarist Artie Villasenor. In 1991 Discos MM released their album *Sonido Básico*, which Lummis marketed to no avail to major U.S. labels.

When MMV restructured in 1991, Lummis took over and brought manager, promoter, and booking agent Max Silva into the company. Silva replaced Gottschalk as executive producer of CDs, and Lanphier and I took over as music producers. Soon after this, Discos MM signed the Hometown Boys, from Lubbock. Leading a neotraditionalist resurgence in Tex-Mex conjunto, they soon triggered another wave of Gold Records.

Thus, with a solid string of hits, SugarHill Studios established itself as a recording center for Spanish-language productions during the 1990s. Until its popularity crested and began to fade near the end of the decade, Tejano music remained our primary source of success with Latino styles. But other musical possibilities *en español* would soon emerge.

THE LATE 1980S TO MID-'90S BROUGHT increasingly diverse projects to SugarHill Studios. From madcap sessions with Australian rock bands to more staid productions for educational services to long-running relationships with eclectic record labels and continued development in the Latino market, we worked with all kinds of clientele.

The first Aussie group to utilize the facility was called Weddings Parties Anything, which briefly recorded there while representing their homeland on stage at the 1988 Houston International Festival. One of the tracks, "Goat Dancing at Falafel Beach," appeared on a twelve-inch vinyl EP called *Goat Dancing on the Tables*, released in Australia on the WEA label. That single resurfaced also on the EP *No Show without Punch*, issued in Europe by Utility Records. But these lads would soon be followed by some of their countrymen with bigger projects at hand.

Thompson continued to find new sorts of clients for SugarHill. One such was the Educational Enterprises Recording Company (EERC), founded and operated by Paul and Blanche Harrison. Since the 1970s they had been creating and marketing recordings of rehearsal instrumentation and vocal demos for the Texas All-State Choir. With a new repertoire established each year by the Texas Music Educators Association, EERC recorded the required accompaniment and produced the vocal demos. Starting in the early 1990s EERC began adding other states as clients, including Florida, South Carolina, and New Mexico. Since 1994 Debbie Talley, alto vocalist and pianist, has produced the sessions. While this type of work is not glamourous, it is quite valuable for an independent studio operation.

Nonetheless, SugarHill Studios primarily catered to individuals and groups producing albums for the popular or alternative music marketplace.

Guitarist and composer Erich Avinger (b. 1956) self-produced his first solo album at SugarHill. With emphasis on jazz improvisation and drawing from an international palette of musical influences, he called it *Heart Magic*. Issued in 1989, it became the first CD on the Heart Music label, owned by Tab Bartling. Since then Heart Music has used SugarHill to produce over a dozen CDs, consistently placing titles on *Billboard*'s jazz charts and the Gavin national jazz radio charts. For example, its first two releases by saxophonist Tony Campise, *First Takes* and *Once in a Blue Moon,* both reached number three in the Gavin rankings. Moreover, the latter stayed on the *Billboard* jazz Top 20 list for three months.

In 1989 the independent producer Randall Jamail formed Justice Records, which Thompson joined as vice president and A&R man. Hence, a whole new chapter in studio history began. Jamail explains the genesis and development of his label:

> I was getting ready to record Kellye Gray at the time, and I decided to record that first album at SugarHill. . . . *Standards in Gray* featured a lot of the best jazz cats in Houston: David Catney, piano, Sebastian Whittaker, drums, David Craig, bass, and others. We cut that record live to two-track. No overdubs, just great performances captured live in the studio, just like in the old days in New York. We made a great record, but at that point there was no destination for it. . . . So I decided to form my own company and put out the record myself.

Jamail thereafter aggressively promoted the record, getting airplay on local radio, good reviews in regional publications, and effective self-distribution in the area. He continues,

> It seems surreal how this label has moved through the years. We recorded exclusively at SugarHill for at least the first three years. In 1990 we recorded five jazz albums, and three of them went to number one on the jazz charts. We were also named the number one debut jazz label by R&R [Radio and

Records] and Gavin, the two radio reporting charts. We did at least eight albums in 1991, which included guitar legend Herb Ellis.

Regarding his reasons for recording so many of his initial projects at SugarHill Studios, Jamail adds,

There is something about the A room at SugarHill, which is very comfortable and intimate. I have worked at the Power Station in New York and Ocean Way in Los Angeles. It is harder to maintain that communication and intimacy in those big rooms. . . . All those records . . . made in that funky old house studio with all the history have a feeling and warmth to them that says creativity was at work. Those early Justice albums were recorded in an environment that was comfortable, unpressured, loose, and spontaneous. The musicians all enjoyed the vibe at SugarHill.

Drawing first from talent in Houston's largely underrated jazz scene, Justice seemed to be defining itself by a single genre. But that would change. Jamail says,

We were becoming a preeminent independent jazz label. That was certainly not my intention. My background was more in singer-songwriter music, rock, and Texas blues. The jazz direction was not planned but was a huge blessing because those first dozen albums were live to two-track analog tape or direct to two-track DAT digital recordings. . . . All of those early albums sounded top-notch. . . . Audiophile magazines and *Billboard* always gave us very high marks for the recordings. . . .

I made the shift towards roots music after a couple of years of jazz albums. I released both the orphaned Emily Remler [1957–1990] CD, completed prior to her untimely death in Australia on tour, and a two-volume tribute album that was recorded in New York and Houston. While working on those albums I met Dr. John in New York. I asked him if there were any young blues guitar players that I might want to take a look at. He led me to Tab Benoit.

We then signed [Benoit] and brought him to Houston to record [at SugarHill] . . . the album *Nice and Warm*. We anticipated that it would sell around 5,000 units, and it actually sold close to 90,000. At the time it was the most successful album in our catalogue.

While Benoit would continue to record for Justice Records, Willie Nelson would soon supplant him as the label's best-seller. His 1994 Justice release *Moonlight Becomes You* received a Grammy nomination and, as Jamail says, "put the label on a different footing. We had broken a new blues artist and now we had signed an international icon." Thereafter Justice also signed Waylon Jennings, Kris Kristofferson, Billy Joe Shaver, and other major artists. Various "demos and preproduction sessions for those projects" were staged at SugarHill Studios, Jamail says.

As Justice Records expanded, it mainly used SugarHill for the Houston-based artists it recorded. That roster included the veteran jazz vibraphonist Harry Sheppard (b. 1928), who issued several acclaimed CDs. Justice also has introduced multiple albums by younger jazz artists, such as pianist Dave Catney (1961–1994) and drummer Sebastian Whittaker (b. 1966).

As for SugarHill's role in these recordings, Tim Carman, in a review of Whittaker's album *First Outing*, says,

> It would be an understatement if you said they got the sound right. It required some wizardry from engineer Bradley and co-producers Jamail and Whittaker, but they managed to record *First Outing* live and direct to two-track in less than two days. The result is a warm, deeply rich record that belies the fact that most of the musicians who played on it weren't even born when the legendary Blue Note jazz label was at its creative peak.

Similarly, Rick Mitchell writes in a *Houston Chronicle* feature article, "Justice sound quality is comparable to what comes out of the high-tech studios in New York or Los Angeles. Jamail works closely with engineer Andy Bradley at Houston's SugarHill Studios."

As for Catney, following his 1990 album *First Flight,* he issued *Jade Visions.* I also engineered his final CD, *Reality Road,* recorded at Rice University's Stude Concert Hall, released posthumously in 1995. Performing solo on a nine-foot Steinway grand piano, Catney played a set of raw and emotional pieces for this gem, which was recorded directly to analog two-track with Dolby SR, using two Neumann tube U-67 microphones.

Now a subsidiary imprint distributed by Buddha Records, Justice Records has recorded an eclectic mix of artists—and many in collaboration with SugarHill Studios, the place where it staged its early productions.

BY 1990 MMV DETERMINED THAT A SINGLE studio room was insufficient for the collective needs of its record label, jingle company, and public recording studio company. So, we rebuilt the smaller studio, replacing most walls with a checkerboard layout of pine shingles and large squares of sound-absorbent polyurethane foam. We carpeted the floor—but left exposed the area with the gold star design. Also we remodeled the isolation booths and upgraded lighting and wiring.

In the control room we installed new wall paneling or absorbent tiles, as well as new shelving. Having refurbished the Auditronics console and wiring, we improved supporting equipment by adding an Otari MX-80 twenty-four-track machine, along with twenty-four tracks of DBX noise reduction (to make the two studios compatible), plus a two-track Otari MTR-10.

After acquiring more analog and digital processors plus a second drum kit, SugarHill had two fully operational studios, manned by either Lanphier or J. R. Griffith.

In 1991, shortly after Studio B came on line, more Australians arrived, starting with the rock group Hitmen DTK—a musical spin-off of the defunct and legendary Radio Birdman. The lineup featured guitarist Chris Masuak, singer Johnny Kannis, bassist Shane Cook, and drummer Gerard Pressland—but former Birdman Deniz Tek made a special guest appearance too. The result was the 1991 album *Moronic Inferno,* released in Australia on Zeus Records (and in Europe under the title *Surfing in Another Direction*).

Tek explains his involvement in this project:

> I hadn't talked to Chris in quite a few years. We had a huge falling out when Birdman broke up in 1978. . . . However, I was keen on rekindling the friendship. . . . He suggested that I come down to the sessions in Houston from Montana. So he sent me demos of the songs, and I went to work practicing and getting my chops back.

Given Radio Birdman's lofty status in the annals of Australian rock, this reunion at SugarHill Studios was historic. Moreover, according to Tek, it reinvigorated his improvisational instincts—and made him eager to develop a solo project that, too, would involve SugarHill. He says,

> I was given the liberty to do a couple of my songs while I was there. With Chris and his band, I cut "Pushin' the Broom" and a couple of other songs that appeared on an [1992] EP, *Good 'nuff* [Red Eye/Polydor #63-889-2], released in Australia. One of the highlights . . . was the jam session we did one night after all the songs had been recorded, which was officially dubbed "Coors Live." Some of that night also appeared on an [1999] EP and a single released in Europe, [by] Deniz Tek and Chris Masuak: "Let the Kids Dance" [Undead Records #002]. . . .
>
> I realized how much fun I was having in the studio with the creative process and being with friends. On top of that, I also realized what a great place SugarHill was. The more I found out about it, the more I wanted to come back and do some more work. . . . I immediately started planning my album and my return to Houston. I knew I would do it at SugarHill. . . . Chris had to be involved—because the chemistry was back. And I wanted to do it with [Andy Bradley] because [he] knew what was going on.

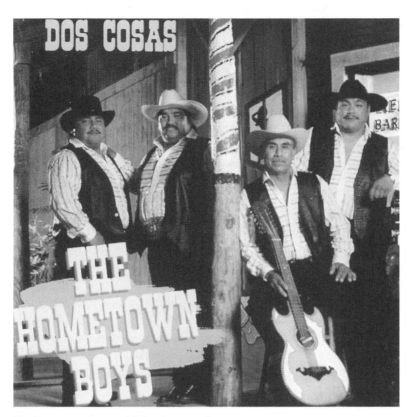

The Hometown Boys, publicity photo, 1996

Tek and Masuak returned in early 1992 to begin working on Tek's first solo CD, *Take It to the Vertical,* on Red Eye/Polydor Records. Houston master saxophonist Grady Gaines performed as a special guest, soulfully blending his Gulf Coast R&B sound with that of these former punk rockers. Tek tells more about this project:

> Chris was the obvious choice to be the other guitar/keyboard player/coproducer on the album following the recementing of our relationship. I picked Scott Asheton [ex-drummer for Iggy Pop and the Stooges] and [Phil] "Dust" Peterson on bass because I'd played with both of them in the past. . . . We were able to put together a band spirit almost immediately, and the recording worked. My wife, Angie Pepper, came down and sang a co-lead vocal and some harmonies on the album.

One good vibe led to another. During Tek's sessions, Chris recruited him and studio drum technician Robbie Parrish to record an additional four tracks with him. These eventually appeared on a CD credited to the Juke Savages on Phantom Records, Australia (#20).

These SugarHill sessions collectively played a key role in Tek's 1990s reemergence as a performer and recording artist. They also led directly to a highly touted Radio Birdman reunion tour in 1996, the first in eighteen years—which later triggered other international touring and new recordings elsewhere. Like myriad music breakthroughs before, this one started at the old studio complex on Brock Street.

Tek adds some final comments on that place:

> I have met some amazing people at SugarHill . . . Grady Gaines . . . Huey P. Meaux. . . . I also remember the day that we went up to the tape archives. . . . That was completely mind-blowing to me because to just walk in and see the multitrack tape of "She's About a Mover"—it was like being in a gold mine of sound.

Meanwhile the MMV-owned Discos MM label rode to new levels of Tejano success with its recent *conjunto nuevo* signee, the Hometown Boys. Over the course of a dozen or more CD recordings at SugarHill (all engineered, produced, or coproduced by Lanphier), the Homies racked up major sales and numerous awards, including Gold Records for 1994's *Tres Ramitas* and 1995's *Mire Amigo.*

As a result of the Hometown Boys' success, we also recorded a veteran conjunto group called Los Dos Gilbertos, plus a younger band called Los Pecadores.

I coproduced Discos MM's recording of the group David Olivares and XS. That project spawned a cross-cultural wonder, for Meaux suggested converting some 1960s rock into contemporary cumbia. Drawing from studio history, we Latinized "She's About a Mover," and it became a regional hit.

At this point MMV underwent another restructuring, which left Lummis, Silva, and Leavitt in charge. They decided to close the SugarHill Sound jingle company and concentrate more fully on the Latino music market. Then in early 1993, with Lummis exiting to the corporate banking world, MMV next elected to scale back certain operations. It also closed Studio B, selling much of its gear and investing the proceeds in new sound equipment for the Hometown Boys, with whom Lanphier departed to work full time.

Now on my own in charge of studio operations, I began searching for a possible short-term lessee for Studio B, which was otherwise used only for rehearsals. Seeing that historic chamber empty again depressed me. Moreover, given recent business decisions, I was uncertain about the future of MMV's relationship with the studios. But more changes lay ahead.

Emergence
of a RAD Idea

ONCURRENTLY WITH MMV RECONSIDERING its commitment to studio ownership, I crossed paths with several people who would influence the next phase of SugarHill's history. Through a series of fortunate affiliations, a new company would be born.

It started when Robbie Parrish, who was producing a CD for singer Tony Villa, brought in Rodney Meyers to add keyboard effects on Villa's album. Meyers, a college professor in audio technology, was also doing freelance work in digital mastering and editing—and seeking proper space in which to establish his business.

So Meyers, Max Silva, and I convened to discuss and arrange a lease agreement whereby Meyers's independent mastering company would become a tenant in the SugarHill building. We determined that he would occupy the second-floor site where International Artists had once maintained offices—the same place where Bill Quinn had originally installed the upstairs control room for the big studio.

Meyers gutted the space, soundproofed it, and created an acoustically correct environment for processing audio. His company, Sound Engineering, began operations on site with a mastering room, a small office, and a small production room. It was one of the first digital mastering facilities in Houston, fittingly located in the city's oldest continuously operating studio.

Meanwhile, we briefly leased Studio B to independent producer Dan Yeaney, who staged some freelance sessions there. Upon his departure, MMV sold the final vintage Auditronics console, leaving only a set of Altec monitors and a two-track MCI JH-110 analog tape deck.

However, musician and independent sound engineer Dan Workman was also searching for a place to move his own studio business. He says,

It was 1994, and I was recording at my home studio called the Big House. . . . It was getting difficult to use the whole house for sessions. So I thought about moving to a studio and doing my work there. . . . I decided to call Robbie [Parrish]. He was Mister Network. . . . He says, "Why don't you call Andy Bradley over at SugarHill? I think Studio B is just being used as a rehearsal place."

Having a stable tenant in Studio B was good news at SugarHill. "When I first came over," Workman says, "Rodney Meyers was putting in sheetrock upstairs in what was to become the mastering facility, Sound Engineering. . . . At the time I thought it was very cool that there would soon be a full-fledged mastering room in the building." In fact, mastering had not been done at 5626 Brock since Jim Duff left Gold Star in late 1968. Through the 1980s the norm was that vinyl record pressing plants handled mastering. However, in the later 1980s and the 1990s specialized independent mastering facilities became more common, especially with the digital revolution changing the nature of sound recording.

Thus, SugarHill Studios came to house two new tenants with separate but complementary business interests. As part of the agreement with Workman, his company and SugarHill shared equipment and any overflow of customers. Since his client base had little if any overlap with mine, our two studio companies could collaborate effectively without being rivals.

A Mackie twenty-four channel/eight-bus console and a Fostex sixteen-track analog deck that ran one-half-inch tape anchored Workman's studio space. He also brought in a number of excellent microphones and outboard processing units. Monitoring speakers were the classic Altec 604Es, Yamaha NS10Ms, Tannoy 6.5s, and Auratone sound cubes. As he transitioned into digital engineering, Workman added Tascam DA-88 modular digital recorders.

"It took a little while to build up my client base," Workman says. "I started to pull in a number of bands that I met at the Urban Art Bar, where I worked sound." These included Pull My Finger (later known as Ultramaag) and Badger (later known as The Tie That Binds). He went on to work with Planet Shock, Beat Temple, Bon Ton Mickey, Brian Jack and the Zydeco Gamblers, his own band Culturcide (on the album *Home Made Authority*), I-45, Moses Guest, and David Brake and That Damn Band, to name a few.

Having Workman and Meyers as tenants of the MMV-owned SugarHill Studios building developed a tripartite business affiliation that made sense. As each company pursued its own interests, we interacted regularly via referrals and consultations. We had developed, more or less organically, without foresight or intention, a symbiotic relationship.

AMONG THE SUGARHILL STUDIOS clients during this era, blues-rock guitarist Bert Wills was a regular. He recounts the artist-studio relationship:

> In late 1992 I came in with Jerry Lightfoot to record his first solo album *[Burning Desire]*. Jerry was a legend in the blues scene in Texas, both white and black. . . . It is right about this time that I discovered the reverb chambers in [the] hallway. . . . and how beautiful the reverb was that could be created in them. From that day on, it became a signature sound on all of our albums. . . .
>
> I had [previously] been recording over at Limelight Studios. . . . They had just switched over to the early ADAT digital recording, and I didn't like the sound or the difficulty with which those clunky machines operated. That early digital recording was harsh and unforgiving in its sound. I really missed the warmth of analog tape. So I lobbied to go over to SugarHill— because [they] were using analog tape. . . . For my first album, *Mr. Politician* [1993], we figured that a few of the cuts done at Limelight were acceptable and cut the other two-thirds of the album at SugarHill. . . .
>
> I remember showing up the day after the famous Huey incident [i.e., Meaux's arrest] to do guitar and vocals overdubs on the *Special Session* album. . . .
>
> The third album we did together was the surf record, *Pavones Sunset*. . . . [We] recruited Robbie Parrish and Rick Robertson to be the band for the album, and like the previous records, we used Paul English on keyboards and Kuko Miranda on Latin percussion.
>
> The last album I did for Goldrhyme Records was *Tell Me Why*. . . . in mid-1999. We recorded the drums out in the room, behind the drum booth where the organ's Leslie speaker lived. We got a great live kind of retro-ish sound that fitted perfectly with those songs.

Studio drummer and independent producer Parrish worked sessions with various artists in this time period, ranging from the country-rockabilly bandleader Jesse Dayton and his group the Road Kings to the New Age singer-songwriter-pianist Anita Kruse.

Meanwhile, the MMV-owned label Discos MM remained active. One of the new artists it introduced was a Tejana singer and her band, Annette y Axxion. They eventually recorded three CDs at SugarHill, all released on Fonovisa Records. Moreover, Meyers's Sound Engineering company took over the mastering engineering for Discos MM products, including the various releases by the Tejano band Xelencia, which continued to record at SugarHill on an almost annual basis.

Another project for Discos MM involved a live recording of two groups, the Hometown Boys and Los Dos Gilbertos, at a huge south Houston night-club called Hullabaloos. We contracted Malcolm Harper and Reel Sound Recording from Austin to provide and operate a mobile truck unit outfitted with a vintage MCI console and two twenty-four-track MCI analog tape decks. Malcolm and I collaborated on the engineering while Steve Lanphier handled the live mix, with Ramon Morales working the monitors. From those recordings MMV produced three different CDs, one of each band performing separately and another combining tracks by both. All three albums, leased to Capitol/EMI Records, were big sellers.

In 1996 a New York label commissioned a Jones Hall recording of the Houston Symphony Orchestra, with Christof Eschenbach conducting. After transporting and installing the necessary gear, I coengineered the project with producer Michael Fine, recording three separate three-hour sessions over two days. The result was the album titled *Schubert,* featuring the Schubert-Berio composition "Rendering" (from *Sketches for 10th Symphony*) and the Schubert-Joachim *Symphony in C Major, Grand Duo,* on Koch Records (#3-7382-2).

Working on recording projects with symphony orchestras, Tejano sensations, rock bands, and other such groups kept those of us based at SugarHill Studios immersed in the music. But some business issues had to be settled if we were going to keep it up.

EARLY 1996 BROUGHT A SERIES of transformations to SugarHill Studios. Meyers changed the name of his digital editing and mastering company to Essential Sound. Workman's Big House company had established itself as a site for digital multitrack recording—recently abetted by upgrades, including a third Tascam DA-88 recorder, a twenty-four-channel extender for the Mackie eight-bus console, Amex/Neve and API preamps, and a pair of Genelec 1030A monitors. Workman's embrace of digital technology was counterbalanced to some degree by my preference for old-fashioned analog.

But the biggest change occurred in April 1996 when Silva announced that MMV had decided to limit its interests to the Discos MM label, artist management, and music publishing—and thus sell SugarHill Studios. He said that MMV wished, if possible, to maintain offices and continue recording in the building as tenants of the new ownership.

Meyers, Workman, and I had recently achieved a productive synergy, but now we realized that it all could quickly fall apart. So Meyers proposed that we pool resources and purchase the place as partners. And what could have been a crisis became an opportunity.

Using the initial letter in each of our first names, we became RAD Audio, Inc., a Sub-chapter S Texas corporation. In October 1996, along with two additional investors, Tom Littman and Jon Bradley (no relation to the coauthor), RAD then purchased the SugarHill Studios name and complete inventory of equipment from MMV—but not the real estate itself.

Given MMV's asking price for the old structure and its obscure location, we had another idea—and began scouting the metropolitan area for a more prominently situated space to establish a new recording facility bearing the time-honored SugarHill name.

Until we found it, RAD and its recently acquired assets remained temporarily and precariously housed at the old SugarHill site. MMV, of course, continued to offer the structure and land for sale but allowed RAD to pay for utilities and maintenance and remain there in the interim.

Over the next several months, the RAD partners searched fruitlessly for the right site to launch the envisioned new incarnation of SugarHill Studios. At the same time, we got surprisingly negative feedback from some of our clients regarding our plans. Again and again, people expressed dismay or disappointment that we would be moving from the historic Gold Star/SugarHill site. These factors prompted us to question the wisdom of our plans—when suddenly there was a breakthrough as MMV chose to lower its selling price significantly.

In November 1997 MMV accepted our counteroffer. Thus, already possessing its name and gear, RAD purchased the real estate that had been SugarHill Studios. We had also come to believe that it was the right thing to do, keeping all the major components of the venerable studio company intact and rooted to the ground at 5626 Brock Street.

23

Millennial Destiny

AS NEW SUGARHILL STUDIOS OWNERS, RAD Audio first extensively remodeled the structure and the studio chambers. It was a time of fresh beginnings, both in terms of the upgraded building and the styles of music recorded there. As was customary, there remained a diverse range of clientele, but the biggest hits would now come from a younger generation of artists performing contemporary pop, R&B, and rap.

The remodeling started with roof replacement, installation of new air-conditioning units, and cosmetic painting. In 1999 we also completely overhauled and redesigned the Studio B control room, including the installation of new wall surfaces, a rebuilt raised floor, racks, and desk. The room was equipped with a Sony MCI JH-24 analog tape recorder with twenty-four channels of Dolby SR noise reduction and four Tascam DA tape recorders providing thirty-two channels of digital recording capacity. Speakers were Altec 604s, Yamaha NS10s, and Genelec 1040s. Outboard preamps included Amek/Neve, API, Demeter, Benchmark, and Bellari. We had DBX, UREI, TubeTech, and Manley compressors, plus several Lexicon reverbs.

Upon completing Studio B's renovation, in October 1999 we temporarily closed Studio A to do the same there. We sold the Neotek IIIC console and commissioned Martin Sound to build us a new Neotek Elite board. As he had done in Studio B, Rodney Meyers redesigned, rewired, and outfitted the control room—creating a multipurpose booth, a machine room for analog and digital tape decks, and a computer room. He also installed air locks on studio and control room doors to improve isolation. By February 2000 the new board was installed, capping RAD's major refurbishing campaign.

Some of RAD's new clients included progressive Celtic ensembles, such as the band Clandestine, an eclectic group featuring Emily Dugas, Jennifer

Hamel, E. J. Jones, and Greg McQueen. Early on in the new SugarHill owner-ship, Clandestine recorded the album *The Haunting*, followed a year later by *To Anybody at All* (produced by Irish musician Jerry O'Beirne). In 1999 the Rogues—featuring Randy Wothke, Brian Blaylock, Lars Sloan, and Jimmy Mitchell—recorded their acclaimed album *Off Kilter* at SugarHill.

But it was not all bagpipes and bodhrans. Nineteen ninety-eight also brought us the Chinese American Christian organization known as the New Heart Music Ministry, directed by Yen Schwen Er. He was a doctoral candidate in violin performance at Rice University who first performed at SugarHill on "sweetening" sessions to enhance various recordings. That led to New Heart recording its first CD, *You Are My God*, at SugarHill. Since then, we have recorded roughly one album per year for this internationally touring group, which includes a full choir with lead vocalists, drums, bass, guitar, piano, electronic keyboards, percussion, violin, viola, flute, Chinese flute, oboe, cello, and French horn.

The California-based pop-rock band Smash Mouth visited SugarHill twice to cut special tracks for radio or film. Dan Workman recalls they first recorded "a punk-rock version of 'Take Me Out to the Ball Game'" for promotional use by Major League Baseball on Clear Channel Radio stations, and their producer was enamored of the vintage equipment and historic studio. Later, Smash Mouth returned to cut vocals for a song for the 1998 film *Half Baked*. Workman adds, "The vocals were recorded on top of a track sent by [the British electronic duo] the Chemical Brothers, who were the producers of the movie soundtrack."

Having signed to a new label, Vanguard Records, blues guitarist Tab Benoit returned to SugarHill Studios to recapture the magic he had previ-ously cooked up there on his acclaimed 1992 debut disc. Coproducing with Benoit, I engineered the session live in the studio with his band, resulting in the well-received 1999 album *These Blues Are All Mine*.

By then, RAD had added Ramon Morales to the general engineering staff, replacing Steve Lanphier, who was mainly recording and producing Tejano groups for Discos MM. Steve Christensen, who started as an intern in 1998, would later replace Morales.

While we made many other late-1990s recordings, none topped those by a young female vocal group from Houston who would go on to dominate the *Billboard* charts with a string of SugarHill-produced hits like no artist since Freddy Fender.

BY THE TURN OF THE PRESENT CENTURY, Destiny's Child had become a pop cultural phenomenon. These singing and dancing teenage girls had de-buted with an eponymous CD on Columbia Records in 1998. They scored successively bigger sales with the multi-Platinum follow-up albums: 1999's

The Writing's on the Wall and 2001's *Survivor.* In 2003, the most famous member, Beyoncé Knowles (b. 1981), issued *Dangerously in Love,* her first solo CD, winner of five Grammy Awards. By 2005, the global superstar trio—Knowles, Kelly Rowland, and Michelle Williams—were mainly pursuing independent careers, but they were still hugely popular. In her 2005 article "Destiny's World Domination" Julie Keller reports that they "were the big winners at this year's World Music Awards, taking home trophies for Best-Selling Pop Group, Best-Selling R&B Group, and Best-Selling Female Group of All Time."

Along their way from anonymity to unprecedented success, there were some controversial personnel changes, well-publicized disputes, lawsuits, and settlements—which sparked some negative backlash among fans and in the media. Yet Destiny's Child, conceived and managed by Knowles's father, never wavered in their rapid climb to the highest peak on the pop cultural landscape, and the three core members continue today to enjoy multimedia success in a variety of ventures.

Yet during a key phase in their metamorphosis into a triumvirate of world-famous music and fashion icons, they recorded some of the most noteworthy Destiny's Child tracks at SugarHill Studios.

Workman collaborated extensively with Destiny's Child on their second and third albums and with Knowles on her solo debut. He explains the group's SugarHill connection:

> Ron Wilson sent Matthew Knowles and Destiny's Child to us. . . . They [already] had a Top Ten hit with "No No No," which was produced by Wyclef Jean on their first album. They were working on their second record and wanted to find a more comfortable place to do their recording.
>
> He first brought Beyoncé in here to see if she would be comfortable. Beyoncé came in, and I did vocal karaoke sessions with her. . . . We did several sessions like that, and then Matthew brought the rest of the girls in to begin working on their second album.
>
> That's when we rented all the gear from Dream Hire in Nashville for their producer, Kevin Briggs, alias "She'kspere." He was from Atlanta and had just come off the [girl group] TLC's [hit] record, which was huge. We set up shop in Studio B . . . [and] we recorded six or seven songs, [four of which] wound up on that record *Writing's on the Wall.* I did most of the sessions, but . . . Ramon Morales covered a session, and . . . was hired away from us to tour with them and handle all their live sound needs.

When Morales departed, Christensen took his place. He describes his involvement in the Destiny's Child sessions:

I did a lot of interning with Dan Workman and Ramon Morales as they worked on the *Writing's on the Wall* CD for Destiny's Child. Later I engineered the Bee Gees cover they did called "Emotion." I also did a song for them that went off to Disney Productions. I was the engineer for Dan when he cut the guitar parts for the song "Dangerously in Love 2" that became the title track for Beyoncé's first solo album. I worked with her sister Solange on a number of tracks. In between all of that, I subbed for Ramon on their first European tour.

SugarHill Studios thus played an important behind-the-scenes role in the major phase of Destiny's Child's ascension. By engineering numerous hit tracks in the studio, as well as providing talent for their sound needs on tour, we were participants in their success.

The megahit album *The Writing's on the Wall* included the SugarHill-produced tracks "So Good," "Hey Ladies," "She Can't Love You," and "Bug-a-Boo," the last of which peaked at number thirty-three on the *Billboard* Hot 100 pop singles. That album reportedly sold approximately eight million copies in the United States and another twelve million worldwide.

SugarHill Studios was even more involved in production of *Survivor*, with six of its songs recorded there. Of those, four became Top 10 singles. "Independent Women Part 1" and "Bootylicious" both reached number one on the charts; meanwhile, the title track single went to number two, and "Emotion" peaked at number ten. The two other SugarHill-recorded tracks were "Gospel Medley" and the original version of "Dangerously in Love." The album debuted at number one on the *Billboard* charts and reportedly sold over three million copies in its first two months of release, eventually reaching the rarefied quadruple-Platinum status.

Workman recalls the SugarHill sessions for that album:

For their third album, *Survivor*, . . . the recording took place over a much longer period of time. The previous record with She'kspere was done in a concentrated chunk of time. By now Beyoncé was really producing the group. They were buying tracks from highly qualified programmers and writing words for them. The sessions took place in Studio A and B. . . .

Beyoncé would be driving over to the studio listening to all these tracks that had been sent to her, and she would pick out her favorite. When she got here, she would immediately start writing lyrics for the song and finish it right there in front of me. For the song "Bootylicious" she wrote all the lyrics for it right in our Studio A. Then she taught the song to Kelly and Michelle, and all three of them worked on the vocals together. Unlike the previous album where Beyoncé did 95 percent of the vocals, for this their third album, the other girls were much more involved.

"Bootylicious" started out with the Fleetwood Mac sample "Edge of Seventeen," and I thought that it turned into a phenomenal song. I remember Matthew calling me the next day and asking me what had the girls done. The day before had been a fourteen-hour day in the studio, and we had finished the song completely. So I told him that we had done the song "Bootylicious." He said, "What?" And I said, "Bootylicious." And he said, "Bootylicious?" I could tell he didn't like the sound of that at all. That all changed when he actually heard it, and, of course, it became a big hit.

In addition to being impressed with Beyoncé's on-the-spot skills as a lyricist and producer, Workman also was awestruck by certain aspects of her musicianship, particularly regarding timing. For example, he says,

"Gospel Medley," [which] was released on the *Survivor* album, . . . was also placed on Michelle's solo [2002] gospel record, *Heart to Yours,* and that was done here. . . . Before we started recording it, I asked Beyoncé if she wanted a click track, or metronome, for the song. She said, "No, it is a *rubato* song with tempo changes."

Then I said, "Well, would you like some kind of pedal tone or synthesizer pad to sing over to use as a pitch reference?"

She said, "Oh no." . . . I thought, wow, this could be a big mess. Well, I was wrong. She sang it perfectly in tune, and the timing was great. She put all her parts on it flawlessly, and so did Kelly and Michelle when it was their turn. It turned out to be an astonishingly beautiful multilayered gospel medley.

The good working relationship established between Destiny's Child and SugarHill Studios even led to a recording project for national television. Workman provides the context:

MTV did a special called *The Road Home.* It was about stars going to play in their hometown . . . [and] one of the shows was on Destiny's Child. . . . The concert was at the Cynthia Woods Mitchell Pavilion. MTV called us to record the live performance. I assembled a combination of J. P. Rappenecker's remote recording rig and ours to do a forty-eight-track digital tape recording of the concert that could be locked up to video.

Given the group's moneymaking success, Destiny's Child's manager Matthew Knowles eventually bought a valuable block of real estate (contain-

Destiny's Child, publicity photo, 2002

ing a three-story nineteenth-century house and other buildings) in Houston's Midtown district; there he established his Music World Entertainment offices and installed a state-of-the-art private recording studio. But prior to that, we staged one last SugarHill session to record a remixed version of "Dangerously in Love" for Beyoncé's first solo album. The new treatment of the song, called "Dangerously in Love 2," won a Grammy Award for Best Female R&B Vocal Performance, while the album earned the Grammy for Best Contemporary R&B Album in 2003.

Workman describes how he came to play on that song:

I was cutting vocals for it and doing mixes of it. I noticed that the nylon string guitar sample was so bad that it was embarrassing to listen to. Beyoncé really liked the song a lot. . . . So I called Matthew and told him that vocals were going well, but that the guitar part on the song was really bad and that I could cut it again and make it better. He said, "Do it." . . . It was my first credit as a studio musician on a Platinum-selling single and album.

Despite the excellent track record that Destiny's Child and Beyoncé had established as clients of SugarHill Studios, that relationship ended once Knowles created his Music World Entertainment compound. "Ramon Morales, who used to work for us, was engineering in their studio," Workman notes, adding, "So basically our run with Matthew and Destiny's Child was pretty much over."

But what a fine run it had been for SugarHill, one that enabled it to start a new millennium as a reenergized hit-making studio.

IN ADDITION TO RECORDING BEST-SELLING material for the contemporary R&B and pop market, in the early twenty-first century SugarHill Studios got involved in the rap scene. That transformation started with our brief affiliation with the New Orleans–based label called Cash Money Records. Founded in the early 1990s, Cash Money achieved a 1997 pressing and distribution deal with Universal Records. Several of its artists—including Juvenile (b. Terius Gray, 1975), Lil' Wayne (b. Dwayne Michael Carter, 1982), and producer Mannie Fresh (b. Byron O. Thomas, 1974)—have now risen to superstar rapper status, and SugarHill played a role in one large production.

That opportunity arose at the suggestion of musician Rick Marcel (b. 1966). In March 2001 he came to SugarHill to record the foundation tracks for a song in an upcoming Universal film release, which starred several Cash Money recording artists. Marcel produced all the instrumentation and sang the scratch vocals. We then sent the tapes to Sigma Studios in Philadelphia, where the group Unplugged added the final vocals. This small project led, in April and May of 2001, to a gathering of various so-called "Dirty South" rappers at SugarHill Studios. Workman explains,

They found us through guitar and bass wizard Rick Marcel. Rick had been working with them at Carriage House Studios in Florida, and they had been talking about going to Houston. Rick Marcel steered them towards us. . . . They wound up staying for about two and a half weeks, working around our regular clients.

The presence of a large assemblage of self-proclaimed gangsta rappers proved difficult for the SugarHill staff. Cash Money had booked studio time for one week but actually took over twice that long, conflicting with other scheduled productions. "Those guys would show up five or six hours late for almost every session, like it was no big deal," says Christensen. "It's like a giant parade when they arrive somewhere." Workman adds,

> They were the most disrespectable bunch, and we had just a miserable time with them. . . .
> Amazingly, they told us when they left that they had never gotten so much work done before. A lot of that had to do with the quality of the engineering staff they were working with. Part of it had to do with the fact that we didn't have a swimming pool, or pool tables, or a basketball goal so that people could slack off and leave the engineer sitting waiting for the next session. I must say that none of the sessions ever started on time, and they certainly finished way later than we expected.

Among this large entourage of Cash Money artists were Lil' Wayne and Mannie Fresh, as well as label cofounder Brian "Baby" Williams (b. 1974, aka Birdman) and the West Coast rapper called Mack 10 (b. Deadrick D'Mon Rolison, 1971). Various others were there, including an all-girl group called S5 and a boy band named Unplugged (aka Official). Workman elaborates on the sessions:

> Lil' Wayne was the most talented, and Mack 10 was the aggressive, bad-attitude guy. Mannie Fresh was the resident producer for all the rappers, and Baby was the chief musical programmer. I think we had as many as thirty reels of two-inch tape working with DA-88 digital slave tapes, and Pro-Tools sessions all running simultaneously. On some days they were using both rooms at the same time.

While the Cash Money sessions at SugarHill Studios yielded a lot of material, we have never ascertained most of the titles or details of subsequent publication. "I am quite certain that some of the songs that we started and some that we finished wound up being released—and may even have been hits in the rap world," says Workman. However, given its lax documentation of session details and titles, Cash Money has left us clueless. "Their organization did not take the time and care that Sony [owner of Columbia Records] and Destiny's Child did to keep track of what was recorded and where," he explains.

Christensen offers some additional details:

> The first people [to record] were producer/drum programmer Mannie Fresh, keyboardist Wolf, and bass guitarist Rick Marcel. None of the songs was cre-

ated offline beforehand. Baby and Slim, the owners of Cash Money Records, were real good at keeping the rappers, the posse, and various other visitors away down the hall or outside while this crew was working. From an engineering point, it was cool working with the music bunch. They approached it like a band creating a song. In four hours we would have four songs done, recording to twenty-four-track analog. That took us to midnight. So then those guys would split until the next day.

Then in came the rappers and vocal producers. Everything changed at that point. The guys were all jerks. But they were outstanding rappers and got the job done. . . . We worked on songs for Mack 10's upcoming CD release *Bang or Ball,* which featured Lil' Wayne, Turk, and B.G.

One of the few results we have been able to trace, the *Bang or Ball* album from Cash Money/Universal Records, made it to number four on the *Billboard* R&B/hip-hop albums chart in January 2002.

In addition to the Cash Money crew, a Jamaican-born reggae-dancehall rapper also cut a hit record at SugarHill Studios in 2001. Robert Minott, sometimes billed only by his surname, had recorded there in the late 1980s, but when he returned in the new millennium he brought with him tracks on analog tape, Pro Tools files, and other digital platforms. Over a period of about six months we worked on finishing seventeen songs. Six had been recorded in Jamaica, four were created at SugarHill, and the rest came from different programmers in Houston. We did the vocals for most of the songs in Studio B, with mixing done in Studio C. Errol McCalla, who had programmed "Independent Women" for Destiny's Child, also worked on this project, which resulted in Minott's album *Playing the Game Right* on the World Beat Records label. The sound of this record blended Jamaican pop with contemporary urban influences, including hip-hop. Minott scored a Top 10 hit with the track "Playa Playa (Playing the Game Right)," which peaked at number eight on the *Billboard* rap singles chart in September 2001, while simultaneously hitting number sixteen on the separate *Billboard* R&B/hip-hop singles chart.

Thus, in the early phase of RAD Audio ownership, SugarHill Studios asserted its continuing relevance through best-selling projects featuring new R&B or hip-hop music and mostly younger, African American performers. By late January 2002, Destiny's Child, Mack 10, and Robert Minott all simultaneously had singles and/or albums on the *Billboard* charts.

Though times and tastes had changed, the facility—in its sixth decade of operations—was still a house of hits.

Still Tracking in
the Twenty-first Century

WHILE A NEW GENERATION OF HIT PERFORMERS infused SugarHill Studios with fresh styles of contemporary urban music to start the new millennium, the facility also retained its no-zoning tradition. That is, the company regularly recorded—and still does—music from a multicultural mix of genres, including country, blues, jazz, rock, pop, Celtic, gospel, classical, Latin, R&B, rap, and other forms and mutations. In addition to working with hundreds of artists from the Houston scene, in recent years the facility has continued to host a diverse roster of high-profile visitors. Those range from R&B and rap sensation Brian McKnight to alt-rocker Frank Black to the mysterious experimental composer Jandek to Texas folk hero Willie Nelson to veteran pop singer Ann-Margret to country singer Clay Walker, and many others.

Walker (b. 1969) was one of the biggest country stars of the 1990s, a Beaumont native who seemingly went straight from obscurity to the national limelight. As Stephen Thomas Erlewine writes in *All Music Guide*, "Walker immediately established himself as a commercial success . . . racking up no less than five number one singles in the first three years of his career." From his 1993 debut through 1999, Walker had released a total of six albums (including a *Greatest Hits* compilation) on Giant Records, all recorded elsewhere. Then in 2001 he came to SugarHill Studios to record some vocal tracks for his last Giant project, the CD *Say No More*, which reached number fourteen on the *Billboard* country album chart. Dan Workman explains some details of those sessions:

> Doug Johnson was the head of Giant Records and also Clay's producer. Doug . . . flew down to Houston and brought his favorite microphone and

preamps and an engineer by the name of Chip Matthews. . . . Among the songs that were recorded for that album are "Could I Ask You Not to Dance," "She's Easy to Hold," and "Texas Swing."

Matthews returned a few months later to mix the audio tracks recorded during Walker's recent performance at the Houston Livestock Show and Rodeo—a concert that was sold to Direct TV for satellite broadcast. Then in 2003 Walker staged vocal sessions at SugarHill for his album *A Few Questions,* produced by Jimmy Ritchey and released on RCA. This one rose as high as number three on the 2004 country album rankings by *Billboard.*

In October 2006 the Texas Country Music Hall of Fame singer-songwriter Johnny Bush returned after a twenty-one-year absence to record the CD *Kashmere Gardens Mud: A Tribute to Houston's Country Soul.* Produced by Rick Mitchell, this fourteen-track concept album features Bush originals and classic covers that all connect in some way to the city. These songs cover a spectrum of stylistic shadings, including a fine treatment of "Born to Lose" (written by Houston native Ted Daffan) with the Calvin Owens Blues Orchestra. "I have never been part of a session that big in my life. They had a rhythm section, fourteen horns, and a string section," Bush marvels, adding, "And it was all being done in the same room where Mickey Gilley and I recorded 'Ooh Wee Baby' in 1956!"

Some of the other noteworthy guest performers on this album include Willie Nelson, Jesse Dayton, Bert Wills, Paul English, Dale Watson, Frenchie Burke, Brian Thomas, and Bush's brother, the Rev. Gene Shinn.

The well-received *Kashmere Gardens Mud* led directly to a country music summit of sorts at SugarHill Studios. It involved three alumni of the 1950s-era band known as the Cherokee Cowboys—its leader, singer Ray Price (b. 1926), Nelson, and Bush. The resulting album, *Young at Heart,* is a collection of standards (arranged by Owens, English, and Nelson Mills). Bush explains its origin and concept:

> When we finished the *Kashmere Gardens Mud* album, I played the two big band songs that we recorded with the Calvin Owens Blues Orchestra to Willie. His ears perked up, and his eyes kind of sparkled and he said, "You know, we need to do a whole album of songs like that. . . . old established hit records that are recognizable." . . . This album is not old country or new country. It's not really pop music. It is a hybrid of pop, jazz, and country in a big band situation.

Slated to be released on Nelson's Pedernales Records label and distributed by MCA, this recording is a direct by-product of the cross-cultural musical environment that Bush discovered at SugarHill.

Other notable country artists to record at SugarHill in recent years include singer Kelly Schoppa, whose *Let's Go Dancing* was released in 2005. There was also the fiddle player and singer Jeff Chance, a Nashville veteran who had formerly recorded on the Mercury and Curb labels. He paired with guitarist Randy Cornor in 2007 to cut tracks for an album project. The country-folk singer-songwriter Glenna Bell recorded her 2007 CD *The Road Less Traveled*, featuring a duet with Bush, at SugarHill. Meanwhile, the Honky Tonk Heroes and their special guest James Burton (b. 1939, a Rock and Roll Hall of Fame guitarist) came there to record 2008's *Paybacks Are Hell*. In the last few years SugarHill has also hosted sessions by the River Road Boys, a western swing ensemble that includes fiddler and singer Clyde Brewer.

The versatile John Evans has been grounded in country music and rockabilly, both as a singer-songwriter and a producer. But drawing from other influences he has also crafted a rock sound, as evidenced on albums recorded at SugarHill, such as *Circling the Drain* (2004) and *Ramblin' Boy* (2006)—which engineer Christensen describes as "the first of his big production rock records."

In the blues genre, one of the most prolific clients was the late maestro and trumpeter Calvin Owens. In a professional career that reached from the 1940s till his 2008 death, Owens worked with numerous major figures, most famously with B. B. King. But Owens first recorded in the late 1940s at the site where Bill Quinn founded his historic recording enterprise. Though Owens did some Duke-Peacock 1960s session work there and some early 1990s overdubbing too, it was not until the twenty-first century that he came there to produce and perform on projects featuring the Calvin Owens Blues Orchestra and many special guests.

His first major undertaking at SugarHill Studios was the 2002 album *The House Is Burnin'*, released (as were all of his projects) on his own Sawdust Alley label. Owens coarranged the selected songs with trombonist Aubrey Tucker and saxophonist Horace A. Young. In addition to the horn-heavy nineteen-piece band, members of the Houston Symphony string section and guest soloists such as saxophonist Grady Gaines augmented the instrumentation. Featured vocalists, besides Owens, were Trudy Lynn, Gloria Edwards, and Leonard "Lowdown" Brown.

The 2004 CD called *The Calvin Owens Show* showcased his orchestra with singers Edwards and Lynn, plus special guests saxophonist Wilton Felder (b. 1940, a founding member of the Crusaders), guitarist Bert Wills, harmonica ace "Sonny Boy" Terry Jerome, and the then eighty-eight-year-old Conrad Johnson, who delivered a masterful alto saxophone solo on "The Hucklebuck."

Around this time, I also helped remix Owens's debut solo CD, *True Blue*. Originally released in 1993, the remastered version was issued in 2005.

Among the many distinguished guests to appear on *True Blue* are the guitarists B. B. King and Johnny Copeland, as well as jazz star David "Fathead" Newman (b. 1933) on tenor sax.

We then remixed a set of tracks Owens had previously recorded with rappers such as South Park Mexican, Big Snap, and Valdemar. Some of these were originally released on the 2000 album *Stop Lyin' in My Face,* an unusual fusion of rap with Owens's big band blues. However, Owens had used guest rappers on several other CDs too. The remixed compilation was issued in 2006 on the European label called Sabam Records.

The passionate intensity that Owens brought to his many productions fueled a surge of new Sawdust Alley releases in the final years of his life. His most characteristic album of 2006 was *I Ain't Gonna Be Your Dog No More: The Calvin Owens Show, Volume Two.* Owens also worked on, in his own words, "another rap CD with Rasheed, Valdemar, and the Classic Thugs," as well as "a Spanish-language blues album," plus "an album featuring Trudy Lynn singing with the Calvin Owens Blues Orchestra." That last one, titled *I'm Still Here,* garnered finalist consideration for 2007's Best Soul Blues Album in the Memphis-based Blues Foundation's Blues Music Awards. His burst of creativity not yet slaked, Owens went on to make the 2007 album *Houston Is the Place to Be* with his full orchestra and special guests such as Barbara Lynn, Rue Davis, Pete Mayes, and others. That CD was released simultaneously with the debut album by an Owens protégé—the bilingual Mexico-born blues singer and saxophonist, Evelyn Rubio. Also recorded at SugarHill, *La Mujer Que Canta Blues* was credited to Rubio "y Calvin Owens Orqestra Azul."

The close relationship Owens had with SugarHill Studios caused him to recommend the facility to one of his former colleagues—the current bandleader and trumpeter in B. B. King's band. So in January of 2007 James Bolden recorded his first solo album there. Called *Playing to the King,* it is a tribute to the guitar-wielding bluesman he has backed for many years. Bolden tells how it came to be:

> I live in Houston even though I'm on the road worldwide with B.B. for over two hundred dates a year. My cousin, Rocky White, who was the drummer for the Mercer Ellington Orchestra, also lives in Houston. So in mid-January of 2007 [B.B.] came into Galveston to play two dates at the Opera House. This was a perfect opportunity to record, as we were in the area for about five days. . . . [We] recorded ten great songs that were either B.B's or my compositions. Rocky was the drummer, and the rest of the guys were from B.B's band.

Highlighted by senior artists such as Owens and Bolden, SugarHill Studios recorded some impressively grand blues and jazz in the first decade of the

Barbara Lynn and Calvin Owens, at SugarHill Studios, 2006

new millennium. But there were performers from the next generation too—perhaps best exemplified by the fine blues-rock singer Tommie Lee Bradley. Supported by experienced musicians such as Erich Avinger, Bert Wills, Kenny Cordray, Paul English, Anthony Sapp, and Kelly Dean, Bradley recorded all the tracks for her 2005 album, *Soul Soup,* at SugarHill.

One jazz session came about following Hurricane Katrina's destruction of New Orleans. In October 2005 Nonesuch Records booked studio time at SugarHill to record tracks for *Our New Orleans 2005: A Benefit Album,* released one month later. New Orleans–based engineers Mark Bingham and Drew Vonderhaar worked with producer Doug Petty to record two of the Crescent City's recently displaced jazz stars, clarinetist Michael White (b. 1954) and trumpeter Kermit Ruffins (b. 1964), for the project.

Meanwhile, jazz pianist and vocalist Kellye Gray continued to make SugarHill Studios her recording base. Having previously been there to make her first two CDs (*Standards in Gray* on Justice Records and *Tomato Kiss* on Proteus Recordings), she used the SugarHill staff again in 2002 for live sessions at Ovations, a Houston club. We did the location recording with freelance engineer J. P. Rappenecker, producing enough quality tracks to make two CDs. The first, released in 2002, was called *Blue* and featured the ballads,

Latin, and gentle songs. The second CD, released in April 2003, was named *Pink* and featured the bebop, high-energy blues, and funk grooves.

The sibling vocal trio known as the Champion Sisters first brought their blend of pop-jazz standards to SugarHill in 2004. (Forty-eight years earlier, their father, George Champion, had recorded at the same site with George Jones.) Featuring a tight three-part harmony that evokes the Andrews Sisters, the three Champion women—Molly, Brenda, and Sandra—cut tracks for their 2005 debut album *In the Mood,* which included a guest appearance by jazz saxophonist Kirk Whalum. In 2006 the sisters returned—again with Paul English as arranger, keyboardist, and producer—to record their follow-up album, *Christmas with the Champion Sisters* (2007).

WHILE COUNTRY, BLUES, AND JAZZ have remained staples of SugarHill sessions in recent years, there have also been various manifestations of postmodern rock and even avant-garde music, as well as an ongoing relationship with rap.

Perhaps the most unusual of all the artists in these categories is the internationally famous-for-being-obscure atonal music phenomenon known simply as Jandek. A mostly one-man operation based in Houston, Jandek released his first self-produced album in 1978. As of 2008, he has now issued over fifty weird art-rock albums, many of which have been mixed and mastered at SugarHill.

While Jandek's music resists simple classification, *Texas Monthly* writer Katy Vine reveals that Jandek favors the description "pentatonic refractive dissonance." Reclusive and elusive, Jandek has steadfastly shunned publicity and the revelation of his true identity, disappearing instead behind his corporate identity as Corwood Industries, the name of his homemade label. Moreover, despite a growing worldwide cadre of fans, Jandek made no public performances until October 2004, when he played at an unpublicized event in Scotland. Since then, Jandek has occasionally but rarely played live elsewhere. *Houston Chronicle* writer Andrew Dansby, who observed a 2007 concert, describes the live sound as "dark, naturally; loud; and, for those who like their music served up with performance-artish rough edges intact, sharp as shorn metal . . . like deconstructed mountain music run through monster amps."

I first met Jandek in 1981 at ACA Studios when he hired me to mix and master his third album, *Later On.* Since then, I have mixed a tremendous volume of his music—and since 1984, all at SugarHill Studios. Jandek has confirmed that I handled mixing and mastering for the Corwood releases #0741 through #0769, and then for #0783 and all subsequent releases to date. As Dansby points out, "there's some untainted allure to the music." And despite its strangeness and the mystique of the Jandek persona, in some respects he is one of the most successful artists currently engaging the services of SugarHill Studios.

Speaking of unusual personae, the famous alternative rocker known variously as Frank Black and Black Francis, of the influential late 1980s–early '90s postpunk band the Pixies, graced SugarHill Studios with a session during his Fall 2006 tour. Via his pseudonyms, Black (b. Charles Mitchell Kittredge Thompson IV, 1965) has been a major presence on the national scene for over two decades. Christensen recalls the night Black recorded at SugarHill:

> Billy Block, a drummer . . . all during the 1980s here in Houston, called [Andy Bradley] to talk about a recording session. It turns out that he is both the manager and drummer for Frank Black. . . . They were in town playing a show at the Meridian [and] wanted to cut a couple of new songs. . . . They brought in an engineer named Billy Mumfrey . . . and I worked as his assistant. . . . The band arrived by taxi from the Meridian about midnight. . . . They just jumped in the studio and went to work and knocked out the two music tracks like a well-oiled machine. . . . As soon as we finished the tracks, Frank went into the vocal booth. I had the Neumann U-67 [microphone] set up, and he just sang and screamed Frank Black–style.

As often occurs when touring visitors briefly use the studio, Black departed with the only copy of the recorded tracks—and provided SugarHill with no song titles or identifying details. However, because Christensen recalls overhearing that this session was for a "live" album, it seems likely that these two tracks may have appeared on the Frank Black *Live Session* EP that was created during that same tour.

Sometimes traveling artists come to SugarHill Studios, and sometimes SugarHill comes to them. In July 2007, members of the Australian Rock and Roll Hall of Fame group Radio Birdman toured the United States, and we recorded both of their Texas gigs for broadcast on the *SugarHill Sessions* series on Houston's KPFT-FM radio. Some of those tracks may eventually appear on a special-edition CD called *Live in Texas*.

On the local front, the band called Spain Colored Orange—which mixes elements of indie rock, jazz, psychedelia, and pop—emerged around 2005, winning numerous "Best of" categories in the 2006 *Houston Press* Music Awards. Later that year the group came to SugarHill to record their first CD, *Hopelessly Incapable of Standing in the Way,* for release on Lucid Records. They made the 2008 follow-up album, *Sneaky Like a Villain,* there too.

The versatile, nontraditional Celtic group called the Rogues have continued to use SugarHill Studios to record their high-energy music. In 2001 they cut all the tracks there for the album 5.0. Then in 2003 SugarHill made on-site multitrack digital recordings of a Rogues concert at the Houston venue called McGonigel's Mucky Duck, preserved on the double CD called *Made in Texas*. The group returned to SugarHill in 2005 to make the album *Rogue Trip*, as well as in 2008 to record tracks for the CD *American Highlander*.

Thus, SugarHill continues to function as the professional recording base of choice for various local groups engaged in creating and dispensing new tracks. Other representative examples include the Texas jam band called Moses Guest, which first recorded there in 1999, and returned in 2002 to make an eponymous double album. In 2003 the ever-popular early rock and R&B connoisseurs called El Orbits did more sessions there. "Enough material was recorded for two CDs of Orbit music. The first, *Flyin' High with The El Orbits*, was released in early fall of that year on Freedom Records [#1026]," says band founder David Beebe, adding, "The Christmas album was called *The El Orbits Holiday Album*." In recent years SugarHill has also staged sessions for albums by indie rock singer-songwriters such as Chet Daniels, Sarah Sharp, and Ray Younkin, as well as Latin rock ensemble Jesse Flores and Vudu Café and the psychedelic rockers Southern Backtones.

Yet despite the prevalence of different offshoots of rock at SugarHill Studios in the new century, the site has continued to draw rappers and contemporary R&B performers too. Among those, one high-profile figure is the Grammy-nominated singer and multi-instrumentalist Brian McKnight (b. 1969), who came to SugarHill to collaborate with rap mogul Jermaine Dupri (b. 1973). Christensen also engineered those sessions and shares these recollections:

> They were cutting a new song for Brian McKnight, and Jermaine Dupri was producing. Brian was on tour and had a day off in Houston. The control room was a wall of keyboards. Between the keyboards and the speakers, it looked like we had built a bunker. They came in with nothing prepared and a few ideas. They started playing and programming and soon had built up a great track. Meanwhile Brian was writing lyrics and working on melodies. As soon as they finished the music, he went into the studio and laid down all the vocals.

Around the same time, Christensen also recalls working at SugarHill with the Chicago rapper known mainly as Twista (b. Carl Terrell Mitchell, 1973). "He rapped so fast that doing punch-ins to his tracks was brutal," he says. "The song he did with us was called 'Rubber Band Man'"—probably the remix version that premiered in 2004 featuring, in addition to Twista, the rappers called T.I., Trick Daddy, and Mack 10.

Among other hip-hop artists to cut tracks at SugarHill recently is the New Orleans gangsta rapper known as C-Murder (b. Corey Miller, 1971), who recorded "The Truest Shit I Ever Said" for 2005 release on Koch Records. Houston-based Latino rapper Rob G used the facility to record his debut CD for Latium Entertainment (distributed by Universal Records). The Caucasian rapper called Origino recorded his 2007 album *Leave the Ground Behind* (L&O Records) at the studios, including his remix of the hit single "What Do You Get?" (featuring guest appearances by fellow rappers Paul Wall and G-reg). Finally, studio personnel such as Workman and James Garlington have recently collaborated on tracks for two albums by the Houston rapper, now a convicted felon, known as South Park Mexican, alias SPM (b. Carlos Coy, 1970). The first is the 2008 CD titled *The Last Chair Violinist,* for which the vocals were recorded via telephone while Coy awaited trial. The other is called *The Country Boys,* scheduled for release in 2009. Both are on the infamous rapper's own Dopehouse label.

DEPARTING STRIKINGLY FROM THE GRITTY realities of the rap world, SugarHill also staged sessions for a country-and-western-flavored gospel album by the Swedish-born singer and actress Ann-Margret (b. 1941). In October 2001 she was in Houston for an extended run of the touring musical *The Best Little Whorehouse in Texas.* During that time she also recorded the vocal tracks for her album *God Is Love: The Gospel Sessions,* which ultimately included the vocal group the Jordanaires, the western swing legends the Light Crust Doughboys, and country singer James Blackwood. Christensen explains the format for these SugarHill recordings:

> Art Greenhaw from the Light Crust Doughboys was the producer . . . with Ann-Margret as featured vocalist. . . . She and Art would go out in the studio and jam through the songs. He played piano, and she sang, and it was all done live with her in the room with the piano. Some of the songs were one-takers. . . . Once they had finished, Art took the tapes to Nashville and built [the rest of the album] on top of those piano and vocal tracks.

A marked departure in her forty-plus-year career, Ann-Margret's *God Is Love* album ultimately received a Grammy nomination for Best Contemporary Gospel album and a GMA Dove Award nomination for Best Country Album.

Finally, while the work has not occurred on site at 5626 Brock Street, for most of the twenty-first century SugarHill Studios has overseen recordings during the annual classical music extravaganza produced by the International Festival-Institute at Round Top, Texas. Over one hundred top students gather there each summer for six weeks of intense musical study—the results of which are featured in weekend performances by a symphony orchestra, a chamber orchestra, and numerous smaller ensembles. The Institute was founded in 1971 by James Dick, an internationally renowned concert pianist and teacher. He explains,

> It started as a ten-day festival. We got some press, some notoriety, and we were successful. . . . We were able to find our first 6 acres here in Round Top, which has now grown to 210 acres. We are a nonprofit educational organization . . . and offer full scholarships to the students that come here from all over the United States and parts of the world.

Situated in a gorgeous Hill Country setting, the Institute showcases the musicians in an acoustically stellar concert hall that includes a state-of-the-art sound-recording booth. Utilizing the in-house equipment and supplemental gear from SugarHill, we prepare all the concert recordings for duplication and radio broadcast on Houston's KUHF-FM classical station, Austin's KMFA-FM, and National Public Radio's *Performance Today* series—as well as for an internationally distributed series entitled *Live from Festival Hill*.

SINCE THE EARLY 1940S, THE HOUSTON-BASED studio company founded by Bill Quinn has been making recordings. As this book has endeavored to show, in terms of longevity, the volume of business, the diversity of musical styles, and the number of influential hits and classic tracks it has produced, this continuously operated enterprise is phenomenal. Like the no-zoning metropolis that it calls home, the Gold Star/SugarHill recording facility has played a unique role in Texas history and American music.

Catalogue of Interviews

Except where otherwise indicated, all interviews were conducted in person and tape-recorded by Andy Bradley in Houston, Texas.

Archer, Warren. August 13, 2004.
Barber, Glenn. Via telephone. January 6, 2005.
Barkdull, Wiley. November 16, 2004.
Bartlett, John David. Via telephone. May 24, 2004.
Becker, Carl. Via telephone. November 12, 2005.
Beebe, David. February 9, 2004.
Benson, Ray. Written notes. Austin, Texas, November 13, 2003.
Bernard, Rod. Via telephone. September 11, 2004.
Bolden, James. September 21, 2007.
Brady, Pat. September 21, 2003.
Brewer, Clyde. January 23, 2003.
Bush, Johnny. November 3, 2006, and February 12, 2008.
Calvert, Craig. September 24, 2004.
Champagne, Don. November 15, 2004.
Chance, Jeff. Via telephone. September 19, 2007.
Christensen, Steve. August 16, 2007.
Clagett, Paul. Via telephone. January 14, 2004.
Clark, Guy. Via telephone. February 24, 2004.
Clement, Jack. Via telephone. May 15, 2004.
Cordray, Kenny. October 3, 2002.
Davis, Frank. Via telephone. August 17, 2004.
Dick, James. Round Top, Texas, January 15, 2005.
Dillard, Bill. Telephone interview by Andrew Brown. Tape recording. 2006.
    Used by permission.

Douglas, Mel. October 11, 2005.

Drachenberg, Don. Via telephone. July 24, 2007.

Duff, Jim. December 11, 2003.

Fliegel, Rafael. August 9, 2003.

Frazier, Skipper Lee. August 27, 2004.

Gilley, Mickey. Via telephone. June 12, 2004.

Gregory, Rex. September 30, 2005.

Harris, Roger. Via telephone. May 24, 2004.

Head, Roy. Written notes. September 23, 2002.

Jackson, Melvin. Via telephone. June 25, 2006.

Jamail, Randall. March 9, 2006.

James, Mark. Via telephone. October 12, 2004.

Jones, Doyle. September 11, 2002, and October 14, 2002.

———. Via telephone. January 11, 2003.

Jones, Jon. Via telephone. June 4, 2006.

Juricek, Frank. Brenham, Texas, January 5, 2005.

Kurtz, Gene. September 23, 2002.

LaBeef, Sleepy. April 9, 2004.

———. Via telephone. March 4, 2004.

LaCroix, Jerry. June 13, 2004.

Lam, Hank. September 22, 2004.

Landes, Rob. December 13, 2002.

Latimer, Gaylan. Via telephone. June 14, 2003.

Linhof, Kurt. Via telephone. November 23, 2003.

Mayes, Pete. June 11, 2006.

McCracklin, Jimmy. Via telephone. October 16, 2007.

McLain, Tommy. Via telephone. November 13, 2004.

Miller, Frankie. Via telephone. May 5, 2004.

Mims, Connie. September 12, 2004.

Moody, Mickey. April 22, 2008.

Needham, Dean. March 9, 2004.

Norris, Slick. November 16, 2004.

O'Gwynn, James. Via telephone. November 13, 2004.

Oldrieve, Bob. December 14, 2004.

Olivier, Jim. Via e-mail correspondence. September 30, 2006.

O'Neil, Leo. April 16, 2004.

Ornelas, Willie. Via telephone. February 9, 2004.

Owens, Calvin. June 19, 2004, and November 22, 2004.

Parrish, Robbie. March 11, 2005.

Payne, Gordon. Written notes. August 18, 2007.

Poole, Hank. Via telephone. May 19, 2004.

Poole, Trent. April 23, 2003.

Potter, Todd. Via telephone. October 12, 2003.

Preston (Courville), Johnny. Via telephone. November 17, 2003.

Remington, Herb. June 19, 2003.

Romano, Rock. July 16, 2004.

Rush, Ray. December 12, 2003.

Russell, David. Via e-mail correspondence. June 24, 2004.

Singleton, Shelby. Via e-mail correspondence. September 11, 2003.

Smith, Bobby Earl. Via telephone. August 12, 2004.

Snead, Doak. Via telephone. July 22, 2004.

Storm, Warren. Via telephone. November 21, 2004.

Strachwitz, Chris. Via telephone. June 19, 2003.

Taylor, Mike. Via telephone. November 11, 2005.

Taylor, Susan. Via telephone. October 22, 2005.

Tck, Deniz. Via telephone. October 11, 2003.

Thomas, Bubbha. November 13, 2003.

Thomas, Danny. Via telephone. September 24, 2004.

Thompson, Mayo. Via telephone. April 2, 2003.

Tucker, Aubrey. November 12, 2004.

Versay, Flery. Via telephone. March 11, 2004.

von Steiger, Marilyn. Via telephone. October 16, 2004.

Webb, Cassell. Via telephone. October 22, 2005.

Webb, Joyce. Via telephone. January 11, 2007.

Wills, Bert. August 13, 2004.

Workman, Dan. July 15, 2004.

Wothke, Randy. Written notes. March 12, 2005.

Young, Don Michael. Via telephone. June 11, 2005.

Chart Records
from the House of Hits

The first section documents many, but not necessarily all, of the recordings known to have ranked on the national charts. Following the corresponding date, the highest chart position for each recording is indicated, preceded by the # symbol. Except when otherwise noted, each entry in this section refers to the *Billboard* singles chart in the primary genre category for the designated artist(s). In cases where a recording charted in two different genre categories, we indicate both parenthetically. Unfortunately, we have insufficient historical chart data regarding gospel hits (particularly for the Peacock label) recorded at the facility—and thus are unable to include them here.

The second section lists songs recorded or mixed at Gold Star/SugarHill Studios that had significant regional popularity, grouped by decades.

I. Gold Star/SugarHill recordings known to have ranked on the national charts

DATE	CHART POSITION	ARTIST AND SONG/LP	LABEL
1/4/47	#4	Harry Choates and His Fiddle, **"Jole Blon"**	Gold Star 1314
11/8/48	#8	Lightnin' Hopkins, **"T-Model Blues"**	Gold Star 662
11/16/48	#7	Lil' Son Jackson, **"Freedom Train Blues"**	Gold Star 638
2/12/49	#13	Lightnin' Hopkins, **"Tim Moore's Farm"** [released from Gold Star 640]	Modern 20-673
1/9/54	#5	Jimmy Heap & The Melody Masters with Perk Williams, **"Release Me"**	Capitol 2518
10/29/55	#4	George Jones, **"Why Baby Why"**	Starday 202

DATE	CHART POSITION	ARTIST AND SONG/LP	LABEL
1/28/56	#7	George Jones, **"What Am I Worth"**	Starday 216
3/10/56	#93	Jimmy Heap & The Melody Masters with Perk Williams, **"Butternut"**	Capitol 3333
7/14/56	#7	George Jones, **"You Gotta Be My Baby"**	Starday 247
8/4/56	#2	Benny Barnes, **"Poor Man's Riches"**	Starday 262
10/20/56	#3	George Jones, **"Just One More"**	Starday 264
1/26/57	#10	George Jones & Jeanette Hicks, **"Yearning"**	Starday 279
3/9/57	#10	George Jones, **"Don't Stop The Music"**	Mercury 71029
6/10/57	#13	George Jones, **"Too Much Water"**	Mercury 71096
8/4/58	#3 R&B #6 Pop	The Big Bopper, **"Chantilly Lace"**	D 1008/ Mercury 71343
10/20/58	#16	James O'Gwynn, **"Talk to Me Lonesome Heart"**	D 1006
12/1/58	#72	The Big Bopper, **"Little Red Riding Hood"**	Mercury 71375
12/8/58	#38	The Big Bopper, **"Big Bopper's Wedding"**	Mercury 71375
12/15/58	#14	Eddie Noack, **"Have Blues Will Travel"**	D 1019
12/29/58	#28	James O'Gwynn, **"Blue Memories"**	D 1022
4/13/59	#5	Frankie Miller, **"Blackland Farmer"**	Starday 424
10/5/59	#7	Frankie Miller, **"Family Man"**	Starday 457
10/12/59	#1 Pop #3 R&B	Johnny Preston, **"Running Bear"**	Mercury 71474
12/18/59	#7	Claude Gray, **"Family Bible"**	D 1118
6/12/61	#22	Benny Barnes, **"Yearning"**	Mercury 71806
7/17/61	#15 Country #82 Pop	Frankie Miller, **"Blackland Farmer"**	rerelease of Starday 424
10/30/61	#53	Gene Thomas, **"Sometime"**	Venus 1439/ United Artists 338
3/9/63	#14	Country Johnny Mathis, **"Please Talk to My Heart"**	United Artists 536
10/12/63	#89	Joe Hinton, **"Better to Give Than Receive"**	Back Beat 539
8/15/64	#13	Joe Hinton, **"Funny (How Time Slips Away)"**	Back Beat 541
1/30/65	#34	Joe Hinton, **"I Want a Little Girl"**	Back Beat 545
1/30/65	#30	Lee Lamont, **"The Crying Man"**	Back Beat 542
4/3/65	#13	Sir Douglas Quintet, **"She's About a Mover"**	Tribe 8308

DATE	CHART POSITION	ARTIST AND SONG/LP	LABEL
6/5/65	#36	Junior Parker, **"Crying for My Baby"**	Duke 389
7/24/65	#6 R&B #86 Pop	O. V. Wright, **"You're Gonna Make Me Cry"**	Back Beat 548
9/4/65	#1 R&B #2 Pop	Roy Head & The Traits, **"Treat Her Right"**	Back Beat 546
11/16/65	#7 R&B #95 Pop	Jimmy McCracklin, **"Think"**	Imperial 66129
11/20/65	#32	Roy Head & The Traits, **"Apple of My Eye"**	Back Beat 555
1/2/66	#8 R&B #62 Pop	Bobby Bland, **"I'm Too Far Gone (to Turn Around)"**	Duke 393
1/29/66	#31	Sir Douglas Quintet, **"The Rains Came"**	Tribe 8314
?/26/66	#47	Pozo Seco Singers, **"Time"**	Edmark/Columbia
3/26/66	#99	Roy Head & The Traits, **"My Babe"**	Back Beat 560
?/66	#110	Roy Head & The Traits, **"Wigglin' and Gigglin'"**	Back Beat 563
3/17/66	#95	Roy Head & The Traits, **"To Make a Big Man Cry"**	Back Beat 571
8/20/66	#25	Buddy Ace, **"Nothing in the World Can Hurt Me"**	Duke 397
12/10/66	#13	Bobby Bland, **"Back in the Same Old Bag Again"**	Duke 412
12/24/66	#27	Junior Parker, **"Man or Mouse"**	Duke 413
2/11/67	#33	Buddy Ace, **"Hold On (To This Old Fool)"**	Duke 414
4/15/67	#6 R&B #88 Pop	Bobby Bland, **"You're All I Need"**	Duke 416
4/22/67	#4 R&B #80 Pop	O. V. Wright, **"Eight Men, Four Women"**	Back Beat 580
8/12/67	#25	O. V. Wright, **"Heartaches, Heartaches"**	Back Beat 583
8/26/67	#48	Junior Parker, **"I Can't Put My Finger on It"**	Mercury 72699
11/25/67	#19	John Roberts, **"Sockin' 1-2-3-4"**	Duke 425
2/24/68	#23 R&B #96 Pop	Bobby Bland, **"Driftin' Blues"**	Duke 432
2/15/69	#14	Bubble Puppy, **"Hot Smoke & Sassafras"**	International Artists 128
1969	#176	Bubble Puppy, *A Gathering Of Promises*	International Artists IALP10

DATE	CHART POSITION	ARTIST AND SONG/LP	LABEL
5/27/72	#15	Little Royal, "Jealous"	Tri-Us 912
7/14/73	#88	Little Royal, "I'm Glad to Do It"	Tri-Us 916
10/27/73	#5 R&B #42 Pop	Bobby Bland, "This Time I'm Gone for Good"	Dunhill/ABC 4369
1/11/75	#1 Country #1 Pop	Freddy Fender, "Before the Next Teardrop Falls"	ABC/Dot 17540
3/1/1975	#20	Donnie King, "Mathilda"	Warner Bros. 8074
6/21/75	#1 Country #8 Pop	Freddy Fender, "Wasted Days and Wasted Nights"	ABC/Dot 17558
10/4/75	#10 Country #45 Pop	Freddy Fender, "Since I Met You Baby"	GRT 031
10/11/75	#1 Country #20 Pop	Freddy Fender, "Secret Love"	ABC/Dot 17585
1975	#1 Country #20 Pop	Freddy Fender, *Before the Next Teardrop Falls*	ABC/Dot
11/8/75	#72	Donnie King, "I'm a Fool to Care"	Warner Bros. 8145
1976	#1 Country #41 Pop	Freddy Fender, *Are You Ready for Freddy*	ABC/Dot
1976	#10	Freddy Fender, *Since I Met You Baby*	ABC/Dot
1/10/76	#13	Freddy Fender, "Wild Side of Life"	GRT 039
2/7/76	#1 Country #32 Pop	Freddy Fender, "You'll Lose a Good Thing"	ABC/Dot 17607
5/22/76	#7 Country #59 Pop	Freddy Fender, "Vaya Con Dios"	ABC/Dot 17627
7/31/76	#91	Donnie King, "Stop the World (and Let Me Off)"	Warner Bros. 8229
9/18/76	#2 Country #72 Pop	Freddy Fender, "Living It Down"	ABC/Dot 17652
10/16/76	#100	Doug Sahm, "Cowboy Peyton Place"	ABC/Dot 17656
11/20/76	#38	Asleep At The Wheel, "Miles and Miles of Texas"	Capitol 5347
1976	#3 Country #59 Pop	Freddy Fender, *Rock 'N' Country*	ABC/Dot
3/19/77	#4	Freddy Fender, "The Rains Came"/ "Sugar Coated Love"	ABC/Dot 17686
7/30/77	#11	Freddy Fender, "If You Don't Love Me (Why Don't You Just Leave Me Alone)"	ABC/Dot 17713

DATE	CHART POSITION	ARTIST AND SONG/LP	LABEL
11/26/77	#18	Freddy Fender, "Think about Me"	ABC/Dot 17730
1977	#4	Freddy Fender, *If You're Ever in Texas*	ABC/Dot
1977	#4	Freddy Fender, *The Best of Freddy Fender*	ABC/Dot
3/11/78	#34	Freddy Fender, "If You're Looking for a Fool"	ABC 12339
6/17/78	#13 Country #103 Pop	Freddy Fender, "Talk to Me"	ABC 12370
11/4/78	#26	Freddy Fender, "I'm Leaving It All Up to You"	ABC 12415
1978	#34	Freddy Fender, *If You Don't Love Me*	ABC/Dot 2090
2/17/79	#22	Freddy Fender, "Walking Piece of Heaven"	ABC 12453
6/23/79	#22	Freddy Fender, "Yours"	Starflite 4900
10/13/79	#61	Freddy Fender, "Squeeze Box"	Starflite 4904
1979	#44	Freddy Fender, *Swamp Gold*	ABC
1/12/80	#83	Freddy Fender, "My Special Prayer"	Starflite 4906
4/5/80	#82	Freddy Fender, "Please Talk to My Heart"	Starflite 4908
2/19/83	#87	Freddy Fender, "Chokin' Kind"	Warner 29794
10/8/88	#97	Don Lafleur, "Beggars Can't Be Choosers"	Worth 102
1989	#5 Gavin Jazz	Kellye Gray, *Standards In Gray*	Justice
1990	#1 Gavin Jazz	Sebastian Whittaker, *First Outing*	Justice
1990	#10 Gavin Jazz	Harry Sheppard, *Viva Brazil*	Justice
1990	#1 Gavin Jazz	David Catney, *First Flight*	Justice
1990	#3 Gavin Jazz	Tony Campise, *First Takes*	Heart Music
1991	#24 Gavin AAA	Erich Avinger, *Sí*	Heart Music
1991	#1 Gavin Jazz	Herb Ellis, *Roll Call*	Justice
1991	#15 Gavin Jazz	Harry Sheppard, *This-a-Way, That-a-Way*	Justice
1991	#4 Gavin Jazz	Various Artists, *Tribute to Emily Remler, Vol. One*	Justice
1991	#1 Gavin Jazz	Stefan Karlsson, *Room 292*	Justice
1991	#7 Gavin Jazz	Various Artists, *Tribute to Emily Remler, Vol. Two*	Justice
1991	#1 Gavin Jazz	Sebastian Whittaker, *Searchin' for the Truth*	Justice
1991	#20 Gavin Jazz	King & Moore, *Impending Bloom*	Justice

DATE	CHART POSITION	ARTIST AND SONG/LP	LABEL
1992	#1 Gavin Jazz	Stefan Karlsson, *The Road Not Taken*	Justice
1992	#1 Gavin Jazz	David Catney, *Jade Visions*	Justice
1992	#3 Gavin AAA	Tab Benoit, *Nice and Warm*	Justice
1992	#3 Gavin Jazz #19 Billboard Jazz	Tony Campise, *Once in a Blue Moon*	Heart Music
1992	#10 Gavin Jazz	Harry Sheppard, *Points of View*	Justice
1992	#1 Gavin Jazz	Sebastian Whittaker, *One for Bu*	Justice
1993	#1 Gavin Jazz	Stefan Karlsson, *Below Zero*	Justice
1993	#3 Gavin Jazz	David Catney, *Reality Road*	Justice
1993	#19 Gavin Jazz	Tony Campise, *Ballads, Blues, & Bebop*	Heart Music
2/24/94	#8	Elsa Garcia, **"Ni Mas, Ni Menos"**	Discos MM/ Capitol-EMI Latin
6/2/94	#42	Elsa Garcia, *Ni Mas, Ni Menos*	Discos MM/ Capitol-EMI Latin
ca. early 1995	#37	The Hometown Boys, *Tres Ramitas*	Discos MM/ Fonovisa
6/24/95	#39	The Hometown Boys, **"Mire Amigo"**	Discos MM/ Fonovisa
9/22/95	#25	The Hometown Boys, *Mire Amigo*	Discos MM/ Fonovisa
1996	#17 Gavin Jazz	Kellye Gray, *Tomato Kiss*	Proteus
1996	#3 Gavin Jazz	Joe Locascio, *A Charmed Life*	Heart Music
1997	#11 Gavin Jazz	Elias Haslanger, *For The Moment*	Heart Music
1998	#4 Gavin Jazz	Elias Haslanger, *Kicks Are for Kids*	Heart Music
9/25/99	#33	Destiny's Child, **"Bugaboo"**	Columbia
1999	#5	Destiny's Child, *The Writing's on the Wall*	Columbia
9/23/00	#1	Destiny's Child, **"Independent Women Part 1"**	Columbia
3/17/01	#2	Destiny's Child, **"Survivor"**	Columbia
2001	#1	Destiny's Child, *Survivor*	Columbia
6/9/2001	#1	Destiny's Child, **"Bootylicious"**	Columbia
9/17/01	#8 Rap #16 R&B	Minott, featuring Kurupted Seed, **"Playa Playa (Playing the Game Right)"**	World Beat

DATE	CHART POSITION	ARTIST AND SONG/LP	LABEL
9/29/01	#10	Destiny's Child, **"Emotion"**	Columbia
11/17/01	#14	Clay Walker, *Say No More*	Giant
1/19/02	#4	Mack 10, *Bang or Ball*	Cash Money/ Universal
2002	#25	Destiny's Child, *This Is the Remix* [album, UK]	Columbia
2002	#57	Michelle Williams, *Heart to Yours*	Columbia
2003	#1	Beyoncé Knowles, *Dangerously in Love*	Columbia
6/2003	#57	Beyoncé Knowles, **"Dangerously in Love 2"**	Columbia
10/23/04	#3	Clay Walker, *A Few Questions*	RCA

II. Selected regional hit singles recorded or mixed at Gold Star/SugarHill Studios

Those which did not register on the national charts yet had significant regional popularity, grouped by decade

1940s	
Lightnin' Hopkins, **"Short Haired Woman"**	Gold Star 3131
Lightnin' Hopkins, **"Unsuccessful Blues"**	Gold Star 656A
Aubrey Gass, **"Kilroy's Been Here"**	Gold Star 1318

1950s	
James O'Gwynn, **"Losing Game"**	Starday 266
James O'Gwynn, **"Muleskinner Blues"**	Mercury 71066
James O'Gwynn, **"Two Little Hearts"**	Mercury 71234
Link Davis, **"Sixteen Chicks"**	Starday 235
Albert Collins, **"The Freeze"**	Kangaroo 103

1960s	
C.L. & The Pictures, **"For the Sake of Love"**	Kirk 635
Champagne Brothers, **"Stranger to You"**	Typhoon 2002
Champagne Brothers, **"It's Raining"**	Typhoon 2003
Charlie Booth, **"Fishin' Fits"**	Lori 9534
Sleepy LaBeef, **"Tore Up"**	Wayside 1654
Johnny Copeland, **"Down on Bending Knees"**	Golden Eagle 101

Johnny Williams, **"Long Black Veil"**	Pic 1 105
B. J. Thomas & The Triumphs, **"Garner State Park"**	Joed 117
Neal Ford & The Fanatics, **"All I Have to Do Is Dream"**	Tantara 1104
The Bad Seeds, **"All Night Long"**	J-Beck 1004
Zakary Thaks, **"Face to Face"**	J-Beck 1009
1970s	
Tommy McLain, **"Jukebox Songs"**	Crazy Cajun 2027
Warren Storm, **"King of the Dance Halls"**	Crazy Cajun
1980s	
Kelly Schoppa, **"Amarillo by Morning"**	Bellaire
Kelly Schoppa, **"Does Ft. Worth Ever Cross Your Mind"**	Bellaire
Tommy McLain, **"Daddy Said Roses Don't Grow Here Anymore"**	Crazy Cajun 2087
Little Joe y La Familia, **"Cuatro Caminos"**	Leon
1990s	
Jerry Rodriguez & Mercedes, **"El Pinguino"**	Capitol/EMI Latin
David Olivares and XS, **"She's About a Mover"**	Fonovisa

Selected Discographies:
A Partial History

The following discographies document only a portion of the thousands of historical recordings made at the Gold Star/SugarHill Studios facility—including those (that we know of) from its earliest incarnation as Quinn Recording Company and all of those from its brief (1968–1970) identity as International Artists Recording Studios. Most of the groupings presented here, arranged chronologically, reflect productions for certain regional labels that had particularly long or otherwise noteworthy affiliations with Gold Star/SugarHill Studios. Please note that numerous recordings discussed in this book are not documented here—because they were made for other labels and because of limitations of space.

Much of this information was researched by, and provided courtesy of, Texas music historian Andrew Brown.

I. Gulf Records

Singles produced at Quinn Recording, 1944–1946

100A/100B	Woody Vernon, "I'm Lonesome But I'm Free"/"A Rainy Sunday Night"	1944–1945
103A/103B	Jerry Irby, "Nails in My Coffin"/"You Don't Love Me Anymore"	1945
105A/105B	Al Clauser & His Oklahomans, "Soldier's Return"/"Dream Rose"	1945–1946
3000A/3000B	Jesse Lockett & His Orchestra, "Boogie Woogie Mama"/"Blacker the Berry"	1946

II. Gold Star Records

Singles produced at Quinn Recording or (as it became known) Gold Star Studios, 1946–1951

GOLD STAR 1300 SERIES (COUNTRY)		
1313/ 1314	Harry Choates and His Fiddle, **"Basile Waltz"/"Jole Blon"**	1946
1315/ 1316	Tex Looney and His Western Stars, **"I Left a Rose"/"Blue Eyes"**	ca. late 1946
1317	Leon Jenkins and The Easterners, **"Drinkin' My Life Away"/"Blue Schottische"**	ca. December 1946
1318	Aubrey Gass with The Easterners, **"Kilroy's Been Here"/"Delivery Man Blues"**	ca. February 1947
1319	Harry Choates and His Fiddle, **"Allons a Lafayette"/"Port Arthur Waltz"**	ca. March 1947
1320	Woody Vernon and Southern Stars, **"What Happens Next"**/ The Southern Stars, **"Million Dollar Polka"**	ca. March 1947
1322/ 1323	Al Terry with The Goldstar Band, **"I'll Be Glad When I'm Free"/"If You Want a Broken Heart"**	ca. March 1947
1324	Virgil Bozman & His Oklahoma Tornadoes, **"Just a Year Ago Today"/"Grinding for You Darling"**	ca. April 1947
1325	Gold Star Trio, **"Baruska"/"Ostang"**	1947
1326/ 1330	Harry Choates and His Fiddle, **"Fa-De-Do Stomp"/"Rubber Dolly"**	1947
1332	Oklahoma Tornadoes, **"La Prison"**/ Hokey Pokey Trio, **"Hokey Pokey"**	1947
1333	Harry Choates and His Fiddle, **"Wrong Keyhole"/"Missing You"**	1947
1334	Gold Star Band, **"Green Bayou Waltz"**/ Sons of The South, **"Hawaiian Two-Step"**	1947
1335	Harry Choates and His Fiddle, **"Bayou Pon Pon"/"Lawtell Waltz"**	1947
1336	Harry Choates and His Fiddle, **"Louisiana"/"Poor Hobo"**	1947
1337	David Gray and The Gold Star Band, **"Talk of the Town"**/ Gold Star Band, **"Gold Star Polka"**	ca. 1947
1338	Phil Marx and The Texans, **"The Stars, the Moon, and You"/"Forgive Me"**	ca. 1947
1339	Byrd & Bingo and The Swynett Swingsters, **"I'm Afraid of Horses"/"It's a Natural Thing"**	ca. 1947

1340	Harry Choates and His Fiddle, "Rye Whiskey"/"Devil in the Bayou"	ca. 1947
1341	Hank Locklin, **"Rio Grande Waltz"**/ **"You've Been Talking in Your Sleep"**	ca. 1947
1342	Frances Turner, **"The Moment I Found You"**/ **"The Curse of an Aching Heart"**	1947
1343	Harry Choates and His Fiddle, **"Draggin' the Bow"**/**"Te Petite"**	1947
1343	Harry Choates and His Fiddle, **"Draggin' the Bow"**/**"Sidewalk Waltz"**	ca. 1947–1948, issued late 1950/early 1951
1344	Tennessee Van and The Cumberland River Boys, **"Tonight I Wonder"**/**"Going Back Home"**	1948
1345	Buddy Duhon with Harry Choates and His Fiddle, **"Old Cow Blues"**/**"Nobody Cares for Me"**	1948
1350	Harry Choates and His Fiddle, **"Mari Jole Blon"**/**"Honky-Tonkin' Days"**	ca. 1948–1949
1352	Eddie Noack and The Road Buddies, **"Gentlemen Prefer Blondes"**/**"Triflin' Mama Blues"**	ca. 1948–1949
1357	Eddie Noack and Bill Byrd, **"Pyramid Club"**/**"Simulated Diamonds"**	1949
1370	Ray and Ina Patterson, **"Brown Eyes"**/**"Sunny Side of Life"**	1949
1371	Eddie Noack, **"Raindrops in the River"**/**"Hungry But Happy"**	1949
1380	Harry Choates & His Fiddle, **"Louisiana Boogie"**/**"Sidewalk Waltz"**	1949
1381	Cotton Thompson with Deacon (Rag-Mop) Anderson and The Village Boys, **"How Long"**/**"Hopeless Love"**	1950
1382	Gene Jones (Okie Jones), **"Stop, Look, and Listen"**/**"Foolish Heart"**	1950
1385	Harry Choates & His Fiddle, **"Harry Choates Blues"**/**"Chere Mon"**	1950
1386	Johnny Nelms and The Sunset Cowboys [sic: Johnny Nelms], **"I'll Learn Ya, Dern Ya"**/**"I'm So Ashamed"**	1950
1387	Don Thorpe with Mary and Her Merrymakers, **"Country Corn"**/Dude Barnett with Mary and Her Merrymakers, **"Sometimes (I Get So Lonesome)"**	ca. 1950
1388	Harry Choates & His Fiddle, **"It Won't Be Long"**/**"Maggie Waltz"**	ca. 1950–1951
1389	Jimmy Choates, **"French Waltz No. 3"**/**"French Waltz No. 1"**	ca. 1950–1951
1390*	Margaret Mabry, **"I Lost a Souvenir"**/**"Streets of Gold"**	ca. 1950–1951

1390	Johnny Royal, **"Golden Wedding Waltz"**/ Dick Gottleibe, **"Cross Roads"**	ca. 1950–1951
1391	Eddie Noack and Gig Sparks, **"Greenback Dollar"**/ Eddie Noack and Bill Byrd, **"Tragic Love"**	1951
1392	Grady Hester with Caller, George Reese, **"Cindy"**/**"Split Your Corners"**	1951
1394	Wink Lewis and Martha Lynn, **"Won't You Come Back"**/**"I'll Take You Back"**	1951
1395	Cole Sisters, **"Texas Waltz"**/**"I'll Wait and Watch"**	1951

* Note: Apparently inadvertently, Gold Star assigned its 1390 catalogue number twice.

GOLD STAR 600 SERIES (BLUES)		
613	Lightnin' Hopkins, **"Ida Mae"**/**"Shining Moon"**	ca. June 1947
614	L. C. (Lightnin' Jr.) Williams, **"Trying, Trying"**/**"You'll Never Miss the Water"**	ca. July 1947
615	Thunder Smith, **"Cruel Hearted Woman"**/ **"Big Stars Are Falling"**	ca. July 1947
616	Lightnin' Hopkins, **"Mercy"**/**"What Can It Be"**	ca. August 1947
618	Curtis Amy & His Combo, **"Realization Blues"**/**"Sleeping Blues"**	ca. August 1947
622	Conrad Johnson & His Orchestra, **"Howling on Dowling"**/**"Fisherman's Blues"**	ca. September 1947
623	L. C. Williams, **"Hole in the Wall"**/**"Boogie All the Time"**	1947
624	Lightnin' Hopkins, **"Lonesome Blues"**/**"Appetite Blues"**	ca. October 1947
626	Peppermint Nelson [Peppermint Harris], **"Peppermint Boogie"**/**"Houston Blues"**	ca. October 1947
628	Leroy Ervin, **"Rock Island Blues"**/**"Blue, Black, and Evil"**	ca. November 1947
632	Perry Cain/Skippy Brown/Edwin Pickens, **"All the Way from Texas"**/**"Cry, Cry"**	ca. January 1948
633	Henry Hayes and His Band, **"Bowlegged Angeline"**/**"Baby Girl Blues"**	ca. February 1948
634	Lightnin' Hopkins, **"Walking Blues"**/**"Lightning Blues"**	ca. March 1948
635	Southland Quartet, **"Go 'Long for a Long Time"**/**"Have a Time"**	ca. April 1948
636	Roy Brown, **"Deep Sea Diver"**/**"Bye Baby Bye"**	ca. July 1948
637	Lightnin' Hopkins, **"No Mail Blues"**/**"Ain't It a Shame"**	ca. August 1948
638	Lil' Son Jackson, **"Roberta Blues"**/**"Freedom Train Blues"**	ca. August 1948
640	Lightnin' Hopkins, **"Tim Moore's Farm"**/**"You Don't Know"**	ca. September 1948

641	Lightnin' Hopkins, **"Treat Me Kind"**/**"Somebody's Got to Go"**	ca. September 1948
642	Lil' Son Jackson, **"Ground Hog Blues"**/ **"Bad Whiskey, Bad Women"**	ca. October 1948
644	Thunder Smith, **"Santa Fe Blues"**/**"Temptation Blues"**	ca. October 1948
645	Andy Thomas, **"Angel Chile"**/**"My Baby Quit Me Blues"**	ca. November 1948
646	Lightnin' Hopkins, **"Baby Please Don't Go"**/**"Death Bells"**	ca. November 1948
647	Sherman Williams and His Band, **"Why Don't You Tell Me So"**/**"No One in My Heart"**	ca. December 1948
648	L. C. (Lightnin' Jr.) Williams, **"Black Woman"**/ **"I Won't Be Here Long"**	ca. December 1948
650	Will Rowland Orchestra, **"Cold Blooded Woman"**/ **"Run Mr. Rabbit Run"**	ca. December 1948
651	Lee Hunter, **"Back to Santa Fe"**/**"Lee's Boogie"**	ca. January 1949
652	Lightnin' Hopkins, **"Mad with You"**/**"Airplane Blues"**	ca. February 1949
653	Lil' Son Jackson, **"Gone with the Wind"**/**"No Money, No Love"**	ca. March 1949
656	Lightnin' Hopkins, **"Mad with You"**/**"Airplane Blues"**	ca. March 1949
657	Will Rowland & His Band, **"Reefer Blues"**/ **"Don't Lose Your Mind"**	ca. March 1949
658	Jimmie Lee's Band, **"Bobby Sox Bop"**/**"Club Raven"**	ca. April 1949
659	Andy Thomas, **"In Love Blues"**/**"Walking and Crying"**	ca. April 1949
660	Buddy Chiles, **"Mistreated Blues"**/**"Jet Black Woman"**	ca. April 1949
661	D. C. Washington [D. C. Bender], **"Rebob Boogie"**/**"Happy Home Blues"**	ca. June 1949
662	Lightnin' Hopkins, **"Jailhouse Blues"**/**"T-Model Blues"**	ca. July 1949
663	Lil' Son Jackson, **"Cairo Blues"**/**"Evil Blues"**	ca. September 1949
664	Lightnin' Hopkins, **"Lightnin' Boogie"**/**"Unkind Blues"**	ca. October 1949
665	Lightnin' Hopkins, **"Fast Life Woman"**/**"European Blues"**	ca. October 1949
666	Lightnin' Hopkins, **"Automobile"**/**"Zolo Go"**	ca. late 1949
667	L. C. Williams, **"Strike Blues"**/ **"You Can't Take It with You Baby"**	ca. late 1949
668	Lil' Son Jackson, **"Gambling Blues"**/**"Homeless Blues"**	ca. early 1950
669	Lightnin' Hopkins, **"Old Woman Blues"**/**"Untrue Blues"**	ca. early 1950
670	Link Davis, **"Joe Turner"**/**"Have You Heard the News"**	ca. early 1950
671	Lightnin' Hopkins, **"Henny Penny Blues"**/**"Jazz Blues"**	1950
673	Lightnin' Hopkins, **"Jackstropper Blues"**/**"Grievance Blues"**	1950

GOLD STAR 100 SERIES (GOSPEL)

113	Tex Moon, **"In the Garden"/"Near the Cross"**	1947/48
114	Elder Bonds, **"Prayer for the Sick"/"Can't Make the Journey"**	1947/48
115	Madam Ernestine, **"While the Blood Runs Warm"/** **"I'll Never Turn Back"**	1949
116	Elder Bonds, **[titles unknown]**	

GOLD STAR 400 SERIES (MEXICAN AMERICAN)

| 401 | Conjunto de Maxie Granados (with Fred Zimmerle, accordion, Mike Garza, contrabajo), **"Houston Polka"/"Flora Perdida"** | |

GOLD STAR 500 SERIES (SQUARE DANCE)

501	Grady Hester and The Texsons, **"8th of January"/"Give the Fiddler a Dram"**	
502	Russell McKnight, **"Sally Goodin'"/"Bill Cheatem"**	ca. 1949
503– 505	Grady Hester And The Texsons, **[titles unknown]**	

GOLD STAR 700 SERIES AND MISCELLANEA

711	Eddie Noack, **"Frown on the Moon"/"Unlucky Me"**	
712	Smith Spadachene, **"Moving On"/"Spanish Two-Step"**	
713	Woody Vernon, **"My Happiness"**/Pete Marchiando, **"Latin Medley"**	
714	Corman Harris, **"Bolero De Diablo"/"Swanee Bolero"**	
715	Buster Dees, **"Please, Dear"/"The Moment I Found You"**	1949
717	Buster Dees, **"White Roses"/"Forgotten"**	1950
813	Ray Krenek Orchestra, **[titles unknown]**	
888	Leon Jenkins, **"Hot Pretzels"/"Green Corn"**	
1628	Tommy Wilson with Sammy Incardona Orchestra, **"My Texas Girl"/** Little Sammy Incardona and His Orchestra, **"You're Lonesome and I'm Blue"**	1947
3131	Lightnin' Hopkins, **"Short Haired Woman"/"Big Mama Jump"** *	ca. May 1947

* Note: Lightnin' Hopkins also recorded scores of additional tracks at Gold Star Studios, not documented here, for release on other labels.

III. Gold Star Masters, 1953–1963

In late 1953, Bill Quinn began assigning a sequential numeric code to the masters that he created at Gold Star. The numbering sequence started at 1000 and continued until Quinn's retirement in 1963. The highest known Gold Star master number is 1699, dating from a session in June 1963. Beginning in 1964, under new management, the studio facility's mastering numeration started again at 1000.

The record label and corresponding catalogue number for each entry (if known) is indicated parenthetically. (Note: The Gold Star mastering numbers may or may not be the same as the issuing record companies' assigned catalogue numbers.)

1953		
1003	Slim Jones, **"Texas Woman"**	Blue Light 1003

1954		
1004	V. Cecil Williams, **"Two Timin' Baby"**	Gilbert 1004
1005	V. Cecil Williams, **"Maurine"**	Gilbert 1005
1010	Deacon Anderson, **"Daddy's Waltz"**	Bayou 1010
1011	Deacon Anderson, **"Just Looking through These Tears"**	Bayou 1011
1012	Eddie Noack, **"How Does It Feel to Be the Winner"**	TNT 110
1013	Eddie Noack, **"Too Hot to Handle"**	TNT 110
1016	Sonny Corner, **"Darling Goodbye"**	Pilgrim 1016
1017	Bill Lister & Del Dunbar, **"There's a Million Ways to Say I Love You"**	Pilgrim 1016
1020	Doyle Brothers, **"Wedding Day"**	TNT 113
1021	Doyle Brothers, **"TNT Baby"**	TNT 113
1032	Woody Simmons, **"Hold Back the Dawn"**	Pacific 210
1033	Woody Simmons, **"Coney Island Lights"**	Pacific 210
1038	James O'Gwynn, **"Bottle Talk"**	Nucraft 2020
1039	James O'Gwynn, **"Love in an Old Fashioned Way"**	Nucraft 2020
1042	Randy Reeks, **"I'm Gonna Call"**	Robin 1042
1043	Randy Reeks, **"Give Me Back My Heart"**	Robin 1043
1056	Lightnin' Hopkins, **"Unsuccessful Blues"**	reissue of Gold Star 104
1057	Lightnin' Hopkins, **"Grieving Blues"**	reissue of Gold Star 104
1060	George Edgin & Leon Jenkins, **"The Goober Song"**	Unique 1060
1061	George Edgin & Leon Jenkins, **"Only a Tear"**	Unique 1061
1062	Toni Rose, **"Let's Love"**	Lightning 301
1063	Toni Rose, **"My Heart Says"**	Lightning 301

1066	Bill Heyman, **"Easy Way Out"**	Lightning 111
1067	Bill Heyman, **"I Want My Baby"**	Lightning 111
1070	Stoney Paige, **"Second Hand Sweethearts"**	Zip 1070
1071	Stoney Paige, **"It Seems Unfair"**	Zip 1071
1072	Floyd Tillman, **"Save a Little for Me"**	Western 1072
1073	Link Davis, **"Big Houston"**	Western 1073
1074	Wanda Gann, **"Little Miss Claus"**	Nucraft 2028-4
1075	Wanda Gann, **"So Nice"**	Nucraft 2028-5

1955

1086	High Pockets, **"Then We'll Be Happy"**	Rainbow 1086
1087	High Pockets, **"Boy Crazy Jane"**	Rainbow 1087
1092	The Scholars, **"The Poor Little Doggies"**	Cue 7297
1093	The Scholars, **"What Did I Do Wrong"**	Cue 7298
1098	Johnny Carroll, **"The Stars Came Down from Heaven"**	J.M.C. 1098
1099	Johnny Carroll, **"Think of You"**	J.M.C. 1099

1956

1103	Smith Spadachene and Band, **"Ivory Tower"**	Nucraft 132
1104	Smith Spadachene and Band, **"I Love You Mama Mia"**	Nucraft 132
1107	Jimmy Duncan, **"Sing Me No Sad Songs, Sam"**	Cue 7929
1108	Jimmy Duncan, **"Here I Am"**	Cue 7929
1113	Arlene Irby w/ Becky Barfield, **"Come Back to Me"**	Sylvia
1114	Arlene Irby, **"You Don't Think about Tomorrow"**	Sylvia
1119	Sir Cedric Fatwallet, **"What Is a Waitress"**	Tone 1119
1120	Sir Cedric Fatwallet, **"Honest John Crabmore"**	Tone 1120
1121	Wink Lewis, **"More Times Than One"**	Tone 1121
1122	Wink Lewis, **"Zzztt...Zzztt...Zzztt"**	Tone 1122
1125	Louisiana Lannis, **"Tongue Twister Boogie"**	Snowcap 1125
1126	Louisiana Lannis, **"Walking Out"**	Snowcap 1126
1132	Becky Barfield, **"Blue Guy in Town"**	Pilgrim 1132
1133	Wayne Forest, **"Maybe You Know"**	Pilgrim 1132
1135	Tex Cherry, **"Dirty Jim Blues"**	Mel-O-Tone
1136	Tex Cherry, **"Cannon Ball–Fox Chase"**	Mel-O-Tone

1137	Walton & The Silver Lake Boys, **"Man, What a Party"**	Lael
1138	Walton & The Silver Lake Boys, **"Don't Tell Me"**	Lael
1139	Larry Wheeler, **"Sittin' Here Drinking"**	Mel-O-Tone
1140	Larry Wheeler, **"Cry Woman Cry"**	Mel-O-Tone 1140

1957

1145	Don Mahoney, **"Saddle Up Your Rocky-Horse"**	Enterprise 1145
1146	Don Mahoney, **"Old Shep"**	Enterprise 1146
1148	Bobby Muncy, **"When the Chips Are Down"**	Enterprise
1149	Bobby Muncy, **"Empty Heart"**	Enterprise
1152	Charles Drake, **"I'm Gonna Take Life Free"**	Enterprise
1153	Charles Drake, **"You're the One I Dream About"**	Enterprise
1172	Wayne Henderson, **"Won't You Hold Me in Your Arms Again"**	Circle 1172
1173	Wayne Henderson, **"Walking in Circles"**	Circle 1173
1174	Joe Nettles, **"Oh, Baby!"**	Circle 1174
1175	Joe Nettles, **"Give Us a Chance"**	Circle 1175
1180	Harold Young, **"Rock and Roll Dice"**	Wagon Wheel 1180
1181	Harold Young, **"Louisiana Baby"**	Wagon Wheel 1181
1182	Bobby Collins, **"What Do I Miss"**	Enterprise
1183	Bobby Collins, **"After Laughter Came Tears"**	Enterprise
1195	Johnny Nelms, **"Mr. Freight Train"**	Tilt 1195
1196	Johnny Nelms, **"Hurt Is the Heart"**	Tilt 1196
1203	Ernie Hunter w/ Hal Harris, **"Boy Crazy"**	Rainbow 1203
1204	Ernie Hunter w/ Hal Harris, **"Kissing Your Picture"**	Rainbow 1204
1205	Dido Rowley, **"When the Chips Are Down"**	Enterprise 1205
1206	Dido Rowley, **[title unknown]**	Enterprise 1206

1958

1207	Tony Farr, **"You're the Only One"**	Enterprise
1208	Tony Farr, **"What's the Use"**	Enterprise
1211	Tony Farr, **"There's No Sense Marrying Me"**	Enterprise
1212	Tony Farr, **"Why Don't You Try to Love Me"**	Enterprise
1219	Big Charles Green, **"Rocking on the Moon Tonight"**	Hitt 180
1220	Big Charles Green, **"You Excite Me Baby"**	Hitt 180

1223	Charles Drake, "Got to Pay My Income Tax"	Enterprise
1224	Charles Drake, "My Baby Just Told Me Goodbye"	Enterprise 102

1959

1225	Duane Schurb, "You're a Fool"	Enterprise
1226	Duane Schurb, "Rolly Polly"	Enterprise
1231	Clyde Easley, "You Ask Me Darling"	Enterprise
1232	Clyde Easley, "Drive in Baby"	Enterprise
1233	Floyd Lee, "Go Boy"	Enterprise 1234
1234	Floyd Lee, "Give Your Love to Me"	Enterprise 1233
1244	Jerry Irby, "The Sea"	Hi-Lo 1244
1245	Jerry Irby, "Nails in My Coffin"	Hi-Lo 1245
1246	Harold Casner, "That Is Why"	Gulf 101
1247	Harold Casner, "Marker in Your Heart"	Gulf 101
1264	Joey Ambra, "One Love"	Teen 1005
1265	Joey Ambra, "I Don't Know"	Teen 1005

1960

1400 (?)	The Aces Wild, "Baby Don't Go"	Big T 1400
1401 (?)	The Aces Wild, "Forever My Darling"	Big T 1400
1414	Richie Richardson, "The Jump"	Galaxy 103
1415	Richie Richardson, [?, unknown title]	Galaxy 103
1432	Charlie Booth, "Fishin' Fits"	Lori 9534
1433	Charlie Booth, "Gonna Find Some Lovin'"	Lori 9534
1439	Gene Thomas, "Sometime"	Venus 1439
1440	Gene Thomas, "Every Night"	Venus 1440

1961

1445	Bill Mraz, *Festival Album*, Side One	Mraz LP 502
1446	Bill Mraz, *Festival Album*, Side Two	Mraz LP 502
1463	Joe Bee, "Angel of Love"	All Star 7223
1464	Joe Bee, "What Good Would It Do"	All Star 7223
1467	Henry Moore, "Pretty Baby"	Master 101
1468	Henry Moore, "I Believe in You"	Master 101
1488	Jack Moore, "Bad, Bad Blues"	Trojan 5001
1489	Jack Moore, "Cry, Cry (I Cry Night and Day)"	Trojan 5001

1500 (?)	Link Davis, **"Ferry Ride"**	Al's 1500
1501 (?)	Link Davis, **"Rice and Gravy"**	Al's 1501
1506	Mel Douglas, **"Since You Walked Away"**	SAN 1506
1507	Mel Douglas, **"Cadillac Boogie"**	SAN 1506

1962

1510	Link Davis, **"Johnny Be Good" [sic]**	Al's 1503
1511	Link Davis, **"My Last Goodbye"**	Al's 1503
1554	Ernest Netti, **"With Open Arms"**	Gentry 101
1555	Ernest Netti, **"Happy Days"**	Gentry 101
1556	Gene Thomas, **"Mysteries of Love"**	Venus 1443
1557	Gene Thomas, **"That's What You Are to Me"**	Venus 1443
1603 (?)	Melvin Gayle, **"You're in Love"**	Castle 1603
1604 (?)	Melvin Gayle, **"Kruschev Twist"**	Castle 1603
1620	Richie Richardson, **"The Frog"**	Spotlight 451
1621	Richie Richardson, **"Someone's Been in Love"**	Spotlight 451
1628	Jack Moore, **"Debbie"**	Caprock 121
1629	Jack Moore, **"Baby Don't Cry"**	Caprock 121
1630	Mel Douglas, **"Dream Girl"**	Gulf 1630
1631	Mel Douglas, **"Forever My Darling"**	Gulf 1631
1638	Woody Bridges, **"Rich Man's Servant (Poor Man's Wife)"**	Royce 1638
1639	Woody Bridges, **"Old Old Man"**	Royce 1639
1640	Lucy Lynn, **"Ist Es Den Liebe"**	Gulf 1640
1641	Lucy Lynn, **"Bright Lights"**	Gulf 1641
1651	Sleepy LaBeef, **"Ride On Josephine"**	Wayside 1651
1652	Sleepy LaBeef, **"Walkin' Slowly"**	Wayside 1652
1653	Tommy LaBeff, **"Lonely"**	Wayside 1653
1654	Tommy LaBeff, **"Tore Up"**	Wayside 1654

1963

1681	Mel Douglas, **"There Must Be a Way"**	Tamel 11
1682	Mel Douglas, **"Pounding Heart"**	Tamel 11
1688	Eddie Noack, **"Christ Is the Only Ark"**	Rivera 33
1689	Eddie Noack, **"When I Get to Nashville"**	Rivera 33
1691	Fred Richardson & Monroe Fields, **"Locked Away (From Your Heart)"**	Rivera 34

1692	Fred Richardson & Monroe Fields, **"Twisting the Chimes"**	Rivera 34
1698	Dodie Cherry, **"He Taught Me How to Yodel"**	Empire 495
1699	Dodie Cherry, **"The Girl in My Home Town"**	Empire 495

IV. Nucraft Records

Singles produced at Gold Star Studios, 1953–1959

113	Harmon Tucker and His Sunset Playboys, **"Streets of Unwanted"**/**"You Can't Win"**	
114	Harmonica Kid and The Sunset Playboys, **"Martha Lea"**/**"I Wish You Was My Darlin'"**	
115	Railroad Earl and His Railroaders, **"Pretty Baby"**/**"Foldin' Money"**	
116	Gibbs Sisters, **"The Lonely Pigeon"**/**"Mama Leave Daddy Alone"**	
121	Bud & Bud Hooper and Their Musical Buddies, **"Please Don't Cry"**/**"You Traveled Too Far"** [reissue of Azalea 101]	
130	Harmonica Kid & Ranch Boys, **"I Didn't Do Nothing"**/**"Little Dutch Girl"**	
132	Smith Spadachene and Band, **"Ivory Tower"**/**"I Love You Mama Mia"**	
2020	James O'Gwynn and His Cry Babies, **"Love in an Old Fashioned Way"**/**"Bottle Talk"** [2020-B was reissued in 1959 as Mercury 101-B.]	1954
2021	Harmonica Kid, **"Parakeet Love Song"**/**"My Dear Son"**	
2022	Harmonica Kid, **"Jole-Blon"**/**"Coo-Coo-Coo"**	1954–1955
2023	James O'Gwynn and His Crybabies, **"I Wish You Wuz My Darling But You Ain't"**/**"Love Made Slave"** [also issued as Azalea 2023]	1954–1955
2024	Fred Hawkins and His Copycats, **"Everybody's Doing It"**/**"Tears"**	
2026	Link Davis, **"Grasshopper"**/Floyd Tillman, **"Magnolia Garden Waltz"**	1955
2028	Wanda Gann, **"Little Miss Claus"**/**"So Nice"**	
2029	Wayne Henderson, **[titles unknown]**	
100	Harmonica Kid [and] Fay Froelich, **"I Can Always Tell"**/Harmonica Kid [and] M. T. Schultz, **"Little Dutch Girl"**	1959

V. Starday Records

Singles produced at Gold Star Studios, 1954–1957

152	Sonny Burns & The Western Cherokees, **"Waltzing with Sin"/"Another Woman Looking for a Man"**	7/17/54
156	Fred Crawford, **"Each Passing Day"/"Never Gonna Get Married Again"**	8/21/54
159	Eddie Noack, **"Take It Away Lucky"/"Don't Trade"**	9/11/54
160	Peck Touchton, **"Let Me Catch My Breath"**/ George Jones, **"Let Him Know"** [A-side credited to George Jones]	1954
162	George Jones, **"You All Goodnight"/"Let Him Know"**	9/25/54
163	Eddie Eddings and The Country Gentlemen, **"Smoochin'"/"Yearning (To Kiss You)"**	1954
164	Red Hayes, **"A Satisfied Mind"/"Doggone Woman"**	10/16/54
165	Sonny Burns, **"Tell Her"**/ Sonny Burns & George Jones, **"Heartbroken Me"**	11/6/54
166	Glenn Barber, **"Ring around the Moon"/"Ice Water"**	11/6/54
167	R. D. Hendon and His Western Jamboree Cowboys, **"You Traveled Too Far"/"Return My Broken Heart"**	1954
169	Eddie Noack, **"Left Over Lovin'"/"I'll Be So Good to You"**	1955
170	Fred Crawford, **"You Gotta Wait"/"I Just Need Some Lovin'"**	1955
174	Bill Nettles, **"Wine-O Boogie"/"Gumbo-Mumbo (Papa Had to Go)"**	1955
175	Sonny Burns, **"Invitations (To Your Wedding)"**/ **"Let's Change Sweethearts"**	1955
178	Biff Collie, **"What This Old World Needs"/"Lonely"**	1955
179	Sonny Fisher, **"Rockin' Daddy"/"Hold Me Baby"**	March 1955
186	Melvin Price, **"The Pace That Kills"/"Maybe It's Because I Love You"**	5/7/55
187	Harry Choates, **"Jole Blon (French)"/"Jole Blon (English)"** [reissue of Gold Star masters]	1955
188	George Jones, **"Hold Everything"/"What's Wrong with You"**	1955
189	Sonny Burns, **"Six Feet of Earth"/"You'll Look a Long, Long Time"**	1955
190	Sonny Fisher, **"Hey Mama"/"Sneaky Pete"**	5/14/55
192	Smokey Stover, **"You Wouldn't Kid Me, Would You"**/ **"It's Easier Said Than Done"**	1955
194	R. D. Hendon and His Western Jamboree Cowboys, **"Big Black Cat"/"Four Walls (Around My Heart)"**	June 1955
196	Glenn Barber, **"Poor Man's Baby (And a Rich Man's Dream)"**/ **"Married Man"**	1955

197	Jack Hammonds, **"Mr. Cupid"**/**"That's the Way to Fall in Love"**	1955
198	Gene Tabor, **"A Real Gone Jesse (I'm Hot to Trot)"**/**"I'm Not the Marrying Kind"**	1955
199	Fred Crawford, **"Cain't Live with E'm!! (Cain't Live without E'm!!"** [sic]/**"What's on Your Mind"**	8/20/55
201	Eddie Noack, **"Wind Me Up"**/**"If It Ain't on the Menu"**	1955
202	George Jones, **"Why Baby Why"**/**"Seasons of My Heart"**	8/22/55
203	Biff Collie, **"Goodbye, Farewell, So Long"**/**"Look on the Good Side"**	1955
204	Jimmy Lee Durden and The Drifters, **"What Can I Say"**/**"Reconsider"**	1955
205	Jack Derrick, **"Rainbow of Love"**/**"Waitin' and Watchin'"**	1955
207	Sonny Fisher, **"Rockin' and Rollin'"**/**"I Can't Lose"**	Sept. 1955
208	Leon Payne, **"I Die Ten Thousand Times a Day"**/**"We're on the Main Line"**	1955
209	Sonny Burns, **"A Real Cool Cat"**/**"Frown on the Moon"**	9/24/55
212	Harry Choates, **"Poor Hobo"**/**"Opelousas Waltz"** [reissue of Gold Star masters]	1955
213	Eddie Noack, **"Fair Today, Cold Tomorrow"**/**"Don't Worry 'Bout Me Baby"**	1955
214	Glenn Barber, **"Ain't It Funny"**/**"Livin' High and Wide"**	11/19/55
215	Leon Payne, **"Christmas Love Song"**/**"Christmas Everyday"**	Dec. 1955
216	George Jones, **"What Am I Worth"**/**"Still Hurtin'"**	1/14/56
218	Fred Crawford, **"Just Another Broken Heart"**/**"Me and My New Baby"**	1956
219	Buddy Dee And String Band, **"Swamp Water Drag"**/**"Cherokee Ride"**/**"String Band Rag"**/**"Shuffle the Blues"** [EP]	1956
220	Leon Payne, **"You Are the One"**/**"Doorstep to Heaven"**	1956
223	Sonny Burns, **"Satan's a-Waitin'"**/**"Girl of the Streets"**	1956
224	Harry Choates, **"Port Arthur Waltz"**/**"Honky Tonk Boogie"** [reissue of Gold Star masters]	1956
225	Eddie Noack, **"When the Bright Lights Go Dim"**/**"It Ain't Much But It's Home"**	1956
228	R. D. Hendon and His Western Jamboree Cowboys, **"We Smiled"**/**"Don't Push Me (Let Me Fall)"**	3/24/56
229	Rudy Grayzell, **"The Moon Is Up (The Stars Are Out)"**/**"Day by Day"**	3/17/56
230	Biff Collie, **"Doodle Doo"**/**"Empty Kisses"**	1956
231	Bill Mack, **"Fat Woman"**/**"Kitty Kat"**	March 1956
232	Leon Payne, **"Two by Four"**/**"You Can't Lean on Me"**	1956
233	Larry Nolen and His Bandits, **"Ship Ahoy"**/**"Lady Luck"**	1956

234	George Jones, **"Your Heart"**/**"I'm Ragged But I'm Right"**	1956
235	Link Davis, **"Sixteen Chicks"**/**"Deep in the Heart of a Fool"**	4/21/56
236	Benny Barnes, **"Once Again"**/**"No Fault of Mine"**	5/5/56
237	Neal Merritt, **"What's the Difference"**/**"You Had to Do Me Wrong"**	1956
238	Johnny Nelms, **"Tribute to Andy Anderson"**/**"Everything Will Be Alright"**	1956
239	Jimmy Lee Durden and The Drifters, **"I Miss Her So"**/**"Since Yesterday"**	1956
240	Thumper Jones [George Jones], **"Rock It"**/**"How Come It"**	5/5/56
241	Rudy "Tutti" Grayzell, **"Duck Tail"**/**"You're Gone"**	5/5/56
242	Link Davis, **"Sixteen Chicks"**/**"Grasshopper Rock"**	5/12/56
243	Fred Crawford, **"Rock Candy Rock"**/**"Secret of My Heart"**	1956
244	Sonny Fisher, **"Little Red Wagon"**/**"Pink and Black"**	6/9/56
245	Rock Rogers [Leon Payne], **"Little Rock Rock"**/**"That Ain't It"**	1956
246	Eddie Noack, **"For You I Weep"**/**"You Done Got Me"**	1956
247	George Jones, **"It's OK"**/**"You Gotta Be My Baby"**	1956
248	R. D. Hendon and His Western Jamboree Cowboys, **"The Waltz of Texas"**/**"Lonely Nights"**	1956
249	Glenn Barber, **"Shadow My Baby"**/**"Feeling No Pain"**	1956
250	Leon Payne, **"All the Time"**/**"One More Chance"**	1956
251	Biff Collie, **"Joy Joy Joy"**/**"All of a Sudden"**	1956
252	Bill Mack, **"Cat Just Got in Town"**/**"Sweet Dreams Baby"**	7/28/56
253	Rocky Bill Ford, **"Have You Seen Mabel"**/**"Mad Dog in Town"**	July 1956
254	Sonny Burns, **"Think Again"**/**"If You See My Baby"**	1956
255	Link Davis, **"Don't Big Shot Me"**/**"Trucker from Tennessee"**	1956
256	George Jones, **"Boat of Life"**/**"Taggin' Along"**	8/11/56
257	Amos Como, **"Hole in the Wall"**/**"Heartbroken Lips"**	Sept. 1956
259	Larry Nolan And His Bandits, **"Golden Tomorrow"**/**"I Wonder"**	1956
260	Neal Merritt, **"No One But You"**/**"Someday You'll Pay"**	1956
262	Benny Barnes, **"Poor Man's Riches"**/**"Those Who Know"**	1956
263	Johnny Tyler, **"Lie to Me Baby"**/**"County Fair"**	10/6/56
264	George Jones, **"Gonna Come Get You"**/**"Just One More"**	9/15/56
265	Bob Doss, **"Somebody's Knocking"**/**"Don't Be Gone Long"**	10/13/56
266	James O'Gwynn, **"Losing Game"**/**"If I Never Get to Heaven"**	1956
267	Leon Payne, **"A Prisoner's Diary"**/**"Sweet Sweet Love"**	1956

268	Louisiana Lannis, **"Much Too Much"**/**"Muscadine Eyes"**	1956
270	Rudy "Tutti" Grayzell, **"You Hurt Me So"**/**"Jig-Ga-Lee-Ga"**	11/3/56
271	Jeanette Hicks, **"Extra-Extra"**/**"Cry Cry (It's Good for You)"**	1956
272	Fred Crawford, **"Lucky in Cards"**/**"I Learned Something from You"**	1956
273	Harry Choates, **"Allons a Lafayette"**/**"Draggin' the Fiddle"** [reissue of Gold Star masters]	1956
274	Smokey Stover, **"Now"**/**"My Building of Dreams"**	1956
275	Link Davis, **"Bayou Buffalo"**/**"Would You Be Waiting"**	Dec. 1956
276	Eddie Noack, **"The Worm Has Turned"**/ **"She Can't Stand the Light of Day"**	1956
277	Harry Carroll, **"Checkerboard Lover"**/**"Two Timin'"**	1956
278	Tibby Edwards, **"I Don't Want to Say I Love You"**/**"Fool That I Was"** [reissued on Mercury]	1956
279	George Jones and Jeanette Hicks, **"Yearning"**/ Jeanette Hicks, **"So Near (Yet So Far Away)"**	1956
280	Bill Mack, **"It's Saturday Night"**/**"That's Why I Cry"**	2/2/57
281	Neal Merritt, **"I've Got to Cry"**/**"The Funniest Feeling"**	1957
282	Slim Watts, **"Painted Lady"**/**"Tu-La-Lou"**	Feb. 1956
283	Larry Fox, **"Don't Hold Me Close"**/**"Guilty Heart"**	1957
284	Harry Choates, **"Tondelay"**/**"Basile Waltz"** [reissue of Gold Star masters]	1957
285	Jimmy Lee Durden, **"Time Heals Everything"**/**"No Mistake"**	1957
286	Jimmy Logsdon, **"No Longer"**/**"Can't Make Up My Mind"**	1957
287	Margie Singleton, **"One Step (Nearer to You)"**/**"Not What He's Got"**	1957
292	Sleepy LaBeef, **"All Alone"**/**"I'm Through"** [reissued on Mercury]	May 1957
293	Link Davis, **"Slippin' and Slidin' Sometimes"**/**"Allons a Lafayette"**	May 1957
294	Eddie Skelton, **"Let Me Be with You"**/**"My Heart Gets Lonely"**	5/27/57
295	Herbie Remington, **"Remington Swing"**/**"Ragged But Right"**	1957
299	Jimmy and Dorothy Blakely, **"Runaway Heart"**/ Jimmy Blakely, **"Crazy Blues"**	June 1957
301	Utah Carl, **"Sometime"**/**"Lovin' You"**	1957
302	Arlie Duff and The Duff Family, **"What a Way to Die"**/ **"You've Done It Again"**	July 1957
309	Margie Singleton, **"My Picture of You"**/**"Love Is a Treasure"**	1957
310	Jack Cardwell, **"Once Every Day"**/**"Hey, Hey Baby"**	8/26/57
313	Bill Mack, **"Million Miles Away"**/**"Cheatin' on Your Mind"**	9/30/57

314	Fred Crawford, **"You're Not the Same Sweet Girl"**/**"By the Mission Wall"**	8/26/57
315	Eddie Skelton, **"That's Love"**/**"No Sweetheart Tonight"**	9/16/57
316	Eddie Noack, **"Scarecrow"**/**"Think of Her Now"**	1957
319	The Davis Twins [with] Sleepy Jeffers, **"Pretending Is a Game"**/ **"My Blackbirds Are Blue Birds Now"**	8/26/57
320	The Marksmen, **"You Hurt Me So"**/**"Don't Gamble with My Heart"**	Sept. 1957
321	Rudy "Tutti" Grayzell, **"Let's Get Wild"**/**"I Love You So"**	Sept. 1957
322	Utah Carl, **"Stormy Skies"**/**"Don't Go Wrong"**	1957
323	Margie Singleton, **"Take Time Out for Love"**/**"Beautiful Dawn"**	1957
331	Link Davis, **"Waltz of the Jambalaya"**/**"Big Coonie"**	1957
332	Herbie Remington, **"Station Break"**/**"Slush Pump"**	1957
334	Eddie Noack, **"Dust on the River"**/**"What's the Matter Joe?"**	1957
336	Cecil Bowman and The Arrows, **"Blues around My Door"**/**"Too Late"**	1958
356	Roger Miller, **"Can't Stop Loving You"**/**"You're Forgetting Me"**	late 1957
401	Benny Barnes With The Echoes, **"You Gotta Pay"**/**"Heads You Win (Tails I Lose)"**	1958
424	Frankie Miller, **"Blackland Farmer"**/**"True Blue"** [recorded 1956, released 1959]	1956–1957
718	Roger Miller, **"Playboy"**/**"Poor Little John"**	late 1957

VI. Starday Records

Long-play albums containing tracks recorded at Gold Star Studios, 1956–1969

101	George Jones, *Grand Ole Opry's New Star* [same title reissued on Mercury]	1956
102	Various Artists, *Hillbilly Hit Parade*	1956
125	George Jones, *The Crown Prince of Country Music*	1961
151	George Jones, *The Fabulous Country Music Sound of George Jones*	1962
335	George Jones, *George Jones*	1965
344	George Jones, *Long Live King George*	1965
366	George Jones, *Story*	1966
401	George Jones, *Songbook & Picture Album*	1967
440	George Jones, *Golden Country Hits*	1969

VII. Mercury Records

Long-play albums containing tracks recorded at Gold Star Studios, 1957–1965

20282	Various Artists, *Hillbilly Hit Parade* [different material than the Starday LP of same title]	1957
20306	George Jones, *14 Top Country Favorites*	1957
20328	Various Artists, *Hillbilly Hit Parade Vol. 2*	1958
60621	George Jones, *Greatest Hits 1*	1961
60624	George Jones, *Country and Western Hits*	1961
60793	George Jones, *Novelty Side*	1963
61048	George Jones, *Country and Western No. 1 Male Singer*	1965

VIII. D Records

Singles produced at Gold Star Studios, 1957–1964

1000	Tommy Wood [aka Eddie Noack], **"My Steady Dream"**/**"Can't Play Hookey"**	1957
1001	Al Travis, **"He Brought Us Together"**/**"Mom and Dad Love You Too"**	1/1/58
1002	Wortham "Slim" Watts, **"Lonesome"**/**"Cotton Picker"**	5/31/58
1003	Utah Carl, **"Treasured Memories"**/**"Never Meant for Me"**	4/29/58
1005	Tony Douglas, **"World in My Arms"**/**"Baby, When the Sun Goes Down"**	6/30/58
1006	James O'Gwynn, **"Changeable"**/**"Talk to Me Lonesome Heart"**	6/30/58
1007	Margie Singleton, **"Shattered Kingdom"**/ **"I Want to Be Where You're Gonna Be"**	1958
1008	The Big Bopper, **"Chantilly Lace"**/ **"Purple People Eater Meets the Witch Doctor"**	6/30/58
1009	Sonny Hall & The Echoes, **"My Big Fat Baby"**/ **"Gonna Pack Up My Troubles"**	1958
1010	Les Cole & The Echoes, **"Rock-a-My Baby"**/**"Bee Boppin' Daddy"**	1958
1011	Johnny Dollar, **"No Memories"**/**"Walking Away"**	1958
1012	Ray Jackson, **"Texas-Alaska"**/**"Alaska"**	7/14/58
1013	The Four B's, **"Love Eternal"**/**"I Played the Fool"**	2/3/58
1014	Bobby Moncrief, **"Don't Hold Me to a Vow"**/**"Here Is My Heart"**	1958
1016	Eddie Bond, **"The Blues Got Me"**/**"Standing in Your Window"**	8/7/58
1017	Glenn Barber, **"Hello Sadness"**/**"Same Old Fool Tomorrow"**	1958

1018	Doug Bragg & The Drifters, **"Daydreaming Again"**/ **"If I Find My Dream Girl"**	1958
1019	Eddie Noack, **"Have Blues Will Travel"**/**"The Price of Love"**	1958
1020	Dee & Patty, **"Ohh-Wow"**/**"Sweet Lovin' Baby"**	1958
1021	Johnny Forrer, **"Fool's Paradise"**/**"Understand"**	1958
1022	James O'Gwynn, **"Blue Memories"**/**"You Don't Want to Hold Me"**	1958
1023	Harry Choates, **"Draggin' the Fiddle"**/**"Allons a Lafayette"** [reissue of Gold Star masters]	1958
1024	Harry Choates, **"Jole Blon"**/**"Corpus Christi Waltz"** [reissue of Gold Star masters]	1958
1024	Harry Choates, **"Jole Blon"**/**"Draggin' the Bow"** [second reissue]	1961
1025	Ray Jackson, **"Tears of Tomorrow"**/**"Echo Mountain"**	10/27/58
1026	Royce Porter, **"Lookin'"**/**"I Still Belong to You"**	1958
1027	Country Johnny Mathis, **"Lonely Nights"**/**"I've Been Known to Cry"**	1958
1029	Ted Doyle, **"He Made You Mine"**/**"I'm All Wrapped Up"**	1958
1030	Rufus Thibodeaux, **"Cameron Memorial Waltz"**/**"Mean Autry"**	1958
1033	Patsy Timmons, **"I Understand Him"**/**"Step Aside Old Heart"**	1958
1035	Sonny Hall, **"Men Do Cry"**/**"The Day You Walked Away"**	1958
1036	Dave Edge, **"I Kept It a Secret"**/**"I Didn't Think It of You"**	1958
1037	Eddie Noack, **"I Don't Live There Any More"**/**"Walk 'Em Off"**	11/11/58
1038	Gaston Ponce Castellanos, **"Que-Chula-Estas"**/**"Si-Yo-Te-Quiero"**	1959
1041	Jerry Lynn, **"Bugger Burns"**/**"Queen of the Moon"**	1/4/59
1042	Merle Kilgore, **"It'll Be My First Time"**/**"I Take a Trip to the Moon"**	1/5/59
1043	Harry Choates, **"Poor Hobo"**/**"Opelousas Waltz"**	1/29/59
1044	Harry Choates, **"Port Arthur Waltz"**/**"Honky Tonk Boogie"**	1/30/59
1047	Ray Campi, **"Ballad of Donna & Peggy Sue"**/**"The Man I Met"**	2/6/59
1048	Cecil Bowman, **"Man Awaitin'"**/**"Justice of Love"**	2/10/59
1052	Benny Barnes, **"Happy Little Blue Bird"**/**"Gold Records in the Snow"**	2/25/59
1053	Bill Kimbrough & The Townsmen, **"Chantilly Lace Cha Cha"**/**"Egg Head"**	3/6/59
1054	Country Johnny Mathis, **"From a Kiss to the Blues"**/ **"Since I Said Goodbye to the Blues"**	3/7/59
1055	Ray Jackson, **"Tea Leaves Don't Lie"**/**"What Makes You Cry"**	3/10/59
1057	Ted Doyle, **"One More Heartache"**/**"Just for the Thrill"**	3/22/59
1060	Eddie Noack, **"A Thinking Man's Woman"**/**"Don't Look Behind"**	4/2/59
1064	Rufus Thibodeaux, **"Sauce Piquant"**/**"Louisiana Festival"**	4/22/59

1066	Dee Mullins, **"I've Really Got a Right to Cry"**/**"The World's a Lie"**	4/22/59
1069	Glenn Barber, **"Most Beautiful"**/**"Your Heart Don't Love"**	May 1959
1074	Johnny Forrer, **"My Blues"**/**"The Real Thing"**	6/10/59
1076	Tommy Durden, **"Deep in the Heart of a Fool"**/ **"The Bee (That Won the Baseball Game)"**	6/16/59
1078	Country Johnny Mathis, **"I Don't Know How I Can Live"**/**"Run Please Run"**	6/20/59
1079	Patsy Timmons, **"Answer to Life to Go"**/**"I've Got It"**	6/20/59
1080	William Tell Taylor with Jimmy Heap & The Melody Masters, **"I Can't Ever Free My Mind"**/**"Uh Huh"**	6/25/59
1081	Tibby Edwards, **"Memory of a Lie"**/**"One More Night"**	6/26/59
1085	Cecil Bowman, **"Cotton"**/**"Curse of Wine"**	7/10/59
1089	Jimmy & Johnny, **"My Little Baby"**/**"All I Need Is Time"**	8/13/59
1090	Margie Word, **"Takes a Lot of Heartaches"**/**"I Shot Sam"**	8/16/59
1093	Claude Gray, **"Loneliness"**/**"Best Part of Me"**	8/22/59
1094	Eddie Noack, **"Man on the Wall"**/**"Relief Is Just a Swallow Away"**	8/23/59
1095	Ted Doyle, **"One Step Ahead of Sorrow"**/**"Just One More Glass"**	8/24/59
1097	Dave Edge, **"Wham Bam"**/**"Nights of Loneliness"**	8/28/59
1098	Glenn Barber, **"New Girl in School"**/**"Go Home Letter"**	8/27/59
1099	Shirley Rucker, **"I Hear Your Footsteps"**/**"You Take More Than I Can"**	8/30/59
1105	William Tell Taylor, **"Angel of Love"**/**"Love Is Everywhere"**	10/18/59
1108	Leon Payne, **"Brothers of a Bottle"**/**"Mitzie McGraw"**	10/22/59
1109	Patsy Timmons, **"Branded for Life"**/**"My Philosophy"**	10/23/59
1110	Cecil Bowman, **"Sweet Cake & Kisses"**/**"Tea Leaves Don't Lie"**	10/21/59
1114	Johnny Nelms, **"Yoshe"**/**"Memories for a Pillow"**	11/26/59
1118	Claude Gray, **"Family Bible"**/**"Crying in the Night"**	12/18/59
1119	Country Johnny Mathis, **"Come On In"**/**"The Chances Are"**	1/2/60
1124	Eddie Noack, **"Shake Hands with the Blues"**/**"Sunflower Song"**	2/5/60
1128	Glenn Barber, **"The Window"**/**"Another You"**	2/19/60
1129	Herbie Remington, **"Coo Coo Creek Hop"**/**"Chime Out for Love"**	2/24/60
1130	Country Johnny Mathis, **"Caryl Chessman"**/**"Tears and Gold"**	2/29/60
1131	Willie Nelson, **"What a Way to Live"**/**"Misery Mansion"**	3/11/60
—	Paul Buskirk & His Little Men featuring Hugh [Willie] Nelson, **"Nite Life"**/**"Rainy Day Blues"** [unissued: independently released on Rx Records 502]	March 1960

1132	Harry Choates, **"Basile Waltz"/"Tondelay"**	3/12/60
1133	William Tell Taylor, **"Sweet Dreams of You"/"Seeing Is Believing"**	3/3/60
1134	Danny Ross, **"The Things I Cannot Change"/"Jose"**	3/14/60
1135	Link Davis, **"Waltz of the Jambalaya"/"Big Coonie"**	3/14/60
1137	Reece Brothers, **"Jail Break"/"Run Away"**	3/31/60
1138	Leon Payne, **"There's No Justice"/"With Half a Heart"**	4/1/60
1144	Claude Gray, **"Leave Alone"/"My Party's Over"**	5/6/60
1145	Cecil Bowman, **"Most Beautiful"/"Whispering Lies"**	5/20/60
1146	Ted Doyle, **"The Life You've Lived"/** **"My Baby's Gone Again"**	May/June 1960
1148	Eddie Noack, **"Too Weak to Go"/"Firewater Luke"**	June 1960
1149	Charles Drake, **"A Fool's Careless Life"/"She Wore Another Name"**	June 1960
1150	Leon Payne, **"Blue Side of Lonesome"/"Things Have Gone to Pieces"**	June 1960
1152	Country Johnny Mathis, **"When I Came through Town"/** **"Only Time Will Tell"**	6/12/60
1153	Perk Williams, **"You Traveled Too Far"/"You're Not My Angel Anymore"**	7/21/60
1154	Claude Gray, **"Homecoming in Heaven"/** **"When the Light Shines in the Valley"**	Aug. 1960
1157	Fitz Morris, **"Fishing Tales"/"Edge of Paradise"**	Aug. 1960
1165	Mac McGee, **"A Lock without a Key"/"I've Closed the Door"**	10/6/60
1166	Al Dean, **"Handful of Ashes"/"Horses Carry Tales"**	10/10/60
1168	Nick Williams & The Treece-Reece Trio, **"Springtime in Heaven"/"How Many Heartaches"**	11/8/60
1177	Treece-Reece Trio, **"When the Hurt Hurts No More"/** **"Teen Age Loneliness"**	1/21/61
1178	Johnny Nelms, **"Old Broken Heart"/"I've Never Had the Blues"**	2/3/61
1182	Perk Williams, **"What More"/"Are You Trying to Tell Me Goodbye"**	2/7/61
1186	Herbie Remington, **"Fiddleshoe"/"Soft Shoe Slide"**	3/3/61
1191	Link Davis, **"Come Dance with Me"/"Five Miles from Town"**	3/31/61
1192	Al Dean, **"I Need No Chains"/"A Girl at the Bar"**	5/2/61
1195	Johnny Nelms, **"Picture in My Heart"/"Half Past a Heartache"**	7/1/61
1203	Booth Kinner, **"This Lonesome Pillow"/"So Lonesome"**	7/1/61
1204	Mac McGee & The Texas Ramblers, **"Move Over Conscience"/"I'd Better Run"**	6/6/61
1205	Cecil Bowman, **"Lay Your Hoe Down"/"This World Will Be So Lonely"**	7/14/61

1206	Danny Reeves, **"I'm a Hobo"**/**"Bell Hop Blues"**	7/25/61
1218	Al Dean, **"I'll Win Again"**/**"One Heartache from the Blues"**	9/29/61
1220	Eddie Noack, **"It's Hard to Tell an Old Love Goodbye"**/ **"Love's Other Face"**	10/18/61
1222	Harry Choates, **"Oh-Meon"**/**"Big Woods"**	10/29/61
1225	Dave Edge, **"Chained to a Love"**/**"Tears That I Wasted"**	11/29/61
1226	George Jones, **"Maybe Next Christmas"**/**"New Baby for Christmas"**	11/30/61
1235	George Cooper, **"I Finally Broke the Spell"**/**"The Ways of Life"**	3/26/62
1236	Jerry Jericho, **"Just for the Thrill"**/**"Tears Fall Again"**	4/9/62
—	Eddie Noack, **"The Same Old Mistakes"**/**"You've Got a Woman"** [unissued]	
1239	Billy Western, **"Worn Out Words"**/**"His and Hers"**	6/6/62
1240	Al Gressett & The Texas Ramblers, **"Do You Realize"**/**"You Gotta Hurry"**	8/23/62
1245	Billy Western, **"My Blue Room"**/**"Say When"**	2/8/63
1247	Johnny Nelms, **"I'm So Ashamed"**/**"The Sulfur Queen"**	3/12/63
1248	Tex Wayne, **"Angel with a Pony Tail"**/**"Standing at the Crossroads"**	4/20/63
1252	Billy Western, **"Home's Not Where My House Is"**/**"Love Enough"**	6/22/63
1256	Tex Wayne, **"She's Lying Again"**/**"My Party's Over"**	2/20/64
1257	Truitt Forse & Jerry Lynn With Benny Leaders Band, **"Searching for Someone"**/**"Fool You Fool"**	3/10/64
1260	Don Gilbert, **"Your Time for Tears"**/**"With Open Arms"**	3/27/64
1270	Stoney Stark,**"Face in the Crowd"**/**"Your Conscience Will Hurt"**	10/21/64

IX. Kangaroo Records

Singles produced at Gold Star Studios, ca. 1958–1959

101/102	The Dolls, **[?, unknown titles]**
103/104	Albert Collins And His Rhythm Rockers, **"Freeze"**/**"Collins Shuffle"**
105/106	Joe Hughes and His Orchestra, **"I Can't Go On This Way"**/ **"Make Me Dance Little Ant"**
107/108	Henry Hayes and Orchestra, **"Two Big Feet"**/**"Call of the Kangaroo"**
109/110	Henry Hayes And Orchestra, **"It Takes Money"**/**"Stop Smackin' That Wax"**
111/112	Little Joey Farr, **"I Want a Big White Cadillac for Christmas"**/**"Rock 'n' Roll Santa"**

X. Gulf Records (Label reactivated by Bill Quinn)

Singles produced at Gold Star Studios, ca. 1959–1962

101	Harold Casner, **"That Is Why"/"Marker in Your Heart"**	
62760/62761	Sleepy LaBeef, **"I Can't Get You Off My Mind"/"I Found Out"**	
62762/62763	Jerry Bryan [And The] Houndogs, **"Vampire Daddy"/"Walking Out"**	
1630/1631	Mel Douglas and The Nu-Notes, **"Dream Girl"/"Forever My Darling"**	1962
1633	Virgil Gage, **"I'm Still in Love with You"/"I Live You"**	1962
1640/1641	Lucy Lynn, **"Ist Es Den Liebe"/"Bright Lights"**	1962

XI. Sarg Records

Singles produced at Gold Star Studios, 1955–1960

136	Link Davis, **"Cockroach"/"Big Houston"**	1955
137	Floyd Tillman, **"Baby I Just Want You"/"Save a Little for Me"**	1955
—	Coye Wilcox, **"Bird's Nest on the Ground"/"Don't Take My Love"** [unissued]	1955/56
140	Al Parsons & The Country Store Boys, **"Wait for Me Baby"/"Memories of Yesterday"**	May 1956
144	Johnny Carroll, **"The Stars Came Down from Heaven"/"I'll Think of You"**	1956
147	Al Parsons & The Country Store Boys, **"Darling, I Still Dream of You"/"Why Can't You Be True"**	1956
148	Al Urban, **"Lookin' for Money"/"I Don't Want to Be Alone"**	1956
154	Al Parsons & The Country Store Boys, **"You've Done Her Wrong"/"I Got You Where I Want You"**	1956
155	Dick Fagan, **"Love Is Like the Sun"/"My Aim in Life"**	1956
158	Al Urban, **"Won't Tell You Her Name"/"Gonna Be Better Times"**	1958
—	Dick Fagan, **"This Lonesome Road"/"Blues in My Heart"** [unissued]	1958
174	Al Urban, **"The Last Heartache"/"Street of Memories"**	1960

XII. Various labels owned by Huey P. Meaux

Singles recorded and produced at Gold Star/SugarHill Studios, 1964–1988 for American Pla-Boy, Crazy Cajun, Jetstream, Pacemaker, Pic 1, Teardrop, Tribe, Tri-Us, Typhoon, Ventura

AMERICAN PLA-BOY RECORDS *		
1977	Heather Black, **"There"/"Circles"**	1972
1980	Doug Sahm, **"El Paso Train"/"Ain't Nothing Wrong with You"**	1976
1983	Donny King, **"I Played That Song for You"/"Mathilda"**	
1984	Jesse Lankford, **"I'll Have to Be with You Again"/"Take Your Time"**	
1984	Ron Arledge, **"Woman of the World"/"You Can't Get There from Here"**	
1985	John Craig Stout, **"Louisiana Funk Homegrown"/"Lovin' Cajun Style"**	1975
1986	Clarence Henry, **"We'll Take Our Last Walk Tonight"/"In the Jailhouse Now"**	
1986	Ron Wayne, **"Country's Got the Slows"/"Warmed Over Coffee"**	
1987	Jerry Biscamp, **"Since Baby's Back Again"/"You're the One I Love Tonight"**	
1988	Sandra Morrison, **"It's You"/"What Might Have Been"**	
1989	Tommy Mclain, **"Baby Jesus"/"Carefree Moments"**	
1990	Clarence Henry, **"We'll Take Our Last Walk Tonight"/"You Can Have Her"**	
1991	The Nashville Rebels, **"A New Girl in Town"/"The Rains Came"**	
1992	Heather Black, **"Cajun Blue"/"Harris County Jail"**	
1992	John Craig, **"JJ"/"We've Seen Worse Times"**	
1993	Tommy McLain, **"Real Rock & Roll"/"Sister Caroline"**	
1994	Tommy McLain, **"Wild Side of Life"/"When It Rains"**	
1995	Billy Johns, **"Dreams"/"Feel It"**	
1995	Harvey Thompson, **"Ride This Train"/"What I Want What I Need"**	
1996	Tommy McLain, **"Dim Lights Thick Smoke"/"Just Out of Reach"**	
2025	Donny King, **"The Flame of Love Too Low"/"Woman of the Worlds"**	
2026	Freddy & Manuel, **"I'm Up on the Right Track"/** **"Flying My Way Back to Texas"**	
2031	Johnny Cantrell, **"Come to Me"/"I'm Lonestar Lonesome Tonight"**	1986
8000	Mel Garrett, **"Hello Whiskey Again"/"I Can't Hold a Candle"**	

* Note: This label inexplicably twice assigned the catalogue numbers 1984, 1986, 1992, and 1995—in each case to a different artist performing a different pair of songs.

526	Link Davis, **"Big Mamou"**/**"Cajun Honey"**
2001	Alvin Crow, **"Retirement Run"**/**"Country Ways"**
2002	Freddy Fender, **"Before the Next Teardrop Falls"**/**"Waiting for Your Love"**
2004	Doug Sahm, **"Hot Tomato Man"**/**"If You Really Want Me to I'll Go"**
2006	Freddy Fender, **"Esta Noche Mia Seras"**/**"Vivo en un Sueño"**
2007	Tracy Friel, **"Missing You"**/**"If You're Ever in Texas"**
2008	Joe Barry, **"There's a Crowd"**/**"I Started Loving You Again"**
2012	Sherri Jerrico, **"If You Fake It I Might Make It"**/**"Mind Can't Control Baby"**
2014	Freddy Fender, **"No Toquen Ya"**/**"I Love My Rancho Grande"**
2015	Tommy McLain, **"Good Morning Louisiana"**/**"Mama Send Me a Dollar"**
2018	Tommy McLain, **"Honky Tonk"**/**"Tender Years"**
2019	Freddy Fender, **"Vaya Con Dios"**/**"No Soy El Mismo"**
2024	Floyd Tillman, **"She Loved Me"**/**"Paper Flowers"**
2025	Tracey Balin, **"A Man Would Be a Face"**/**"These Hands You're Holding Now"**
2027	Tommy McLain, **"Jukebox Songs"**/**"Leaving This Town"**
2029	June Terry, **"Wheel of Fortune"**/**"Someday"**
2031	Tommy McLain, **"Send Me the Pillow"**/[?, B-side title unknown]
2033	Tommy McLain, **"I Cried"**/ Freddy Fender, **"Bartender Play Me Some Freddy Fender"**
2036	Donny King, **"I Don't Want Nobody"**/**"Beer Barrel Polka"**
2037	Freddy Fender, **"Going Out with the Tide"**/ Tommy McLain, **"Fannie Mae"**
2038	Warren Storm, **"I Walk Alone"**/**"Don't Fall in Love"**
2041	Willie Tee, **"Misery Loves Company"**/**"Sick and Tired"**
2042	Harvey Dubois, **"Gettin' Baby off My Mind"**/**"I'm Not Just Woman Hungry"**
2043	Berly Hanks, **"Cowboys Never Use Their Hearts"**/**"Dum Dum"**
2044	Tommy McLain, **"They'll Never Take Her Love Away from Me"**/ **"Lose the Blues"**
2045	Harvey Wray, **"Woman I'm Leaving"**/**"Unattended Love"**
2051	Arch Yancey, **"Rose of Ol' Pawnee"**/**"Cadillac"**
2053	Warren Storm, **"I've Shed So Many Tears"**/**"We'll Sing in the Sunshine"**
2054	Harvey Dubois, **"Hole in the Boat"**/**"In Memories of You"**

2055	Willie Tee Trahan, **"Before the Next Teardrop Falls"**/ **"My Tears Are Falling Tonight Love"**	
2056	Tommy McLain, **"They'll Call Me Daddy"/"Please Mr. Sandman"**/ **"I'll Change My Style"/"Crazy Baby"** [EP]	
2057	Freddy Fender, **"She's Still My Mexican Rose"/"Come On Home"**	
2060	Freddy Fender, **"Goin' Honky Tonkin'"/"My Confession"**	
2061	Warren Storm, **"They Won't Let Me In"/"You Can't Get There from Here"**	
2063	Tommy McLain, **"Goin' Honky Tonkin'"/"It's the Same Old Thing"**	
2065	Warren Storm, **"Jealous Woman"/"Old Honky Tonks"**	
2072	Burton Gaar, **"Don't Fan the Flame"/"Sugar Roll Blues"**	1984
2074	Tommy McLain, **"Parlez Vous France"/"Baby Dolls"**	1985
2075	Val Lindsey, **"Big Basile"/"Val's Cajun Fiddle"**	1985
2076	Pat Straza, **"Sing Me a Song Papa"/"She Don't Know about Love"**	1985
2077	Freddy Fender, **"Pobre Viejo Papa"/"Vaya Con Dios"**	1985
2078	Johnny Winter, **"Holidays & Weekends"/"Driving Me Crazy"**	1985
2079	Dave Dudley, **"I Wish I Could Sprechen Sie Deutsch"**/ Chubby Wise, **"Maiden's Prayer"**	
2080	Tracer, **"Take Me All the Way"/"Meet Me at Midnight"**	1985
2081	Freddy Fender, **"Keep It a Secret"/"I Might as Well Forget You"**	
2082	T. K. Hulin & Smoke, **"You've Been Bad"/"She's Got a Love Hold on Me"**	
2083	Tommy McLain, **"I'll Change My Style Crazy Baby"**/ **"They'll All Call Me Daddy"**	
2086	Joe Barry, **"Today I Started Loving You Again"/"Three's a Crowd"**	
2087	Tommy McLain, **"Louisiana People"/"Roses Don't Grow Here Anymore"**	
2088	Warren Storm, **"I'm Not Just Woman Hungry (I'm Starving to Death)"**/ **"Sometimes a Picker Just Can't Win"**	1986
2089	Benny Barnes, **"Foolin' Myself"/"You're Telling Me Lies"**	1986
2090	Doug Kershaw, **"It Takes All Day"/"That Real Old Cajun Me"**	1987
2091	Susan Watson, **"What Comes after Love"/"Bad Girl"**	
2092	William Burton Gaar, **"You Go Crazy All Alone"/"Two Timed"**	1987
2093	Warren Storm, **"The Rains Came"**/ **"You Need Someone Who'll Be Mean to You"**	
2094	Brian Collins, **"Nickel's Worth of Heaven"/"Love Is the Key"**	
2095	Mel Garrett, **"Forgive Me I've Sinned (Short Version)"**/ **"Forgive Me I've Sinned (Long Version)"**	

2097	William Burton Gaar, **"Teardrop from Heaven"**/**"After All These Years"**	
2098	Mel Garrett, **"I've Had Enough"**/**"I Just Need Someone to Hold Me Tonight"**	1988
9024	C. L. & The Pictures, **"Love Will Find a Way"**/**"I'm Sorry"**	

JETSTREAM RECORDS

827	Sonny Raye & Fancy, **"(Come On) Git-Wut-I-Got"**/**"I Wanna Be Good to You"**	
828	Barbara Lynn, **"Takin' His Love Away"**/**"How Do You Think I Can Live without Love (After What I've Been Used To)"**	
829	Barbara Lynn, **"Disco Music"**/**"Movin' on a Groove"**	
830	Flesch, **"Freaky Love"**/**"Take It Out on Me"**	
831	Sonny Raye & Fancy, **"I Got You Babe"**/**"Where Did We Go Wrong"**	
832	Ira Wilkes, **"Love the One You're With"**/**"Never Miss Your Good Thing"**	
833	Oscar Perry, **"Has Anybody Seen Her"**/**"People Are Talking"**	
900	Oscar Perry, **"Love Everything about You"**/**"Danger Zone"**	
901	Oscar Perry, **"(She's an Upsetter) Bad Bad Motor Machine"**/**"She Needs Love"**	

PACEMAKER RECORDS

260	Sir Douglas Quintet, **"Sugar Bee"**/**"Blue Norther"**	1964
262	Yesterday's Obsession, **"Complicated Mind"**/**"The Phycle"**	
1973	Freddy Fender, **"Wasted Days and Wasted Nights"**/**"Just Bidin' My Time"**	
1982	Reggie Forch, **"Filled Up to My Neck"**/**"Love War"**	

PIC 1 RECORDS

105	Johnny Williams & the Jokers, **"Long Black Veil"**/**"Won't You Forgive"**	
111	Devons [Sir Douglas Quintet], **"Wine Wine Wine"**/**"Joey's Guitar"**	1966
119	Dawgs, **"Shy"**/**"Won't You Cry for Me"**	

TEARDROP RECORDS

3030	Champagne Brothers, **"It's Raining"**/**"Robin"**	
3042	Champagne Brothers, **"Let's Live"**/**"I'll Run Away, Far Away"**	1964
3046	Champagne Brothers, **"Christmas Time without You"**/**"Snow on the Old Bayou"**	
3058	Ivory Joe Hunter, **"Heart Don't Love Her Anymore"**/**"I've Asked You for the Last Time"**	
3059	Champagne Brothers, **"Old Enough to Break a Heart"**/**"Raining in My Heart"**	
3065	Ivory Joe Hunter, **"Up on Heartbreak Hill"**/**"Most of All"**	
3086	Champagne Brothers, **"The Love I Lost"**/**"I Love the Go-Go Girls"**	1964

3108	Champagne Brothers, **"Don't Ask Me Why"/"My Love & the Seasons"**	
3123	Sunny & the Sunliners, **"Cheatin' Traces"/"No One Else Will Do"**	
3124	Clifton Chenier, **"Oh Lucille"/"You Know That I Love You"**	
3125	Clifton Chenier, **"Shake 'Em Up Baby"/"My Little Girl"**	
3479	Doug Sahm, **"Who Were You Thinking Of"/"Velma from Selma"**	1982
3480	Doug Sahm, **"Love Taker"/"Life in the City"**	1982
3481	Doug Sahm, **"I'm Not a Fool Anymore"/"Don't Fight It"**	1982
3482	Doug Sahm, **"I'm Not a Fool Anymore"/"Don't Fight It"** [reissued, with picture sleeve]	1983

TRIBE RECORDS

8308	Sir Douglas Quintet, **"She's About a Mover"/"We'll Take Our Last Walk Tonight"**
8309	Doty Roy, **"I'm Not That Kind of Girl"/"He's My Ideal"**
8310	Sir Douglas Quintet, **"The Tracker"/"Blue Norther"**
8312	Sir Douglas Quintet, **"The Story of John Hardy"/"In Time"**
8314	Sir Douglas Quintet, **"The Rains Came"/"Bacon Fat"**
8317	Sir Douglas Quintet, **"Quarter to Three"/"She's Gotta Be the Boss"**

TRI-US RECORDS

912	Little Royal, **"Razor Blade"/"Jealous"**	
913	Little Royal, **"I'll Come Crawling"/"You'll Lose a Good Thing"**	
915	Little Royal, **"I Surrender"/"Soul Train"**	
916	Little Royal, **"I'm Glad to Do It"/"My Love Needs Company"**	
917	Little Royal, **"Don't Want Nobody Standing over Me"/ "Keep on Pushing Your Luck"**	1973

TYPHOON RECORDS, 1963

| 2002 | Champagne Brothers, **"Stranger to You"/"Chickawawa"** |
| 2003 | Champagne Brothers, **"It's Raining"/"Robin"** |

VENTURA RECORDS

| 722 | Bob & Gaylan, **"It Belongs to You"/"Don't Go in My Room, Girl"** |

MISCELLANEOUS LABELS NOT OWNED BY MEAUX BUT TO WHICH HE LEASED TRACKS

| ABC/Dot 17656 | Doug Sahm, **"Cowboy Peyton Place"/"I Love the Way You Love"** | 1976 |
| ABC/Dot 17674 | Doug Sahm, **"Cryin' Inside Sometimes"/"I'm Missing You"** | 1976 |

Chrysalis 2504	Doug Sahm & The SDQ, **"Sheila Tequila"/"Who'll Be the Next in Line"/"Wooly Bully"/"She's About a Mover"** [EP]	1981
Collectables 4253	Doug Sahm & The SDQ, **"Mendocino"/"She's About a Mover"**	1986
Cadette 8005	C.L. & The Pictures, **"Then You'll Know"/"Love Will Find a Way"**	
Epic 9849	Bobby Sharp, **"Walk Think Cry"/"I Don't Want to See You Again"**	
Scepter 12154A	B. J. Thomas, **"Bring Back the Time"/ "I Don't Have a Mind of My Own"**	1967
Kingfish 525	Warren Storm, **"They Won't Let Me In"/ "Sitting Here on the Ceiling"**	
London REU-1010171	Sir Douglas Quintet, **"She's About a Mover"/"We'll Take Our Last Walk Tonight"/"The Tracker"/"Blue Norther"** [EP]	1965
London DL20888	Sir Douglas Quintet, **"She's About a Mover"/"The Rains Came"**	1966
Mercury 6817-062	Sir Douglas Quintet, **"Mendocino"/"She's About a Mover"**	1970
Mercury PRA 115 (Australia)	Sir Douglas Quintet, **"Mendocino"/"Dynamite Woman"/ "She's About a Mover"/"Quarter to Three"** [EP]	1970

XIII. Various labels owned by Don Robey

Singles recorded for and produced at Gold Star Studios
or Back Beat, Duke, Peacock, and Sure Shot

BACK BEAT RECORDS	
1963–1964	
539	Joe Hinton, **"There's No In Between"/"Better to Give Than to Receive"**
540	Joe Hinton, **"There Oughta Be a Law"/"You're My Girl"**
541	Joe Hinton, **"Funny (How Time Slips Away)"/"You Gotta Have Love"**
542	Lee Lamont, **"The Crying Man"/"I'll Take Love"**
543	Roy Head & The Traits, **"Teenage Letter"/"Pain"**
544	O. V. Wright, **"I Don't Want to Sit Down"/"Can't Find True Love"**
1965	
545	Joe Hinton, **"I Want a Little Girl"/"True Love"**
546	Roy Head & The Traits, **"Treat Her Right"/"So Long My Love"**
547	Joe Hinton, **"Everything"/"Darling Come Talk to Me"**
548	O. V. Wright, **"You're Gonna Make Me Cry"/"Monkey Dog"**
550	Joe Hinton, **"A Kid Named Joe"/"Pledging My Love"**

551	O. V. Wright, **"Poor Boy"**/**"I'm in Your Corner"**
552	Bobby Adeno, **"It's a Sad World"**/**"The Hands of Time"**
553	Fanatics, **"Dancing to the Shotgun"**/**"You're Moving Too Fast"**
554	Coastliners, **"Wonderful You"**/**"Alright"**
555	Roy Head & The Traits, **"I Pass the Day"**/**"Apple of My Eye"**
556	Jeanette Williams, **"A Friend of Mine"**/**"You Didn't Know Then"**
558	O. V. Wright, **"Gone for Good"**/**"How Long Baby"**
560	Roy Head & The Traits, **"My Babe"**/**"Pain"**
563	Roy Head & The Traits, **"Wigglin' and Gigglin'"**/**"Driving Wheel"**
565	Joe Hinton, **"I'm Waiting"**/**"How Long Can I Last"**
566	Coastliners, **"She's My Girl"**/**"I'll Be Gone"**

1967

571	Roy Head & The Traits, **"To Make a Big Man Cry"**/**"Don't Cry No More"**
574	Joe Hinton, **"If I Had Only Known"**/**"Lots of Love"**
577	Coastliners, **"California on My Mind"**/**"I See You"**
579	Bobby Adeno, **"I'll Give Up the World"**/**"Treat You Like a Queen"**
580	O. V. Wright, **"Eight Men, Four Women"**/**"Fed Up with the Blues"**
581	Joe Hinton, **"You've Been Good"**/**"Close to My Heart"**
583	O. V. Wright, **"Heartaches, Heartaches"**/**"Treasured Moments"**
586	O. V. Wright, **"What about You"**/**"What Did You Tell This Girl of Mine"**
587	Jeanette Williams, **"Longing for Your Love"**/**"Something Got a Hold on Me"**

DUKE RECORDS

1964

373	Buddy Ace, **"It Makes You Want to Cry"**/**"You've Got My Love"**
378	Ernie K-Doe, **"My Mother-in-Law (Is in My Hair Again)"**/**"Looking into the Future"**
381	Buddy Ace, **"My Love"**/**"True Love Money Can't Buy"**
382	Miss La-Vell, **"Everybody's Got Somebody"**/**"The Best Part of Me"**

1965

389	Junior Parker, **"Crying for My Baby"**/**"Guess You Don't Know (the Golden Rule)"**
391	Buddy Ace, **"Inside Story"**/**"Just to Hold My Hand"**
392	James Davis, **"Bad Dreams"**/**"Ain't It Great"**
393	Bobby Bland, **"I'm Too Far Gone (to Turn Around)"**/**"If You Could Read My Mind"**

397	Buddy Ace, **"It's Gonna Be Me"**/**"Nothing in the World Can Hurt Me (except You)"**
398	Junior Parker, **"Goodbye Little Girl"**/**"Walking the Floor over You"**
399	Clarence Green & The Rhythmaires, **"Keep a Workin'"**/**"I Saw You Last Night"**
400	Ernie K-Doe, **"Boomerang"**/**"Please Don't Stop"**
401	Buddy Ace, **"Who Can Tell"**/**"Baby Please Don't Go"**

1966

410	Clarence Green & The Rhythmaires, **"I'm Wonderin'"**/**"What Y'all Waiting on Me"**
411	Ernie K-Doe, **"Dancin' Man"**/**"Later for Tomorrow"**
412	Bobby Bland, **"Back in the Same Old Bag Again"**/**"I Ain't Myself Anymore"**
413	Junior Parker, **"Man or Mouse"**/**"Wait for Another Day"**
414	Buddy Ace, **"Come On in This House"**/**"Hold On to This Old Fool"**
416	Bobby Bland, **"You're All I Need"**/**"Deep in My Soul"**
419	Buddy Ace, **"Something for These Blues"**/**"I'm Counting on You"**

1967

| 432 | Bobby Bland, **"Driftin' Blues"**/**"A Piece of Gold"** |

PEACOCK RECORDS

1964

1935	Little Frankie Lee, **"Taxi Blues"**/**"I Gotta Come Back"**
1937	Don Fletcher, **"Two Wrongs (Don't Make a Right)"**/**"I'm So Glad"**
1938	Reuben & The Chains, **"Ain't You Gonna Love Me"**/**"Answer These Questions"**

1965

1939	Bud Harper, **"Mr. Soul"**/**"Let Me Love You"**
1944	Minnie Epperson, **"It'll Last Forever"**/**"Nothing But the Facts"**
1945	Al "TNT" Braggs, **"Earthquake"**/**"How Long Do You Hold On"**
1946	Lonnie Woods Trio, **"Shakin' Sugar, Part 1"**/**"Shakin' Sugar, Part 2"**

PEACOCK RECORDS 3000 GOSPEL SERIES

1964

3011	Loving Sisters, **"Sing Your Troubles Away"**/**"Don't Let My Running Be in Vain"**
3014	Sunset Travelers, **"Blind Bartimaeus"**/**"There's a Change in Me"**
3025	Mighty Clouds Of Joy, **"I'll Go, Part 1"**/**"I'll Go, Part 2"**
3027	Loving Sisters, **"Fix Me"**/**"Trying Time"**
3039	Sunset Travelers, **"Another Day"**/**"On Jesus' Program"**

	1965
3047	Loving Sisters, **"Man on the Other Side of Jordan"**/**"God Don't Like It"**
3050	Mighty Clouds of Joy, **"A Friend in Jesus"**/**"Two Wings"**
3052	Gospelaires of Dayton, Ohio, **"Remember Me Jesus"**/**"Never Turn Back"**
3053	Sensational Nightingales, **"His Great Love"**/**"Cleanse My Soul"**
3055	Rev. Cleophus Robinson, **"Elijah Rock"**/**"God's Sons and Daughters"**
3060	Loving Sisters, **"He That Believeth"**/**"An Unfailing God"**
3063	Gospel Keys, **"Let Him Come into Your Life"**/**"I Come to Thee"**
3064	Mighty Clouds of Joy, **"He's Able"**/**"Swing Low"**
3071	Rev. Cleophus Robinson, **"Silent Night"**/**"Amen"**
3074	Sunset Travelers, **"Wonderful Jesus"**/**"Hide Me"**
3075	Pilgrim Jubilee Singers, **"Turn You 'Round"**/**"Pearly Gates"**
3078	Josephine James, **"Lord I Believe"**/**"Look Down upon Me"**
3079	Gospelaires of Dayton, Ohio, **"When I Get in Glory"**/**"Never Grow Old"**
3080	Mighty Clouds of Joy, **"Nobody Can Turn Me Around"**/**"Touch Me Lord"**
3081	Loving Sisters, **"God's Eagle"**/**"Jesus Is All I Need"**
3082	Rev. Cleophus Robinson, **"Unfolding Book of Life"**/**"Only Believe"**
3084	Dixie Hummingbirds, **"The Old Time Way"**/**"Gabriel"**
3085	Gospel Keys, **"I'm Not Ashamed"**/**"Back to Dust"**
	1966
3092	Rev. Cleophus Robinson, **"Rusty Old Halo"**/**"Lord I'm Your Child"**
3094	Awakening Echoes, **"Another Day"**/**"Born Again"**
3099	Mighty Clouds of Joy, **"I'm Glad about It"**/**"Let Jesus Use You"**
3100	Rev. Cleophus Robinson, **"Why (Am I Treated So Bad)"**/**"He's Done Great Things"**

SURE SHOT RECORDS

	1963
5001	Verna Rae Clay, **"He Loves Me, He Loves Me Not"**/**"I've Got It Bad"**
	1964
5003	Bobby Williams, **"Play a Sad Song"**/**"Try Love"**
5005	Bobby Williams, **"Keep on Loving Me"**/**"You Waited Too Long"**

	1965
5008	Malibus, **"Chance for You and Me"**/**"Strong Love"**
5012	Bell Brothers, **"Don't You Know She's Alright"**/**"Not Your Kind of Love"**
5013	Bobby Williams, **"When You Play (You Gotta Pay)"**/**"It's All Over"**
5014	Malibus, **"Two at a Time"**/**"I Had a Dream"**
5016	Bobby Williams, **"I'll Hate Myself Tomorrow"**/**"The Last Time"**
5017	J. J. Daniels, **"Mr. Lonesome"**/**"Deep Down Inside"**
5023	Bell Brothers, **"Look at Me"**/**"Pity Me"**
5025	Bobby Williams, **"Baby I Need Your Love"**/**"Try It Again"**
5026	Rhonda Washington, **"Swingtown USA"**/**"What about Love"**
	1966
5028	Malibus, **"Gee Baby (I Love You)"**/**"What's This Coming"**
5030	Lee Mitchell, **"Where Does Love Go"**/**"You're Gonna Miss Me"**
5031	Bobby Williams, **"I'll Hate Myself Tomorrow"**/**"I've Only Got Myself to Blame"**

XIV. Long-play albums containing tracks recorded at Gold Star Studios

Issued by various labels owned by or affiliated with Don Robey

BACK BEAT RECORDS		
BLP 60	Joe Hinton, *Funny (How Time Slips Away)*	1965
BLP 66	O. V. Wright, *Eight Men, Four Women*	1967
DUKE RECORDS		
DLP 79	Bobby "Blue" Bland, *The Soul of the Man*	1966
DLP 83	Junior Parker, *The Best of . . .*	1967
DLP 90	Bobby "Blue" Bland, *If Loving You Is Wrong*	1968
DUNHILL RECORDS (RELEASED AFTER ROBEY SOLD HIS CATALOGUE TO ABC/DUNHILL)		
50163	Bobby "Blue" Bland, *His California Album*	(1973)
PEACOCK RECORDS		
	1965	
PLP 121	Mighty Clouds Of Joy, *A Bright Side*	
PLP 122	Sunset Travelers, *On Jesus' Program*	

| PLP 125 | Loving Sisters, *Trying Time* |
| PLP 126 | Rev. Cleophus Robinson, *God's Sons and Daughters* |

XV. International Artists Records

Singles produced at Gold Star Studios, 1968–1970

101	The Coastliners, **"Alright"**/**"Wonderful"**	October 1965
123	Beauregard, **"Popcorn Popper"**/ **"Mama Never Taught Me How to Jelly Roll"**	1968
124	The Rubayyat, **"If I Were a Carpenter"**/**"Ever, Ever Land"**	1968
125	Lost & Found, **"When Will You Come Through"**/**"Professor Black"**	1968
126	13th Floor Elevators, **"Will the Circle Remain Unbroken"**/ **"I'm Gonna Love You Too"**	1968
127	Lightnin' Hopkins, **"Mr. Charlie"**/**"Baby Child"**	1968
128	Bubble Puppy, **"Hot Smoke and Sassafras"**/**"Lonely"**	1968
129	Endle St. Cloud In The Rain, **"Tell Me One More Time (What's Happening to Our World)"**/**"Quest for Beauty"**	1969
130	13th Floor Elevators, **"Livin' On"**/**"Scarlet & Gold"**	1969
131	Sonny Hall, **"Poor Planet Earth"**/**"The Battle of the Moon"**	1969
132	The Shayds, **"Bring Your Love"**/**"Search the Sun"**	1969
133	Bubble Puppy, **"Beginning"**/**"If I Had a Reason"**	1969
134	Endle St. Cloud, **"This Is Love"**/**"Professor Black"**	9/25/69
136	Bubble Puppy, **"Days of Our Time"**/**"Thinkin' about Thinkin'"**	1969
137	Shayde, **"A Profitable Dream"**/**"Third Number"**	1969
138	Bubble Puppy, **"Hurry Sundown"**/**"What Do You See"**	1969/70
139	Endle, **"She Wears It Like a Badge"**/**"Laughter"**	1970
141	Arnim-Hamilton, **"Pepperman"**/**"Walkin' Midnight Coffee Break"**	1970
142	Ginger Valley, **"Ginger"**/**"Country Life"**	1970

XVI. International Artists Records

Long-play albums containing tracks recorded at Gold Star Studios, 1968–1970

IALP6	Lightnin' Hopkins, *Free Form Patterns*	1968
IALP7	Red Krayola, *God Bless the Red Krayola and All Who Sail with It*	1968

IALP8	13th Floor Elevators, *Live* [track mixing only]	1968
IALP9	13th Floor Elevators, **Bull of the Woods**	1969
IALP10	Bubble Puppy, **A Gathering of Promises**	1969
IALP12	Endle St. Cloud, **Thank You All Very Much**	1970

XVII. Crazy Cajun Records

Long-play albums recorded or mixed at SugarHill Studios, 1975–1985

CA. 1975	
CCLP 1001	Pappy (Te Tan) Meaux, **True Cajun Blues: Moi-tu-sul**
CCLP 1002	Clifton Chenier, **Bayou Soul**
CCLP 1003	Sir Douglas Quintet, **The Best of . . .**
CCLP 1004	Papa Link Davis, **Big Mamou**
CCLP 1005	Floyd Tillman, **Golden Hits**
CCLP 1006	Mickey Gilley, **Mickey Gilley**
CCLP 1007	Ronnie Milsap, **Vocalist of the Year**
CCLP 1008	Freddy Fender, **Before the Next Teardrop Falls**
CCLP 1009	Johnny Winter, **Early Winter**
CCLP 1010	Clifton Chenier, **Clifton Chenier**
CCLP 1011	Freddy Fender, **Love Me Tender**
CCLP 1012	Freddy Fender, **Canta**
CCLP 1013	Freddy Fender & Sir Douglas, **Re-Union of the Cosmic Brothers**
CCLP 1014	Champagne Brothers, **My Love and the Seasons**
CCLP 1015	Oscar Perry, **Moods of the Man**
CCLP 1016	Benny Barnes, **The Best of Benny Barnes**
CCLP 1017	Sunny & The Sunliners, **Live in Las Vegas**
CA. 1977–1978	
CCLP 1018	Rocky Gil & The Bishops, **Soul Party**
CCLP 1019	Chuck Price, **Chuck Price**
CCLP 1020	El Curro, **Flamenco Guitar**
CCLP 1021	The Singin' Nurses, **The Singin' Nurses**
CCLP 1022	Roy Head, **His All Time Favorites**
CCLP 1023	Mexican Blood, **Streets of Laredo**

CCLP 1024	The Ascots, *Color Me Soul*
CCLP 1025	The Cate Bros., *Friendship Train*
CCLP 1026	Danny Epps, *Laid Back Country Picker*
CCLP 1027	Joey Long, *The Rains Came*
CCLP 1028	Tommy McLain, *If You Don't Love Me & His All Time Favorites*
CCLP 1029	Sir Douglas Quintet, *The Tracker*
CCLP 1030	Warren Storm, *Family Rules*
CCLP 1031	Shirley & Co. and Jesse Hill, *You'll Lose a Good Thing*
CCLP 1032	Various Artists, *Country Classics*
CCLP 1033	Danny Epps, *He's a Drifter*
CCLP 1034	Sweet Smoke, *How Sweet It Is*
CCLP 1035	Jesse Lankford, *We'll Take Our Last Walk Tonight*
CCLP 1036	Jesse Lankford & C. L. Weldon, *Houston's Natural Gass*
CCLP 1037	Dr. John, *The Night Tripper*
CCLP 1038	Fiddlin' Frenchie Burke, *Big Mamou*
CCLP 1039	Freddy Fender, *Live*
CCLP 1040	Dr. John, *Malcolm Rebenneck*
CCLP 1041	Freddy Fender, *Since I Met You Baby*
CCLP 1042	C. L. Weldon, *I'm Asking Forgiveness*
CCLP 1043	Co Co Ryan, *Bad News on the Radio*
CCLP 1044	B. J. Thomas, *His All Time Favorites*
CCLP 1045	B. J. Thomas, *Didn't It Rain*
CCLP 1046	B. J. Thomas, *Luckiest Man in the World*
CCLP 1047	Johnny Copeland, *Sings the Blues*
CCLP 1048	Danny Ezba, *Green Grass of Home*
CCLP 1049	Joey Long, *Flying High*
CCLP 1050	Tommy McLain, *Good Morning Louisiana*
CCLP 1051	Henry Moore, *It's My Own Tears That's Being Wasted*
CCLP 1052	Tracey Balin, *Standin' on a Mountain Top*
CCLP 1054	Co Co Ryan, *Back on the Road*
CCLP 1055	T. K. Hulin, *As You Pass Me By . . . Graduation Night*
CCLP 1056	Triumphs, *Gotta Keep My Cool*
CCLP 1057	Reginald Forch & Jesse Harrison, *Reginald Forch & Jesse Harrison*
CCLP 1058	Glenn Stillwell, *Parody of the Mountain Climber*

CCLP 1059	The Phinx, *Sometimes*
CCLP 1060	Charles Berry, *Neighbor Neighbor*
CCLP 1061	Oscar Perry, *Mend a Broken Heart*
CCLP 1062	Margo White, *I've Got a Right to Lose My Mind*
CCLP 1063	Bobby Sharp, *Autumn Leaves Must Fall*
CCLP 1064	Bobby Sharp, *Walk, Think, Cry*
CCLP 1065	David Owens, *Sunshine Go Lightly*
CCLP 1066	Various Artists, *Juke Box Hits of Garner State Park*
CCLP 1067	Roy Head, *Boogie Down*
CCLP 1068	Mark James Trio, *She's Gone Away*
CCLP 1069	Sherri Jerrico, *Country Heartaches*
CCLP 1070	Chris Crosby & Johnny Fitzmorris, *We'll Take Our Last Walk Tonight*
CCLP 1071	Gloria Edwards, *Anything You Want*
CCLP 1072	Trudy Lynn, Faye Robinson, Mintee Mitchell, Lois Cotton, *Silk 'n' Soul: Big City Nights*
CCLP 1073	Roy Head, *Rock 'n' Roll My Soul*
CCLP 1074	Allison & The South Funk Boulevard, *Allison & the South Funk Boulevard*
CCLP 1075	Danny Ezba, *Try Jenny*
CCLP 1076	Tiny Skaggs & His Pop Country Big Band, *Tiny Skaggs & His Pop Country Big Band*
CCLP 1077	Bobby Michaels, *Came the Rain, Came the Change*
CCLP 1078	Oscar Perry, *I Think They'd Sell the Sunshine*
CCLP 1079	Joe Pipps, *Last Train Ride*
CCLP 1080	Tommy McLain, *Show Time*
CCLP 1081	Tommy Stuart, *What Makes Mary Go Round*
CCLP 1082	Tommy Stuart, *Tommy Stuart & His Band of Friends*
CCLP 1083	South Funk Boulevard Band, *South Funk Boulevard Band*
CCLP 1084	Warren Storm & Johnnie Allen, *Warren Storm & Johnnie Allen*
CCLP 1085	Joe Medwick, *Why Do Heartaches Pick On Me*
CCLP 1086	Rod Bernard, *This Should Go On Forever and Other Bayou Classics*
CCLP 1087	Wiley & Jesse Barkdull, *The Gospel Truth*
CCLP 1088	Tiny Fuller, *My Guitar Does the Singin'*
CCLP 1089	Tracey Balin, *Love Me Tonight*
CCLP 1090	Lowell Fulson, *Lowell Fulson*

CCLP 1091	Tiny Cato, *My Kind of Blues*
CCLP 1092	B. J. Thomas, *Loving You*
CCLP 1095	Don Goldie with The Sir Douglas Quintet, *Don Goldie with the Sir Douglas Quintet*
CCLP 1096	Doak Snead, *Think of Me Sometime*
CCLP 1097	Mandrake, *Mandrake*
CCLP 1098	Mary McCoy & Misty Adams, *Mary McCoy & Misty Adams*
CCLP 1099	Donny King, *Mathilda*
CCLP 1100	Freddy Fender & Tommy McLain, *Friends in Show Business*
CCLP 1101	Alvin Meaux & Anything Goes, *Alvin Meaux & Anything Goes*
CCLP 1103	Leon Rausch, *Doin' It Bob's Way*
CCLP 1104	Big Mama Thornton & Clifton Chenier, *Live and Together*

CA. 1979–1985

CCLP 1106	Freddy Fender, *Live in Las Vegas*
CCLP 1108	Johnny B & The Bad Boys, *Dirty Leg*
CCLP 1109	Val Lindsey, *Cajun Classics*
CCLP 1110	Val Lindsey, *Modern Day Cajun*

XVIII. Other (i.e., non–Crazy Cajun Records)

Long-play albums by Freddy Fender (or, in one case, contributed to by him) containing tracks recorded at SugarHill Studios, released on various labels as indicated

Mercury SR 61253	*The Good, the Bad and the Ugly* [compilation of songs by various artists]	
ABC/Dot 2020	*Before the Next Teardrop Falls*	
ABC/Dot 2044	*Are You Ready for Freddy*	1975
ABC/Dot 2050	*Rock 'N' Country*	1976
ABC/Dot 2061	*If You're Ever in Texas*	1976
Pickwick International JS6195	*Your Cheatin' Heart*	1976
ABC/Dot 2079	*The Best of Freddy Fender*	1977
ABC/Dot 2090	*If You Don't Love Me*	1977
ABC/Dot 2101	*Merry Christmas/Feliz Navidad*	1977
ABC AA1062	*Swamp Gold*	1978
Teevee TV1020	*20 Greatest Hits*	1979

ABC AY1132	*Tex Mex*	1979
Starflite/CBS AL36284	*Together We Drifted Apart*	1980

XIX. Various other labels

Singles produced at SugarHill Studios, 1974–ca. 1980

S.B.I. 1007	Soul Brothers Inc., **"Let's Shack Up"**/**"Ugly to the Bone"**	1974
King 6400	Gloria Edwards, **"Keep Up with My Man"**/**"Anything You Want"**	
Polydor 2-14025	Jesse Lankford, **"We'll Take Our Last Walk Tonight"**/ **"What's a Matter Baby"**	
ABC/Dot 12370	Freddy Fender, **"Please Mr. Sandman"**/**"Talk to Me"**	
ABC/Dot 17540	Freddy Fender, **"Before the Next Teardrop Falls"**/ **"Waiting for Your Love"**	
ABC/Dot 17558	Freddy Fender, **"Wasted Days and Wasted Nights"**/ **"I Love My Rancho Grande"**	
ABC/Dot 17585	Freddy Fender, **"Secret Love"**/**"Lovin' Cajun Style"**	
Plantation 134	Lee Emerson, **"The Gospel Truth (Like It 'Tis [sic])"** [one side mono, the other stereo]	
ABC/Dot 17607	Freddy Fender, **"You'll Lose a Good Thing"**/**"I'm to Blame"**	
ABC/Dot 17652	Freddy Fender, **"Living It Down"**/**"Take Her a Message"**	
ABC/Dot 17686	Freddy Fender, **"The Rains Came"**/**"Sugar Coated Love"**	
ABC/Dot 17713	Freddy Fender, **"Thank You My Love"**/**"If You Don't Love Me"**	
ABC/Dot 17730	Freddy Fender, **"Think about Me"**/**"If That's the Way You Want It"**	
ABC/Dot 17734	Freddy Fender, **"Christmas Time in the Valley"**/ **"Please Come Home for Christmas"**	
ABC/Dot 17581	Tracey Balin, **"You Don't Have Far to Go"**/ **"I'll Always Be Missing You"**	1975
ABC/Dot 17725	Joe Barry, **"If You Really Want Me to I'll Go"**/**"You're the Reason"**	
ABC 12453	Freddy Fender, **"Walking Piece of Heaven"**/**"Sweet Summer Day"**	1979
WB 8100	Donny King, **"You Can't Get Here from There"**/**"Cheating Traces"**	
WB 8150	Bob O'Donnell, **"Jimmy"**	1975
WB 8229	Donny King, **"Stop the World"** [one side mono, the other stereo]	
Smash/Polygram 884-828-7	William Burton Gaar, **"Somewhere between Mama's and Daddy's"**	
Smash/Polygram 888-089-7	William Burton Gaar, **"I'm Gonna Rise Up through These Ashes"**	

XX. Starflite Records

Long-play albums produced at SugarHill Studios, 1979

LP2001	Freddy Fender, *Hits By (Vol. 1)*
LP2002	Jimmy Donley, *Born to Be a Loser*
LP2003	Doug Kershaw, *Louisiana "Cajun" Country*
LP2004	T. K. Hulin, *Hit Memories By*

XXI. Modern Music Ventures productions

Long-play albums/CDs produced at SugarHill Studios, 1989–2001, released on Discos MM (DMM) and/or other labels

DMM 1001	Mary Maria, *Un Poco de Todo de Toda Mi Vida*	1989
DMM 1002	Valentino, *Valentino*	1989
Polygram/Mercury Latino 842979-2	Rick Gonzalez & The Choice, *La Primera Vez*	1990
Polygram/Mercury Latino 846296-2	Jerry Rodriguez & Mercedes, *Rebelde*	1990
Capitol/EMI Latino	The Hometown Boys, *It's Our Turn*	1990
Capitol/EMI Latino H2H42522	Elsa Garcia, *Simplemente*	1991
DMM 1003	The Basics, *Sonido Basico*	1991
Capitol/EMI Latino H2H42524	Jerry Rodriguez & Mercedes, *No Somos Criminales*	1991
Capitol/EMI Latino	The Hometown Boys, *El Poder de una Mujer*	1991
Capitol/EMI Latino H2H42596-2	Rick Gonzalez & The Choice, *Por Ti*	1991
Capitol/EMI Latino	Elsa Garcia, *Ni Mas, Ni Menos*	1991
DMM 2710 (Capitol/ EMI Latino)	The Hometown Boys, *Somos Dos Gatos*	1992
DMM 2837 (Capitol/ EMI Latino)	The Hometown Boys, *Hombre Innocente*	1993
DMM 1826 (Fonovisa)	David Olivares Y Grupo XS, *Tu y Yo*	1994
DMM 0647 (Capitol/ EMI Latino)	The Hometown Boys, *Tres Ramitas*	1994

Capitol/EMI Latino H2-7243-8-31462-2-2	Los Dos Gilbertos, *Live*	1994
DMM 1149 (Capitol/ EMI Latino)	The Hometown Boys, *Live*	1994
Fonovisa Tejano 12001	Annette Y Axxion, *Llama Equivocada*	1995
Fonovisa Tejano 12005	David Olivares Y XS, *Aqui Esta*	1995
DMM 2002	The Hometown Boys, *Mire Amigo*	1995
Fonovisa Tejano 14002	Elsa Garcia, *Tu Solamente Tu*	1995
Fonovisa Tejano	David Olivares Y XS, *Amiga Mia*	1996
Fonovisa Tejano 12016	Los Dos Gilbertos, *La Gata Blanca*	1996
DMM 1201	The Hometown Boys, *Dos Cosas*	1996
Fonovisa Tejano 12012	Annette Y Axxion, *Dejame Vivir*	1996
DMM 9551	The Hometown Boys, *Eres Mia*	1997
DMM 1997	Angel Flores, *El Firi Firi*	1998
DMM 1998	Los Vencedores, *Esquinas del Frente*	1998
DMM 9679	The Hometown Boys, *Como Nunca*	1998
DMM 7243	Various Artists, *Tejano Treasures*	1999
DMM 1999 (EMI-Fonovisa)	The Hometown Boys, *Vestida de Blanco*	1999
DMM 1946	The Hometown Boys & Friends, *Country and More*	1999
DMM 4001	The Hometown Boys, *Luces de New York*	1999/2000
DMM 0104	Los Monarcas, *Como Quisiera*	2000
DMM 5653	Los Pekadorez, *Recuerdos de Ti*	2000
DMM 1900	Los Vencedores, *Eres Toda Una Mujer*	2000
DMM 4004	The Hometown Boys, *Puro Tesoro*	2000
DMM [?]	Los Fantasmas Del Valle, *Bellos Recuerdos de Los Fantasmas*	2000
DMM 1346	David DeAnda Y La Ley, *La Chancla*	2000
DMM 1996	The Hometown Boys & Friends, *Puras Polkas*	2000
DMM 5614	Los Yoyo's, *Mi Unico Camino*	2000
DMM [?]	The Hometown Boys & Los Dos Gilbertos, *Live: Mano a Mano* [originally recorded in 1994]	2000
DMM 2000	The Hometown Boys, *Ten Years/Diez Años*	2000
DMM 1463	Los Dos Gilbertos, *Y Sus Rancheras*	2001

XXII. Heart Music

Long-play albums/CDs produced at SugarHill Studios, 1989–2000

HMEA 001LP	Erich Avinger, *Heart Magic*	1989
HMEA 002CD	Erich Avinger, *Sí*	1991
HMTC 021	Tony Campise, *First Takes*	1990
HM 004	Tony Campise, *Once in a Blue Moon*	1992
HM 005	Tony Campise, *Ballads, Blues and Bebop*	1993
HM 006	Tony Campise, *Ballads, Blues, Bebop and Beyond*	1994
HM/Tafford Music 791481234625	Joe Locascio, *A Charmed Life*	1996
HM 020	Elias Haslanger, *For the Moment*	1997
HM 0020600182	Joe Locascio, *Home*	1997
HM 000206001726	Elias Haslanger, *Kicks Are for Kids*	1998
HM 023	Erich Avinger, *Poets, Misfits, Beggars, and Shamans*	2000

XXIII. Justice Records

Long-play albums/CDs produced at (or recorded at performance site by) SugarHill Studios, 1989–1997

JR 801012	Kellye Gray, *Standards in Gray*	1989
JR 0201-2	Sebastian Whittaker, *First Outing*	1990
JR 0301-2	Harry Sheppard, *Viva Brazil*	1990
JR 0401-2	David Catney, *First Flight*	1990
JR 0601-2	Wendi Slaton, *Turn Around and Look*	1990
JR 1001-2	Herb Ellis, *Roll Call*	1991
JR 0302-2	Harry Sheppard, *This-a-Way That-a-Way*	1991
JR 0502-2	Various Artists, *Just Friends: A Gathering in Tribute to Emily Remler, Vol. One*	1991
JR 0701-2	Stefan Karlsson, *Room 292*	1991
JR 0503-2	Various Artists, *Just Friends: A Gathering in Tribute to Emily Remler, Vol. Two*	1991
JR 0702-2	Stefan Karlsson, *The Road Not Taken*	1991
JR 0202-2	Sebastian Whittaker & The Creators, *Searchin' for the Truth*	1991
JR 0801-2	King & Moore, *Impending Bloom*	1991

JR 0402-2	Dave Catney, *Jade Visions*	1991
JR 0002-2	Various Artists, *Justice Records Sampler: The First Year*	1992
JR 1201-2	Tab Benoit, *Nice and Warm*	1992
JR 0203-2	Sebastian Whittaker & The Creators, *One for Bu*	1992
JR 0602-2	Wendi Slaton, *Back Here Again*	1992
JR 1401-2	David Rice, *Orange Number Eight*	1992
JR 0802-2	King & Moore, *Potato Radio*	1992
JR 0003	Various Artists, *Strike a Deep Chord: Blues Guitar for the Homeless*	1993
JR 0703-2	Stefan Karlsson, *Below Zero*	1993
JR 0006-2	Various Artists, *Hellhole*	1994
JR 0204-2	Sebastian Whittaker & The Creators, *The Valley of the Kings*	1995
JR [?]	David Catney, *Reality Road*	1994
JR 1003-2	Herb Ellis, *Down Home*	1996
JR 0304-2	Harry Sheppard, *Standards Unleashed*	1997
JR 1204-2	Tab Benoit, *Live: Swampland Jam*	1997
AE 8802-2	The Road Kings, *Live at the Satellite Lounge* [site performance recorded by SugarHill Studios]	1997

Chronology of Gold Star/ SugarHill Engineers

1941–1963, Bill Quinn (owner)	**1974–1976,** Pat Brady
1963–1964, Walt Andrus	**1975–1981,** Mickey Moody
1961–1964, Dan Puskar	**1977–1979,** Carlton Blake
1963–1967, Bert Frilot	**1981–1984,** Lonnie Wright
1963–1967, J. L. Patterson	**1982–1986,** Lindon Hudson
1964, Jack Clement	**1982–1984,** Jack Duncan
1964–1965, Doyle Jones	**1984–present,** Andy Bradley (co-owner)
1964–1967, Louis Stevenson	**1986–1993,** Rod Thibault
1964–1966, Robert Lurie	**1987–1992,** J. R. Griffith
1965–1966, Bill Holford	**1988–1990,** Bill Holford
1965–1966, Gaylan Shelby	**1989–1990,** James Grosso
1966–1969, Jim Duff	**1991–1998,** Steve Lanphier
1967–1968, Dennis Trocmet	**1994–2000,** Ramon Morales
1968–1969, Fred Carroll	**1994–present,** Dan Workman (co-owner)
1968–1969, Hank Poole	**1994–2007,** Rodney Meyers (co-owner)
1970–1971, Kurt Linhof	**2000–present,** Steve Christensen
1970–1971, Dennis Bledsoe	**2001–present,** John Griffin
1972–1986, Huey P. Meaux (owner)	**2000–2003,** Michael Martin
1972, Mike Taylor	**2004–2007,** Leigh Crane
1972–1974, Dennis "Crash" Collins	**2004–present,** Josh Applebee
1972–1974, Hank Lam	**2004–2008,** James Garlington
1972–1973, Roger Harris	**2004–present,** Tyson Sheth
1972–1976, Robert Evans	**2005–2006,** Heba Kadry
1973–1976, Gaylan Shelby	**2008–present,** Chris Longwood

Bibliography

Allen, Bob. *George Jones: The Saga of an American Singer.* New York: Doubleday, 1984.

Ames, Roy C. Liner notes to *Blues to the Bone* by Loudmouth Johnson and Johnny Winter. Collectables (CD COL-0675), 1996.

Ankeny, Jason. "The Mighty Clouds of Joy." *All Music Guide.* 4th ed. Edited by Vladimir Bogdanov, Chris Woodstra, and Stephen Thomas Erlewine. San Francisco: Backbeat Books, 2001: 609.

Bardwell, S. K., and Lisa Teachey. "Accused Child Molester Back in Houston to Face Charges." *Houston Chronicle,* March 8, 1996, sec. A.

————. "Meaux Arrested after Being Traced to Mexico/Fugitive Will Be Returned to Houston." *Houston Chronicle,* March 6, 1996, sec. A.

Barthelme, Frederick. "The Red Crayola." *Oxford American:* Web Extras. Available at http://www.oxfordamericanmag.com/content.cfm?ArticleID=287&Entry=Extras (accessed August 1, 2008).

Benicewicz, Larry. "Remembering Bert Frilot." Available at http://www.bluesworld.com/BFRILOT.html (accessed July 27, 1998).

Benson, Ray. "Artist's Song Notes: 'Miles and Miles of Texas.'" *Lone Star Music.* Available at http://www.lonestarmusic.com/lsmsongnotes.asp?id=1240 (accessed August 8, 2008).

Brooks, Tim. Rev. of *Duke/Peacock Records: An Illustrated History with Discography* by Galen Gart and Roy C. Ames. *ARSC Journal* 22, no. 2 (Fall 1991). Also available at http://www.timbrooks.net/reviews-music/gartDUKEREV.cfm (accessed July 14, 2008).

Brown, Andrew. "Allstar." *American Song-Poem Music Archives.* http://www.songpoemmusic.com/labels/allstar.htm (accessed July 2, 2008).

————. Liner notes to *Benny Barnes: Poor Man's Riches (The Complete 1950s Recordings).* Bear Family (CD 16517), 2007.

————. Liner notes to *Harry Choates: Devil in the Bayou (The Gold Star Recordings).* Bear Family (CD 16355), 2002.

————. Liner notes (in the form of a hardback book) to *The Sarg Records Anthology: South Texas 1954–1964*. Bear Family (CD 16296), 1999.

————. "RE: TCF." E-mail response to Roger Wood. July 23, 2008.

————. "Texas Rancher: The Tony Sepolio Interview." *Taking Off: Musical Journeys in the Southwest and Beyond*, no. 1 (Spring 2005): 2–22.

Callahan, Mike, Dave Edwards, and Patrice Eyries. "International Artists Album Discography." *Both Sides Now Publications*, 2007. Also available at http://www.bsnpubs.com/texas/internationalartists.html (accessed July 30, 2008).

————. "The Musicor Records Story." *Both Sides Now Publications*, 2006. Also available at http://www.bsnpubs.com/ua/musicorstory.html (accessed July 22, 2008).

Cano, Ray, Jr. "Gold Star Studios." *Texas Music History Online*. http://ctmh.txstate.edu/attraction.php?cmd=detazil&attrid=22 (accessed May 9, 2008).

Carman, Tim. Rev. of *First Outing* by Sebastian Whittaker. *Houston Post*, July 12, 1990.

Cartwright, Garth. "Sonny Fisher: Singer-Songwriter Who Fused Country Music with the Blues to Produce Rockabilly." *The Guardian*, October 26, 2005, sec. Obituaries. Also available at http://www.guardian.co.uk/news/2005/oct/26/guardianobituaries.artsobituaries (accessed June 17, 2008).

Case, Keith. "Guy Clark Biography." Keith Case & Associates. http://www.keithcase.com/profiles/guy/bio.html (accessed July 12, 2008).

Coffey, Kevin. Liner notes to *That'll Flat Git It!, Vol. 19: Rockabilly from the Vaults of D and Dart Records*. Bear Family (CD 16408-AH), 2000.

Cogan, Jim, and William Clark. *Temples of Sound: Inside the Great Recording Studios*. San Francisco: Chronicle Books, 2003.

Corcoran, Michael. *All Over the Map: True Heroes of Texas Music*. Austin: University of Texas Press, 2005.

Dahl, Bill. "Grady Gaines: Biography." *Allmusic.com* (2008). Available at http://www.allmusic.com/cg/amg.dll?p=amg&sql=11:hbfixqu5ldoe~T1 (accessed August 12, 2008).

————. Liner notes to *The Johnny Copeland Collection: Working Man's Blues*. Fuel 2000 (CD 302-061-260-2), 2002.

Dansby, Andrew. "SXSW: It's Been a Musical Feast." *Houston Chronicle*, March 19, 2007. Available at http://www.chron.com/CDA/archives/archive.mpl?id=2007_4307474 (accessed August 22, 2008).

Davidson, Dan. "Rudy 'Tutti' Grayzell." *A Rockabilly Hall of Fame Presentation*. http://www.rockabillyhall.com/RudyGrayzell1.html (accessed June 17, 2008).

DeRogatis, Jim. "The Great Albums: *The Psychedelic Sounds of the 13th Floor Elevators*." April 21, 2002. Available at http://www.jimdero.com/News2001/GreatElevators.htm (accessed July 31, 2008).

Dickerson, Deke. Liner notes to *A Man Like Me: The Early Years of Roger Miller*. Bear Family (CD 16760-AH), 2006.

Dougan, John. "Radio Birdman." *All Music Guide to Rock*. Edited by Michael Erlewine, Vladimir Bogdanov, and Chris Woodstra. San Francisco: Miller Freeman Books, 1995: 632.

Drummond, Paul. *Eye Mind: The Saga of Roky Erickson and the 13th Floor Elevators*. Los Angeles: Process Media, 2007.

Eder, Bruce. Rev. of *Texas Battle of the Bands. AllMusic.com* (2008). Available at http://www.allmusic.com/cg/amg.dll?p=amg&sql=10:hcfwxqrhldoe (accessed July 26, 2008).

Eder, Bruce, and Richie Unterberger. "The Bad Seeds." *AllMusic.com* (2008). Available at http://www.allmusic.com/cg/amg.dll?p=amg&sql=11:j9foxqr5ldae~T1 (accessed July 27, 2008).

Edwards, David, Mike Callahan, and Patrice Eyries. "The Starday Records Story." *Both Sides Now Publications*, 2002. Also available at http://www.bsnpubs.com/king/stardaystory.html (accessed May 30, 2008).

Erlewine, Stephen Thomas. "Clay Walker." *All Music Guide*. 4th ed. Edited by Vladimir Bogdanov, Chris Woodstra, and Stephen Thomas Erlewine. San Francisco: Backbeat Books, 2001: 716.

———. "Faithful." *All Music Guide*. 4th ed. Edited by Vladimir Bogdanov, Chris Woodstra, and Stephen Thomas Erlewine. San Francisco: Backbeat Books, 2001: 348.

———. "Pappy Daily." *Allmusic.com* (2008). Available at http://www.allmusic.com/cg/amg.dll?p=amg&sql=11:gvfyxqu5ldke~T1 (accessed June 4, 2008).

Escott, Colin. Liner notes to *The Complete D Singles Collection: The Sounds of Houston, Texas, Vol. 1*. Bear Family (CD 15832-1), 1995.

Fancourt, Les, and Bob McGrath. *Blues Discography 1943–1970*. West Vancouver, B.C.: Eyeball Productions, 2006.

Flippo, Chet. "Texas Rock & Roll Spectacular." *Phonograph Record* (March 1974): 22–23.

Gart, Galen, and Roy C. Ames. *Duke/Peacock Records: An Illustrated History with Discography*. Milford, N.H.: Big Nickel Publications, 1990.

George, Nelson. *The Death of Rhythm and Blues*. New York: Plume, 1988.

Govenar, Alan. *Meeting the Blues: The Rise of the Texas Sound*. Dallas: Taylor, 1988.

Gray, Christopher. Rev. of *Paint the Town Brown* by Banana Blender Surprise. "Texas Platters." *Austin Chronicle*, July 7, 2006. Also available at http://www.austinchronicle.com/gyrobase/Issue/review?oid=oid%3A384116 (accessed August 12, 2008).

Hall, Michael. "A Long, Strange Trip." *TexasMonthly.com*, December 2001. Available at http://www.texasmonthly.com/2001-12-01/feature3.php (accessed July 31, 2008).

Harris, Sheldon. *Blues Who's Who*. New Rochelle, N.Y.: Arlington House, 1979.

Hartman, Gary. *The History of Texas Music*. College Station: Texas A&M University Press, 2008.

Haworth, Alan Lee. "Big Bopper." *The Handbook of Texas Music*. Austin: Texas State Historical Association, 2003: 20.

———. "Hopkins, Lightnin'." *The Handbook of Texas Music*. Austin: Texas State Historical Association, 2003: 142.

Head, James. "Sahm, Douglas Wayne." *The Handbook of Texas Music*. Austin: Texas State Historical Association, 2003: 281.

Hellinger, Linda. "Daily, Harold W. [Pappy]." *Handbook of Texas Online*. Available at http://www.tshaonline.org/handbook/online/articles/DD/fdaaf.html (accessed May 14, 2008).

Hickinbotham, Gary. "A History of the Texas Recording Industry." *Journal of Texas Music History* 4, no. 1 (Spring 2004): 18–32.

Hoffman, Lawrence. Liner notes to *Mean Old World: The Blues from 1940 to 1994.* Smithsonian (RD 110/MSd4-35974), 1996.

Holtzman, Vivian. "Nowsounds." *Houston Post,* February 4, 1968.

Huey, Steve. "Lucinda Williams: Biography." *Allmusic.com* (2008). Available at http://www.allmusic.com/cg/amg.dll?p=amg&sql=11:gifexqr5ldfe~T1 (accessed August 12, 2008).

Johnson, Stephen. "Meaux May Have His Bond Revoked." *Houston Chronicle,* February 7, 1996, sec. A.

Keller, Julie. "Destiny's World Domination." *E! Online,* September 1, 2005. Available at http://music.yahoo.com/read/news/23584356 (accessed August 18, 2008).

Kienzle, Rich. Liner notes to *The Essential George Jones: The Spirit of Country.* Legacy/Epic (E2K 52451), 1994.

Koda, Cub. "Clifton Chenier." *All Music Guide.* 4th ed. Edited by Vladimir Bogdanov, Chris Woodstra, and Stephen Thomas Erlewine. San Francisco: Backbeat Books, 2001: 860.

Koshkin, Brett. "Rocks Off: Slip Inside This House." *Houston Press Blogs,* July 30, 2008. Available at http://blogs.houstonpress.com/rocks/2008/07/slip_inside_this_house_mp3s_fr_1.php (accessed July 30, 2008).

LaBate, Steve. "Just for the Record: 10 Classic Sessions and the Studios That Shaped Them." *Paste Magazine,* no. 10 (June 2004). Also available at http://www.pastemagazine.com/action/article/1274/feature/music/just_for_the_record (accessed May 27, 2008).

Leadbitter, Mike, ed. *Nothing but the Blues.* London: Hanover Books, 1971.

Liebrum, Jennifer. "Meaux Enters 'Not Guilty' Pleas to Drug, Sex Charges." *Houston Chronicle,* March 12, 1996, sec. A.

Liebrum, Jennifer, and George Flynn. "Meaux Pleads Guilty to All Charges, Gets 15 Years." *Houston Chronicle,* June 1, 1996, sec. A.

Lomax, John, Jr. Liner notes to *Look, It's Us!* Jester Records LP, 1963.

Lomax, John Nova. "Catfish Reef: *Happy Woman Blues.*" *Houston Press Blogs,* February 20, 2007. Available at http://blogs.houstonpress.com/rocks/2007/02/catfish_reef_happy_woman_blues.php#more (accessed July 22, 2008).

Lonergan, David. "Kinky Friedman." *St. James Encyclopedia of Pop Culture.* Available at http://findarticles.com/p/articles/mi_g1epc/is_bio/ai_2419200432 (accessed August 11, 2008).

Lynskey, Dorian. "The Man Who Went Too High." *The Guardian,* June 8, 2007, Features. Also available at http://www.guardian.co.uk/music/2007/jun/08/popandrock2 (accessed July 31, 2008).

McComb, David G. "Houston, Texas." *The Portable Handbook of Texas.* Austin: Texas State Historical Association, 2000: 437–441.

McCord, Jeff, and John Morthland. "The 100 Best Texas Songs." *Texas Monthly* (April 2004). Also available at http://www.texasmonthly.com/2004-04-01/feature.php (accessed May 26, 2008).

Malone, Bill C. *Country Music, U.S.A.* Second rev. ed. Austin: University of Texas Press, 2002.

Marek, Ted. "Houston Hits the Disk Mart." *Houston Chronicle* (Rotogravure: Sunday magazine), February 3, 1957.

Millar, Bill. "That Rockin' Daddy." *New Kommotion* 2.2 (Summer 1976): 17–18.

Millar, Jeff. "Recording Session." *Houston Post,* September 9, 1965.

Mitchell, Rick. "There's Justice in Jazz." *Houston Chronicle,* July 20, 1990. Also available at http://www.chron.com/CDA/archives/archive.mpl?id=1990_717358 (accessed August 14, 2008).

Morthland, John. "Wasted Days." *Texas Monthly,* October 1995. Available at http://www.texasmonthly.com/1995-10-01/music.php (accessed August 8, 2008).

Moser, Margaret. "Hey, Hey, Hey!: Roy Head and Gene Kurtz Still 'Treat Her Right.'" *Austin Chronicle,* August 31, 2007. Available at http://www.austinchronicle.com/gyrobase/Issue/story?oid=oid%3A531654 (accessed July 20, 2008).

Noack, Eddie. "Talkback with Noack." Interview by Bill Millar. *New Kommotion* 2.2 (Summer 1976): 17–18.

Paterson, Beverly. "An Interview with Chris Gerniottis." In liner notes to *Form the Habit* by Zakary Thaks. BeatRocket (CD 131), 2001.

Patoski, Joe Nick. "Sex, Drugs, and Rock & Roll." *Texas Monthly,* May 1996, 116–125.

———. *Willie Nelson: An Epic Life.* New York: Little, Brown, 2008.

Prince, Rod. "The Tale of Bubble Puppy 1966–1972." Available at http://bubblepuppy.com/BubbleTale.html (accessed August 2, 2008).

"Producer's Profile." *Cashbox,* October 25, 1969: 64.

"Quinn." Obituary. *Houston Post,* January 6, 1976.

Rock and Roll Hall of Fame. Induction statement for Bobby "Blue" Bland. 1992. Available at http://www.rockhall.com/inductee/bobby-blue-bland (accessed July 16, 2008).

Ruhlmann, William. Rev. of *Blowin'* by the Noel Redding Band. *Allmusic.com* (2008). Available at http://www.allmusic.com/cg/amg.dll?p=amg&sql=10:3xfqxqy5ldde (accessed August 11, 2008).

Salem, James M. *The Late Great Johnny Ace and the Transition from R&B to Rock 'n' Roll.* Urbana: University of Illinois Press, 1999.

Schultz, Barbara. "Producer's Desk: Arhoolie Records' Chris Strachwitz." *Mix,* August 2002. Available at http://mixonline.com/recording/interviews/audio_arhoolie_records_chris/ (accessed July 24, 2008).

Shadwick, Keith. *The Encyclopedia of Jazz and Blues.* London: New Burlington Books/Quintet, 2001.

Smith, William Michael. "Gold Star Studios—Houston, Texas (1948): Lightnin' Hopkins—'T-Model Blues.'" *Paste Magazine* 10 (June 2004). Also available at http://www.pastemagazine.com/action/article/1277/feature/music/gold_star_studios_houston_texas_1948 (accessed May 27, 2008).

Strachwitz, Chris. Liner notes to *Lightning Hopkins: The Gold Star Sessions, Vol. 1.* Arhoolie (CD 330), 1990.

———. Liner notes to *Texas Blues: The Gold Star Sessions.* Arhoolie (CD 352), 1992.

Sullivan, Ruth K. "Robey, Don Deadric." *Handbook of Texas Online.* Available at http://www.tshaonline.org/handbook/online/articles/RR/fropc.html (accessed July 16, 2008).

Tottenham, John. "Rudy: Elvis Liked What He Saw and Offered the Performer a Job." *The Sunday Oregonian,* April 21, 1996. Also available at http://www.rocka billyhall.com/RudyGrayzell1.html (accessed June 17, 2008).

Tynan, John. "The Mercury-Starday Story." *Country and Western Jamboree* (March 1957): 12–13, 28.

United States Court of Appeals, Fifth Circuit. *United States of America, Plaintiff-Appellee, v. J. L. Patterson, Jr., Defendant-Appellant.* 528 F.2d 1037, Docket 75-3143. Decided March 18, 1976. Available at http://bulk.resource.org/courts.gov/c/F2/528/528.F2d.1037.75--3143.html (accessed July 31, 2008).

United States Court of Appeals, Second Circuit. *United States of America, Appellee, v. M. Perry Grant and Service Securities, Inc., Appellants.* 462 F.2d 28, No. 577, Docket 71-2198. Decided May 25, 1972. Available at http://bulk.resource.org/courts.gov/c/F2/462/462.F2d.28.71-2198.577.html (accessed July 31, 2008).

Unterberger, Richie. "Zakary Thaks." *All Music Guide to Rock.* Edited by Michael Erlewine, Vladimir Bogdanov, and Chris Woodstra. San Francisco: Miller Freeman Books, 1995: 845. Also available at http://www.allmusic.com/cg/amg.dll (accessed July 27, 2008).

Vine, Katy. "Jandek and Me." *Texas Monthly,* August 1999. Available at http://www.texasmonthly.com/1999-08-01/music.php (accessed August 22, 2008).

Wadey, Paul. "Obituary: Joe 'Guitar' Hughes." *The Independent,* May 26, 2003. Also available at http://findarticles.com/p/articles/mi_qn4158/is_20030526/ai_n12685293 (accessed July 7, 2008).

Wesolek, Barbara. "The Pappy Daily Story." *Glad Music Company* (July 15, 1977). Also available at http://www.gladmusicco.com/PappyDaily.htm (accessed May 14, 2008).

Winters, Aubrey. "Music Beat." *Nashville City Beat* (January 1976): 5.

Wood, Roger. *Down in Houston: Bayou City Blues.* Austin: University of Texas Press, 2003.

———. *Texas Zydeco.* Austin: University of Texas Press, 2006.

Wynn, Ron. "Roy Head." *All Music Guide to Rock.* Edited by Michael Erlewine, Vladimir Bogdanov, and Chris Woodstra. San Francisco: Miller Freeman Books, 1995: 373.

Zolten, Jerry. *Great God A'mighty!: The Dixie Hummingbirds.* New York: Oxford University Press, 2003.

Zuniga, Jo Ann, Rick Mitchell, and Jennifer Liebrum. "Record Producer Charged in Child Porn Case." *Houston Chronicle,* January 30, 1996, sec. A.

Index